BOUND FOR DISTANT SEAS

A Voyage Alone to Asia
Aboard the 28-Foot Sailboat Atom

JAMES BALDWIN

Atom Voyages • Brunswick, Georgia

Contents

Introduction

I recently turned 55 years old, and she was pushing 50. We had spent our lives together since our youth, always looking after one another as we made our way twice around the world. Though I had carelessly neglected her in recent years and had even flirted with others, she stood patiently by with the unspoken promise she was always there for me.

Often I was pulled into this reflective state as I worked on refitting my 50-year-old 28-foot sailboat *Atom* as she sat on her trailer under a canopy of shady oaks in our backyard. Like a long-lasting marriage, we served each other's needs. She was built to sail, and apparently so was I. Memories of those days of our adventures together on the open seas remained as ever-present and sustaining as my own heartbeat.

The task of unbolting the deck hardware and stripping *Atom* apart piece by piece was comparable to an archaeological dig, uncovering the stories of an earlier time. I thought of past loves I had won and lost while *Atom* stayed true and constant by my side, providing a home and the means to travel. I paused in my labors to lay my hands on her weathered deck, smiling inwardly as I thought: "We've had a good run of years together, ol' girl, and beaten up and aged as you are, as we both are, I can't deny I'm still in love with you."

Sanding through old layers of paint unleashed memories into the dusty air. First, there was the white surface coat of paint I had applied in South Africa in 1995 as I prepared for the stormy passage around the African Cape to re-enter the Atlantic and complete my second circumnavigation. Little did I know at that time that a fortune teller's remarks to a bright young woman I had known in Taiwan had set into motion a life-altering path for both of us. The next layer to emerge was the off-white paint that I'd applied several years earlier with the help of a girlfriend in the Philippines. Taking me deeper into the past, that coat of paint had weathered longer than did her relationship with this self-interested solo sailor. My world then was still narrowly focused on my own sailing odyssey. Sanding further, I uncovered the blue paint I'd applied to *Atom's* hull in Michigan before our first voyage around the world together. That darkest blue, I later discovered, heated the interior of the boat much like a solar oven under the tropical sun. As yacht designer Nat Herreshoff reportedly said, "There are only two colors to paint a boat, black or white, and only a fool would paint a boat black."

The memories flooded back in a rush. It seemed only a moment ago that it was 1986. I was 28 years old and had recently returned home to Florida from a solo two-year circumnavigation only to find myself unhappy at the prospect of remaining ashore in the United States. I sorely missed the excitement, the challenge, and the simple joys I'd known while bound for distant seas. Though I had circled the world under sail in the previous two years, as described in my earlier book *Across Islands and Oceans*, I had not seen nearly enough of it and knew that there remained many mysteries out there for me to discover. The obvious and strange thing about circumnavigating is that I ran as far from home as it was possible to go and yet the journey brought me right back to where I started, at least in the physical sense. A further incentive to go again, if one was needed, was finding that back home the stagnant American economy held limited job opportunities. I still possessed a fierce need to be my own master, which left me even less employable than when I'd departed the country two years earlier. Like many shore-bound sailors, I felt an affinity to Herman Melville's Ishmael who, after being ashore too long with society's heavy hands around his neck, suddenly felt an irrepressible urge to knock the hats off the heads of people he passed on the street.

So within months of returning to Florida after my solo world voyage, I was itching to get back to sea, to have a new adventure. By sailing mainly in the southern hemisphere on my first trip, I had bypassed Asia. Now, the idea of a voyage alone to China began to intrigue me. Rumors were in the air that the communist Chinese government had just begun to crack open its doors to foreign cruising yachts. I was determined to be one of the first solo navigators to explore those exotic ports and attempt to take *Atom* on an extensive journey up the Pearl River whose tributaries run inland hundreds of miles through the southern Chinese provinces. Beyond that, the winds of fate could carry me wherever they wished. Along the way, those erratic winds pushed me off course and carried me further than I could have imagined.

Perhaps one day you too may awaken from your dreams to find yourself bound for distant seas.

James Baldwin
Brunswick, Georgia
May 2015

BOUND FOR DISTANT SEAS

MODIFICATIONS TO *ATOM*

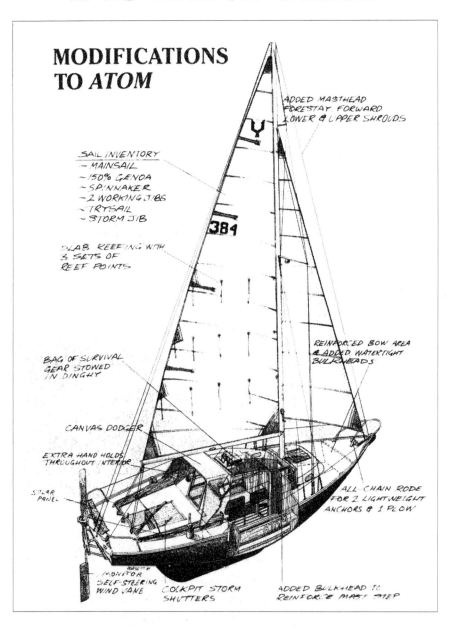

ADDED MASTHEAD FORESTAY, FORWARD LOWER & UPPER SHROUDS

SAIL INVENTORY
- MAINSAIL
- 150% GENOA
- SPINNAKER
- 2 WORKING JIBS
- TRYSAIL
- STORM JIB

SLAB REEFING WITH 3 SETS OF REEF POINTS

384

REINFORCED BOW AREA & ADDED WATERTIGHT BULKHEADS

BAG OF SURVIVAL GEAR STOWED IN DINGHY

CANVAS DODGER

EXTRA HAND HOLDS THROUGHOUT INTERIOR

SOLAR PANEL

ALL CHAIN RODE FOR 2 LIGHTWEIGHT ANCHORS & 1 PLOW

MONITOR SELF-STEERING WIND VANE

COCKPIT STORM SHUTTERS

ADDED BULKHEAD TO REINFORCE MAST STEP

1 *Atom* Unplugged

Go to the sea and reach for new horizons.

Atom's route to Panama

Once *Atom* cleared the breakwaters and the rushing motorboat traffic of Florida's Fort Lauderdale inlet, a light breeze filled in, and I cast off the towline from my friend's sailboat. He turned off his motor now and sailed silently alongside us for another mile before waving farewell and turning back to port. I took a long last look at the line of beach topped by a jagged concrete skyline of condos. Then I turned and stared and stared at the empty seascape before me. I was like a man starved of freedom, now set free. *Atom*'s bow dipped to the swell. A wave broke with a light slap against the hull. I sharpened my focus on the magical interplay of wind, wave, and sails. *Atom* and I were bound towards Panama and the Pacific, carrying a heart full of joy and high expectations as the sea's fresh salt breeze cleansed the air of the hazy stench of the city.

I convinced myself that no one really needed me back there, though that wasn't completely true. My recently divorced mother probably felt differently about my hurried departure after only a few months at home. I was her only child. She never spoke of her needs, and I was too self-absorbed to ask. She understood my compulsion to follow rainbows and seek the poetry of life, just as she had done in her youth, and she outwardly encouraged me to undertake this voyage because she knew it was what I had to do.

Less than a year earlier I had sailed back to Fort Lauderdale after a two-year voyage alone around the world. Having grown accustomed to roaming the world under sail, I suddenly found myself unfit to remain long on shore. Mostly I went back to sea because I was still in love with her: I longed for the outlandishly painted sunsets and silvery moonrises over open horizons, the blissful calms and terrifying tempests, *Atom*'s dance with the waves under a big sky, the joyous arrivals, and even the sad goodbyes. I loved the sea despite her unforgiving tendency to punish the unprepared. As in any one-sided love affair, her indifference to me would have been heartbreaking if we had been kept apart any longer.

I did make a halfhearted attempt to come ashore at least long enough to earn the money needed to begin another voyage. Within a few days of returning from the first circumnavigation, I moved *Atom* to a boatyard in Fort Lauderdale to tackle some long overdue maintenance issues. Before this work could begin I needed money. At that point the savings I had earned building a wooden sailboat for an expat owner while I was waiting out the cyclone season in New Guinea had all but disappeared. Fortune has always smiled on me, though she's been known to ignore me until I'm holding my last dollar.

This time my savior was Dan Spurr, an editor at *Cruising World Magazine* and the former owner of a Pearson Triton, the same model boat as *Atom*. When he heard about my return to the states he asked me to write a feature-length article describing my voyage and its preparations. I was eager to relate my sea stories, and to be paid for the task was almost too good to be true. Although I was a voracious reader, I was an untrained writer. I decided then to make writing my next immediate goal and wished that I had paid more attention to my unappreciated high school English teachers.

Dumpster Diving; Mean Streets; Rough Seas

By day I stripped *Atom* apart. One of my first tasks was removing her old mahogany plank rudder, so riddled by the wood-boring toredo worm that pieces of it came apart in my hands. I built a new one of laminated tapered plywood sheathed in fiberglass. More items, such as that fine piece of marine plywood, came to me from digging through piles of jettisoned yacht gear in the boatyard dumpsters than came through the gilded doors of the local marine store.

At night I worked as a security guard for the boatyard. Sitting alone in my phone booth-sized, lighted guard station each night, I outlined and wrote up my magazine article. Despite my efforts, I can see now that I had a long way to go before I developed a readable style. Luckily, my editor found the interesting content outweighed the flawed delivery. He mailed me a check for $400 and scheduled it for publication a few months later. This early success taught me that most readers will forgive imperfections of style, providing you have something worthwhile to say.

Meanwhile, my mother, who still lived in a north Detroit suburb, arranged for me to make a telephone interview with her reporter friend at the *Detroit News*. In the 1980s, a local boy sailing alone around the world was considered novel enough to warrant a page two story on a slow news day. I hoped that this unpaid interview outlining the highlights of my two-year voyage might open more doors on the path to a future writing career. An official at the Detroit Yacht Club read the news article and called me to offer free air fare plus a $500 speaker's fee for a lecture and photo slide presentation at their club one evening.

This was too good an opportunity to pass up. Even so, I felt uncomfortable when I gave my awkward presentation to such an affluent crowd. My audience of white collar lake racing sailors and their bored wives looked more stunned than entertained as I recounted in pictures and words how I had sailed as a penniless gypsy on my ill-equipped little boat from one distant island to the next, climbing the remote mountains to live among tribal peoples. As I stood before them in my outdated suit pulled from a storage box in my mother's closet, I couldn't help feeling some irony. That evening I was a respected guest at the same exclusive club that had thrown me off its property five years earlier. While sailing *Atom* on her first trip around the lakes, I had innocently pulled up to the yacht club fuel dock to buy a few gallons of gas and to top up the water tank. A club member from a nearby motor yacht scowled at me from under his braided yachting cap as I secured my lines. The security guard quickly marched over and announced, "This is private—for DYC yachts only," as he cast off my dock lines and set me adrift in the river currents. At that time I wished to be a member of the club, that privileged class who these few years later honored me as their paid guest speaker. I had earned my way into their ranks, at least for one night, which was long enough to reveal to them that, despite my sailing achievements, I was still not of their breed.

I followed up on the presentation at the DYC with other paid slide presentations and talks, including at the public library across the street from my old high school in the Detroit suburb of Mt. Clemens. Revisiting my high school and some of my old friends and teachers reminded me of how at 16 I had been a miserable student, prone to skipping class to be anywhere else. After tenth grade, with the reluctant permission of my permissive parents, I fled the tedium of school and the Michigan winter to catch a Greyhound bus to California. There I rented a spare room from an unknown friend of a friend in a Latino suburb of L.A.

On some weekends I walked the streets of Hollywood, bemused and bewildered at the bizarre human wreckage that lined the sidewalks at night. A couple times I hitchhiked to Huntington Beach and, lacking a wet suit and surfboard, watched from shore with longing as surfers rode the cold Pacific waves. During the week I hunted for jobs around L.A. The best I could find in the down economy was a few days a week as a temporary laborer for $10 a day. For a couple weeks the job finder company bused me into a factory with other marginally employable men to be used as hated strikebreakers, pushing our way through the angry, shouting faces of the union picket lines. The streets I walked were not filled with the golden opportunities I had imagined. California Dreamin' had turned into a hard dose of reality for a boy with few friends and no money. The indifferent and overcrowded city had rejected me. I returned home malnourished in body as well as in soul, resigned to finishing high school and learning a trade. By applying myself as I had never done before, I crammed the remaining two years of high school into one year of night classes while I worked at a string of other jobs during the day. After graduating from metalworking and welding school, I worked for two years to save the money to buy my boat. A boat I could live aboard would not only take me to all the foreign lands I hungered to see but also insulate me somewhat from relying on a steady stream of money and other people's good will.

A couple of my high school teachers showed up at my library lecture and congratulated me with that look of perplexity that a student so disruptive, truant, and demonstrably below average could ever do anything notable with his life. Gaining that sudden minor public attention made me uneasy, as if I were an undeserving fraud. There I was, busily spinning a web for some unknown purpose, only to risk entangling myself. I soon gave up the act to return to *Atom* and prepare for another voyage. At sea alone, you are who you are. There is no one to impress, no one to let down but yourself.

But why again go alone? Hadn't I seen enough loneliness and danger on my earlier passages? A person can end up waiting a very long time before finding a compatible crewmate who has the time and inclination to travel the route you seek to follow. It helped that I viewed the sea not only as a blue highway to transport me to new lands but also as a solitary retreat. Like a Tibetan monk trekking through the mountains on a solo pilgrimage to some isolated shrine, I embraced each mindful step of the journey as a meditation borne in the solitude of the sea. The navigator stands at the center of a circle of sea and sky, using his mind, muscle, and senses to deliver him to some imagined new place and new awareness. None of us lives his entire life alone, but how uplifting and transforming it is to indulge this quest for oneness of self and environment from time to time.

Back in Fort Lauderdale, my voyage preparations continued with a major overhaul of *Atom*'s vital components. On my first circumnavigation, during nights rushing blindly through the darkness, I often worried about hitting reefs or collisions with large floating objects such as semi-submerged shipping containers or even loitering whales. That anxiety increased when I narrowly escaped without damage after running over an uprooted drifting tree in the Gulf of Panama. It can be unnerving to be alone in mid-ocean when all that stands between you and the bottom of the sea is a half-inch skin of fiberglass. To reduce my worries, if not all the risk, I now built a watertight collision bulkhead in the bow section under the v-berth. The tight budget and my quest to remain self-reliant ensured that there would be no life raft or emergency rescue beacon aboard.

For several months *Atom* sat drying out on her trailer in a Fort Lauderdale boatyard as I replaced bad rigging with slightly less bad rigging from the dumpster, applied new paint and varnish, rebedded leaky deck fittings, and did a hundred or more other jobs. After my overland visit to Michigan, I returned to the boatyard and sealed the hull below the waterline with three coats of epoxy barrier coat. The hull had so far shown no signs of that dreaded blistering of the fiberglass laminate known as osmosis. I had read that this epoxy sealing would help preserve the fiberglass for decades to come, so it seemed to be worth the time and expense.

During the eight years I had owned the boat I continually repaired *Atom*'s cranky antique four-cylinder gasoline inboard engine. For the most part, I used it only when entering ports and in some limited coastal motor-sailing situations. It remained such an uncooperative and inscrutable beast that I now decided to remove it and sail engine-free. It was an added incentive that I was able to sell the engine to another sailor for $300. That was a permanent fix to my years of engine troubles and repair expenses. Unfortunately for the buyer, his costs in ongoing maintenance time and money were just beginning. Like watching an ex-wife move in with a new man, I hoped that they fared better together than we had. Besides the concerns of my wallet, my temperament was better suited to waiting for a fair wind than waiting for a mechanic and suffering the frustration of a broken engine letting me down one day when I most counted on it. *Atom*'s finely-crafted hull would sail better without dragging a propeller through the water, and I no longer needed to worry about getting our propeller tangled up in fishing nets or crab traps. My main motivation, however, was that I now felt ready to tackle this sport on a more fundamental level—to place as little as possible between myself and the sea. I did carry a 13-foot wooden sculling oar I had built on the dock in Mauritius two years earlier. Instead of a standard double-oared rowing motion, the single sculling oar over the transom was operated by a twisting push and pull motion of the arms while standing facing forward and gripping the oar under one arm. By applying just the right oar twisting technique, I could move *Atom* along in a calm harbor at just over one knot. Either an hour of hard labor on the oar got me across the harbor, or complete exhaustion brought the boat to a halt.

The world of sailing has become so corrupted by auxiliary engine propulsion that "engineless" is the only word we use to define a pure sailing craft. The word implies that a vessel lacks something unquestionably fundamental when in fact an inboard engine is the chief impediment to becoming a competent sailor. The motorized sailor reaches for his ignition key at the slightest sign of boredom when progress is slow. He also expects the engine to get him in and out of every conceivable situation when, more often than not, sail power would serve equally well.

Nowadays, getting away from it all seems to require frequent contact with "it all" via satellite phones offshore and cell phones along the coast, SSB radio, and shipboard email messaging. At that time, most of those distracting devices were not available. I'd like to think it wouldn't have mattered if they were, because I imagined an experience aboard *Atom* alone as a sea-going attempt to emulate Henry David Thoreau's elemental sojourn at his self-built cabin at Walden Pond in the mid 19th century. Whereas Thoreau dirtied his hands in the soil and traipsed through the woods around his cabin with wide-open eyes and fertile mind, I roamed the seas and its islands. We both sought to know our place in the world intimately and, in doing so, to cultivate the man within.

As I prepared to disengage temporarily from society, so too *Atom* became unplugged. On a quest to rid myself of many of the superfluous contrivances that stand between man and nature, I ruthlessly stripped *Atom* of all her electrics. Out went the electric lights and radios, even the main batteries and the hundreds of feet of copper wires making up the boat's 12-volt electrical system. I used a one-burner kerosene stove for cooking and kerosene lamps for lighting. I did bring a video camera to document portions of the trip, but its batteries required recharging on visits ashore. The marine toilet, with all its leaky valves, pump, and hoses went overboard to be replaced by an honest bucket in a wooden box. For entertainment I had my harmonica and acoustic guitar aboard. My ability with both instruments was so limited that they perfectly suited a solo journey.

Sailing alone and without an engine or distracting electric gadgets would eventually teach me whatever I hadn't learned about sailing and my own abilities during my first circumnavigation. That journey had taught me how rich our lives become when our needs remain few. What you don't have, you likely don't need. Now I took that lesson one step further.

Sailing stripped to its bare essentials is hard to justify to most people. They feel it's not a practical choice for them, and so they try to convince people that it's not practical for anyone. Either you have an innate understanding of the value of a particular adventure, or you sit back and scoff at the impracticalities of it. Those who need to ask why are unlikely to be satisfied with any explanation. I also remind myself that my dream is no one else's and that my choices are not lifetime commitments, so I don't waste time trying to convince others to follow my wayward path. Our nature is to evolve—each physical path or philosophical corridor inevitably broadens or leads to another.

As I set out from Fort Lauderdale to cross the Straits of Florida in early March 1987, I intended to continue 1,500 nautical miles nonstop southeast through the Bahamas and then south through the Windward Passage to Panama. We crossed the Gulf Stream current that first day and entered Bahamian waters. Now sitting in my home office looking over my journal and the tattered, saltwater-stained logbook from that passage, I read that the winds soon settled into the northeast at Force 4–6 (11–27 knots). The logbook takes me back, and I visualize the choppy head seas striking the bow, the boat heeling to increasingly gusty winds as I reefed down the mainsail and replaced the largest #1 headsail with the smaller #2, then the #3 a few hours later, and finally the #4 jib. The only smaller sail remaining to set in even stronger winds was a storm jib that was not much bigger than a diagonally folded tablecloth. It required that many different sized jibs to allow the Triton's small, relatively light, and low-freeboard hull to balance the heeling force of the varying wind

Atom departs Fort Lauderdale

strengths with the boat's counterbalancing keel. When that correct balance is found, the boat drives forward with minimal leeway. It's also much drier on deck to sail less heeled, and slowing her down when possible with smaller sails puts less strain on the rigging, deck, and hull. There is only so much punishment an old boat can take before she starts to come apart. Knowing his boat's limits is a sailor's top priority.

Without the luxury of a modern furling headsail that reefs down in size by rolling the sail up incrementally on a headstay tube, I was obliged to go through a simple but often drenching sail-changing routine. On that first day at sea my third sail change began by easing out the sheet line attached to the sail's lower aft corner, called the clew. Sailors have a strange language that they use to precisely identify each item on their ship. Having that secret language also provides entertainment as it befuddles the lubbers aboard. As the rising wind flogged the sail I rushed forward with the smaller sail in its bag. By that time the building seas were topped with breaking crests. The boat leapt off a wave top and fell heeling over with an unsettling bang into the next wave trough. My lifeline harness tether kept me attached to the boat as my legs slid out under the lifelines into the warm sea. I lashed the bag to the windward lifeline on the heeling deck and released the jib halyard, which allowed me to claw the sail back down the headstay mast wire. Crawling forward crab-like on the plunging deck, between dousings of saltwater from waves striking the side of the bow, I disconnected the sheets and halyard, unhooked the bronze piston hanks from the leading edge of the sail, and stuffed it rough, wrinkled, and wet into its bag, which I lashed to the lifeline. Having lost a sail over the side in my first year of sailing, I never again failed to secure a bag on deck. Then I reversed the process with the smaller sail, scrambled back to the cockpit with the sail bag under one arm, and tightened the sheet on the leeward cockpit winch until the sail was trimmed tightly enough to stop its flogging. Finally, I took a deep breath. The next sail change might be needed at any moment.

Obviously, the lighter the winds are, the easier a sail change becomes, and when *Atom* is sailing downwind the process can sometimes be done without even getting wet. The older I got the less concerned I was about losing a bit of ground to windward, so more and more often I resorted to turning the boat downwind to change sail and then resumed course when safely back in the cockpit.

My sails were all over twenty years old, and some of them were very much older, so I carried a sail repair kit to hand stitch loose seams and patch tears as needed. Before beginning this trip, I needed to replace my ancient sails, which were so rotten I could push my finger through the material. I had nursed them along for years, but it was obvious they would not see me across another ocean. I wrote a note to the Triton Association newsletter (a group of sailors who owned the same model boat as *Atom*), offering to buy a set of used sails from another owner. Perhaps someone into racing was replacing his sails because they were somewhat stretched out of shape for racing but still serviceable for cruising duty. I was happily surprised when a man I had never met sent me his used mainsail and genoa as a "gift for *Atom*."

Cruising sailors are like that; they help out other sailors in need. I recall when I had last arrived in Panama, seeing a sailboat hauled out at the repair yard with a group of sailors working to patch several large holes in the bottom of the boat. The owner had been sailing alone, overslept, and struck a reef near the coast, sinking the boat in shallow water. Like me, he had little money and no other home. As soon as word of the incident got out, several of the sailors in the anchorage got together to see if they could rescue the boat. Working in rough waters on the top of a dangerous reef, they somehow managed to refloat the boat using empty oil drums they flooded and lashed to the hull below the water and then filled with compressed air from their scuba tanks. Once afloat they towed the boat with their dinghies to the boat yard, pumped it dry, and patched it up with donated materials. You could easily see the relief and gratitude of the young sailor, who had his home and his dreams unexpectedly returned to him.

I kept *Atom*'s nose pressed hard on the wind despite the hull-pounding waves as we tacked and threaded our way through the Bahamas in the Northwest and Northeast Providence Channels. I knew this route well, having sailed the same path on my first voyage to Panama. Vigilance for shipping and unlit reef-girt shores became my main concern. On my third day out, strong easterly winds had reduced me to storm jib and triple-reefed main as I tacked back and forth between the low sandy islands and surrounding reefs. With each tack, first one deck rail was under water, then the other. As the boat slammed into the seas, her bow cut through the wave tops and flung sheets of spray through the air. When possible, I ducked for some shelter behind the folding canvas dodger that shields the companionway entrance to the cabin. I grew fatigued from lack of sleep as well as constantly trying to hold myself from being flung from one side of the boat to the other. "Easier days to come," I told myself, which turned out, as always, to be at least partly true.

Suddenly the jib halyard broke at a chafe point on its mast sheave and dropped the thrashing sail onto the deck with part of it dragging in the sea. My budget didn't include replacing all the lines before departure, but I did have the spinnaker halyard available, which I quickly transferred to rehoist the jib. This was only a temporary solution, and if I somehow lost the spinnaker halyard, I would be unable to hoist any jib at all. I needed a calm harbor in order to climb the mast and pull a spare line through the hoisting block. My lockers held an ample supply of used and very used lines that I had rescued from an early death in the Florida marina dumpsters. The shoestring sailor is a master of recycling, or he is going nowhere.

I also needed a calm day to unbolt and repair the Aries mechanical windvane attached to the transom. Having a reliable self-steering device was essential to free me from the drudgery of non-stop hand steering. But during these first few days I had noticed it held an unsteady course, causing *Atom* to dodge about on its course like a hunted rabbit. A few days before departure I had hurriedly disassembled the gears to replace worn bushings and had somehow misaligned the gear teeth during reassembly. Every little detail counts.

Meanwhile, the northeast winds had increased to a steady and punishing Force 7. To resolve both issues, I diverted course to anchor in a protected cove at the Bahamas uninhabited Royal Island. Several other American cruising sailboats lay at anchor there waiting out the strong winds before continuing their island-hopping cruises. As the winds lashed the palm fronds on shore and rattled *Atom*'s rigging, I made a heaping plateful of curried vegetables and rice. It was the first time I had lit the stove in the past two days due to the bone-jarring motion of beating into wind and sea. I was half asleep before I finished my meal. The next thing I recall was waking up 10 hours later, and feeling fully recovered.

I met the other sailboat crews when we all dinghied ashore the next morning. Among the vacationing couples was a skipper who shared with us the voice weather forecast and weatherfax image download that he had just received on his SSB radio. The near gale force winds and rough seas, he told us, were expected to gradually die down over the next few days.

The Humorless Frau; Reef Anxiety; Night Encounters

I had stopped briefly at Royal Island with a couple of passengers during my trip to the Bahamas five years earlier. With me aboard *Atom* was a newly wedded German couple in their late twenties who had answered my note on a Nassau marina bulletin board asking for crew willing to "share expenses." Actually, this was more of a ruse to do a bit of unlicensed chartering. What cash-poor sailor doesn't dream of sailing his boat around tropical isles while being paid and complimented by generously tipping tourists? What I didn't realize was how unsuited my small boat and my independent nature were to the demands of tourists. The husband came out by water taxi to where *Atom* lay anchored off the marina, and we negotiated a one-week trip around the islands for the bargain price of $200. With me supplying the food and fuel, the profit margin was pretty slim but better than my other options. The next morning I pulled alongside the dock where he and his bride hopped aboard with two huge suitcases. I shoved their hard baggage into the tiny forward cabin and showed them how they could sleep on the same V-shaped bunk after shifting the bags to the side. His frau let us know immediately that this was not her idea of a nice honeymoon when, with Germanic zeal, she dragged a finger along the galley counter, brought up some specks of dust, and shrieked in my face, "You live like filsey pig!" Her husband reassured her that all would be perfect as I bit my tongue and scrubbed the countertops.

The three of us sailed along the string of islets east of Nassau some 45 miles to Royal Island. No sooner was the anchor down in this perfectly tranquil honeymoon location and my invitation issued to go snorkeling than the shrew demanded, "Vere's zis casino und restaurant?" Charter business was not so easy after all. She eventually drove me to the unkind thought that there was still a remote chance a shark would carry her off before the trip was over, saving her new husband a lifetime of tongue lashings.

The next morning I prepared a pot of boiled oats for their breakfast. Handing our lady a bowlful of steaming oats in the heat of the still and humid morning air brought another shriek of disgust as she dumped it overboard: "Vat is zis sheet? Zis is baby food. I haf teats, ya! Ve Germans do not boil zee oats into dis deesgustink goo!"

"Yes, I know you have teats," I replied calmly. "But I can't serve you raw oatmeal."

Our cheerless frau instructed me to mix the raw oats with a couple spoons of nonfat milk powder; add tepid water, cinnamon, and sliced bananas; and let the concoction soak a few minutes. I hated to admit it, but the overbearing wench taught me something. My Nordic mother had regimented me, as her mother had regimented her, to boil all oatmeal into a pot of barely palatable porridge that might have doubled for lumpy wallpaper paste. Though I never grew to actually like the stuff, it was at least cheap and nutritious and well-suited to an unrefrigerated boat pantry. Tradition is hard to overcome, but I never boiled oats again and learned to enjoy the meal more after adding in a few spoons of muesli or granola. When I do get caught in a cold climate and want a hot breakfast, I pour heated water over the oats, but still don't cook them. Sorry, mom.

I could not endure the punishment a moment longer, so since *Atom* still had a motor at that time, the next day I put it to good use by motor-sailing as fast as I could back to Nassau. The husband had been in non-stop apology mode to that wretched woman since the moment we got underway. At least I think he was apologizing by his repeated demands to her of "*verzeihung, bitte*" (forgiveness, please). To the ears of non-Germans, an apology in German can be indistinguishable from an insult. I imagine he is still *verzeihung*-ing to this day. My guests threw their luggage onto the dock and leapt from the deck before I could get the boat stopped and take a line ashore. They did not even pay a portion of the agreed $200 for the shortened charter trip, or thank me for my trouble. And so ended my only attempt at a chartering career.

My current visit alone to Royal Island was relatively enchanting as I walked the trails across the low hills on the narrow 4-mile-long island, passing stone and coral block ruins of a previous settlement now partly hidden and overgrown with vines and coconut trees. In the past 300 years the island and its superb sheltered harbor once hosted pirates, then Royalist privateers during the American Revolution, later becoming an enterprising Englishman's private estate and sheep ranch. A thick, low limestone wall severed the island on its narrow north/south axis. Humans to one side and sheep to the other, I presumed. At first glance the island seemed devoid of life, aside from the coarse scrubby brush and coconut palms. Then a rooster trumpeted his presence. I encountered his flock running wild all over the island, as well as a couple forgotten goats. Next to the stone quay at the harbor stood the abandoned plantation house, a workshop, and a saloon with two collapsed billiards tables. Nearby sat the ultimate folly for a nearly roadless island—the broken rusted heap of a Model T Ford, complete with a young tree sprouting from its open trunk. The old plantation had obviously been here a long time before being abandoned to the ravages of weather and vandals.

As I rinsed the sea salt from my clothes with buckets of freshwater pulled from the island's well, I felt what must be an almost universal inclination to move ashore, claim the island as my own, and put things back in order. It was just as well that in the financial sense I was impoverished, because I could surely fall victim to mad schemes such as this. I already knew that the more you possess, the more you become possessed. The island that had sustained and sometimes broken the early settlers, I left as I had found it—a ghostly haunt to visiting yachties.

Underway again, I tacked into a rising wind toward open waters east of the Bahamas and then turned south. A vicious but short-lived thunderstorm pinned me down with pellet-like sheets of wind-driven rain. I clawed and climbed my way to the mast to triple reef the mainsail, which tamed it enough for *Atom* to regain some balance. With rain-stung eyes I clung to the bow pulpit rail to attach and then hoist the storm jib, which I sheeted to windward to arrest our forward movement. Lying hove to in this way, I rode out the squall from the security of the cabin while peering through the portlights at the violent display of nature's beauty.

By nightfall, I was sailing at a safe distance along the windward coast of Eleuthera Island. The snake-like Eleuthera is approximately 90-miles long and averages only two to three miles wide. On earlier voyages I had spent many happy days sailing along the shallow banks of clear, calm waters of its western shore, anchoring in quiet harbors behind the low limestone hills. Now as I skirted the coasts of the neighboring Cat Island, San Salvador, and Samana Cay, I felt as if I was sailing in familiar home waters. Scholars still dispute which of these little islands was the site of Columbus's first landfall in the Americas. In the five centuries since, for better and worse, we have reshaped much of the pristine New World in the image of Old World Europe. The native Lucayan people of the Bahamas, unskilled in warfare, had been occasionally hunted and eaten, so the story goes, by the aggressive Carib warrior tribes who inhabited the larger Caribbean islands to the south. But it took Spanish slave hunters only 30 years after Columbus's arrival to exterminate all the Lucayans in the Bahamas. Fortunately for us modern sailors, a few of these out-islands of the New World remained otherwise little changed from when the peaceable Lucayans inhabited their shores.

A day later, on a cloudy black night, my feelings of familiarity changed to high anxiety as I blindly sailed through the narrow passages between the smaller islands of the southern Bahamas. I was less than a mile off the fringing reef of the low Mayaguana Island before I discerned it by a faint light on shore. By dawn, Mayaguana was eight miles astern and already lost to sight because of its lowness to the sea. Light north winds carried me slowly south. By the next evening, somewhere directly ahead, I knew, lay the unlit and uninhabited Little Inagua Island. I remained on deck all night straining to make out the shape of land or hear the muted sound of surf boiling over the reefs. A break in the clouds finally revealed a dark shadow of land emerging directly ahead. Minutes later a pale moon outlined the silvery white line of surf foaming on the reef. At that moment the fitful wind fell nearly calm. I caught my breath as I sensed an unseen current pulling us towards destruction on the bony coral fingers ahead. I jumped forward and hoisted our largest headsail. The light breeze stretched the deep wrinkles from the sail. Gradually we gained enough speed to pull clear of the danger.

As I entered the Windward Passage near the coast of Cuba the following night, a line of squalls caught me asleep in my bunk. We were under full sail when suddenly the boat heeled over at a crazy angle accompanied by a chaotic drumming noise of wind on flogging sails, spars, and rigging. I clambered over the canvas and rope leecloth that held me in my bunk and clipped on my safety harness as I charged up the companionway steps and into the maelstrom. As I yanked down the sails, the wind kept increasing, pulling the wet flogging sailcloth from my hands. The painful sting of rain and salt spray on my face told me it must be blowing over 60 knots. I let *Atom* run straight downwind to the southwest under bare poles. The wind dropped somewhat after the initial squall line had passed. But the stirred-up sea remained laced with streaks of wave break spindrift as it continued to blow at least 40 knots (a Force 8 gale) for several hours. The force of the wind on her hull, deck, and bare rig pushed us along at about three to four knots as I peered into the blackness. Meanwhile, I debated with myself whether I needed to dig out the storm sails from the cockpit locker or wait out the blow a bit longer.

Suddenly out of the rain a few hundred yards ahead appeared a freighter crossing in front of us. What the ship did next seemed inexplicable. The captain's actions nearly cost me my life. Maybe he saw me on radar or noticed the dim light of my kerosene lantern bobbing from the backstay above my head in the cockpit and wanted to investigate. In any case, the ship reversed its engine and came to a stop dead ahead with *Atom* heading straight for the center of its broad hull. Someone shined a searchlight at us, apparently to see if we were a lifeboat in distress. If I hadn't been in distress before, I surely was now because we were locked on a collision course.

At first I dared hope we might slip astern of the ship's high iron hull if I could steer a few degrees to starboard. As *Atom* scudded inexorably forward, pushed by the strong winds at our back, I yanked the tiller to turn the boat. There was no response because we had no sail up to give steerageway. As I stared ahead, paralyzed for a long moment by fear and indecision, the black hull grew larger and more ominous. I briefly directed my flashlight beam on the leviathan's bridge and then aimed it back at my empty mast, hoping to indicate my helpless and perilous state.

There was perhaps one minute remaining before we crashed into the ship's side—no time to hoist and sheet a storm jib or rig the storm trysail that could be raised in place of the mainsail. I jumped forward to the mast, desperately fighting the knots that bound the mainsail to the boom and managed to hoist the sail a few feet before something jammed it in place. The sail flogged loose as I leapt back to the tiller, hoping we had enough sail area up to provide some steerage. *Atom* turned sideways to the wind and sat stubbornly in place, as if resigned to her fate. Seconds before the wind drove us into the wall of steel now towering above us, her skipper finally realized his mistake and put his engine into full ahead. We slid by so close under her stern that *Atom* swirled in her prop wash like poop about to go down a toilet.

The encounter left me with a dry throat and rubbery knees. If I hadn't fully realized it before, I knew now that this would be no easy voyage. A radio to contact the ship or an engine aboard *Atom* might have prevented the near disaster. That incident highlighted the danger of sailing without them. On the other hand, if I had prepared the storm trysail earlier and had it ready to hoist for such a situation, we would have been able to safely maneuver regardless of the ship's movements. It is always better to maintain the ability to direct your boat and your destiny rather than rely on another skipper to avoid hitting you. No matter how long and far you sail, there are always lessons the sea can teach you.

The next morning the dark 7,000-foot mountains of Haiti were backlit by the sunrise on our port beam. To starboard the purple, cloud-capped coast of Cuba hove into view. Cuba was still off-limits to American yachts at the time. I was thankful for the strong and fair wind that carried us quickly and safely away to the south. *Atom* slid down these growing waves at a great speed, slowing momentarily in the troughs, as if to catch her breath, before climbing the back of each passing wave. On the wave crests the wind moaned in the rigging as streaks of spray flew around us. That lively wavetop ballet marked our stage entrance into the theater of the northeast trade winds.

Not a single ship came into view all that day. But I did have companions of another sort in the fish and bird life that surrounded me. For hours I watched a school of yellowfin tuna that closely followed the boat. From time to time their orderly soldier-like march was broken by a frenzy of activity as the fleet hunters tore into passing schools of smaller, slower fish. Seabirds noisily dived and fought over the remaining scraps. After the slaughter, the tuna took to the air in long graceful arcs, as if from sheer love of flight or in celebration of a successful hunt. There were so many taking to the air at once that I thought we might scoop one up in our sails.

The winds and seas settled down enough so that I shook out a reef in the sail. *Atom* reeled off well over a hundred miles each day under a singing wind as seabirds wheeled in the sky around us. The harmless rolling seas topped with white foamy crests presented themselves in endless procession. These are the happy days of easy progress that sailors long for and remember best.

In contrast, on my first voyage to Panama I had sat becalmed for the better part of three days in that very spot as a low-pressure system disrupted the trade winds. That calm was memorable, however, because of the chance encounter I had there with a huge square-rigged ship lying motionless beside me for several hours. Its canvas hung limp, barely pulsing as the heavy spars lazily rolled high above the ocean swell. Her skipper told me over the VHF radio that I had at the time that his charter vessel was bound north to Bermuda. We discussed and guessed at when the wind might return. His diesel engine had broken down, leaving him helpless like the ancient pirate ships he resembled. When a light breeze popped up a few hours later we continued on our opposite tracks.

Out here I had the freedom I sought, real freedom, unattached to conditions and limits. You might think that a small boat is confining compared with a house on land. While the average American house is measured in the thousands of square feet and small apartments in the hundreds of square feet, *Atom*'s cabin floor space was a narrow corridor some eight feet long. The forward three feet of that floor was in the head and forward cabin where the coachroof was too low for a person over five feet to stand up. Lockers, bunks, and a mini galley took up the remainder of the useable space. My galley counter held a sink only big enough to accommodate hand washing or to place one pot or a couple dishes. But on deck, beyond the confines of the cabin, lay access to a whole world that moved by as I roamed it while wrapped tortoise-like in my protective shell.

I settled into my sea routine. During the days and nights I took brief naps, awakening to the insistent ringing of my kitchen timer alarm to take visual scans of the horizon. The more distance I put between myself and the shore and shipping lanes the more time I gave myself between rings of the alarm clock. Days were filled with cooking meals on my kerosene stove, exercising, meditating, making journal notes, reading from my library, adjusting course, and trimming sails to a wind that remained between north and east. I couldn't count the number of hours I stood with one arm around the mast for support, gazing out on the endlessly fascinating rolling seascape.

An hour or two each day were devoted to navigating by sextant. The sun was commonly available and easy to shoot. But the stars and planets were the navigator's true trophy. The big, glowing sphere of Venus was often visible as it tracked forever within 47 degrees of the sun's setting or rising. The first, brightest stars to appear in evening twilight formed as yet incomplete constellations. Nevertheless, I knew them all by name and their relative place in the sky. I lifted the sextant like a shaman raising his magic scepter on the temple mount and brought the distant stars down to earth where I measured their precise angle to one sixtieth of one degree of arc, and to one precise second of time. From there I converted these observations to hopeful lines of position on my chart. The act brought feelings of belonging, of power, to command the stars to mark my place on the naked sea.

On March 21, eleven days out from Royal Island, *Atom* approached the coast of Panama. Remembering too well my last landfall at Panama, when a strong coastal counter-current had swept me ten miles to the east, this time I compensated by adjusting course to bring me slightly west of the canal entrance. But this year the current was non-existent, and I made landfall ten miles west of my target at Limon Bay. Once the error was discovered, I tacked back east until we sailed past the ships of a dozen nations' flags moored off the breakwater entrance to the Panama Canal. I dropped anchor among the other yachts in Cristobal Harbor and fell into the deep and satisfying sleep of a sailor finally arrived in safe harbor.

2 The Gates of Panama

Where the seas of east and west meet and the land divides us no longer.

The Caribbean and Pacific coasts of Panama and her outlying islands offered an unspoiled cruising ground for sailboats, and I'd often dreamed of cruising the area fully. But if I was going to reach Hawaii before the summer hurricane season, I had little time to linger and enjoy the sights. Instead, as I'd learned from my first canal transit three years earlier, I'd be busy enough restocking the boat with provisions and trying to outfox the gauntlet of paper shuffling bureaucrats, wharf thieves, and street muggers who preyed on the unwary yachtfolk transiting the canal.

In 1987 the United States still remained in control of the Panama Canal Zone—a five-mile-wide slice of territory bordering the canal itself. Despite the American overlords, the mix of Panamanian and American permit stampers managed very well to mimic the out-of-control bureaucracy common to much of Latin America. Since *Atom* had passed this way before and carried the ship identification card issued on her first transit, I was now at least allowed to skip some of the more tedious procedures, such as bringing aboard an official to measure our tiny cargo capacity with tape measure and calculator.

Alerted by the yellow quarantine flag hoisted on my mast, a Panamanian Customs launch motored out to *Atom*. After a brief look around the boat for contraband, the officers handed me a stack of forms to fill out in triplicate and then cleared me to come ashore. I launched my 6-foot plastic dinghy from its resting place—lashed upside down to the cabin top—and went first to visit a 41-foot plywood and fiberglass trimaran anchored next to me. There I met Gary and Donna Matsushima who were bringing back the new-to-them, used boat from Key West to their home port of Kaneohe Bay, Hawaii. Meeting them was a lucky coincidence because I too was planning to visit Kaneohe

Bay on my trip across the northern Pacific. The young couple briefed me on mooring options in Hawaii and provided an update on canal procedures. From them I heard the canal had just closed its lock doors to yachts for the next eighteen days due to maintenance. What at first seemed an annoyance turned out to be a useful interlude to give me time to prepare my boat and locate a crew of four that each yacht was required to have to act as line-handlers in the locks.

Panama Pandemonium; Three Sisters; Esmeralda's Eyes

One more complication Gary and Donna informed me about was that yachts were now required to spend two days transiting the 50-mile-long canal instead of one long day as I had done on my first trip. This meant that I needed to find space aboard my already snug 28-foot boat for the four additional crew to sleep as we anchored overnight in Gatun Lake, midway through the canal.

Next I rowed ashore to the dinghy dock at the small and informal Panama Canal Yacht Club. I spent two days beyond its protective gates, running around the squalid, dangerous streets of Colón, filling out paperwork, and paying fees averaging a few dollars each to various Panamanian and American canal officials. After soccer, document stamping is the chief national sport of Latin America, and the Canal Zone was at the top of their game. For example, the Port Captain issued me clearance only after I had returned from taking his paperwork across town to another office where they affixed to the forms a five-dollar stamp. Apparently the Port Captain's office could not be trusted to collect the fee. The total cost was under $100, leaving me about $1,400 in savings. This was all the money I had in the world—no credit cards occupied my thin wallet—but what of that? I was still three times richer than when I had set sail on my first world voyage with only $500 in my pocket. And as before, I always expected to find work when I needed it, on other boats or on shore. Being broke in a foreign land was always the best motivator to meet the people there and find a job.

To transit the Panama Canal requires an engine, of course. I had departed Fort Lauderdale engineless, but I had a plan on how to get through the canal. Before leaving, I had bolted an adjustable outboard motor bracket to *Atom*'s transom. In the Cristobal anchorage I arranged to rent a dinghy motor for $25 from a friendly yacht-owner, who agreed to drop it off to me on the morning of our transit. He was scheduled to transit on the same day, so I could return his motor when we both reached the Pacific side of the canal.

At the yacht club bar I met Juan, a friendly Colombian guy about my age with curly locks of black hair sticking out from under his baseball cap. Juan worked as crew on another larger yacht that was based here. He spoke basic English, and after we had gotten to know each other for a few minutes, he agreed to join me for the transit and to help find the other three crew I needed. The next day Juan showed up in a dinghy with three lovely teen-aged Panamanian sisters. As I lent a hand to pull them aboard, I was introduced to Marisol, Mariluna, and China (the last pronounced "Cheena," a Hispanic nickname for a girl with oriental eyes) —all as alluring as their dreamy-sounding names. Their dark skin and oriental features revealed their far-flung ancestry: Spanish mixed with the African, Indian, and Chinese laborers brought here a century earlier by the French and then the Americans to build the canal. To entertain our guests for their first time aboard a sailboat, I hoisted anchor, and we sailed around the flat waters of the three-mile-wide Limon Bay. Beyond their beauty, they were enthusiastic crew, running back and forth to help set the sails, exploring the layout of the cabin, and laughing at the novelty of it all. When I noticed they were good on their feet and could handle the lines on cue, an idea formed in my head that I may have just found my canal line-handlers. I was so dazzled by my lively crew that I nearly let *Atom* run aground under self-steering when we too quickly reached the far end of the bay. Once back at anchor, the girls prepared vegetables and rice Spanish style, that is to say, with plenty of tongue-blistering hot chili peppers.

The following evening the girls took me to the outskirts of Colón to be entertained by a traveling carnival that had come to town. Around midnight I brought the girls back by taxi to their farmhouse outside the city. At the door waited their mother. I could tell from her forced tight-lipped smile and piercing black eyes that sized me up disapprovingly from my flip-flop sandals to my military haircut, that she did not approve of transient canal zone sailors running around with her young daughters. I should have known when she kept me standing awkwardly at the bottom of the porch after our introduction, that I was out of luck. But I went ahead anyway and asked permission to have her daughters accompany me as crew for the canal transit.

"*Tal vez*" (Perhaps), their mother replied sternly without the hint of her previous forced smile. Her apparently ambiguous response was translated to me by the pouting Mariluna as a definite "No." It was clear that the idea of a lusty gringo sailor proposing to take her daughters away for two days and nights on the canal trip had not charmed the lady at all. My fun with the sisters was over, and I still lacked three crew members.

Juan and I had to hustle. The next day Juan found Patricio, a young Panamanian who worked as a vendor at the city's vegetable market, who agreed to come along for $20 cash and a bus ticket back home from the other end of the canal.

This left me short by two line handlers. In our search, Juan and I risked the thief-infested streets of Colón where we met a Colombian friend of his who he thought might be willing to come along on our trip. On the sidewalk in front of a seedy-looking district near the center of town, Juan introduced me to Armando and his 18-year-old sister, Esmerelda. Armando had been a policeman in Colombia until a month ago when he and his sister had fled to Panama. With Juan interpreting, Armando described how the mafia in his hometown had threatened to kill him and his family over some cocaine trafficking incident he had inadvertently gotten caught up in. Here in Colón, the only job Armando and his sister had found was selling cigarettes and candy at a leased sidewalk concession. The wooden table in front of us held single pieces of gum, hard candy, and loose cigarettes sold one at a time to passersby who could not afford to buy the whole pack. After they paid the rent on the table and merchandise, their average two-dollar daily profit went to pay for their cheap hotel room. Almost nothing remained for food. Armando spoke in such a friendly, even hopeful manner, and his sister's smile was so devastating that I wished I could afford to give them more than the couple dollars I spent on candy at their street stand, which I passed out to a circle of begging children. I stretched my budget again when I offered to hire Armando and Esmeralda to be my final two line-handlers, which they eagerly accepted. To escape the blistering hot streets of town, the four of us went for a sunset sail in the bay and had a party aboard *Atom* that night to celebrate our new friendship.

The afternoon before our transit, Armando and Esmeralda were to show up to meet me at the yacht club as planned. They were a little late. Then a lot late. The thought of having no crew when the canal pilot arrived had my stomach knotted. Off I ran through the tough streets of Colón searching for them for hours until that evening I got a tip that Armando had been seen going into the Olympia Bar. With some apprehension of going alone into a Colón bar at night, I stepped through the doors of the Olympia into blasting disco music and flashing lights. An aroma of tobacco smoke, stale beer, and urine filled my nostrils. What I saw next shocked the modesty of this young sailor who had never before been inside a real honest-to-God whorehouse.

Lined up elbow-to-elbow along the bar, like crows perched on a fence, were about 50 black-haired Colombian women, whose faces of various shades of brown were highlighted with gaudy make-up. Some wore mini-skirts, and others wore jeans fitting as tightly as grape skins. They had all quickly turned as one to size up the new customer when I first opened the door. At this early hour there were few other men there. The dusky women pounced on me like starved vultures pecking into a newly discovered carcass. Seeing me hesitate, with my hand still frozen on the door handle, they formed a scrum and jostled me deeper inside the bar. Several clung to each arm, pulling in different directions, waving their other hands and clucking to each other excitedly in Spanish. This may have been some sailor's vision of a great night out, but my sober innocence put me in a sudden cold sweat. A writhing mass of painted lips, heaving cleavage, and tight jeans loudly demanded/implored/begged/pleaded that this gringo buy everyone drinks (apparently, the commission on drinks increased their thirst). Each in turn gazed suggestively and offered we should go upstairs "for short time." I no longer drank alcohol at that time, and the hulking bartender/bouncer/pimp raised both eyebrows when, hoping to avoid a case of Montezuma's Revenge from dirty ice cubes, I asked meekly for an unopened can of tonic water.

Eventually, my eyes adjusted to the flashing lights. Through the smoky air I noticed Armando sitting with his sister at a table in a dark corner of the room, apparently trying not to be seen. I pulled away from the girls and joined them. Speaking in our mixture of English and Spanish, Armando explained they couldn't crew for me on the canal trip. He went on to explain that, after being unable to afford a room to keep them off the street any longer, he had signed a contract to sell his virginal sister into sex slavery at this foulest of Colón's nasty nightclubs. In return, he had received $100 and was allowed to hang out in the bar each night in hopes of making Esmeralda's new job slightly less traumatic for her. He seemed only saddened rather than angry at how fate had conspired to ruin their lives.

My jaw hit the table. I shouted above the music: "You sold your own sister as a prostitute?" I repeated it again in broken Spanish, as if expecting a different reply. Armando slowly and silently nodded his downcast head.

While we talked my eyes kept returning to Esmerelda. So young and alive and full of promise. She was utterly beautiful. Like an Indian princess, with her long straight black hair tied back to flow over the back of her lacy white dress, she looked as innocent as a painted doll. I hated the thought of what would happen to her here. How long before she would be transformed into a hard-hearted whore like the ones still circling around our table hoping to tempt me? I asked Esmerelda to quit this place and come with us on the trip through the canal. She replied that she would, but if she left the bar for more than a couple hours at a time she would be fined, and probably beaten, by the owner. The bar owner had taken her passport and would not return it unless they paid him $500. She was a prisoner now and would remain so until the shine of her youth had worn off, when she would be discarded as human refuse in the alleys of Colón.

God, how I wished I could buy her freedom for her. But I reminded myself that I was on a voyage alone. I had little enough money to get myself out of here, and if I bought her freedom for the $500, they would be right back in the same position a few days later. As we talked, she reached across the table and held my hand. She seemed resigned to her fate, but as I looked at her sad smile and dreamy eyes she said something to me in Spanish that sounded like, "Give me a sign, and I will run away with you and follow you wherever you go." Or maybe I had only imagined her speaking what her eyes were telling me. If we try, any of us can remember one or more turning points that shaped the rest of our lives. Roads taken or not taken, as they say. This moment was one of mine. I was so strongly affected by this girl that, even though we would momentarily part and pursue our separate and very uncertain futures, she became a powerful symbol for one of life's roads not taken. I thought back to my girlfriend Dolores on the Indian Ocean island of Mauritius. We had parted two years earlier with the promise to meet again one day. We corresponded by mail that first year, and then eventually my letters went unanswered. I could not sail the great physical and metaphorical distance back to her, and now apparently she had moved on. I too gave up on that dream and set a new path.

We like to say that we are directed by fate or circumstance, when in reality we are both pilot and passenger of our choices; we choose to move forward or to blindly follow past decisions we may no longer believe in. When I think of absent loves honestly lost to one's chosen life path, a poem by Khalil Gibran whispers to me:

> *But let there be spaces in your togetherness,*
> *And let the winds of the heavens dance between you.*
> *Love one another, but make not a bond of love:*
> *Let it rather be a moving sea between the shores of your*
> *souls.*

My wanderlust had left actual seas between myself and the souls I loved.

A Masterful Bluff; Tucked into Taboga

I walked with broken heart back to the yacht club bar. Later that night, still lacking two crew, I met a South African couple about thirty years old, from the fair-haired white Afrikaner tribe of Africa. They were looking to gain experience on a practice run before bringing their own sailboat through the canal and agreed to come along at this last minute, for no charge.

Early the following morning, Juan and Patricio arrived by dinghy. They brought the rented outboard motor, which we attached to *Atom*'s motor bracket. The Afrikaans couple, André and Amanda, were aboard as well, and . . . well . . . I had forgotten to tell them that they would be spending two days in my crowded boat with Patricio, who was black. In 1987, the strict race segregation insanity of South African apartheid was André and Amanda's home rule of law. Fortunately, the crisis was averted because my guests had already traveled enough out in the real world to know the segregation lie they had been fed. We all got along fine, which proves good people can rise above an evil culture, once they are removed from that culture and its oppressive laws.

In the minutes before our canal pilot (called an Adviser in canal-speak) arrived, I attached the fuel line and started the outboard motor. The minimum speed requirement for yachts in the canal was 5 knots (about 6 MPH), and a small outboard motor could easily provide adequate propulsion for a boat as small as *Atom*. The motor first ran rough and then died, refusing to start again. A slow simmer of panic rose within me at the thought of having no running motor when the pilot arrived. I would incur a heavy fine, and my transit would have to be rescheduled. My hard-won precious line handlers would scatter and new ones would have to be recruited—eventually. I got on André's handheld VHF radio and hastily arranged to pay another skipper, who was now picking up his pilot, to tow us if necessary. When our Panamanian pilot arrived and said, "Start the engine and let's get going," I took a risk and honestly told him the outboard motor would be slow and that with this fair north wind we could go faster under sail. That the motor didn't work anyway, I kept to myself.

"Whatever's faster is fine with me," he said to my great relief. Juan pulled my anchor aboard while I hoisted the sails. We sailed across the harbor to the entrance of the first lock, dropped the sails, and rafted along our buddy boat, which pulled us into the first of six immense lock chambers. The double set of steel doors weighing thousands of tons swung shut with a finality that marked our exit from the Caribbean Sea. Canal workers flung messenger lines with monkey's fist ends that landed with a thud on the deck. To the messenger lines we attached our required four 125-foot mooring lines, which the workers hoisted up and tied to bollards. I had adapted two of the lines from my anchor rodes, and André and Amanda had graciously brought the other two. Ahead and behind us were a total of nine other yachts of all sizes from various countries of origin. Even herded together like this we looked minuscule within the walls of the 1,000-foot long by 110-foot wide locks.

Valves turned, and the great aqueducts in the lock floors opened. Beneath us the waters swirled as gravity flooded the chamber with millions of liters of fresh water from the dammed inland river. The boiling turbulence caused our boats to strain like unruly animals on their heavy mooring lines. Two more sets of locks raised us 85 feet to the level of the Gatun Lake reservoir.

The normally dependable canal could be forced to close at any time if the tropical rains ever failed to feed enough water into the reservoir. A few years later, El Niño weather events caused a drought severe enough to disrupt canal shipping temporarily. Deforestation in the Chagres River watershed is probably already responsible for locally diminished rainfall, making the long-term future of the canal look uncertain. Cargo ships and yachts have the alternative route around Cape Horn to reach the Pacific, but few skippers of small yachts will risk facing the Horn's cold and stormy waters. Ship owners would rather transit the canal and pay canal fees up to $250,000 to save the fuel and time pounding through the seas along the Cape Horn route.

We got lucky with a steady following breeze and sailed the entire length of the twenty-two mile long Gatun Lake under spinnaker at our maximum possible speed of seven knots, even passing most of the larger motoring yachts. The freighters we passed as they headed towards the Atlantic seemed out of place, plowing through the jungle lake with a backdrop of drowned forest along the shoreline. To make things even more surreal, our pilot was on the boat for two days and didn't even realize our motor didn't work! I don't think I'd have the nerve to pull that bluff again, particularly with today's heavier fines imposed for not having a functioning motor at the scheduled transit time.

Late that afternoon, at the midway point of the canal, we anchored for the night near the other yachts off the ship channel in Gatun Lake. The canal launch arrived to pick up our pilot who went home for the night and would return the following morning. Before dark the five of us went for a swim in the warm, green waters of the lake. That night I rigged an awning over the boom for Juan and Patricio, who slept on thin cushions on the cockpit benches. I had my regular bunk in the main salon, and André and Amanda fit themselves into the forward cabin v-berth. I placed mosquito nets over the hatches, and for our cockpit crew, I lit mosquito coils next to them whose smoke kept away most of the jungle insects.

To save water at sea I wash dishes by simply leaning over the leeward side of the boat and swishing them in the passing water. Earlier that day when we were underway, I mentioned to André that he could do the same here. I barely concealed my annoyance when André leaned over to rinse out my favorite drinking cup—the one of thick glass with a map of the globe frosted into it—and lost it overboard when our speed through the water snatched it from his hand. To make up for the loss and show me that he had learned his lesson, after we finished my pot of vegetable curry for dinner at the anchorage he insisted on washing the dishes. Butterfingers again! André managed to drop several other pieces overboard. The next day, under my baleful gaze, we ate in shifts, sharing the remaining dishes and silverware, and I made sure to wash them all myself. André was a good man, but he should be confined to using paper plates.

When our pilot returned soon after sunrise, we continued under sail to the end of the lake, where we attached *Atom* to our buddy boat with a towline. We passed through a mountain range at Galliard Cut, a canal dug and blasted through the low point of the Continental Divide, where three more locks returned us to sea level on the Pacific side. We stopped briefly at the Balboa Yacht Club dock where my crew disembarked to catch a bus back to Colón. I continued under tow another half mile until the wind returned, when I cast off to sail alone the final few miles to the nearest anchorage at Taboga Island. A rush of relief and excitement carried me along. Gliding along again under sail in the unlocked open waters of the Pacific, I was finally free from all man-made obstacles. My elation however, was seasoned by the sadness I'd left in Colón.

I anchored *Atom* in her familiar spot—tucked into the corner of the half-moon bay on Taboga Island. The little fishing village was seemingly unchanged since my previous visit. Here I returned to my old habit of immersing myself in the contrasting nature of land and sea by walking across the island. As I made my way up the familiar road over the green hills of Taboga, I was pleased to see that the island remained peacefully free of cars. A farmer on horseback tipped his hat in greeting as he passed. I paused frequently to survey the jungle-clad shores, the harbor, and further out the spots of islands scattered in the gulf. Pelicans roosted noisily by the hundreds in the tangled treetops under the cliffs below me. Farther below, the surf lapped against a rusting steel sailboat, shipwrecked on the reef. Tramping across the countryside here brought back a small taste of what had driven me to walk across all those islands on my previous circumnavigation. Out here I enjoyed a freedom almost like being at sea, coupled with the chance encounters of new flora and fauna, and new friends.

The view from Taboga Island

The little grocery shop in the village was as poorly stocked as I'd found it three years before, so to provision for the next leg of the voyage, I grabbed my largest backpack and caught the ferry boat to Panama City on the mainland. *Atom*'s food lockers were still well-stocked with dry goods from Fort Lauderdale and Colón markets, so once ashore in Panama City I went straight to the sprawling outdoor fruit and vegetable market. I walked past the seafood vendors and attempted to hold my breath as I passed the overpowering aromas of warm raw meats in the open butcher's section. The heavy scent of aging meat and the buzzing flies reminded me how content I was with the vegetarian diet I had followed for several years. I loaded my pack with cabbages, sweet potatoes, onions, garlic, and other foods that keep well without refrigeration. On my way out I filled a handbag with mangoes, limes, and papaya. I made it back to *Atom* on the day's last ferry, found space in hanging nets for some of the more delicate foods, and carefully secured the rest in bags on top of the v-berth.

My preference for vegetarian food stemmed partly from the practicality of not needing to buy and refrigerate expensive meats and partly from an experiment born of a desire to live, at least for a time, in a less contentious state than that of man the hunting animal. Several years earlier I had lost my youthful taste for the sports of fishing and hunting animals, and I had decided more recently not to pay others to slaughter my meals or catch my fish. I was neither an evangelical in my choice nor an overly fussy or demanding type of vegetarian. I did eat some cheese and milk products. When I was invited to another yacht for dinner it was no problem to pick around the pieces of meat and eat the vegetables and grains, however they were served.

At the public water well on Taboga I filled my water jugs, transported them by dinghy, and filled *Atom*'s built-in 24-gallon fiberglass water tank. Then I made another trip ashore to refill the empty jugs, which I secured in lockers for later use. *Atom* sat noticeably lower on her waterline in the sea due to all the provisions and extra water I carried for the long haul ahead across the Pacific.

On my last day anchored off Taboga Island I grabbed mask, snorkel, and fins and swam around the boat with a scrub brush and a stiff putty knife in hand to clean *Atom*'s hull below the waterline. I was happily surprised to find little grass and only a few barnacles stuck to the copper-based anti-fouling paint. What was there came off easily in one stroke of the brush. Apparently *Atom*'s two days in the fresh water of the canal had killed any bottom growth that had begun to colonize the hull. My frequent cleaning of the bottom ensured that the boat was more responsive, and it sailed noticeably faster. A purely sail-powered boat needs every advantage it can get.

Now that I was in the Pacific again, my main goal was to reach Hawaii before the summer hurricane season. Besides the relatives I looked forward to visiting in Hawaii, those islands are situated squarely within the northeast trade winds that would carry me west to the coast of China. My Pilot Charts of the Pacific mark each 300-mile section of ocean with a wind rose depicting expected average wind strength and direction. Thorough study revealed that to reach Hawaii in a boat without an engine at this time of year required avoiding a zone of calms off the Central American coast by first sailing southwest toward the Galapagos. On my first trip across the Pacific, my visit to the Galapagos consisted of heaving to behind San Cristobal Island's Wreck Bay and tossing a packet of letters to another yacht for posting ashore. Lacking Ecuadorian permission to land or the budget to bribe the Port Captain for permission to stay a few weeks, I had chosen instead to sail on nonstop to Polynesia. This time, I determined to go ashore on at least one of those famous and fascinating islands.

3 Galapagos Castaways

Untamed people occupy the untamed lands.

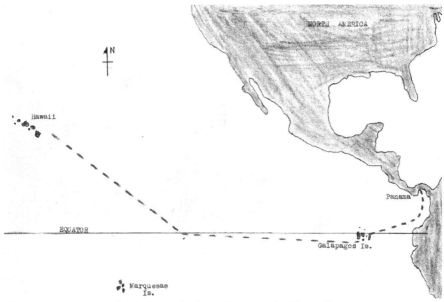

Atom's route from Panama to Hawaii

On a warm April morning, *Atom* glided slowly out of the anchorage at Taboga Island with the light land breeze barely filling her sails. That gentle push was all she needed to send her gracefully on her way at the sedate speed of three knots. The same passage to the Galapagos three years earlier had taken me an exhausting fifteen sleep-starved days of battling contrary currents, shifting winds, and the most continuous thunderstorms I'd encountered on any ocean. I recalled with some foreboding the blackened skies laying down thunderous cannon shots with fire and rain. Now I sailed the same waters six weeks earlier in the year, gambling that an April passage would bring a change for the better in the weather.

As I attempted to sail out the notoriously windless Gulf of Panama, I again encountered calms lasting several hours, as I drifted and dodged the numerous Panamax cargo ships approaching the Panama Canal. The isolated thunderstorms also held my attention as we were alternately drenched and then sun-dried. But overall, the winds were steadier this time and we made fair progress, gaining fifty to one hundred miles per day. Once clear of the cluster of islands and shipping in the gulf, we sailed south into more open waters where there was at least the chance for me to catch up on my sleep. Yet the deep sleep I needed remained elusive, as I caught brief naps with one eye on the telltale compass above my bunk. As on my previous passage, I sailed past and over much floating debris, mostly trees and pieces of timber flushed out to sea from the rain-swollen rivers in the gulf. Scrawled large in the remarks section of my logbook is the terse comment: "ENDLESS TACKING." The following day I wrote and underlined "Tack, Tack, Tack" as winds continued against me.

In calm waters, we could sail at best up to forty-five degrees either side of the eye of the wind. As I sheeted the sails tight for the south wind and got settled on my southwest course, the wind promptly turned southwest, forcing me off to the west. I responded by tacking back to the south. To tack the boat is simple enough. The procedure starts with securing items on deck and below that might shift when the boat changes its heel from one side to the other. Then I release the line from the windvane self-steering and throw the tiller over to leeward. As the boat turns through the eye of the wind, I release the jib sheet, pull the sail across to the other side of the boat, and grind the other sheet in tight on the cockpit winch. During this maneuver I pay attention to the course, steering with one foot on the tiller when my hands are occupied with sheets in order to prevent the boat from falling off on the wrong side of the wind, which would require the process to start over. Finally, I reattach the windvane and adjust it to the new course. All of this is simple enough to do once or even ten times a day, but the process, repeated more times than I could count over the next few days and nights, grew wearying.

The physical act of making numerous course changes was little effort compared with the greater mental chore of keeping track of my position.

I guessed at our average speed and course, neither of which ever remained constant, while going from one tack to the next. After each tack, I recorded the time, estimated course, and distance sailed with a new line on my plotting sheet. The zigzag lines grew into a lightning bolt across the chart. Because the currents pulled this way and that, the accumulated errors could easily be thirty miles a day. A round of sextant sights of stars or sun when the skies cleared enabled me once again to fix our position within two to three miles. Then off we drifted into uncertainty until the next celestial fix.

Not one sailor in a thousand whose boats were fitted with an inboard diesel engine would tolerate countless tacking into such light shifting headwinds. They would choose to motor ahead in search of more favorable winds. But there is a price to pay beyond the fuel expense: with a diesel engine on a small boat you cannot escape the throbbing noise and vibration. Not only do long hours under power burn your limited supply of diesel fuel, but the engine heats the boat until it becomes uninhabitable in the steamy tropical climate. Then its iron mass continues to radiate heat into the cabin for hours after the engine is shut down. After a day or two of motoring, your senses are deadened to the point of insensibility; the subtle messages of the sea are just as lost to you as is the spiritual reward gained in wrestling with nature and ultimately winning the contest as you sail unaided into your next port. I don't say this to belittle sailors who use their engines—I had done so in the past and would again in the future. I merely point out the different mindset and experience it creates.

After several days I had tacked my way to within seventy miles of the coastal border between Colombia and Ecuador. One morning in this area, I watched off the port bow as a fishing boat twice the length of *Atom* appeared to be passing safely ahead. Suddenly he altered course and stopped dead in front of us to lower his nets. With a wide-open ocean around us he chose this one spot to stop, apparently oblivious to the little sailboat bearing down on him. I tacked the boat away and kept a watchful eye on his erratic course until he disappeared well astern. I knew about part-time fishermen/pirates. Better to sail with eyes open and keep my distance. I also didn't want to risk having his net trip our keel, although we would likely pass harmlessly over the top. In all fairness, though, fishermen and skippers of other motor vessels no doubt view sailboats as the bigger nuisance because we make seemingly capricious course changes as we follow invisible shifting winds.

From here I turned course more to the west. As I sailed across the equator at 87 degrees west longitude, I encountered the northern edge of the southeast trade winds, which sweep fully across the tropical South Pacific at this time of year. I gratefully rode on the edge of that great river of air, in the somewhat light and shifty southeast wind, for the final three days into the Galapagos Islands.

Escort to the Enchanted Isles; Spinnaker Thrills

Spanish mariners of the 17th century named the island group *Las Islas Encantadas* (The Enchanted Isles) after watching the islands apparently change their locations, as unpredictable currents carried their ships away in the light winds. In the years since those early Spanish explorers, a colorful succession of characters has visited the islands: pirates and castaways, handfuls of hardy settlers, adventurers, and even Ecuadorian prisoners sent to one of the world's remotest penal colonies. Although renamed *Archipelago de Colón* by Ecuador, the islands are known by the rest of the world as the Galapagos, the Spanish name for the giant tortoises found there.

I was on full alert for those erratic currents around the islands as first discovered by the captains of gold-laden Spanish galleons. I recalled nearly being shipwrecked on one of these island's uninhabited coasts three years earlier. An unexpectedly strong current had carried *Atom* and her sleeping skipper into the inshore reefs of San Cristobal Island one overcast twilit morning. I had awoken just in time to tack the boat offshore and avoid destruction. This time I passed within sight of that same island's north coast at a safer distance before sunset. My destination, Santa Cruz Island, lay sixty miles ahead. That night I remained awake, carefully navigating around several unlit islets whose dark outlines became visible as I approached in the light of the half moon that rose after midnight.

By morning the wind and current had carried me to within a few miles of Santa Cruz. Blue-footed boobies dove headlong into the waters around us, spearing their bills into the shoals of small fish. Flocks of sleek black frigatebirds skimmed the water's surface, snatching surface fish on the wing with their long, hooked bills and harassing less swift birds to disgorge their own catch in mid-air. The frigatebird's unmatched wingspan-to-body-weight ratio helps them to remain continuously aloft for numerous days at a time, but nature's adaptation also prevents them from regaining flight if they were ever to land in the water. They take their rest from their aerial patrols by nesting in trees or on cliffs from which they can launch themselves into flight. For sailors the sight of the frigatebird is a welcome sign that usually means land is within a few days' sail, if not closer.

A family of dolphins escorted us for over an hour, shooting rapidly from side to side under our keel. Shooting over and under each other, they took turns riding the pressure wave pushed from our bow. I lay prone on the forward deck with my head over the side and fingers reaching into the water off the bow. Within minutes a curious dolphin lifted his glistening gray flank within my reach, and we shared a fleeting fingertip to fin contact. The moment's beauty still lingers in my mind.

I knew from my previous visit to these waters that the increased bird and sea life I saw was attracted by the various upwellings of warm- and cold-water currents carrying nutrient-rich waters from the far reaches of the Pacific. I rode now on the warm currents flowing out the Gulf of Panama. A month or two later in the year, the cold Humboldt Current would shift its pattern around the islands, bringing to them a cooler and wetter climate and different marine species. Eons before, fur seals and the miniature Galapagos Penguins had ridden this cold current from the high latitudes of South America to become the only penguins and fur seals to make their home under an equatorial sun.

Approaching Academy Bay under spinnaker

Within ten miles of the entrance to Academy Bay, the wind fell so light that the sails quivered and pulsed as each ocean swell sent the mast rolling in a slow arc. Our progress nearly stopped, so I dropped the jib and hoisted our large, brightly colored spinnaker in its place. This was a risky move because the balloon-shaped spinnaker only works for sailing downwind, and I would soon need to turn the boat upwind in the confines of an unknown harbor full of other anchored boats. My hand-copied chart showed the harbor's approximate location, but it included no details of the harbor itself. I would need agility and some minute's precious time to drop the spinnaker within the mainsail's wind shadow and to remove its aluminum pole without tangling the various control lines or hopelessly twisting the sail around the forestay. The spinnaker, which had been left aboard by the boat's previous owner, was best used with a crew of two or more. A single-handed sailor is better off with a flatter-cut, light air sail that can be hoisted and doused more easily. Lacking funds to replace the spinnaker with something more suitable meant that I had no choice but to use it because, in moments like this, my engineless boat needed every bit of the extra wind-harnessing power that sail provided.

Wind and swell carried me straight into the open anchorage of Academy Bay with the wind accelerating as it funneled along the high sides of the island. I sailed with increasing speed around foaming waters where the waves broke on partly submerged rocks. We recklessly raced past a few anchored sailboats and local fishing and tour boats. My pulse quickened. If I didn't get this right the first time, we would end up on the rocks with yards of spinnaker cloth wrapping the mast. Spying an open spot to anchor before we hit the shallow-trending bottom, I released the line holding the spinnaker pole out so that the sail would lose its grip on the wind by shifting into the shadow of the mainsail. Dropping the tiller, I ran to the mast and released the spinnaker halyard. I stepped to the foredeck to gather the huge billows of sailcloth before it blew into the water and under the keel, then scrambled back to the tiller to turn the boat into the wind. Back I ran to the bow to release the anchor, then to the mast to pull down the mainsail. My heart pounded with excitement. It was an act of controlled chaos that, this time at least, went smoothly according to plan.

As I gathered the lines strewn all over the deck and stuffed the spinnaker back in its bag, the first thing I noticed, was that the anchorage was so exposed and open to the sea that it was little better than anchoring on a mid-ocean shoal. *Atom* and all the boats around her rhythmically lifted their bows to the swells, tugging on their mooring lines unceasingly for the duration of my visit here. Arriving in an anchorage after a long passage, a sailor expects a respite from the heave and roll of the open sea. The agitated Academy Bay was almost enough to make me long for a solid bed on shore. Strong east winds coming into the anchorage were rare in this latitude, but even a moderate east wind or sudden squall could cause some of the boats moored here to drag their anchors, tangle up with each other, and be driven aground. I made a mental note to be prepared to tack my way out of there quickly should the need arise.

The Port Captain's Bite; Darwin's Playground

The coast around me was comprised of an arid strip of lava rock supporting little more than cactus, an occasional stunted tree, and scrubby brush. Next to me on the south side of the bay was Angermeyer Point, where a few rock and timber homes appeared to grow organically out of the cliffs at their backs. Each home had its own dinghy landing because the cliffs blocked easy access to the rest of the island. The main part of town lay on the waterfront across the bay, partially fronted with mangroves. Behind the town, the brown lower slopes were punctuated with volcanic cones wearing an emerald green mantle of vegetation bathed in the moisture of passing clouds.

Yachts and fishing craft shared the anchorage with long-whiskered sea lions that shot through the clear, pale green water, easily catching the small fish they pursued. Playing like a cat with a mouse, a sea lion flipped a fish from his mouth into the air, caught and bit it in half, then purposely flipped the head into my cockpit. I tossed the gift back to him, and he swallowed it in one gulp. Pelicans swooped close over the water and then, seeing their target, tumbled awkwardly into the bay to scoop up any size of fish they guessed would fit in their enormous bills. On the near shore, a dragon-like iguana, three feet from head to tail, basked in the sun on hot black volcanic rocks. When I awoke the next morning, I found a sea lion lounging in my dinghy, as it bobbed on its tether a few felt behind the boat. I had made some friends here even before stepping ashore.

Most of the Galapagos territory was declared a National Park by Ecuador in 1959. Since then, visitors were restricted from venturing outside the two main settled islands of San Cristobal and Santa Cruz without having a permit or being accompanied by a park warden. I learned that the handful of cruising yachts anchored in the harbor were all bound for French Polynesia. The cruising grapevine reported that the local officials were very strict about yachts not staying more than a few days or not wandering around the other islands. Acquiring a Galapagos visa and cruising permit in advance from Ecuador was an exasperating and almost universally unproductive exercise, so most sailors either bypassed the islands or, like me, took a chance on being allowed to visit after stopping unannounced at one of the island group's two ports of entry. Most of the time visitors on yachts were given a three-day temporary visa upon arrival and then were sent on their way. But Ecuadorian policies are as transient and local as morning haze. Each Port Captain feels entitled to interpret them to his wallet's advantage. Crews of the other yachts here told me that a new Port Captain had recently arrived in Academy Bay and that he was granting visa extensions for anyone who could pay his *mordida* (bite) in U.S. dollars.

Academy Bay, known locally as Puerto Ayora, is the principal town of the island group and was home to some 2,500 people. Throughout the past few centuries, the island, as well as the rest in the group, has been renamed a bewildering number of times. First known to the buccaneers as Duke of Norfolk, the Royal Navy felt obliged to change it to Indefatigable Island. Then the captain of the USS Essex named it Porter Island. The Spanish and later Ecuadorian visitors knew it at various times as Valdez, Chavez, and San Clemente. For the moment it is Santa Cruz.

Rowing ashore to the public quay the next morning, I stepped ashore and immediately felt less like I was on a Pacific Island than in any small town in Central America. Along with a smattering of European settlers, most local people had come here from Ecuador and were a handsome mixture of Spanish and South American Indian. At the time of my visit, the capital town looked like a Western frontier outpost. The main street was a dusty dirt road fronted by dilapidated buildings: the post office, bank, a few general merchandise stores, a bakery, and a beer house.

At the bank, I converted $100 U.S. into a fistful of several thousand Ecuadorian sucres. Feeling enriched by the thick wad of sucres, I strolled down the dusty street of wooden shacks and stopped outside the Port Captain's office. I was just in time for the morning ceremony as three soldiers marched out of the shack with high steps, hoisted the yellow, blue, and red national flag of Ecuador, saluted, and stepped smartly back to the Port Captain standing in regal stiffness in a uniform that strained to contain his bulk. Each of the soldiers wore bits and pieces of mismatched uniforms that made them appear like a band of low-cost mercenaries.

Inside the building I handed my passport and clearance papers from Panama to the Port Captain. "You have three days," the Port Captain said solemnly in English as if pronouncing my execution date. Then he added that an extension of stay (or was it a stay of execution?) could be granted for additional "harbor dues." I dumped a pile of sucres on the table to pay. He shoved them back to me and said, "Five dollar U.S. each day."

The sucre was rapidly declining in value against the dollar. "El Porto Capitan" understandably did not want his retirement funded with a worthless currency. It turns out he had good sense as well as good timing because a few years later the sucre bottomed out at 25,000 to the dollar. Eventually the Ecuadorian government gave up the fight and switched to the U.S. dollar, of which I suspect my good port captain already had more than a few. Many Ecuadorians had a tough time getting used to the humiliation—the literal loss of face of their revolutionary war hero, Antonio Sucre, on their currency—as they were now forced to gaze daily upon the strange faces of U.S. presidents and statesmen.

I gave the Port Captain a twenty-dollar bill as a down payment, which he slipped directly into his pocket. We would settle up the account when I returned later for exit clearance. There was no pretense of legitimacy offered by writing up a receipt. In fact, his droopy mustache drooped further when I foolishly mentioned *"Recibo?"* He had probably paid off some official above him to get this coveted post where he could supplement his meager salary by putting the squeeze on visiting gringos. Most Americans who sailed here were outraged at such unabashed corruption. I'm bothered less by occasional open graft than I am by legislators at home in America who feel the need to regulate and collect their so-called legitimate fees on every conceivable human interaction. Most people have been beaten down by the system to the point where they unquestioningly pay any amount to the state for any thing their leaders have decreed from above, provided they receive a paper receipt. In return for our submissiveness, the minions of state legislate a never-ending stream of laws and taxes. I preferred the quick and direct bite from the Port Captain to the slow and unending feast I provide to the tax jackals back home.

Stepping carefully over a man sprawled on the sidewalk taking a *siesta*, I headed toward the police station for an entry stamp in my passport. This particular shack had fist-sized holes through the walls, and the front door lay off its hinges and propped up against the wall. Inside, four tough-looking *hombres* in white T-shirts and green army pants sat around a table, playing cards. An antique tube radio stood silent against the wall next to a pile of equally antique bolt-action rifles. On the table lay some wrinkled bank notes and two pistols, presumably to discourage cheating. Another indiscreet bite here completed the entrance formalities.

The few tourists who came here in the 1980s, arrived either on the slow rolling hell of the supply boat from Ecuador or more often by plane at a U.S.-built WWII military airstrip located on a small, flatter island near the opposite side of Santa Cruz. They then took a ferry across the channel and caught a taxi-van for the twenty-mile ride back to the capital. Tourists usually stayed aboard the small cruise boats that made tours between here and the other nearby islands. There were also rooms for a few people at the edge of town in the Hotel Galapagos, a comfortable hideaway frequented by visiting naturalists.

Next to town was the Darwin Research Institute where various conservation projects were carried out. While thumbing through a shelf of Galapagos-related natural history books, I met a bearded and most serious American professor conducting a three-month long study of the sparrow-like flycatcher bird. "Did you know it is the only representative of its genus on these islands?" he asked while staring at me above thick glasses resting on the tip of his nose. Perhaps he had mistaken me for a fellow ornithologist.

"No, I didn't. But I suppose it catches flies . . . which is a useful trick," I replied, trying to sound intelligent. In return for my polite feigned interest in the boring little bird, I was rewarded with a mind-numbing lecture on all the intimate aspects of a flycatcher's life.

The bird-obsessed professor was one of a long line of naturalists who had come to the Galapagos since the well-known visit in 1835 of English naturalist Charles Darwin. Here he gathered information from the island's unique plant and animal life that, in part, contributed to his Theory of Evolution. Today the Institute carries on his work through research and conservation programs. On its grounds I watched a giant iguana swallow a whole cactus leaf, throat-scratching spines and all! The biggest attraction, though, was the 500-pound tortoises that decorated the park like slowly drifting boulders, feeding on banana tree stalks with the measured, deliberate bites you might expect from an animal whose jaws need to last 150 years or more. Before man arrived, the islands were covered with tens of thousands of these creatures. Then the whaling ships came, and their crews took advantage of this slowly-moving meal, eventually reducing the tortoise population to near extinction. Fresh meat was a rare commodity aboard sailing ships, and the sailors found that tortoises provided large amounts of meat and were easy to catch—provided there were eight men available to carry one back to the ship. In the ship's hold, the tortoise was self-storing because it could live for months without food or water.

The giants of Galapagos

By the 1860s, Galapagos tortoises were as scarce as the hunted whales had become in the South Pacific. Having slaughtered an estimated quarter of a million tortoises, the whalers departed from the islands. With the help of the Darwin Institute, which gathers endangered animals to breed and repopulate, the tortoises are now making a slow comeback. Lonesome George, the last surviving Isla Pinta subspecies of tortoise was found alone on Pinta Island and brought to the institute in hopes that a mate could be found. Thus far, Lonesome George had not found the ladies of the other islands to his liking and remained a celibate bachelor.

The circular, 25-mile-wide, dormant volcano that is the island of Santa Cruz contained only a few small agricultural settlements outside of Puerto Ayora. Itching to see the land beyond the harbor, I loaded my backpack with camping equipment for a two-day trek across the island, laced up my hiking boots, locked the companionway hatch, and double-checked our anchor lines. I looked back uneasily at *Atom* tugging insistently on her anchors as I rowed ashore through the harbor swell with my boots and backpack piled in the dinghy.

In the relative cool of the early morning, I walked the front and back streets of town searching for bread and vegetables for my trip. I visited each little market and food stand in town, but fresh food was brought to town only once a week, and I had picked the wrong day. Eventually, I found some bread at the bakery, and at another shop an elderly lady handed me some carrots while I brushed away the flies and held my breath at the stench of the rotting potatoes lying on the cement floor.

The rising sun of early morning was already sizzling hot as I walked along a narrow dirt road that climbed gently toward the mountainous interior. Lizards slinked across my path, and occasional swarms of lime-green butterflies filled the air. Each island has its own rich mixture of scents. As only a land-starved sailor can do, I soaked them all in as I hiked along: a rare scent of flowers, patches of green grasses in the uplands, and everywhere the heavy odors of baked earth. Black and gray Darwin Finches flittered about, so unafraid of humans that they perched on my hat and shoulders as I walked.

A bus full of people rumbled past me in a cloud of dust. The only other traffic on the road that morning was three *campesinos* (farmers), who rode by on horseback, sitting on hard saddles carved from wood. Following them was their pack of yapping mixed-breed farm dogs. Lashed to the horses' flanks were sacks of the potato-like cassava root and stalks of green bananas that they were transporting to town from their upland farms. One of the men pulled in his reins and stopped to ask me where I was going. He gave me a puzzled smile when I told him I was walking to see the island and meet the people. On my many walks across the islands around the world, people usually seemed amazed or confused by answers like this and would inevitably reply by telling me how many kilometers there were to the next village or end of the road, as if speedy completion of the walk were my main goal.

Within a few hours I had passed from the arid and thorny coastal belt of cactus, prickly pear, and bare rock, through transitional zones of meadow and sparse forest, to the misty high pampas of bracken and ferns. In these highlands, the soil is fertile, though rocky. Temperatures dropped and humidity rose as the mountains squeezed rainfall from the passing clouds. I delighted in the respite from the coastal heat as I walked shirtless in the rain past a field of banana trees.

Beyond a meadow of grazing cattle, I met a light-haired man, obviously Anglo, piling up a stone fence in front of a farmhouse. Mike explained that he was making his second attempt at homesteading. Some years before, he had joined a group of fellow Americans who tried to establish a communal coffee plantation on a neighboring island. The kibbutz-like group was ill-prepared for the realities of the harsh and dry conditions. Within a year they gave up and returned to the easier life in California. "This time I'm back for good," Mike said with determination. "I'll go it alone until I get established, then make a trip to Ecuador to find a wife." His farm, I noticed, had already begun to produce bananas, papaya, coffee, and avocados.

As I walked through the small village of Bellavista, two young Indian boys attached themselves to my sides. I pointed to the mountaintop nearby, and they called out its name together: "Puntudo" (which in this context meant a cone-shaped mountain). They claimed they knew the way to the top, which was the only qualification I required in a guide. The boys led me along a trail toward the mountain. As we brushed through the shoulder-high grasses, ants fell from the leaves onto our exposed skin. The sting of their acid-like secretions urged us to quicken our pace. An hour later we were clear of the high grass and passing over Media Luna, a prominent mountain that bulged from the terrain as though the earth were giving birth to a half moon. Rain clouds rolled in, soaking us as we walked through newly born streams and stepped on thick, spongy carpets of lichen. With spirits a little dampened by the weather, we moved with heads lowered, eyes fixed on the ground directly ahead.

"Puntudo, *arriba, arriba!*" (Upward, upward!) the lead boy shouted as we looked up through a break in the clouds to where a classic volcano cone loomed over us. A final scramble with hands clutching rocks and tufts of grass brought us to the top. The narrow peak was just large enough for the three of us to sit down together. We shared my bread and handfuls of peanuts as we gazed over hills that fell away in misty folds to the cloudless, sun-beaten coast. My map listed this mountaintop at a modest elevation of 2,930 feet, making it the island's highest point.

The boys of Bellavista

I handed the boys 500 sucres ($3 U.S.) for their work. As they scampered off home, I continued alone north across the island. By late afternoon I scouted for a campsite and detoured off the road through thick brush that ended abruptly at the edge of a cliff. Three hundred feet below me was the circular crater of what appeared to be a collapsed volcano, one of a pair of sinkholes called *Los Gemelos* (The Twins). The ground here was either waist-high grass or mud. The only somewhat clear and dry spot to camp was on the very edge of the cliff. The ground sounded hollow when I used a rock to pound in the stakes of my one-person tent, indicating I was perched on a thin overhanging ledge. I needed to remember not to move more than one step away from the tent when I got up in the night. Darwin had stood on this spot looking into these craters, which had no way out if you happened to fall in, and described them as the "antechambers to hell."

That evening I ate my dinner of bread and carrots and tossed my crumbs to the finches fluttering around my head. I recognized the diminutive flycatcher who flew in to join the party as well. When the British ornithologist, David Lack, visited these islands a century after Darwin, he found that the fearless flycatchers boldly attempted to remove hair from the heads of his companions for nesting material. I thought of the professor's speech to me a few days earlier. "Thanks to the professor, I know every clinical detail there is to know about you, my friend, from your mating habits to your penchant for thievery."

I imagined his response: "Ah, but those are mere recited facts. What do you know of my simple joy of flight?"

But facts are what we crave. After sunset I continued reading by flashlight from a book I had borrowed from the Darwin Institute that helped me recognize more of the flora and fauna around me. The clouds lifted later that night. Under the starlight and the music of birds, crickets, and the rustling of the wind in the grass, I luxuriated in the coolness of the mountain air. For the first time in weeks, I noticed the absence of the familiar sounds of the breaking waves of the open ocean or the surf washing the harbor's shores. I lay still on my bed of soft grass and reflected on my purpose for being here. To know an island and its people beyond the superficial requires leaving the tour bus and striking out on foot. The lone traveler on foot is invariably welcomed by the locals as something other than a tourist, whose purpose they see merely as an instrument to pump money into the local economy. On foot you have time to absorb the scenes of the slowly changing landscapes and undisturbed animals. And as after completing a solo ocean passage, you are rewarded for the hard physical effort of clambering over the hills with a sense of fulfillment.

By morning twilight the clouds had moved in to bathe the crater in a frosty, whirling mist. I rolled up my tent and moved silently along the trail to the road where I caught occasional views of the rolling countryside as one cloud drifted by before being replaced by another. It was an easier walk now going downhill. Some hours later the road brought me out of the clouds and again into the arid coastal zone of the island's northern end. My road ended at a dock where I removed my boots to cool my heels in the sea. The fatigue of leg muscles let me know I had walked the length of Santa Cruz. But it was a satisfying fatigue.

An empty bus awaited its load of passengers off the next ferry coming from Baltra Island across the narrow channel. In 1942 the U.S. Air Force constructed this sole airstrip of the Galapagos on Baltra Island to help guard the approaches to the Panama Canal from possible Japanese attack. The Americans referred to the barren land there as "a beachhead on the moon."

I chatted with the bus driver who recognized me as the only pedestrian he had passed on the road during the past two days. "You can ride back for free if you don't have the money," he kindly offered. The ferry docked to unload its passengers—long-haired Indians, other locals, and a couple tourists—who had just arrived from the airport in Quito, Ecuador. As much as I extol the virtues of walking, I had already hiked my way along the only route across this island, so I jumped into the bus and temporarily became an anonymous tourist on the return ride to Puerto Ayora. The potholes and erosion scars of the road became much more noticeable to me as we speedily bounced our way over them on our way back across the island.

While doing research at the Darwin Institute's library, I met Margoth Friere, recently arrived from Quito. She was here studying for a license to be a park tour guide. I suggested she might practice her guide skills by accompanying me on further explorations of the island, and she kindly accepted. We had dinner together aboard *Atom* that night where every little thing about her reminded me how much I missed female companionship.

The next day I met her at the bakery where she worked part time with her cousin. Margoth placed a few sweet rolls in her bag and led me toward her favorite spot on the island, a swimming hole she called "*Las Grietas del Amor*." From a path beginning near the anchorage at Angermeyer Point, the trail led past a secluded cove where a few German families still lived after settling there one or two generations earlier. We continued around patches of cactus and shallow salt-water ponds to trail's end at a stone ledge. An easy scramble down the rocks brought us to a clear pool of water.

"The water is cool and deep," Margoth announced as she pulled off her outer garments, which she laid out on a stone. Then she dove in from an overhanging ledge. I wasn't far behind her. The pool was narrow and long, set between two overhanging cliffs that in places almost touched, blocking out most of the sky. We swam to the opposite end where we reclined on smooth boulders just above the water's surface and looked straight up at our slice of blue sky framed by the cliff's brown edges and a tilted cactus. Neither of us wanted to leave the cool, shaded waters to return to the equatorial heat of the day.

Margoth dove under water and disappeared through a tunnel. I gulped a breath and followed her down. We emerged into another smaller grotto. Like an oasis in the desert, *Las Grietas* contains the only freshwater pond on the entire island, though because fissures in the lava rock at the bottom allow tidal seepage from the sea, the amount of salt in the pond varies with inland rainfall amounts and the water's depth.

We sipped freshwater from the surface of the pond. Then as we swam down into the depths I noticed the water had stratified and tasted salty. Before the island was settled, shipwrecked sailors had survived for months at this life-giving pond where tortoises and even birds could be caught by hand. When I asked why it was called *Las Grietas del Amor* (translated as The Grotto of Love or, more literally erotic, as The Crevices of Love!), Margoth coyly replied, "Young lovers come to this beautiful place to be alone." I again noticed her almond eyes and glistening wet brown skin and knew the moment was perfect.

The Beachcombing Philosopher

Some of the people on Santa Cruz Island are as interesting as the island's better-known wildlife attractions. One day I watched from the cockpit as an older man with shoulder-length gray locks, stood facing forward as he ponderously rowed a heavy wooden skiff across the bay. My wave attracted his attention. He came alongside and introduced himself in English: "Gus Angermeyer, King of Galapagos, welcomes you." Gus was in his mid-seventies, lean of build, with skin tanned and weathered to the point of tortoise leather. His animated face was lively, and his eyes took in everything as he twisted his neck to view inside *Atom's* portlights. Before leaving, he invited me to visit his home in "the cave" he pointed out at the bottom of a cliff face along the shore. I went the next day to see the King, bringing a box of herbal tea as a gift. Made from timber and lava rocks held together with cement, his home did indeed resemble a cave because of how it blended into the cliff side. He prepared the tea for us from a kettle placed over a wood fireplace. The wisps of smoke disappeared up a rock chimney molded into the stone wall.

Gus explained how his parents had wanted their whole family to flee their native Germany in the mid 1930s to seek a simpler life, far from the growing madness of the Nazi regime. His mother had lived through the torment of waiting to learn if her husband had survived fighting in the trenches of WWI, and she did not want to repeat the agony with her precious sons. Gus recalled that he and his brothers had grown up playing Robinson Crusoe, and they always remembered an old sea captain who had told them about the paradise of the Galapagos Islands. The remoteness of the islands appealed to their parents as well, and so they sold their home to buy a forty-year-old wooden ketch, which the five Angermeyer sons, ages 17 to 24, prepared to sail across the Atlantic, through the Panama Canal, and on to the Galapagos. The parents and the boys' sister planned to wait in Germany until the sons could establish a home in the islands and then would join them by ship. The boys, inexperienced sailors, were caught in a storm and dismasted along the English coast. Some months later they found another yacht, but that attempt also failed. The elder brother, Heinlich, returned home to Hamburg due to his failing health from tuberculosis, which for thousands of years had plagued mankind as the untreatable and often fatal "consumption." Gus was now the eldest of the group, and he keenly felt the responsibility of not failing the family.

Finally, in 1937, the four brothers made their way to the Galapagos by steamers. When they landed on Santa Cruz they found no electricity, doctors, or most of the necessities of civilization. The boys labored hard with hand tools and few supplies to build a house and fishing boats. Soon they anticipated the arrival of their parents and siblings. But the war in Europe delayed the family's departure. Then one sad day the brothers received the tragic news that the allied carpet-bombing of Hamburg had killed their entire family. A few years later the ravages of tuberculosis claimed another of the young brothers. The three brothers remained here, as strangers in a strange land, eventually starting their own families and helping each other build separate houses along what is now called Angermeyer Point.

Gus described himself to me as a "beachcombing philosopher." I later heard he had been married for many years to a South American woman named Lucrecia and that he had built her a house nearby. Gus didn't speak of her to me at the time, only telling me he enjoyed living alone, surrounded by his thoughts, a growing library of philosophical books he had been given or had traded for with passing yachts, and a collection of flotsam he had gathered from the beaches and rocky shores over the years.

From his ceiling and wall hung the skeleton of a whale he had found washed ashore during a day of beachcombing. After cleaning the rotting flesh from the huge carcass, he had hauled the bones back one by one and reassembled them in his cave. Shiny tortoise shells hung from the walls, and mummified iguanas perched next to baby sharks preserved in bottles of alcohol. A human skull stared down empty-eyed from a shelf —the sun-bleached remains of a castaway Gus had found along the rocky shore.

I came back again the following day to give Gus some books and spare clothing I had aboard. The town's water supply was known to contain parasites that cause amoebic dysentery, so Gus helped me top up my water jugs with safe rainwater from his cistern. My strongest memory from visiting him over the next several days was of the King seated on his throne of whale vertebrae, reciting to me in his strong and gravelly voice, his own poetry and favorite tracts from philosophers who seemed to span the alphabet from Aristotle to Zeno of Citium. He spoke as if recreating them in his own words as he channeled his friends of mind. I listened entranced as the gregarious old man recounted the stories of a lifetime among these peculiar islands of prehistoric creatures. He pointed to his journals that he had once planned to compile into a book but said the effort became too lonely and exhausting. Holding out a slice of dried goat meat, Gus said, "Come goat hunting with me tomorrow."

"No thanks," I said, "I'm a vegetarian these days, not a hunter."

"Ha! No man in these enchanted islands of mine is vegetarian," Gus bellowed. "Impossible to survive here that way." I wasn't planning on staying here long enough to test his theory.

I told him how much I had enjoyed walking around his island the week before. He remarked, "If you want to see something special, make sure you sail over to Floreana Island before leaving for Hawaii," and then without further explanation handed me an envelope and added, "Go see ol' Margret Wittmer and give her this letter from me."

When I mentioned my lack of a cruising permit to go there, he dismissed the issue with a wave of his hand and the question: "What are you, a tourist to be herded? You have a boat and free will. That's all the permission you need, boy." As I rose to leave the cave that last day, Gus settled a serious gaze on me and offered a final piece of advice: "Mind your navigation in these waters. Beware the silent currents in the darkness, or you may end up like my friend here." He lifted his eyes to the human skull on the shelf above us.

I was now determined, if not actually ordered, to sail to Floreana. But other sailors here had warned me that the Port Captain of Puerto Ayora would deny a request to visit any of the other islands in the group. I decided the King's invitation and the need to deliver *His* letter were all the permission I needed, so I didn't mention my plans when I settled my bill with the Port Captain and cleared out for Hawaii. This was one of those cases best handled by the adage I've followed for so long that it's become my first inclination when dealing with petty venal bureaucrats: never ask permission; never be denied.

4 Floreana Mysteries

From the unknowable mind of God to the mischievous hands of man.

The two weeks I had lived among the friendly and exotic people and animals on Santa Cruz Island had put a sizable dent in my cruising budget. I needed to get back to sea where there was no price of admission beyond what I had already paid to fit out my boat. I was also eager to discover what lay ahead as *Atom* and I zigzagged our way through the moored boats around us and out of Academy Bay with four tacks into the wind. We remained close on the wind with sheets tight, making the 32-mile passage to Floreana Island on a single tack. Midway between the islands, I sailed under sunny skies but could see dark clouds, heavy with rain, that capped the upland peaks of both the island astern and the one ahead. An hour before sunset I anchored at Post Office Bay on Floreana's northern coast. We were alone in the mile-wide bay, facing a land of dark, sun-burnt lava flows sloping gently skyward in the distance.

Blind Seals and Blue Boobies; Darwin's Mystery of Mysteries

As I rowed ashore in the dinghy the next morning, a group of sea lions (*lobos marinos*), numbering more than I could count, swam chaotically through the shallow waters, bodies tumbling over one another in their excitement to have a look at the human interloper. I renamed them *loco lobos marinos* when some of them mischievously bumped into the side of my dinghy. I rowed cautiously among the mob of heads bobbing up and down in the surf, somehow avoiding knocking them in the head with my oar tips. At a sandy spot on the rocky shore, I pulled my dinghy up the beach amid a colony of barking but apparently affable sea lions lying on the black rocks and solidified lava flows. As her pup nursed, a mother raised her head to give me a quick glance, then flopped heavily back down in the sand.

The sea lions of Post Office Bay

Sharing the beach with the sea lions were flocks of clown-like blue-footed booby birds, goose-stepping unconcernedly between their ground nests. Red Sally Lightfoot crabs stood out like splashes of red paint against the dark rocks. Their scientific name, *graspus graspus*, seems equally precious. Land iguanas three-feet long were lazily soaking up the sun. Occasionally, one broke away from the group, venturing inland to feed on cactus plants. Though the giant lizards are timid by nature, their bumpy patches of skin, long claws, horns and swishing tails give them the frightening appearance of little dragons. Reading Darwin's descriptions gave me a chuckle when he referred to them as revolting "Imps of Darkness." The island was a zoo without pens.

The marine iguanas here looked similarly scary, but they live entirely on seaweed and saltwater. Desalination glands in their heads filter out excess salt, which they purge periodically by spraying the crystals in a dragon-like manner out through their nostrils. What a superb adaptation that would be for us sailors as well—to drink from the limitless sea and later sneeze out the salt! In places along the shore of black lava, those cold-blooded creatures gathered tightly together by the hundreds, all facing the sea, motionlessly basking in the sun.

As I set up my camera on a tripod, one of the sea lions silently crept up from behind, bumped into me and nearly knocked me off my feet. I turned to see he was blind with both his eyes completely clouded over. The innocent thing had no enemies on land, but a shark might easily make a meal of him in the water. I walked among and stepped over the resting animals with camera in hand, unable to resist shooting until my two rolls of film were exposed. Suddenly, a bull raised his massive bulk and let loose a fearsome growl in my direction. On Santa Cruz, Margoth had warned me that bulls may charge at a human intruding among his harem of cows. I retreated backwards a few steps, and the bull relaxed. Everywhere, pups nuzzled close to mothers, feeding on them like kittens. Beyond the reach of the bulls, the sociable females put me back at ease with their almost comical whiskered faces of little black noses and sagging ears. They moved about slowly and awkwardly on land, using their back flippers like clumsy feet, in complete contrast to their graceful speed in the water.

For an up-close view of them in their natural environment, I stepped into the calm waters off the beach and swam to deeper water using my mask and snorkel. Several sea lions darted past and then swam in tight circles around me like playful puppies. I tried to mimic their fluid motions, if not their speed. A kaleidoscope of dark, whiskered faces turned to meet mine as they brushed past. On the shore I had been saddened to see so many of the younger sea lions had gone completely blind from weeping sores that had turned their eyeballs a solid white. I wondered: was it some contagious disease sweeping through the colony? I worried they would be unable to hunt, become starved, and end up as shark food. But here in the water I saw that even the blind animals navigated in perfect formation, apparently using their fine-tuned echolocation to sense the movements of other animals and the small fish they eat.

I later learned that a fluke parasite, common in these waters, attached itself to the eyes of sea lion pups and that the oozing white sores on some of the animals were due to a secondary infection. It was a self-limiting disease, and I was happy to learn that most of the animals regained their sight as they grew older.

It is the extraordinary tameness of the creatures of the Galapagos, more than anything else, which gives the islands their magical, arcadian atmosphere. There was a sense of timeless innocence in this place where Darwin began to unfold "the mystery of mysteries, the first appearance of new beings on this earth."

Darwin had observed the same animal life in this bay on his visit in 1835, when he was the twenty-six-year-old, unpaid naturalist on the world voyage of the *HMS Beagle*. Darwin had been studying for the clergy, making him an unlikely candidate for the discoverer of evolution. At the time, he considered geology, botany, and biology as merely his hobbies. At one time the young Darwin and most of his colleagues believed in the now far-fetched calculations made by Archbishop Ussher of Ireland that tell us the world and all its varied creatures were created on Sunday, October 23 in 4004 B.C. Darwin's Galapagos visit changed that notion forever. Through his keen observations and deductive reasoning, Darwin solved the great mystery of man's origins and freed those with open minds from the excesses of pseudo-scientific religious dogma. God may have created the world, but beware of men who tell you how and when he did it.

Due mainly to a lack of fresh water, Floreana's northern coast has resisted a lasting human settlement. As I walked the shoreline towards the opposite side of the bay, I passed the flattened ruins of a Norwegian fishing settlement abandoned in the early 1900s. Nearby, among the leafless and sparse vegetation, I came across an old wooden barrel tied to a tree stump, surrounded by the graffiti of visiting yacht names carved and painted onto pieces of driftwood. The Royal Navy first set up a barrel here in the 1790s as a mailbox for passing sailors. In those days the men of the Pacific whaling fleet were away from their New England homes for years at a time. Outbound ships, which had rounded Cape Horn, left their mail for Pacific ships to pick up on their way back to Atlantic ports. The practice continues to this day—not for whalers or the Royal Navy but as a novelty for the crews of passing yachts and charter boat tourists. Seeing no mail marked for Hawaii, I deposited my own letter here. Within a few weeks, the letter found its way back to my mother in Michigan via a tourist who stamped and posted it upon returning to the U.S.

Irish Pat's Appetite; A Port Captain Like No Other

The first human inhabitant of the Galapagos, and the most notorious person ever to reside on Floreana, was an Irishman by the name of Patrick Watkins, who had been marooned here by a passing English ship in 1805. Watkins built a crude hut along the shore, and survived by hunting and growing vegetables in an upland garden, which he traded for rum to passing whalers. Watkins abducted a black man from an American ship that anchored in the bay and made him his slave until the man managed to escape and was rescued by another ship. A visiting captain described him thus: "The appearance of this man was the most dreadful that can be imagined: ragged clothes, scarce sufficient to cover his nakedness, and covered with vermin; his red hair and beard matted, his skin much burnt from constant exposure to the sun, and so wild and savage in his appearance that he struck everyone with horror."

A few years later, "Irish Pat" kidnapped four sailors and their landing boat from a visiting ship. He and his captives rigged a sail on the little boat and set out with few supplies for a voyage of 600 miles to the South American mainland. Patrick arrived alone in his boat some weeks later at the port of Guayaquil, Ecuador. Presumably, he had killed and eaten his hapless shipmates en route.

The island's dark history continued as a penal colony of Ecuador until 1852, when it was abandoned. In 1870, one final attempt at convict colonization of Floreana ended when the tyrannical commander of the prison was murdered by the convicts who then went on a rampage of rape and murder. The dark and unfortunate island was then again abandoned to the less mischievous native fauna.

Rowing back to the boat, I was inclined to stay in the bay for some days. I had the unreasonable notion that it was my private domain and that leaving prematurely would awaken me from this magical dream. But the sailing season urged me on, and I had one more stop to make before leaving these islands.

To meet the island's reported 53 inhabitants, I sailed six miles around to the settlement of Puerto Valasco Ibarra on the western coast. At first we ghosted along shore, propelled by a light breeze spilling down the cloud-wreathed mountains, whose slopes wore deep, furrowed scars of erosion. Once clear of the bay, I was obliged to beat into a south wind that wrapped around the western coast of the island. While still a mile outside the anchorage at Puerto Ibarra, I watched through binoculars as two men launched a motorboat from shore and sped directly out to intercept me. From the small skiff one of the two young men raised his arm and shouted across the water: "Capitano del Puerto." That sounded like it could be trouble. I feared they were coming to check my papers and warn me away, so I was apprehensive when he waved me to follow him towards shore and then directed me to anchor clear of some submerged rocks lying off the black sand beach.

Had I been sighted in my ramblings at Post Office Bay, and was I now about to be placed under arrest for trespassing without a cruising permit? What punishment would be given? My mind raced with possibilities but came back to two prospects: they could force me to remain until a fine was paid or force me to depart, neither of which appealed to me at all. I was relieved when quite the opposite happened. Once my two anchors were placed according to the Port Captain's specific directions, he climbed aboard and shook my hand with a huge smile on his darkly tanned young face. Armando Burbano introduced himself and his friend, Simon Morales. Neither man spoke English, but their mood was festive. Ignoring his unfriendly assignment of enforcing cruising permits and collecting fees, Armando waived away my passport with *"No problema"* and made it known in Spanish that I was welcome to stay as long as I wished for no charge. To my joy and amazement, my entry here involved no paperwork of any kind. It turned out that at this lonely port a visiting yacht was reason for excitement, not extortion. Seeing my sail on the horizon, Armando had rushed out in his launch to guide me in, fearing that we might sail past without a visit. God bless the sailor's friend Armando and all those of his breed—if any should still exist!

The sole settlement on the eight-mile-wide island was centered on this west coast port, also known as Black Beach. The ever-so-slight indent in the coastline there afforded some marginal shelter from the prevailing winds at that time of year, if not from the long swell running parallel to the coast that set the anchored boats in a perpetual metronomic roll. Five families lived along the shore of that little notch in the coastline of Black Beach. The Port Captain proudly pointed out that there was pure mountain spring water piped to the shore, from which I could fill my water jugs. This was all a refreshing change from the corrupt, germ-ridden, tourist-trodden Puerto Ayora.

Proof of the Port Captain's generous attitude toward visitors was the boat anchored next to me, which was the only other boat at the island. The 27-foot plywood sloop belonged to two penniless Spaniards in their twenties. I invited the rawboned sailors aboard for a meal of meatless spaghetti, which they wolfed down so fast I cooked up another potful. Their scraggly beards indicated less of a desire to grow a full beard than a shortage of sharp razors. They told me they had been marooned here for several months, living off the food they foraged or begged ashore and the fish they could catch in the harbor from their boat. The Port Captain donated what he could, but he was not much better off than they were. The Spaniards were bound for the islands of French Polynesia 3,000 miles to the southwest, but they had run out of money to provision the boat with enough food for the voyage. I gave them ten dollars that they didn't ask for, but I needed to keep a tight control over my own meager funds in order not to end up marooned somewhere soon myself. Their situation was a lesson not to run out of money in a place unsuitable to finding employment.

Jungle Teutonic Dystopia

Of the thirteen main islands in the group, the most interesting and mysterious in terms of human drama is Floreana Island. I had read ominous stories about the island's early inhabitants and hoped to learn more direct from Margret Wittmer, the last of the original settlers. I first saw Mrs. Wittmer from my deck at a distance as she sat on the porch of her sprawling house of wooden planked walls and metal roof facing the shore of Black Beach. I rowed ashore and introduced myself to the gray-haired lady in her eighties, and she invited me to sit with her for tea.

"Here's your letter from King Angermeyer over on Santa Cruz," I said. She set the letter aside unopened and asked me "What else brings you to our island." She listened intently as I told her my story. She seemed as ordinary as any elderly German *haus frau*, instead of the last surviving pioneer of an infamous group of German settlers who had come to the empty island some five decades before.

I had already read some stories of the string of unexplained deaths and disappearances among Floreana's German settlers and have read more about them in recent years. The tale begins in 1929 when a misanthropic German nudist philosopher, Dr. Friedrich Ritter, and his equally humorless disciple, Dore, escaped their unhappy marriages in Germany to create a private utopia together on the uninhabited island of Floreana, or Charles Island as it was also known at the time. With Teutonic fortitude they eked out a rough existence in the forest of the island's interior. In the book she later wrote, entitled *And Satan Came to Eden,* Dore stated that the Nietzsche-obsessed Friedrich claimed people could double man's average lifespan if they followed his ideas on purity of mind to "merge intellect and spirit in the rhythmical movement of the Impersonal All." Among his many eccentricities, Friedrich had prematurely worn his teeth to nubs by masticating his vegetarian diet excessively and then had the remaining stubs and roots extracted to see if he could toughen his gums enough to continue slowly chewing every bite of food.

When sensationalized news of the "Galapagos Adam and Eve" was publicized in Germany, there followed a stream of visitors and would-be settlers to Floreana. Most of them turned back as soon as they saw the harsh reality of existence on an island, which was utterly without the conveniences of modern times.

Margret, several months pregnant at the time, arrived in 1932 with her husband, Heinz, and her stepson, Harry. They had fled a Germany in social and economic chaos in search of the tropical Eden they had read about in the press. At first the family lived in caves once inhabited by pirates as they struggled to build a house in the interior highlands with their limited supplies and tools. Their house was completed just in time for Margret to give birth to the first native child born on Floreana. The Wittmer clan proved to be tough and tenacious as they battled droughts and wild cattle for possession of their gardens, which eventually flourished in the rich volcanic soil. Nearby freshwater springs allowed them to grow a wide variety of fruits and vegetables, which they loaded on mules to carry down the trails to the coast to trade with passing ships. Meanwhile, the odd couple of Friedrich and Dore proved reclusive and unhelpful, treating the Wittmers more as unwelcome trespassers than neighbors.

Soon after the Wittmers arrived, the self-proclaimed Viennese baroness Eloise Von Wagner suddenly appeared with her two male consorts, proclaiming herself the island's "empress" and announcing plans to build a resort for millionaires. The Wittmers were as disgusted with these new arrivals as Ritter had been at them. Within this impossible triangle, the tangled web of concealments and treachery began. The whip- and gun-toting baroness was a drama queen who tried to dominate everyone, by doing everything from stealing the other islanders' mail and food brought in on the supply boats, to feeding outrageous stories about herself and her neighbors to visiting reporters. She went so far as to drive away prospective settlers at gunpoint. In this kind of *Lord of the Flies* story for adults, it wasn't long before her male companions became restless to get away—one she shot, and the other, named Lorenz, sought shelter at the Wittmer house, fearing for his life.

One day the baroness left a message with Margret saying she wanted to speak with Lorenz. He went to meet her and returned two days later, claiming he had found no trace of the baroness. Nobody, furthermore, had seen her leave the island. Lorenz asked the next passing fishing boat to take him off Floreana, but the boat's engine broke down at sea, and Lorenz and the crew's mummified bodies were later found on a nearby island, dead from thirst. Six months later, far short of his expected doubled lifespan, Dr. Ritter died from suspected poisoning. The disillusioned Dore returned to Germany. Years later, the Wittmers' son-in-law mysteriously disappeared one day while collecting firewood. In 1963, an American tourist woman disappeared. Her remains were found almost two decades later, stuffed in a shallow hole in the rocks.

Only Margret remained alive out of the original settlers. She had also managed to outlive several Ecuadorian governors, one of whom had tried unsuccessfully to have the Wittmers evicted. Over the years, their visitors had included well-known American yachtsmen on round-the-world cruises, the crew of cargo vessels that stopped to deliver and pick up mail and deliver supplies, and scientists and naturalists touring the islands. During my visit she lived with her daughter in the house at Black Beach. Every now and then they provided meals and a room for the occasional tourists and yacht crews that passed by. She also acted as postmistress of the island, placing her unique Post Barrel stamp on tourists' letters. A long overdue documentary film, *The Galapagos Affair*, in the style of Darwin meets Hitchcock, came out in 2014. It is said to be "a gripping parable of Robinson Crusoe adventure and utopian dreams gone awry."

There were still no shops or markets here on utopia during my visit. I desperately needed fresh food for the passage ahead. Luckily, the Port

Captain's young Indian friend, Simon, volunteered to guide me up to the island's high fertile slopes where I might purchase vegetables direct from the farmers. We walked past the handful of houses that made up the coastal village. Simon called the road "El Camino," but that seemed too grand for this dirt track of gullies and fist-sized lava rocks. No vehicles used this solitary island road, except one disabled tractor that was parked next to the broken power generating plant. Farther up the road, we stepped onto a footpath, then hopped over a shallow creek and through a gate to the door of a one-room farmhouse. The few scattered farms on the island belonged mostly to immigrants from Ecuador, many of whom had fled the poverty of the mainland only to find worse poverty here. Most returned to Ecuador, beaten physically and spiritually. But a hardy few remained and, through almost ceaseless toil, wrested a living from this ancient land of clinker and thorn.

Simon and I stopped to chat here with Senior Cruz and his wife. They made an odd pair, her large size contrasting sharply with her thin, gray-bearded husband. The Cruzes had lived here since they arrived on the island from Ecuador in 1939. I had met their son Augusto on Santa Cruz and had said I would visit his parents if I stopped at Floreana. The soft-spoken Senior Cruz filled my backpack with a heavy load of potatoes and squash in exchange for a few hundred sucres as his wife served us drinks called *maracuyá*, made of passion fruit mixed with spring water from the stream behind their house. Before leaving, we also sampled the good woman's papaya marmalade served with homemade bread on fine chinaware. After I had assured the couple that all their children and grandchildren on Santa Cruz were alive and well, Simon and I retreated back to the harbor.

That evening I had one quarter of the village population aboard *Atom* for my by now well-known spaghetti dinner. After we had eaten, I brought out my guitar, and my five guests entertained us with lively Latin ballads.

The Cruzes of Floreana

Early the next morning I landed my dinghy at the little stone quay to meet my friend Simon for a walk across the island. Simon set a brisk pace that we did not break until we crested the road's highest point an hour later. It rained heavily on us as we gained further elevation. The rocky road turned into a muddy footpath that itself became a rain-swollen creek that had not existed an hour before. Our feet disappeared into the soft ground at the edge of the stream and made sucking noises as we pulled each foot from the mud. The trail wound close under Cerro de Pajas, its rounded peak thrusting 2,100 feet above the sea. We slogged along for another hour through jungle-like vegetation. Where the trail crested a hill we met father and son *campesinos*, wearing tattered clothing, rubber boots, and cowboy hats and carrying long-bladed machetes. As we passed, they pointed out the best route to the Pirates' Caves just ahead.

The Pirate's Lair; A Campesino's Gift; Margret the Survivor

Within minutes, our trail ended, and we stepped between a narrow cleft in the towering hillside. We walked through a passageway in the smoothly eroded rock walls where overhead a narrow slice of sky let the rain drip down from overhanging vegetation. At one point we turned and climbed up one of the walls using footsteps that had been neatly carved into the stone. I followed Simon up through another fissure in the rock wall, happy to be out of the muddy stream at the cave's floor. We emerged at a clearing on the edge of the mountain. Along this ledge we explored at least six caves that had been enlarged by hammer and chisel into neat little stone houses. From the original overhanging ledges, pirates of the 17th century had carved out these basic lodgings. Into the soft rock they cut benches, beds, shelves, and even a hole through the rock ceiling to serve as a chimney above the fire hearth.

When Simon heard that I planned to stay the night here, he shook his head and made the sign of the cross. He agreed to meet me here in the morning to continue our trek and then quickly left for home. Perhaps

Simon believed in spirits that still inhabited the caves, but fortunately my Spanish was not equal to the task of deciphering his rapid warnings.

Before the modern settlers arrived at Floreana, these mountains had been the domain of pirates who plundered gold from the Spanish galleons that plied the coasts of Peru, Ecuador, and Panama. Rumor had it that treasure is buried in these mountains, as yet unfound. For generations the pirates lived here while they kept a lookout from their mountain perch for passing ships to attack. Later, the caves were occasionally inhabited by escaped convicts from the island's penal colony and doubtless for a time by the fiendish Patrick Watkins himself.

Before the twilight turned to total darkness, I gathered a pile of tall grass to soften a stone bench and unrolled my bivy bag on top. I felt wrapped in the cloak of history; the human events and tragedies that had played out on this tiny mid-ocean island seemed as tactile as the coarse cave walls I ran my hands across. Relatively recent inhabitants here had chiseled their names in the wall next to me. Barely discernible were the dates of 1907 and 1909. Here I slept in comfort, perfectly secure in body and mind as Floreana brooded under the mountain rains and the mysteries of its past.

A few hours after dawn, Simon appeared and shook my hand vigorously with genuine relief at the sight of me apparently unmolested by ghosts and enjoying my breakfast of oats, raisins, and powdered milk. I could have happily stayed another night, even another week if I'd brought more supplies.

Not far from the caves, Simon led us through the heavy forest growth to the abandoned first settlement of the Wittmer family. Stone blocks marked the foundation on which stood an almost miniature wooden house. It was more of a shed than a house actually—one room of rotting wood and rusting tin that was now the haunt of birds and lizards. Outside sat an outhouse and a concrete bathtub and water trough, all of it slowly being reclaimed or buried by the clinging vegetation that pressed in on all sides in an almost menacing way. Simon also knew the tales of the island's dark past, but when I asked for details, he would not speak of them, as if a single word could awaken malevolent spirits. He was clearly anxious to move on, so we continued our brisk walk until we reached the source of the drinking water for the coastal settlement. Here the industrious Heinz Wittmer had constructed a cement catchment to gather the runoff and spring water spilling down from the cliff above. A plastic pipe now carried the island's most precious resource five miles from here to the settlement at Black Beach.

We retraced our path through the corridors of the Pirates' Caves and emerged onto the familiar path leading past short bent trees with limbs draped in moss and a barbed-wire fence marking a pasture. A few cattle grazed under the thick brush, quite unable to manicure all the verdant growth of the pasture.

A boy with his goat

In search of a farmer who might sell me fruit for the voyage ahead, we turned onto a side path heading north. After an hour of sliding on the muddy potholed trails, we spotted a farmhouse on a hill covered in a grove of papaya and banana trees. The farmhouse was one of the crudest shelters possible: a collection of misfit rusting tin sheets on the roof, supported by walls of roughly split timber stuck vertically into the ground and fitting so loosely as to reveal the inhabitants and their piles of debris inside the dwelling. From the doorway a middle-aged Ecuadorian *campesino* emerged with his two young daughters. Juan introduced himself with a warm greeting and handshake. Around us was gathered a crowd of animals: sleeping dogs, grunting hogs wallowing in the mud, and clucking chickens.

A barefoot adolescent girl shyly peered at us through the dirt-floored doorway. Her younger sister clutched her father's hand and stared wide-eyed at the rare visitors. The girls' thin dresses were mostly patches of various materials, all stained the russet color of the earth. There was no greeting or smile from either of the girls as Juan told us his wife and the girls' mother had deserted them some time ago. The isolation and extreme poverty of their situation had driven the woman half mad, and she had "run away to the mainland or who knows where."

Simon spoke to Juan in Spanish, suggesting that I'd like to buy some fruit for a long voyage ahead. He nodded and barked an order to his girls who ran into the house and quickly emerged with his shirt and rubber boots. I don't think there was a single pair of shoes in these highland farms. The choice was either rubber boots or barefoot. As he pulled on his shirt, the youngest girl wiped the caked mud from his boots and handed them to her sister who pushed and pulled them onto her father's feet. It was obviously a familiar chore.

Juan picked up his machete and motioned for us to follow. In the papaya grove we picked enough green fruit to last a couple weeks or more at sea. Then with one mighty stroke of his machete, Juan sliced through the trunk of a 15-foot high banana tree that crashed heavily onto the ground. In less than a year the tree will grow anew through the old trunk and produce another huge bunch of fruit. I was surprised to see how large and numerous the green bananas were. There were well over 200 bananas here. Juan sliced the bunch in half, and Simon and I struggled to lift the awkward 40-pound loads on our shoulders. I now had far more bananas than I could eat, even though I planned to boil

Returning to Atom with the farmer's gift

most of them before they ripened and eat them as a potato substitute. For the rest, our plan was to share with friends back in the village.

Juan gathered several cabbages and some green beans, which he stuffed into my pack. I held out double the sucres of what I guessed the produce was worth, but the proud man shook his head no. Juan told me it was his gift for a man who had journeyed so far alone. Perhaps his fear of being alone in the world was reinforced since his wife had left. I looked into his kind, long-suffering eyes and pressed the money into his cracked and blistered hands. We shouldered our loads to leave as a tear began to well up in my eye. Here was a man living in poverty who was willing to give generously to a relatively wealthy but hungry traveler. The contrast between the grasping selfishness of most people in the city and the deep generosity I received in the poorest frontier regions around the world was a constant wonder to me. On my first circumnavigation I had learned not to fear arriving at a remote island with little money and no friends. As a solo traveler I was universally befriended, and some of the most generous souls were those who possessed even less than I.

Simon knew of a short cut back to the main road. I followed him on a grueling march across muddy valleys and flooding streams. As we lost altitude, the terrain dried out, and we walked among grasses, lava boulders, and then cactus. We labored on under our heavy loads, trying to balance on the rocks shifting underfoot while cactus spines pricked at our legs. That "short cut" was tortuous, and I sighed with relief when we finally returned to El Camino.

Simon took his half of the bananas to the small house he shared with his sister and her young son, who was clutching a baby goat in front of their house. I dropped some bananas with the Port Captain and then handed out more to the hungry Spaniards in the anchorage who seemed to be perpetually engaged in hand-line fishing from their rolling deck.

In preparation to depart for Hawaii I swam around *Atom* with mask, snorkel, and fins to scrape off the few gooseneck barnacles clinging just below the waterline. Fish circled below to feed on them as they drifted down off the end of my scraping blade.

Before leaving I said my goodbyes to the Port Captain and then made a last visit to Frau Wittmer. As she served us tea on her front porch she said, "You remind me of another young fellow who stopped here a few years ago while sailing around the world in his sailboat."

It turned out she was speaking about Robin Lee Graham who had begun a five-year circumnavigation in *Dove* at age 16 and had visited with her on this porch over 20 years previously. Margret had not mentioned if his wife Patti was with him at the time, but I knew she had flown out to Baltra Island for a vacation with Robin before he completed his voyage alone back to California. Like most sailors, I had read the book *Dove* and found much inspiration from it before beginning my own first circumnavigation. From the book it was obvious that long before Robin arrived in the Galapagos he was so lovesick for the American girl he had married in South Africa that he was no longer interested in completing the voyage. For commercial reasons, his father and *National Geographic* magazine, which sponsored his trip, refused to take no for an answer. Robin's story may have been one reason I stayed single as long as I did and for many years preferred to sail alone, where my dreams and my life choices remained my own.

When I delicately asked Margaret about the murders, she looked me straight in the eye and claimed she had no idea who was responsible for the poisoning, shootings, and disappearances. If she had any secrets, she kept them to herself.

Before I stepped down from the Wittmer porch, I said I hoped to return and see her again someday. The old woman matter-of-factly said, "I'll be dead long before you'll circle the world again." Her memoir was published a few years later as *Floreana: A Woman's Pilgrimage to the Galapagos*, and this intrepid lady lived on in Floreana for another decade after that.

5 Empire of Wind, Sea, and Sky

Under the guide star Hokulea, the Polynesian navigators ventured forth beside the wandering frigatebirds that come ashore only to sleep.

I waved goodbye to my two Spanish friends as they fished from their sailboat in the anchorage off Black Beach. I never since heard if they reached Polynesia, stayed on Floreana, or simply disappeared. As it so often goes, when a sailor ups anchor, he sails out of his new friend's lives forever. Each time we set sail we close another chapter in our lives, and the next passage provides ample time to reflect on the events and friendships from the previous island.

My last worldly view of the Galapagos was of the swirling black clouds capping the sleeping volcanic peak of the westernmost island of Isabella as I passed some 20 miles to its south. Isabella and its smaller uninhabited neighbor, Fernandina Island, are the youngest islands in the group, barely a million years old, mere infants in human terms, and contain several still-active volcanoes. Because of their youth, the rocky soil of the hardened lava flows has not broken down sufficiently to support the varied vegetation of their 3–4 million-year-old sister islands to the east. Like most volcanic islands, they are destined to erode back into the sea over the next 20 million years, give or take a hundred thousand human generations. I stared at the receding flanks of Isabella off and on for hours until its image was burned into my memory; this was the last land I would see until Hawaii, over 4,000 solitary miles away.

An orange sun dropped into the waters ahead, bathing the sky and sea around it in fiery reds and yellows. As darkness fell, the kerosene lamp cast a warm golden glow inside the cabin. Above me, the stars of the Milky Way speckled the heavens from horizon to horizon. In the waters below, diamond-like splashes of light marked the movements of jellyfish and other unknown creatures as they disturbed the microscopic blooming phytoplankton. The transition from harbor to sea was punctuated by a soft orchestra of familiar sounds: wave tops lapping against the hull, the jib fluttering momentarily then snapping full of wind, sheets and steering lines creaking under their loads; all signs that we were on course as I was lulled to sleep. The following morning I scanned around an empty seascape. My private empire of wind and sky and open horizons lifted my spirits and heightened my expectation of thrilling adventures to come.

What more could a young man want besides plentiful provisions, a comfortable bunk to lie down in, and his own little ship bound for new adventures? Out here I had a great big dose of solitude and space, freedom from horizon to horizon, a clear sky and pure air, fish below and birds above. We rode on wind and wave as the celestial bodies wheeled overhead. The days were too short, the nights even shorter. Time stood still as it somehow raced away. My circle of solitude was marked by my height of eye—about three miles around the visible horizon or a mile farther when I stood up on the cabin top. If my math is correct, that's 30 square miles of my own backyard!

Navigating a sail-driven boat from the Galapagos to Hawaii is not about following the fixed compass course of a rhumb line, or even the slightly more direct great circle route. Along those paths lurks the sailor's nemesis—that wide region of calms and unsettled weather so aptly named the doldrums, which I had already endured when sailing south from Panama. To avoid the bigger part of the doldrums, my plan was first to sail directly west for 2,000 miles, riding the northern edge of the southeast trade winds, following a course about 100 miles south of, and parallel to, the Equator. Somewhere to the west, the band of doldrums that stretches clear across the Pacific is at its narrowest. That is where I would make a right-angle turn north to cross the windless zone as directly as possible. Contrary and unpredictable currents were to be expected as I turned north across the equator. A few hundred miles farther to the north I expected to find the northeast trade winds that would carry me to Hawaii with fair winds on the beam.

A round of star sights with the sextant at dawn's twilight on the second morning at sea indicated I had covered 158 miles in the preceding 24 hours. I didn't need to consult my logbook to know this was one of the fastest single-day runs we had ever logged. A fresh wind off the port beam and favorable currents had as much to do with the record run as attentive sail handling and a clean hull. I was not a meticulous or technical sailor, which is to say it bothered me little to leave sails less than perfectly trimmed, with outhaul and leech line tension ignored, as long as we had wind and speed to spare. I watched the miles rush beneath the keel and disappear into our boiling wake as if I were in a blissful narcotic trance. Over the next several days our progress slowed to a more typical 120 miles per day as the river-like current slackened and the wind eased slightly.

Phantom Currents; The Doldrums-Inner Peace; Short Rations

Two weeks out of Floreana Island we ran up against an uncharted countercurrent that slowed our progress dramatically. The logbook recorded only fifty miles' progress that day. That foul current had made my decision for me, and I obligingly turned north and sailed across the equator at 123 degrees west longitude. There was no celebration at the crossing of the line; we were heading into the heart of the doldrums. We left the constant trade wind behind us at two degrees north of the equator and entered a region of confused seas. Here the southeast swell met with a northerly and an easterly swell that had the turbulent waters slapping the hull from every quarter. *Atom* mimicked the water's motions and tossed me about with unpredictable lurches that many times nearly knocked me off my feet. To counter the east-flowing current that attempted to carry me backwards 25 miles or more a day, I was forced to shake off my apathy and bring forth that technically minded sailor, patiently adjusting sails and course hour-by-hour and minute-by-minute.

The next day the seas laid down at last. Now began the long days of calm. I dropped and bagged the now-useless jib and sheeted the mainsail tight to stop some of the rhythmic slatting and flapping that tortured the seams as it tested my sanity. Still, I needed to keep some of the mainsail up so that it could act as a giant brake to dampen the boat's eternal rolling.

I watched a jellyfish pass me by. A new and very humbling reality hit me, that when the wind stopped I was even more helplessly adrift than a jellyfish. This is the point when sailors reach for their engine's starter button. I pictured myself motoring through the doldrums to shave a couple days off this passage, but reminded myself that saved days might only be squandered later in perhaps even less productive pursuits. I had sought this challenge and had placed myself in this situation. I would get myself out of it unaided—just not anytime soon. Motor-sailing across the ocean is not a sailing voyage any more than experiencing wilderness from behind the glass and steel of an automobile is a wilderness experience. It is something, to be sure; a passage on the water from point A to B, but it is a distant relation to a true sailing voyage.

I played guitar on deck at sunset, then blew softly into my harmonica as I meditated on the emerging stars. Returning to my bunk I picked up one of sailing mystic Bernard Moitessier's books to read by lamplight. In it he states:

> *I am a citizen of the most beautiful nation on earth. A*
> *nation whose laws are harsh yet simple, a nation that*
> *never cheats, which is immense and without borders, where*
> *life is lived in the present. In this limitless nation, this*
> *nation of wind, light, and peace, there is no other ruler*
> *besides the sea.*

A sedentary person on shore with too many good books at hand is in danger of coming to prefer ideas and stories over action and society. The urge may be to isolate themselves from reality, to overly intellectualize the world. The same danger, magnified ten times, exists for the solo sailor, but at some point the demands of a boat on the sea and the arrival at a new port bring you back to the real world soon enough. From his time at the university of the sea, the sailor may come back with a deeper understanding of himself and bring lessons to share. Some of us go to sea to experience that interface of man and nature. We also go to worship our gods of creation the way I imagine a pilgrim enters Jerusalem or a Mohammedan travels to Mecca.

I read my fill until late that night and, after a final scan of the horizon, slept deeply and relived pleasant memories in dreams for several uninterrupted hours until dawn. After many days alone at sea I was often able to indulge my dreams to an extent I never did when tucked into a four-poster land bed. If some movement or sound of the boat or my alarm clock awoke me mid-dream, I had only to close my eyes and drift back to pick up the same dream where I had left off. At first my dreams led, and I followed. Then at some point I could bring my conscious state into synch with the deep unconscious and alter the course of a dream to whatever outcome I chose. A book on psychoanalytic dream analysis I later picked up gave me insight into those hidden messages and the suppressed thoughts within the musings and images floating in unrecognizable cipher before my sleeping mind. In a computer analogy, it seems that the sleeping brain goes through an offline defragmentation process during a dream state, reorganizing recent memory files for long-term storage. When we dream we reprocess the past to prepare for the future. But then the mind goes beyond the binary functions of a computer to interpret memories and desires and perhaps to guide us through the mental mine field of the entirety of our existence from base reptilian impulse to the moralizing role of the superego. In any case, those dreams at sea were my welcome companions. How could I feel alone when I had all my friends and family within my memories and dreams?

By day I searched the rolling oily swell in vain for signs of wind and then searched again and again, as if seeking could bring back the object of my desire. The only thing moving that day was the angle of the sun. The enflamed yellow disc burned down on me in equatorial ferocity as I hid from it under the shadow of my wide-brimmed straw hat. The sun's rays hit the mirrored surface of the water and reflected back up to burn my skin from below as well as from above. Day after day, there was no sign of the existence of humanity: nary a jet painted its contrail in the sky overhead, and no ship passed to mar the pure seascape canvas. The succession of calm days eventually brought the ever-rolling sea to a nearly level state. Reaching the doldrums in the center of the sea is something of a metaphor for a lone sailor's journey to the deep, unknown center of his own mind. What I found there beneath the surface of things was a timeless unity—the still point of the turning world. The youthful, energetic waves of shallow waters, lashed into movement by each prevailing wind, had at last calmed themselves and found a level balance above the abyss. Eternal questions of where are we going and how we will get there, resolved and then melted away to be replaced by a singular present moment. The trials of the doldrums are felt by one man as frustration and despair and received as a gift of peace to another. It is all perception.

As we rushed along before a fair wind at the beginning of this passage, time had also rushed by. But here the time passed slowly, the way I want time to pass. The long days and longer nights were filled with an acute awareness. These doldrums can teach us something about how to live. Enter them with all the time in the world. Meditate, observe, just be there without desire. Let the calm waters banish your frustrations and reward you with the patience of eternity. The only real danger here comes from within—a feeling of listlessness and creeping depression tried to slink aboard from time to time, coupled with an oppressive, boxed-in claustrophobia that a submariner might feel. It seems odd to feel trapped when you have space that stretches clear to a distant horizon, but the mind knows that this space is unreachable to the body. Fortunately for me, those feelings came only in small fleeting doses. I long ago cultivated an ability to counter them. Being alone and unmoving, I had ample time for meditation. In fact, the entirety of the experience was a prolonged meditation. Here is where acute awareness and calm connectedness meet to carry you from day to day. The wind will return in its own time. Have faith—it will return. And meanwhile, how often does a sailor at sea get to sleep undisturbed through the night, becalmed without and calm within: count it as one of the gifts of the doldrums.

How is it that some people go to sea and find none of these gifts? They complain about the difficulties they faced. They fail and look for excuses. The winds they meet blow over a remorseless sea, driving waves to tumble on troubled shores. The sea brings you face to face with yourself, she gives back only what you bring with you.

I was at that time utterly incapable of understanding the complaints of frustration we always hear from sailors who are becalmed for more than a few hours, particularly when they're short of fuel or their engine quits on a long passage. In their world, a temporary cessation of progress is the worst fate imaginable. Their mind is in a nervous frenzy—will the weather change for the worse? Will I miss my appointments ashore? In time, some of us learn that there are few things in our environment that focused endurance, coupled with a tranquil state of mind, cannot overcome. Rather than feeling frustrated at expectations unrealized, I thrived on the age-old sailor's game of hunting the next zephyr and capturing it to propel me a few more yards on my way. A quote by Henry David Thoreau comes to mind:

> *The sail, the play of its pulse so like our own lives: so thin and yet so full of life, so noiseless when it labours hardest, so noisy and impatient when least effective.*

The windless skies grew overcast. It began to rain and rain. The heavy drops fell so hard, so continuously for two days that at times the liquid air left me short of breath. I opened a valve under the deck drain and attached a short hose to fill buckets and jugs and my freshwater tank with the sweet rainwater that ran along the deck. Tomorrow would be laundry day, though this naked sailor had little to wash beyond a sarong, the sheet on his bunk, and a pillow cover. Plentiful rainfall also meant I could take extravagantly long and frequent showers by standing soaped up on deck during the heavier downpours, or sitting in the cockpit under my solar shower bag hung from the boom.

Even in mid-ocean, far from the centers of man-made pollution, rainwater is less pure than you might think. Each drop of rain begins by moisture in the air condensing around specs of dust and bacteria floating in the atmosphere. As the droplet falls through the lower atmosphere and then runs along the deck of the boat, it picks up more contaminants. I filtered the water through a fine cloth before drinking, but if storing it for longer than a few days I learned to add a few drops of bleach per gallon to prevent a bloom of algae growth in the water tank.

We drifted into a new season; hurricane season had just begun on June 1st. I sat in the center of the tempest's breeding ground, where warm and moist equatorial air uplifting into bands of thunderstorms provided the fuel for the rotation of the earth to spin up these super storms. I frequently tapped my brass barometer to reassure myself we were not being engulfed in a deepening low-pressure system. Brief lashings of wind in the rainsqualls had me dancing all over the deck, trimming and reefing sails to inch our way northward.

Without an engine to speed me on my way, my slow progress began to give me some concern that I could end up on short rations of food before reaching Hawaii. Each week I made an inventory of my food supplies, which by now consisted mainly of weevily flour and corn meal for making bread, rice, beans, onions, potatoes, powdered milk, and the TVP soybean product. The mung beans and alfalfa seeds I intended for daily use were not sprouting well in the hot, humid air. It was at first hugely disappointing, and later alarming, to watch them become moldy and die before they grew large enough to eat. By choice, I carried little processed and canned food aboard. My vegetarian diet kept me from fishing on this voyage, though I had basic fishing tackle aboard, and my skills from earlier years as an avid fisherman might allow me to survive at sea indefinitely, if the need arose.

My state of meditative bliss had been eroded somewhat by the days of continuous rain. Now the blue skies erased the rain, which also

cleared away my spiritual doldrums. I lay down on deck, reaching over
the side to scrape the gooseneck barnacles that were beginning to
colonize the hull near the waterline. I fantasized for a moment about
gooseneck barnacle salad. But I had lost my desire for seafood, and the
barnacles were likely toxic from the anti-fouling paint they clung to.

As I worked, a faint buzzing noise grew in my ears. I stood up to
search the horizon. At first I saw nothing and couldn't place the
unfamiliar sound. As it grew louder I knew it was a type of engine but
not the low throbbing typical of a ship or the distant muted roar of an
airplane. Then, just above the horizon, I spotted a tiny dot that rapidly
grew into the form of a helicopter skimming above the surface of the
water. As he approached, I dropped my scrubbing brush and wrapped a
sarong around my waist as if expecting guests to come aboard. The two
men in the small helicopter circled me once at masthead height and then
hovered just off my stern. The wind from his rotor brushed the sea and
filled our mainsail, causing us to surge forward unexpectedly. In an
instinctual response, I steered us north with one hand on the tiller. The
copilot signaled by hand for me to turn on my radio. I waved my hand
and turned my head side-to-side and shouted back "No radio!" They
couldn't hear me above the howl of the engine but got the message
nonetheless. I had the ridiculous fantasy that if they lingered long
enough, I could ride their rotor wash until clear of the windless zone.
The pilot waved goodbye, and in a few minutes they had completely
disappeared to the east on the reciprocal course from which they came.

I stood on deck watching dumbly until long after they disappeared
over the horizon. I felt strangely sad to be alone after this brief human
encounter and then felt oddly annoyed to have had my spell of solitude
broken so abruptly. They had not realized this piece of ocean had
become my private space, from horizon to horizon. And I wondered:
how and why would a helicopter be out here over a thousand miles from
land? Then I recalled the night before when I had sighted a tight cluster
of white lights on the eastern horizon. That must have been a large tuna
fishing vessel, and this helicopter was their fish spotter. Perhaps they

had intended to invite me over for dinner! No, it was more likely they wanted to ask if any schools of fish had passed our way. I had seen a school of tuna and other fish as recently as the day before. It was just as well that my finned friends had departed and had been saved by my lack of a radio.

Northeaster Salvation; The Star of Joy

We continued our solitary crawl northward at a fitful 1–2 miles an hour. At eight degrees north I entered an area where an upwelling current broke the water's surface into dancing sharp peaks. The turbulent waters hissed audibly. The current, mixed with new wave patterns from the north and east, had me on unsure footing as I moved about the boat in lurches from one handhold to the next. Within a few hours, a random puff of wind brought me out of the choppy current. Then the wind departed to leave me languishing again on a gently rolling sea. During these days of drifting this way and that, even a short-lived movement at the speed of a slow walk felt utterly breathtaking.

Salvation arrived out of nowhere on a cat's-paw, which scratched across the flat surface of the water, a baby's breath that caressed my skin and gave the old sails a facelift as it pulled the wrinkles from the sun-worn Dacron fabric. We heeled almost imperceptibly. An hour later it was upon us—the long-awaited miracle of the northeast trades that blow freely in a thousand mile-wide band across most of the tropical North Pacific. Those winds brushed the surface of the water until little waves rolled along like a field of grain waving in the wind. We rushed along on our course to the northwest. By the next day we were romping along in strong winds just forward of the beam. *Atom* responded by leaning over at a sharp angle, pushing her way ahead at full speed. She flung herself off the building wave tops, landing in the troughs with enough force to make the mast shudder in protest. The unaccustomed speed was exhilarating, so I carried on with all the sail we could carry as we clicked off the miles toward Hawaii. I had spent seven days crossing 300 miles in the doldrums to reach the northeast trades.

Awaiting the first stars of evening twilight

Each night of our northward trek I observed the Southern Cross dipping lower in the southern sky as Polaris, the North Star, rose higher above the horizon to escort me along my way. I greeted Polaris a few times through my sextant's viewfinder at evening or morning twilight. Most casual observers of the night sky know that Polaris indicates the direction of true north. Old-school sailors know that even an uncorrected observed altitude of Polaris equals their current latitude north of the equator within about 45 miles and that applying a few tabulated corrections from the sight reduction tables will reduce that error to two or three miles. Because Polaris is located near earth's north celestial pole, from our perspective it stands motionless in the heavens, with all the stars of the northern sky appearing to rotate around it. Navigators have used it for centuries, though their constant and true guide star has not always been this constant. An ancient Greek navigator noted in 320 B.C. that the northern celestial pole was devoid of stars. In a few more thousand years, due to a cyclic 25,000-year-long wobble of earth's axis, Polaris will again have wandered off to other parts of the sky, leaving future navigators to mourn its passing.

The wandering stars were even more of a concern to me the longer I remained at sea. I carried no radio to get an accurate time signal and relied on two inexpensive quartz wristwatches to time my celestial observations accurately. If there was one minute of error in my watch, I might sail past Hawaii so far off course that I wouldn't even sight the islands. Like two mismatched crewmates of different temperaments, as each day passed, my two watches displayed ever greater disagreements between them, and *Atom*'s navigator grew ever more uneasy. To be certain of sighting Hawaii when my celestial sightings indicated we were getting close, I planned to employ some of the tricks of the bygone Polynesian navigators.

In a true miracle of navigation, around 400 A.D. the ancient Polynesians found their way in their double-hulled voyaging canoes to Hawaii from islands thousands of miles away in the South Pacific. They, of course, carried no clock or sextant or even a compass to guide them. And most challenging of all, they had no charts and no way of knowing if any islands existed that far to the north. These unequaled navigators built their sailing canoes from trees using only stone carving tools. They used sails of woven palm fronds and ropes of twisted coconut fibers. With their finely-honed skills of observation of migratory birds, wind and wave patterns, and direct observation of the stars, the Polynesians sailed the breadth of the South Pacific. They had settled almost all the habitable islands contained there, centuries before Western explorers reached the Pacific. To colonize unknown lands, they carried with them the plants and animals from home that they needed to sustain life, including pigs and chickens, root vegetables, and coconuts. From Tahiti and the Marquesas Islands in present-day French Polynesia, they sailed north to Hawaii on a hunch and luckily found empty islands waiting there. Even more remarkably, after settling Hawaii, some of them found their way back to Tahiti, guided by Sirius, the brightest of all zenith stars, to bring news of the discovery to others who followed.

Having sailed both the North and South Pacific myself, I could imagine the returning Polynesian navigator giving the island chief the sailing directions from their home in the Marquesas Islands to his newly discovered islands of Hawaii: "Sail northeast as close to the southeast wind as possible until you meet the region of calms. Paddle north using your guide stars to where the winds return from the northeast. Hold close to the wind on starboard tack until the star *Hokulea* [the "Star of Joy" known to us as Arcturus] is at your zenith. Sail towards the point of sunset then and look for signs of land from the birds, clouds, and reflected waves. Release your captive frigatebird. If he does not return to the canoe, follow him to the new land." Had the navigator known of the vast area of landless waters to the west, he might have added the warning that if they missed the islands of Hawaii they would perish in the vacant seas beyond his known world.

Mast Stay Failure; Hanging On By One Hand

The thought of my dwindling food supplies whetted my appetite for progress. With the urgency of a Polynesian navigator running low on provisions, I pushed the boat hard by carrying as much sail as I dared. I paid the price for this increased speed with several equipment failures. Unable to take the strain, one or another of the sails required frequent mending. As the old running rigging chafed, I spliced the lines back together.

I kept sailing hard, hoping nothing more serious would break. One day a pin holding the inner headstay wire supporting the mast gave way, and I was forced to reduce sail and attempt to climb the mast to rehang the wire. Although I had a second back-up stay at the head of the mast, the inner stay provided added support and ensured the mast would not fall down if that other stay also failed.

By now I was skilled in free climbing the mast in port by clutching the hanging wires and ropes in my hands and pinching the mast between my thighs and feet to inch my way upwards. Climbing the swaying mast at sea in this fashion was not only terrifying and exhausting but also quite likely to result in a deadly plunge to the deck or into the sea. Pushing thoughts of the dangers from my mind, I determined to make an attempt. I first slackened the mainsail halyard a couple feet to allow me to get footholds on the track slides between the sail and the mast. Then I altered course to follow a more stable downwind run. I extended the tether of my safety harness, placed two shackles and pliers in my pocket, tied the inner stay wire to my belt, and began my climb. Halfway up the mast I paused to rest at the spreaders, which is sailor-speak for the horizontal aluminum tubes that hold the upper shrouds away from the mast. But the strength needed just to hold tight and keep from being pitched into the sea meant I had to get moving again quickly before I was too exhausted to move higher. At 30 feet above the deck, the mast swayed and jerked so violently that I spent long moments focusing every muscle fiber to hold tight.

As I loosened my grip on the mast to attach the wire and shackles, the boat rolled to a larger than normal wave. My body came loose from the mast as I hung by one hand looking down into the sea. With the boat's next roll, I was slammed violently against the mast. Every part of my body cried out in searing pain. My pliers dropped into the sea. I nearly cried at the thought of returning to the deck for more tools. Instantly I decided that getting the shackles finger tight was good enough until better repairs could be made in port. That critical slapdash repair finished, I slithered down to the deck where I sat with my leg and arm muscles twitching uncontrollably with spasms and adrenaline. Blood dripped off one of my fingers from a torn fingernail. I looked up to see spots of blood on the mainsail—proof of a hard-earned passage. The lesson I received was that it is infinitely easier and safer to examine minutely all the rigging and make preventative repairs before departure from port than it is to repair rigging aloft while underway. I told myself I would never climb that high again at sea, no matter the apparent urgency. A couple of years later it proved to be a promise I couldn't keep.

As each 900 miles of longitude passed under the keel, I set my bulkhead-mounted clock back another hour to keep in step with the local time zone. There was no real need to follow local time out here alone where my day was ruled by the solar and lunar clocks overhead, but even the mind of the solo sailor seeks out familiar land-based patterns to follow, and it was one more welcome indication of my progress westwards.

Hawaii at Last!; The Light of Father Damian Shines

On my forty-second day at sea I watched a frigatebird moving erratically, but making progress in a general southwesterly direction where the clouds seemed to be piling up slightly higher than on other points of the horizon. My sextant sights told me I had passed under the Polynesian navigator's "Star of Joy" the night before, and now these other signs pointed towards nearby land. Soon, a long wavy charcoal smudge on the southern horizon grew and defined itself into what I calculated to be the island of Maui. Hours later it was confirmed when I sighted the additional island of Molokai. I sailed close along Molokai's fortress-like landscape of 3,000-foot-high cliffs rising vertically from the sea, their flanks decorated in vegetation and myriad waterfalls born of daily rains squeezed from the passing trade wind-driven clouds. I sailed as close as I dared under what my chart indicated was Kahiwa Falls, its swollen ribbon of water plunging over 1,700 feet directly into the sea with thunderous power. Other smaller cascades vaporized into drifting rainbows in the wind-swirled mists before they even reached the sea.

This rugged, harborless coast appeared exactly as the first Hawaiians had seen it, no doubt marveling as I did at its terrifying beauty. To my land-starved eyes, the awesome presence was almost overwhelming. The magical and mysterious beauty of it was as striking as my first sight of a naked girl and the first touch of her silken thigh. I hooted with a rush of exhilaration and joy as the increasing winds funneled past the mountains to speed us on our way.

Further along, the cliffs yielded to more gentle inclines and steep valleys. These were seemingly empty now but had likely held thriving communities of Hawaiians before their population was severely cut down by disease and alcohol introduced by the crews of whaling ships and other passing sailors. As in many island kingdoms around the world, these native populations struggled in vain to sustain their culture in the face of the Western onslaught.

Just after sunset I sailed past the settlement at Kalawao Village, known for the leper colony that still existed there. Leprosy was another of the curses brought to the islands by passing sailors. By the 1860s, fear of that growing disfiguring and fatal disease caused King Kamehameha V to approve a law banishing all the afflicted lepers of the island group to this narrow peninsula on the north coast of Molokai. Hundreds of islanders who showed signs of the slow consuming disease were arrested, torn away from their loved ones, and forcibly dumped at this nature's prison, guarded on one side by the wild seas of the windward coast and backed with a steep mountain that isolated the peninsula from the rest of the island. Entry by land was along a narrow mule track over a steep mountain range.

In this hopeless, forbidden place of lingering death, in 1873 the Catholic Priest Father Damien began his lifelong exile in the service of the suffering souls of Kalawao. For 16 years Father Damian cared for the physical and spiritual needs of the dying leper outcasts until he too succumbed to the disease in his martyrdom to charity. In recent years, the Catholic Church sainted him as the "Apostle of the Lepers." I can think of none more deserving the title of Saint.

As I sailed past the leper colony, a lone figure near the shore blinked a light at me several times. Perhaps, I mused, he was one of the few remaining lepers who signaled passing ships to let the world know he was there and not to be forgotten. I signaled back by lifting my kerosene lantern, then tacked offshore to cross the 40-mile wide Kaiawa Channel towards Oahu Island.

6 Americanized Eden

Paradise at Bay

At dawn I approached the verdant, sun-soaked windward coast of Oahu. Once the sun had risen high enough behind me to give me good visibility into the water, I threaded my way through the scattered reefs and islets that guard the entrance to Kaneohe Bay. This largest bay in Hawaii affords a rare expansive and protected anchorage in an archipelago comprised of clusters of relatively young circular volcanoes. In addition to the main islands that people are familiar with, the necklace of Hawaiian Islands actually runs from the unvisited Midway Atoll in the northwest, in a 1,500 mile arc to "the Big Island" of Hawaii in the southeast. The island of Hawaii is also big in the vertical sense—15,000 feet from its base on the seafloor to sea level, plus 14,000 feet elevation above the sea—making it a veritable Everest of the Pacific. The islands sit majestically atop the Pacific Plate, which drifts to the northwest several inches a year. Meanwhile, a single fixed volcanic hotspot deep within the earth builds up pressure, occasionally spewing liquid basalt through the crust of the plate, building new islands in new locations across the eons. Midway Island is now in the death throes of a low coral atoll yielding to the erosive forces of wind and water, while the Big Island is yet being born of still active volcanoes with lava occasionally flowing into the sea.

I anchored off the Kaneohe yacht club, 43 memorable days out from the Galapagos and approximately halfway across the 10,000-mile breadth of the Pacific between Panama and China. I managed to arrive with several days' food supply in the lockers and a half-full water tank. I was well-rested and eager to get ashore to visit my cousin and aunt and an extended family unknown to me, who resided here in Kaneohe. Beyond the yacht club, the town of Kaneohe lay squeezed between the bay and the impressive flanks of the Koolau mountain range. A tunnel

Atom sails in Kaneohe Bay

through the mountain connected this side of the island to the unseen tropical megalopolis of Honolulu. As I dinghied ashore, a fighter jet from the Kaneohe Naval Air Station screamed overhead in an abrupt wake up call to civilization's roaring heartbeat.

From the yacht club I first called Customs to report my arrival. They informed me that I needed to come to their office in Honolulu the following day. My next call was to my cousin Judy and Aunt Edie, who years earlier had moved from the harsh climate of the U.S. Midwest to these inviting tropical shores. In a Hawaiian tradition, Judy and her Filipino-Hawaiian husband, Willy Cayaban, their three children, and other relatives were soon showering me with hugs and flower *leis*. It turned out I had many previously unmet relatives of that exotically beautiful blend of European, Asian, and Polynesian races. At Judy's insistence, we moved my boat into the last empty slip they had reserved for me at the single pier of the state-run Heeia Kea Marina. Again at their insistence, I packed my bag to move temporarily into their house a few miles away.

A Month of Bureaucrats and Fiberglass Under My Skin

The following day, my cousin drove me to Honolulu to keep my appointment with Customs. A middle-aged woman in military-style uniform scowled as she visually scanned the dozens of foreign stamps in my passport and then my boat registration. Then she chewed me out like a drill sergeant: "Don't you know you can't sail into Kaneohe until you get clearance here first? All vessels must clear in at Honolulu or Hilo on the Big Island. I'm fining you $200 for that. You also must pay another $25 for State Boat Use Tax."

"Aloha to you as well," I said as I tried to suppress my anger. "First of all, I just sailed here alone from Panama, and my small engineless boat could not safely approach the busy port of Honolulu in the weather conditions at the time. I would have arrived at night, which is dangerous, and if I did sail in here, I couldn't safely sail back around the island against the wind and current to Kaneohe on an engineless boat. I refuse to pay your $200 fine for simply following good seamanship. As for the bogus $25 tax, if you read the fine print of that law, it specifies that it only applies to boats over 30 feet in length, so I'm not going to pay you a damned thing."

From her stunned expression you might have thought I had just said: "I have landed here from Mars, and I have a problem with authority." My cousin became flustered and whispered pleadingly in my ear, "Just pay the woman, Jimmy." The Customs lady glared at me and then reached under the counter as if she were a bartender going for her gun. Instead of a weapon, she pulled up a sheet of paper, which she used like a shield thrust in front of my face. I grabbed the paper, an Application for Appeal, filled it in, left it on the counter and walked out.

I had been spoiled by my painless entry at Floreana Island and had forgotten that some minions of government exist either to shake down the public, to act as the State's obstructionist, or both. A month later, the appeals panel decided to reduce my fine to $100. The implication was that I was only half guilty or maybe crazy enough to deserve some pity. I grudgingly paid the fine from my seriously depleted savings. This reminded me that my plan to stay here in Hawaii for six months, until the end of the typhoon season in the western Pacific, meant I needed to find a paying job. But before doing that I had one big unpaid job to do: repairing *Atom*'s deck.

Ever since buying my boat eight years previously, I had been plagued by leaking deck fittings. On a boat of such low freeboard and propensity to heel generously to moderate winds, the leeward side of the deck was frequently running with seawater from splashing wave tops. The deck of most sailboats, including mine, is constructed of a core of light balsa wood sandwiched between two layers of fiberglass. Dozens of bolts holding cleats, lifeline stanchions, rigging chain plates, tracks, and other fittings penetrated the deck. Over the years, water had leaked past the bolts, rotting the balsa core until the deck became spongy underfoot. At that point, no amount of recaulking the bolts would seal it for long. I had tried every shortcut repair possible, such as drilling numerous holes in the deck and injecting epoxy resin, none of which worked. Imagine life at home if your roof leaked saltwater nearly every day onto your furniture, bed, and all your belongings. I was now more than ready to do whatever it took to have a dry home for a change.

There was only one sure and lasting way to seal the deck again. I needed to remove every deck fitting, cut off the entire top layer of the fiberglass deck in sections, scrape out the rotted balsa, glue in new core material, fiberglass the top layer back down, sand it fair, and repaint. My cousin Judy and her husband Willy, who owned a transmission repair shop in Kaneohe, generously loaned me tools and an electrical generator to power them and drove me into Honolulu for fiberglass supplies. Describing the repair steps makes it look easy, but it took a month working alone full-time to finish the job. Each day after working under the hot Hawaiian summer sun, covered in epoxy resin and fiberglass, I rode my newly purchased, second-hand bicycle back to my cousin's house where I showered long to rinse the fiberglass dust from my skin. Even after scrubbing until my skin turned red, I still scratched and itched through the night. In the end, the luxury of living in a dry boat was well worth the effort.

Essays to Detroit; Working for Rations; The Yhaaa-ting Torquemada

During the evenings I wrote up the story of that first half of my voyage alone to China. After my reporter friend Marie McDougal in Michigan received the article she edited it and published the 12-part series in a Detroit area newspaper. Knowing that I had an audience was about more than stroking the ego; I wanted to share the experience with those who dreamed of adventure and might be inspired to follow, and with those who, for various reasons, would never live their dreams. Not following your dream is a great loss; not having a dream is unimaginable. The future monthly article deadlines gave me further incentive to live an adventure-filled life, one I hoped would be worthy of my readers' attention.

With *Atom* once again fit for sea and my cash savings dwindled to a few hundred dollars, I turned my attention to finding a job. Most of the jobs available were located on the other side of the island in Honolulu, and I considered moving my boat there once I had a job lined up. For several days I walked the docks of the marinas and spoke to everyone I could, but no jobs were offered. Positions of yacht caretaker or shipwright were not generally given to transients. More highly skilled and experienced technicians snatched up the few boat-related jobs in a field where customers were most often referred by word of mouth.

While walking the docks of the Ala Wai Harbor Marina, I passed a 41-foot ketch, named *Horizon*, that I knew belonged to Earl Hinz, the well-known author of a popular cruising guide to the Pacific islands. The boat was buttoned up tightly with an air conditioner buzzing above the forward hatch. I imagined Mr. Hinz inside tapping out another book or magazine article on his typewriter. I didn't dare intrude on what some of his readers called the "Admiral of the Pacific" since he had already blown off an earlier greeting from me by phone.

The esteemed Mr. Hinz and I both belonged to the Seven Seas Cruising Association, a group of over a thousand sailors who travel the world on their yachts. Members often fly the club burgee from their masts and socialize with other members wherever they may meet. Other members, who are temporarily land-based or ensconced long-term in a marina, volunteer as SSCA Port Captains, offering to greet visiting club members and provide local information about their homeport. But the main reason I joined was because in the age before the Internet, the club published a monthly newsletter containing trip reports from members cruising worldwide. The bulletin contained invaluable advice on everything from clearance procedures to the best ports for provisioning, local sailing and weather conditions, and many other details a sailor wants to know. Part of each issue inevitably contained irate members writing in to criticize what someone had written the previous month. If a sailor wrote and mentioned that he gathered coconuts on such and such an island, the next month another sailor would inevitably write in condemning anyone so thoughtless as to touch the fruit that belongs to the locals, and so on. I found the gossip fest strangely entertaining, at least until I unwittingly incurred the wrath of Admiral Hinz when he wrote in to the Bulletin after my departure from Hawaii to complain about what he considered my outrageous behavior.

In my innocent anticipation of meeting Mr. Hinz, I had phoned him soon after my arrival in Oahu. I briefly recounted to him that I was a fellow SSCA member, had sailed solo from Florida, and was en route to China. I asked if he might schedule a time to meet at his boat so that I could ask him a few questions about the islands of Micronesia to which I was next headed. Mr. Hinz told me that he was too busy to meet with me at any time and that I should buy his book instead. He hung up on me faster than if I were a bill collector. As I stood holding the dead phone, I thought, "That's odd. He *volunteered* to be the freaking welcome man for our club!"

His quick dismissal of me happened before he had ever heard of me or even read my report to the SSCA bulletin that he later found so distasteful. After arriving in Hawaii, I had mailed what I thought was a helpful trip report to the bulletin, detailing my passage from Panama and the Galapagos. I mentioned in it that the current Port Captain of Puerto Ayora was allowing sailors to stay for a $5 daily fee and that in Floreana I was welcomed to stay for free and without limits. I also warned readers (without complaining about it) that I was fined in Hawaii for arriving in the wrong port and that others should be careful not to make the same mistake. A month after that was published, I was surprised to read a response to my report in the bulletin from none other than Mr. Hinz. As a yachting version of Torquemada, the Spanish Grand Inquisitor, Hinz pontificated that I should not have stopped in Galapagos without an advance permit (permits that were not being issued), that my payments to the Port Captain made me an accessory to the crime of bribery (in a country where "the bite" is the way of life), that I was stupid not to research the official ports of entry before arriving in Hawaii, and that my trip left an "unclean wake" for those who followed.

My plea? Not guilty on all counts, Your Honor. One of the oft-repeated tenets of the SSCA was that members should "leave a clean wake." Their golden rule meant that we should treat foreign officials as well as the environment, with scrupulous care. I was quite proud of my "clean wake" as I interpreted it and was disappointed that Mr. Hinz and I, despite our common bonds of cruising under sail and being members of the same sailing club, belonged to different worlds. My world was reality focused. His world was bureaucratic compliance to the letter of the law. According to this self-styled expert on blue water cruising and the self-appointed clean wake policeman, I was unclean. I dutifully resigned my membership from the SSCA before Mr. Hinz, whom I came to call Torq the Terrible, could have me ex-communicated. The whole episode reminded me that even within the sailing community there are nearly as many cliques as can be found ashore.

Painting for Dollars; Rich Dreams of Porno, Buys Boat Instead; Atom Goes Solar

Giving up on finding work in Honolulu, I turned to the newspaper classified ads and concentrated on finding work in Kaneohe. I called a local company advertising for an experienced house painter. "Have you worked as a house painter before, and are you residing on the island permanently?" the man asked after he heard my bland un-Hawaiian, Midwestern accent.

I gave vague answers and stretched the truth just enough to get hired. Early each morning I rode my bicycle the five miles from my cousin's home to the business owner's house where his son and one other painter, named Rich, met every morning to load up the pickup truck with equipment and supplies for the drive to whatever house needed painting that day. Mostly we worked on new home construction in the suburbs on the hills overlooking Honolulu and Pearl Harbor. Newly prosperous Japanese businessmen, who were investing heavily at that

time in the relatively inexpensive real estate market of Hawaii, owned
many of these new homes.

When I picked up a brush to paint a porch railing on my first day on
the job, my bearded co-worker Rich, who was about my age and closely
resembled a young Chuck Norris, said, "You're not a painter. I can tell
by the way you hold the brush. Here, don't grip the damn thing like a
dagger, hold the handle between your open palm and thumb like this."
Rich saved my butt by showing me the ropes, and within a couple weeks
I had become the experienced house painter I had claimed to be.

Rich was an entertaining storyteller and commentator on all things
going on in Hawaii, or at least the things that concerned him. Working
with him helped the long days of labor pass easily. He considered
himself a magnet for women and was more obsessed with sex than a
sailor on a one-day shore pass. "I would be great as a porn star. I'm
gonna quit this job as soon as I can find a way into the business," he
repeated to me seriously almost every day. After visiting my boat a
couple times, Rich decided living aboard his own small sailboat in
Kaneohe was better than the rented house he shared with his current
girlfriend and her talkative parrot. Within a couple of weeks he bought a
well-used local fiberglass sloop a foot or two smaller than *Atom* and
moved aboard.

Each day after returning the truck to our boss's house, I biked back
to my cousin's home nestled at the base of the Koolau Mountains. It
amazed me to be riding that busy concrete road through the suburban
sprawl and to look up at the flanks of the mountain that sprouted
instant misty waterfalls and rainbows during the nearly daily but brief
afternoon showers. Occasionally I stopped along the way at a Japanese
temple and garden to stroll among the exotic plants and perfectly
manicured grounds.

As much as I enjoyed the parties and social life at my cousin's house,
now that I was earning money I felt as if I had intruded long enough on
their hospitality. I was also homesick for *Atom*, so I moved back aboard
and anchored her behind Coconut Island next to Rich and one other

resident sailboat. Since this anchorage was only a mile from work, I paddled my newly purchased 16-foot kayak each morning to a landing spot and walked the remaining two blocks to work, carrying the kayak upside down over my head in canoe-portaging style, and left it padlocked to my boss's fence for the day. This kayak was a sit-on-top version of an expedition kayak that I planned to take with me when I sailed out of Hawaii. It would be useful as a second dinghy for exploring the coasts and rivers of the islands ahead.

By working six days a week I managed to save over a thousand dollars a month. Besides the kayak purchase, my newfound wealth permitted me to make some upgrades to *Atom*'s gear. A few miracles of the modern world began to creep aboard when I added a solar panel, battery, and masthead navigation light to increase my visibility in the congested waters of Asia. I also added an inexpensive, portable short-wave radio receiver that could receive the time signals I needed for navigation.

Oahu's Pakalolo and Pavement; Mom Comes to Beautiful Kauai; Samoan Surf Thugs; More Bureau-Brownshirts

When I began planning the walk I expected to make across Oahu just as I had done on every previous island I stopped at, my cousin told me, "You can't walk across *this* island! My God, don't you know those *pakalolo* [crazy tobacco] growers in the mountains will think you're police or stealing their crop or *da kine*, and kill you, *pao*." My cousin and her relatives all seasoned their English with the Hawaiian Pidgin that began among immigrant laborers in old sugarcane plantation days. *Pao* means finished. *Da kine* is a catch-all phrase that means this or that kind of thing, or anything or nothing, and finds its way into almost any sentence. As for the Hawaiian language itself, how can you not love a softly musical language that contains strings of silky vowels punctuated by only a few sparsely used consonants?

I had faced bigger threats than pot growers in places like Papua New Guinea when I walked through malarial swamps or among the warring tribes in the highlands. But the longer I stayed in Oahu, the less enchanted I became with the idea of crossing the island on foot. Oahu is past her paradisiacal prime, they say, which is undeniably true. The vehicle-choked streets of Honolulu and Waikiki, where Authentic Hawaiian Crafts (made in Hong Kong) are flogged to Midwestern tourists, the ribbons of concrete expressways, the resort-blemished coastlines packed with tourists, the heavy military presence, the valleys of endless mechanized pineapple fields—all said she was not the Hawaii of a James Michener novel. I was left with the impression that on an island this developed, I would not discover enough of interest to make a cross-island walk worth the effort.

I did get a taste of rural Hawaii when my mother flew out from Michigan for a vacation. Together we sailed the calm waters of Kaneohe Bay. Then we joined the Cayabans for a plane trip to Willy Cayaban's father's eightieth birthday *luau* at his home in Kekaha Village on the island of Kauai. Grandpa Cayaban had immigrated here 60 years earlier from the Philippines. The leathery old man greeted us with kind eyes and hands toughened and knotty from years of work in the fields. For 44 years he had worked on the Kekaha sugarcane plantation. He and his second wife, Victoria, still lived in his modest wooden house with his wood-fired water heater in the backyard, within sight of the processing plant and sugarcane fields where he had spent a lifetime of hard and honest labor. He amassed no fortune over the years, other than the treasure of a devoted family and the honor of receiving hundreds of visitors for his birthday celebration. When Grandpa's first wife died shortly after giving birth to their fourth child, he took over the job of raising his children. Although he could have had his relatives send him a new bride from the Philippines at any time, he waited 20 years before remarrying in order not to cloud the children's memory of their mother. He raised them alone in a new country with his old-country values.

I joined Grandpa Cayaban and Victoria, on their daily early morning ritual of walking briskly along the coastal road that cut through the village of Kekaha. Along the way they pointed out the local sights and history. This gentle man spoke in Hawaiian Creole, or Pidgin, which was mostly understandable to me by that time. The next day we toured the island with him and went to Waimea Canyon State Park, where we overlooked a miles-wide gorge of mineral-colored and stratified earth. Grandpa pointed out the footpaths in the distance that he used as a young man on pig hunting trips.

But even rural Kauai was changing before our eyes as developers moved in, replacing the fields of coconuts, sugarcane, and the gardens and shacks of the locals with five-star resorts for wealthy tourists. I couldn't help feeling a tinge of sadness at the loss of traditional Hawaiian culture throughout the islands. Although it is not entirely gone, it is well-hidden and mostly overwhelmed by Western culture. While driving through Honolulu each day, I saw the incongruous meeting of the towering high-rise buildings and traffic-jammed streets backed by vistas of palm-fringed beaches and encircling vegetation-draped mountains. Although I visited the Polynesian Cultural Center and museums and read about old Hawaii in books, I met few full-blooded Polynesians. This may have been partly because I was preoccupied with my work and partly because the Hawaiians, who had seen quite enough *haole* (white) intruders, stayed to themselves. I went surfing along the eastern shore of Oahu with Rich a few times and recall the muscular Hawaiian and Samoan surfers, pushing me out of their way as they paddled and surfed past, shouting threateningly, "Off my wave, brah!"

"Those crazy Samoans will beat the crap out of you just for fun," Rich warned and then told me in blow-by-blow detail how it had happened to him before. The bulk and aggression some Samoans cultivated did serve them well as professional American football players. Altogether, Hawaii was a harder, faster, American version of French Polynesia.

At least through the eyes of a sailor, Hawaii is the most beautiful of the 50 states. Yet it was also the most regulated place I had yet seen. Those in control zealously sought to regulate almost every aspect of their constituents' lives. After I had paid my $100 fine for illegal entry into a U.S. state by a U.S. citizen on a U.S.-registered vessel, I was told I couldn't sleep on my boat at the municipal marina. When I moved the boat to a designated anchorage, the Coast Guard came by to tell me not to use my toilet. I almost expected them to wrap me in a diaper. When I hung a small sign on my boat advertising a "Half-day Charter Sail," which as a licensed captain I was allowed to do, officials told me to take it down, without further explanation.

Life ashore is no less complicated and restricted. I was stunned when Judy told me that to ride my bicycle I first needed a license. I learned that mobile homes were forbidden, presumably because they would bring down property values. As a painter, I learned some neighborhoods even had "color codes," not for racial separation as I had experienced in South Africa, but to ensure the color of your house did not clash with what the city council members preferred to look at. As a transient sailor I often felt straightjacketed here, whereas the locals rarely complained of these issues and seemed unaware they had legislated away many of the freedoms Americans once cherished. The lawmakers believe that anything in the "best interests" of the people must be enshrined in law, that we common folk must be protected from every possible hazard in life. In retrospect, I now realize that Hawaii was merely a little ahead of the times as this regulatory orgy becomes the norm throughout the Western world. Freedom and wilderness ashore are racing each other to extinction. At sea you can still find a fleeting taste of both. But move quickly before new government-fed parasites have taxed the wind in your sails, reeducated you to think as they do, legislated your thoughts as well as your movements, and gained control over your very destiny. Although we cannot survive in a state of anarchy, we must have a taste of freedom from time to time to truly live.

The Melting Pot; Polynesian Grudge; Fortress Hawaii

In Pidgin-speak the population of Hawaii is comprised mainly of the white *haole*, with distinctions made for such white sub-classes as *potagee* (Portuguese), the *manong* (Filipino), *pake* (Chinese), *buddha head* (Japanese), native *kanakas* (who number barely ten percent of the total), and an occasional *popolo* (African). These racial groups have mixed over the generations in a true melting-pot culture, all getting along remarkably well. Understandably, the purer Polynesian Hawaiians and Samoans hold a grudge against everyone, especially the *haoles* who stole their land and jailed their beloved Queen Lilioukalani in 1898 in the common colonial era method of gunboat diplomacy.

Aside from privately held estates and plantations, vast amounts of the state are owned or controlled by the U.S. military. For example, the entire island of Kahoolawe was a U.S. Navy bombing range. Imagine an entire 45 square mile tropical island evacuated so it could be used as nothing more than a bombing site! Even at Kaneohe Bay, on most days the skies hosted a parade of low-flying jet fighters, bombers, and helicopters. If it were up to me, I'd be tempted to have the Navy evacuate the people from Honolulu and then bomb that city back to the sand and rock from which it grew and leave Kahoolawe unmolested. When a visiting Canadian yacht anchored near me in the bay, the first thing they asked me was the purpose of the huge military presence. "Welcome to Fortress Hawaii," was all I could say.

As I was sailing to Hawaii from the Galapagos, a group of pro-independence Hawaiians had moved in and claimed the land around the Makapuu Lighthouse on Oahu's eastern point. The governor let them stay a few days and then sent in a S.W.A.T. team to evict and arrest them. "A bad precedent," the local newspaper called it, referring to the militant Hawaiians' land-grab, not the police action. The Hawaiian gripe is even more understandable when you consider that 90% of the non-government land today is held by only 10% of the population. Individuals, mostly descendants of early missionaries and whaling ship captains, own vast estates and tend to lease out their land at prices that drive out the native Hawaiians, rendering them as helpless as medieval serfs on their own land.

Early visitors to the pre-U.S. Hawaii found a different world. When Mark Twain visited the islands in 1866, he called them "the land of happy contentment." In writing about the 19th-century Christian missionaries' efforts to convert the islanders, Twain chided them with his pen in his characteristic deadpan humor: "How sad it is to think of the multitudes who have gone to their graves on this beautiful island, and never knew there was a hell."

Aside from her shortcomings as I judged them, Hawaii had given me new friendships, a welcome family reunion, and a job that allowed me to continue on enriched in spirit and purse, to the less familiar, less Americanized islands of Asia.

7 Nuclear Atolls

Alone again, locked in the warm embrace of sea and sky.

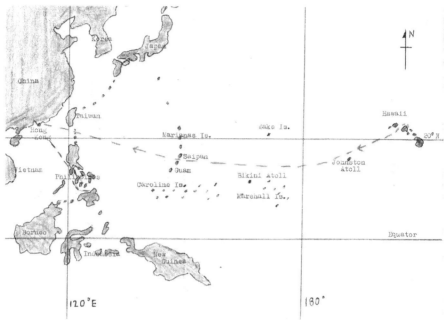

Atom's route from Hawaii to Hong Kong and the Philippines

By January 1988, I'd painted enough houses around Honolulu to fund the next leg of my journey to China, so I gladly quit my job to prepare for my long-awaited departure. On this passage, I planned to visit only one island, Saipan in the Marianas Group. Stops at other islands in Micronesia were tempting but would prolong the trip, putting me into the typhoon season of the western Pacific. Three months' supply of food came aboard as well as charts of the route ahead that I had photocopied from cruising friends. One windless morning, after a farewell meeting ashore with friends and relatives who had come to see me off, I hoisted my two well dug-in anchors onto the deck. Using my single oar, I sculled *Atom* three miles across Kaneohe Bay to anchor behind a sandbar that emerged pristine and born again for a few hours each day at low tide. Sculling a boat this size a few hundred yards in and out of a marina is good exercise. Sculling several miles is more like a sculling marathon. Finally arrived at the sandbar, I scrubbed the patches of barnacles accumulated on the hull and restowed hastily packaged supplies.

Sculling Atom across Kaneohe Bay

A day later, we were ready for sea, but the winds would not cooperate. I vigilantly sniffed the air for signs of the errant trade winds. At night, *Atom* pivoted on her anchor as a whispering cool breeze rolled down the mountains to replace the warm air lifting off the bay. An hour after dawn, the air ceased movement until the afternoon sun heated the mountain air, which rose and pulled in the now relatively cooler air off the bay, resulting in a sea-breeze that lasted until sunset. This land and sea breeze effect is always present to some degree around the larger tropical islands. Because the prevailing trade winds had gone light for a few days, it became the prevailing weather pattern. I was psyched up and restless to get underway. On the other hand, it was dangerous to depart in such fickle winds because, even if I tacked my way out of the harbor in the afternoon, the evening calm could allow currents to pull me back into the reefs. Nothing less than a steady wind would allow me to escape the windward coast for the safety of open water.

Kilauea Sunsets; Keel Meets Reef

While awaiting the return of the trade wind, I paddled my kayak across the bay to an uninhabited island, known locally as Chinaman's Hat. The tip of the cone-shaped islet stood 200 feet above the water and supported little more than scrubby bushes and two mop-headed coconut trees standing as graceful companions. After I had pushed my way through masses of red flowers and shoulder-high bushes laced together with spider webs, my scramble over rocks to the peak rewarded me with a grand view over the expanse of the bay and far out to sea beyond the ribbons of white surf breaking on the reefs. Over a hundred miles away on the Big Island, the Kilauea Volcano erupted, billowing smoke skyward and sending flows of red-hot lava that quenched themselves in explosions of steam when they reached the sea. From here I could see the wide haze of ash that had colored our sunsets blood-red for the past few days.

On my return trip back to the boat, I took a shortcut by paddling directly over the reefs, alternately pulling hard on the double-ended paddle and surfing down the foaming faces of breaking waves. A quarter mile away from me in calmer waters inside the reefs, an eight-man team of the Hawaiian Canoe Club slashed the waters with their paddles, driving their replica outrigger canoe at top speed. Once away from the masses of motorized boats and cars, even over-developed Hawaii had its charms. The beauty of the moment reminded me why I sail and live on the water.

Back aboard *Atom*, I noticed a 40-foot catamaran flying the German flag anchored next to us behind the sandbar. That evening the German couple invited me over to their well-traveled boat for dinner where we shared stories of places seen and future plans. I could see how they enjoyed the expansive living area and stability of two hulls. When I asked what features they liked best about the catamaran, the man said, "This boat doesn't heel and roll like your monohull." He went on to point out his cruising cat's other attributes, such as its shallow draft, buoyancy to remain afloat if holed, and ability to achieve faster speeds than an equivalent-sized monohull. Years later I made a delivery passage on a similar catamaran and learned the list of minuses was just as long as the positives: on a rough sea her low bridgedeck between the hulls slammed against the waves, sending violent, unnerving shudders throughout the boat; performance upwind was even less than my small monohull; cats cost the equivalent of two or more monohulls; and they had the increased maintenance expenses of two engines and two hulls. But their fatal flaw for a singlehanded sailor was the possibility of capsize, however remote, when asleep in a storm. Unlike the monohull, which heels to dump the wind and rolls back up after being knocked down by a wave, the cat's upright stability is matched by her even more obstinate inverted stability. Once over, it won't ever right itself. Fortunately, most cruising cats are built so heavily and with such conservative sail area that a rollover is highly unlikely.

Like many sailors who island-hop through Hawaii, the German couple had stayed here a year longer than first planned. Soon they would be heading south to join what cruisers call the "Coconut Milk Run" across the South Pacific, running in a pack from Tahiti to Tonga or American Samoa, to Fiji, and then on to wait out the cyclone season in either Australia or New Zealand. On whatever sea routes I followed, it was good to have fellow cruising sailors around to share advice and lend a hand when needed. At sea I expected and even welcomed solitude. Once I returned to society, the companionship of fellow cruisers rounded out this lifestyle I had come to love.

On January 23, the trades timidly regained their influence over the island. I hoisted anchor and sails at the first sign of wind, picking my way silently through the reef-studded anchorage. Before long, I discovered I'd left too soon. The wind died as we drifted with the currents. Before I could think of dropping anchor, *Atom* had stopped, her keel planted firmly atop a dead reef. I heaved my anchor over the bow to stop us dragging further aground. The German couple noticed my predicament and sped over by dinghy and generously offered their help. Together we kedged the boat into deeper water by setting out another anchor by dinghy and winching its line tight, and then winching again as we lightly bounced and slid our way to deeper water. The solid fiberglass keel encasing her 3,300 pounds of lead ballast was only scratched by the encounter. By the time we refloated, the wind had filled in again, and I cautiously tiptoed *Atom* along the four-mile passage to exit the bay.

Passing Chinaman's Hat, I continued tacking into the wind and sea for an hour. Further out in the bay, the waves, which were increasing in height, crashed and broke over the reefs on all sides. A rainsquall caught me just as I gained the open sea, laying us over with forceful gusts of wind. I jumped up and double reefed the main and hand steered in the shifting winds. Since my boat didn't yet carry a self-furling jib that mechanically rolled up to smaller size as the winds increased, I quite often had either too much sail up or too little for the wind conditions of the moment. Here again, I was forced to carry too much sail in the gusts, to enable me to continue to move forward as the winds lessened. If I spent ten minutes changing headsails for a brief squall, it could be time to change back to the larger sail even before the first sail change was complete. It was a game of judgment and guesswork.

Steering around the north end of Oahu, I sailed parallel to the jagged slopes of the Koolau Mountain Range until it dropped into the sea at the island's north end. I kept five miles off the coast to stay clear of tiderips and the rising swell that broke dangerously in the shallower waters inshore. A smoky white haze along the coast marked where the swells I rode went on to beat themselves to a furious death along the reefs. A local radio station reported the surf running 30-feet high that day along the Surfing Nirvana of the North Shore: a gift from a distant raging northern Pacific storm. The towering surf even swamped parts of the coastal highway. I was keenly aware that the only thing preventing my own imminent violent death in that surf was a steady wind and our ability to harness it and maintain our course.

By sunset my frayed nerves relaxed as I cleared the coastal dangers. Later that night I watched the blinking beacon from the lighthouse at Kaena Point as it receded towards the east. The labors and stresses of departure had fatigued me enough that I slept soundly between hourly course checks and scans across the horizon for shipping. In the morning the island had vanished from view. My world again became wind, wave, and sky—I felt safe at home. The course was set for Saipan Island, 3,400 miles to the west.

I was finally alone again after months of shoreside hustle. The poet Homer said a sail-filling wind at your back is a good companion for a voyage. In my case, it was my only companion. From my chaotic life ashore I returned monk-like to this solitary existence at sea, yet filled with a boundless joy after being released from land's spider web of limits and ownership. Back there were too many hands in my pockets, too many words/threats/rules. Out here, I was once again totally aware of my place in the richness of space and of time, enjoying an uplifting sense of wonder and a feeling that something good was coming my way. With sails pulling us along, we flew free as the frigatebirds soaring overhead and the flying fish winging across the wave tops.

For three days the wind pushed and shoved *Atom* along at her fastest pace. Rain poured down from gray skies and scudding clouds. I retreated to the dry comfort of the cabin to begin reading from my library of three shelves full of books. Some titles were new to me, and some were classics I returned to over and over again as if having a chat (albeit one-sided) with familiar trusted friends. Finally, the skies cleared, and the wind lightened its touch until it went from rudely shoving us along to a gentle nudge. The sea tune changed from rock-and-roll to slow dance music. Even so, *Atom* continued to cleave her way through at least a hundred miles of water a day. I returned to my routine of tending her needs, which in these halcyon days were little more than sewing a few stitches in the sail seams, checking for loose or chafing rigging, and adjusting course now and then. Hours drifted by as I watched contentedly the countless waves approach—no two of which were exactly alike—and pat us lightly on the stern before fleeing past the bow.

Johnston Atoll; Isle of Dr. Strangelove

Seven hundred miles from Hawaii my course took me past Johnston Atoll, a notorious two-mile long coral island. My research in Hawaii of islands that lay along my course ahead told me this atoll had been a U.S. Nuclear Defense Test Facility and a storage depot for chemical weapons. It was obviously off-limits to civilians on sailboats. I passed the island during the night at a safe distance. A faint glow on the horizon indicated the U.S. military were ashore on the island in their continuing effort to decontaminate the grounds after years of nuclear tests and storage of chemical weapons. In an Orwellian twist, this poisoned atoll was simultaneously listed as a National Wildlife Refuge!

Beginning in the 1950s, Johnston Atoll was used to launch missiles for low- and high-altitude nuclear test explosions. One of these explosions, in 1962, was so powerful, its radiation knocked out several satellites. The fireball could be seen in Hawaii, where its electromagnetic pulse disrupted power and communications. Some other failed launches exploded on or near the ground, further contaminating the island and lagoon with radioactive plutonium for generations to come. When above-ground nuclear testing went out of fashion a few years later, the military found the atoll a useful dumping ground for biological and chemical weapons, including Anthrax, Sarin, and Agent Orange. Leaks and accidental spills drained the deadly brew into the ground and waters of the atoll. Partial cleanups over the years have left the island uninhabitable. It now lies abandoned.

Johnston Atoll was merely a sample of the great lengths to which nations will go to hold the world's population as a nuclear hostage. We were still competing with the Russians at that time, and I wondered, along with much of the world, where our mutual escalating militarism was leading us. My tensions eased as I sailed away from Dr. Strangelove's nuclear wasteland.

Jupiter and the Southern Cross; Time Skips a Beat; Easy Days

The moon was now nearly full, each night adding another hour of its welcome, cool light. With the moon rising astern, *Atom*'s wake stretched out in a shimmering silver ribbon as I sat in the cockpit making journal entries by the ghostly pale light. My course these days was directly into the setting sun, and when it sank below the waves ahead, Venus shone brightly for a few hours until it too dropped into the sea ahead. Next, Jupiter arose to guide me west, followed in the early morning by a sleepy moon. During the night, a glance up at Polaris to starboard indicated true north. Opposite it to port, the Southern Cross hung low in the sky, first lying on its side, then lifting to vertical before corkscrewing back down to the horizon, tracing out endless circles in the southern sky. To read and follow these signposts in the heavens let me slip back to reconnect with the long history of nomadic man who lived as close to elemental nature as I did now.

We sailed across the 180th meridian of longitude and somehow lost 24 hours as I was involuntarily thrust from Tuesday to Thursday. Not a big deal to lose a day, you might say, but this still caused nearly as much consternation to *Atom*'s navigator as it had when I first crossed the dateline three years previously in the South Pacific. An abstract concept so easily grasped while sitting ashore can become perplexing when studied too long, particularly when my star-crossing methods of navigation depended on a supposed continuity of place and time.

Back in the world of islands and oceans, my chart indicated the dozens of atolls and islands of Micronesia lying a few hundred miles to our south. On this voyage I was focused on reaching China and Southeast Asia, but if I ever have the chance to sail across the Pacific again, one of my goals will be to island-hop across the nearly 2,000-mile expanse of Micronesia from the Marshall Islands in the east to Yap and Palau in the west.

The days flitted by easily as my westward reach increased. A perfect gathering of fair wind and mild seas and the navigator's best friend of clear skies gave me the peace of mind to enjoy the routines of the day and sleep well at night. Days were not harried, but adequately filled with exercise, meal preparation, navigating, rig adjustments, reading, then rest and reflection while star-gazing. Almost three weeks out of Hawaii and our food and water supplies were still abundant, thanks to recent rains, a well-stocked galley, and a tray continually brimming over with mung bean sprouts. Not far to our south, my chart indicated a necklace of beckoning little islands forming Bikini Atoll.

Bravo, Bikini Atoll! Paradise in Ashes; You Can't Go Home

Bikini is exceptional among the hundreds of narrow-channeled and often unnavigable atolls in Micronesia because its easy mile-wide entrance leads into a fine anchorage in a spacious lagoon off a palm-lined, sandy motu. That alone would make it a perfect stopping place for sailors crossing this part of the Pacific. Those same attributes made the atoll too perfect for the U.S. Navy to ignore. From 1946 to 1958 the U.S. exploded 23 nuclear bombs on this one-time piece of heaven on earth. The Bikini islanders, all 167 men, women, and children, were conned and bullied into leaving their island home after being assured by Navy officials that they could return to the island permanently after the tests were over. The nuclear explosions, the islanders were told, were needed "for the good of mankind."

The tragedy reached its peak in 1954 with the explosion code-named Bravo. That single bomb was the most powerful weapon we ever created. Its explosive force is said to have exceeded the combined power of all the weapons ever fired in all the wars of history. Hiroshima experienced a mere firecracker 1,000 times weaker than Bravo's 15-megaton blast. It's difficult to believe the entire atoll was not vaporized and the crater filled by the sea to erase all signs of its existence. But nature is tougher than man at his meanest. Her memory of that insult would be long by human terms, but she would overcome. The scientists who created that monster were themselves stunned and quite happy with themselves when the bomb produced three times the blast force they had expected. Bravo sprayed 50,000 square miles of tropic seas and islands with a visible rain of radioactive pulverized coral. Fishermen at sea and hundreds of people on neighboring islands, including the displaced Bikinians themselves, were caught in the fallout. Unwarned children played in the strange "bikini snow," as it came to be called, many dying years later from its cancerous effects. Bravo indeed!

In the years since, the islanders in the region have suffered abnormally high rates of cancers and birth defects. The U.S. military provided little medical treatment for the people but did conduct years of secret medical testing on the islanders for its own purposes. A French lingerie shop manager named his new revealing swimwear the bikini, because, as he said, "Like the bomb, the bikini is small and devastating."

As I sailed past Bikini, 33 years after its evacuation, the surviving islanders continued to mark time on a cramped harborless island 500 miles from home because the soil, water, and plant life on Bikini remained radioactive. The Bikinians belong to a fourth world—that of dispossessed people everywhere. For most of the islanders and their children there is no going back to Bikini. Even if the radioactive contamination were somehow cleaned up, these once proud and self-sufficient people, who voyaged the free seas between free islands in their canoes, will not likely return. After suffering years of near starvation on islands with poor resources, the Bikinians now live as wards of the U.S. government, as addicted to welfare and frozen chicken as are the rest of us. Over the years they lost virtually all of their sailing and fishing skills. The new generation of Bikinians, born after relocation, who have never seen their home island, would prefer to go live in Hawaii. But the Hawaiians do not want them. For now, and perhaps always, these disheartened people can do little but wait in exile.

Too few people in the world know the plight of the Bikinians, and even fewer stand up to champion their cause. We have bigger things to worry about. While we are not all responsible for the crimes committed against these gentle people, we are all responsible for our inaction. I briefly considered sailing into the lagoon without permission, and in an act of righteous civil disobedience, to raise a figurative flag of awareness. Then I realized that the self-irradiating gesture would serve little purpose other than to fill me with rage and possibly some unwanted atoms of plutonium. In the years since I sailed past Bikini, scientists tell us the island has cooled down considerably. It is now likely safe for brief visits by cruising sailors, provided they don't eat the coconuts or drink the well water. Of course, U.S. Naval scientists told the Bikinians a similar story 33-years earlier.

Life at sea is a great spiritual healer, and my disgust with the crazed destructiveness of "advanced civilizations" faded as the winds carried me westward. While I was still several hundred miles from my destination, the wind fell light for three days. Here in the heart of the trades we actually had several hours of unexpected calm. As the wind shifted fitfully from one compass point to another, I shifted sails to pursue each and every puff. In this way I covered no less than sixty miles a day despite the lack of a steady trade. As the weather disturbance passed, the wind returned from the north with stronger than average force, as if to make up for the atmospheric vacuum of the preceding days. With the assist of a fair current, we rushed ahead, covering 145 miles in the next 24 hours.

Magellan—Lost among the Ice and Fire; Mutiny and Death; Rounding the World

During these days at sea I often thought of Ferdinand Magellan, whose carracks in 1521 were the first European vessels to have crossed the entire Pacific Ocean. In contrast to that epic voyage of exploration, my own travails came into perspective as a relative holiday afloat.

Magellan was an adventurer and soldier as well as a skilled seaman. In the book *Magellan*, by Tim Joyner, the Italian scholar Antonio Pigafetta, who accompanied the fleet, was quoted: "So valiant and noble a captain . . . no other had so much natural wit, boldness, or knowledge to sail round the world." His quest was the Spice Islands of the Moluccas, which lie in a remote, almost forgotten part of Indonesia. The trade in pepper and other spices of that region was priceless in Magellan's time. When Manuel I of Portugal refused Magellan's request to equip a fleet for him to journey westward to the Spice Islands, his rival Charles V of Spain stepped in and commissioned Magellan to locate and claim possession of this group of islands for Spain. In his lifetime, Magellan's Portuguese countrymen called him a traitor for sailing under the colors of Spain. Even today, for most Portuguese, he remains a minor footnote in history.

To find his way past the obstacle of South America and into the Pacific, Magellan was determined, if need be, to drive his fleet of five carracks into Antarctic waters. Their clumsy square-rigged ships slowly probed the countless dead-end waterways and channels of Patagonia, sketching their own charts as they went. They searched for safe anchorages amid treacherous currents, rocky shoals, and fierce winds that often whipped the waters into a seething white-capped fury. The harsh elements were only one of Magellan's problems. The Spanish captains assigned to him were prone to treachery. They became increasingly reluctant to navigate without charts or local guides in the worsening weather. Appealing to their patriotism, Magellan urged them on: "Even though we may be forced to eat the cowhide off the yardarms we must go forward and discover what has been promised to the Emperor."

Magellan stood alone in his beliefs as he stubbornly continued his search along the South American coast for the unknown passage into the Pacific. When at last he found it, in the gale-ridden wilderness of the Patagonian channels, deserters fled with his largest ship and the bulk of the fleet's provisions. That ship returned to Spain, where its officers proceeded to poison Magellan's name in order to excuse their cowardly crime. While the remaining fleet lay at anchor, a mutiny arose on another of Magellan's ships. By bold and violent action, Magellan captured the conspirators and had them executed. The remaining ships sailed along Tierra Del Fuego, named "the land of fire" because its miserable inhabitants kept smoky campfires burning at all hours in an attempt to survive the cold temperatures and howling winds of the subpolar climate. Finally, the ships emerged from what we know as the Straits of Magellan. As they made their way northwest to more comfortable latitudes they discovered a sea so calm, Magellan named it *Pacifico.*

The sun burned hotter as the armada sailed into the tropics. Days became weeks, and still there was no sight of land. Salted meat putrefied in the holds. Green scum fouled the water casks, and hunting parties scoured the bilges for rats as the sailors fell dead on the decks from starvation. Yet Magellan's remaining crew stayed loyal. Their commander's indomitable will and superhuman ability to endure patiently, kept them going as much as the knowledge that they surely could not survive the long trip if they turned back. Magellan continued to refuse to submit to defeat even as the ship's crew shrank to just a handful of men still strong enough to hoist a sail.

When halfway across the Pacific, and having sighted only two small waterless atolls, Antonio Pigafetta wrote, "We ate biscuit that was no longer biscuit, but powder of biscuits that was swarming with worms, for they had eaten the good. It stank strongly of rat's urine. We drank yellow water that had been putrid for many days." Magellan's earlier warning that they would continue into the unknown sea even if they had to eat the chafing gear had proven prophetic. "We also ate certain ox hides that covered the tops of the yards, and which had become exceedingly hard because of the sun, rain, and wind. We soaked them in the sea for four or five days, and then placed them briefly on hot ashes, and so ate them; often we ate sawdust. Rats were sold for a half ducat apiece [$200 U.S.], and even so, we could not get enough. I believe that nevermore will any man undertake to make such a voyage."

If you departed the South American coast, and sailed northwest, and were as unlucky in your course as was Magellan, you might sail 8,000 miles or more without sighting habitable land until approaching the Asian continent. If you look at a chart, the tropics of the South Pacific appear filled with islands. So how could the fleet have missed sighting more of them? This illusion of scale results when mapmakers are forced to represent each island of the Pacific on a single sheet of paper in a region where on average it takes days of sailing in empty seas to get from one island to another. An accurate depiction of the scale of land to water would require a chart at least as long as my boat. From a sailor's perspective, the North Pacific is even more devoid of land than the South Pacific. The handful of islands of Hawaii and Micronesia are lost in a sea so vast it could contain all seven continents within its basin. In the watery world of Micronesia any land is precious because of its rarity.

On March 6, 1521, Magellan's fleet sighted the island of Guam. A swarm of sailing canoes came out to greet them. Impressed by the fast and agile canoes, they named the islands, *Islas de las Velas Latinas* (Islands of the Lateen Sails). The ships were no sooner anchored than the curious natives clambered aboard and stole everything they could lay their hands on, ignoring the protests of the starving, skeleton-like Europeans. After they stole one of the ship's longboats, a fight ensued in which seven natives were killed. In retaliation, the natives attacked in a fleet of war canoes, but they were frightened away when Magellan ordered blank shots fired from the ships' canon. After several days of skirmishes, the three remaining ships sailed off under a barrage of stones and insults hurled by the islanders pursuing in canoes. Magellan felt it his duty to warn future explorers and renamed the islands *Islas de los Ladrones* (The Islands of Thieves).

Magellan went on to make landfall in the Philippines where he at first received a warmer reception, until he interjected himself in a squabble between rival tribes and was killed in battle. But the mission of his voyage succeeded. The true breadth of the Pacific was finally realized, and his ships went on to the Moluccas, where they loaded up with spices. After another year of epic adventures and hardships, a single surviving ship returned to Spain, thereby completing the first circumnavigation of the planet. It was the moonshot of its day and arguably the boldest feat of discovery ever undertaken. The value of the spices brought home on that single ship repaid the entire expense of the fleet of five ships, if not the cost of hundreds of sailors' lives.

27 Days Across the Expanse; Saipan; Pacific Repose

On a course paralleling that of Magellan's suffering fleet, 27 days out of Hawaii I sighted a glimmer of lights from Saipan Island during the night. I hove to, and the glow continued to brighten through the night as currents carried me closer to the island. At dawn, the cliff-girt north coast of Saipan appeared a handful of miles ahead, and I resumed course. With increasing winds at my back, we negotiated the tiderips and steep, confused seas that reflected off the island after making their spectacular show of smashing into the base of the cliffs with foam and skyward-shooting geysers of spray. Once past the perils of the northern shore, we glided down the island's leeward coast, running outside a solid white wall of surf over the reef that marked the perimeter of Tanapag Harbor. After several miles, I spotted a wide break in the reefs and entered the sheltered harbor. Progress was slow as I sailed four miles upwind, tacking from the edge of one reef to another. This gave me time for my land-starved eyes to savor the green-cloaked hills unfolding beyond the beaches. The blue water sailor's old yin-yang had begun. When too long at sea I want to behold land. When on land too long, I need to embrace the sea. All too soon the passage was over as I anchored alongside two other sailboats near the commercial docks of the town of Garapan.

In response to my yellow quarantine flag flying from halfway up the mast on the starboard spreader, an off-duty Customs officer appeared in a skiff to inform me that since it was a Sunday I would have to pay overtime charges to clear in. "In that case I'll just wait here until tomorrow," I said. He agreed and told me he'd return the next morning. I was tucked in a comfortable spot and in no hurry to step ashore. I prepared a huge meal of rice and beans and enjoyed eating from a plate without having to brace myself against the rolling sea. Minutes later I fell into a languorous deep sleep that remained unbroken till dawn.

8 The Pied Piper of Saipan

Searching for a lost paradise in the Empire of Death.

Saipan belongs to one of the world's smallest countries, with one of the longest names. The island is part of The Commonwealth of the Northern Mariana Islands, which was formed a year before my arrival when the post-WWII U.S. Pacific Trust Territory was broken up into several independent states. The people of Saipan voted for U.S. Commonwealth status, making it similar politically to Puerto Rico in the Caribbean. The Commonwealth's 17,000 inhabitants lived mostly on Saipan and neighboring Tinian and Rota Islands. Less than a hundred people lived on the smaller islands strung out in an arc to the north. The native Chamorro people here are descendants of Micronesians who intermarried with Spanish, Filipino, Japanese, Chinese, and more recently with their American "trustees." And then there are the Customs officers, whose benign nepotism islandizes a potentially prickly bureaucracy.

Customs, or lack Thereof; Yoko and Ken's Generosity

The morning after my arrival in Saipan, the Customs officer did not appear as promised so in the afternoon I rowed the short distance ashore in my dinghy to clear in. I went first to the Customs shack where the man in charge asked for my "vessel entry permit." Not wanting to make the same expensive mistake I had made when entering Hawaii, I told him that five months earlier I had written to his office from Hawaii for a permit and had not received a reply. This fact he accepted so readily I was tempted to think he had performed the exact same conversation with many sailors before me. His office was another bureaucratic black hole where letters came in but replies never went out. Dropping incoming letters into the trashcan was infinitely easier and more satisfying to them than actually filling out a permit, locating a stamp, and mailing it back. I had no gripe because I'd do the same thing in their shoes. At the immigration office, the same request for my permit was repeated. The officer on duty performed a minor and obligatory bureaucratic tantrum at my admission that I lacked a permit. Then he accepted my explanation along with my $25 entry fee.

That afternoon, as I brought a bow line ashore from my dinghy to moor *Atom* closer to shore, a slightly built Asian woman came running down the pier waving a magazine over her head and calling out "Hello, *Atom!*" I stepped on the pier to meet Yoko and then her husband Ken Kubo who followed several steps behind. "We just read your article about your circumnavigation here in *Cruising World Magazine*," she said with a smile worth crossing an ocean to see. They both welcomed me to Saipan and quickly hustled me back to their house for a meal. We struck up a spontaneous friendship. They insisted on washing my laundry and sent me home with a bag of fresh foods and their Suzuki motorcycle with orders to keep the bike as long as I was on the island. To my further embarrassment, when I picked up my laundry the next day I found Yoko had even patched and sewn the small tears in my clothes.

Yoko was a more gregarious version of my stereotypical image of a Japanese wife: a persistent smile and easy laughter, always busy and devoted to her husband whom she doted on almost as much as she did on me. Yet her desire to explore and her questions about my travels marked her as being of the modern world. The Kubos had relocated to Saipan a few years previously, though they still owned real estate in Tokyo. They were skilled sailors who owned a cruising catamaran they kept in a nearby protected creek, called Smiley's Lagoon. They had ordered it new from the factory in France and shipped it in pieces to their home in Yokohama, Japan, where they had reassembled it before sailing to their retirement home in Saipan. Along the way, they encountered a typhoon at sea, which they rode out attached to a parachute sea anchor for three days. Because their short-wave radio antenna had blown away in the storm, they could not contact their friends who were expecting them on Saipan. Assuming the Kubos had perished in the typhoon, their friends had alerted the Coast Guard. A search was launched, but to everyone's relief Ken and Yoko eventually sailed into Saipan unaided.

Guy Gabaldon—The Warrior-Savior

On my second day on the island, as I was stowing deck gear, a man on the pier called across the water and waved for me to come ashore. A minute later, a tanned and muscular man in his early 60s shook my hand and introduced himself as Guy Gabaldon. He had heard through the rapid island grapevine that a solo sailor and fellow adventurer had arrived, and he thought I might like a tour of the island. He told me he was an American who had fought on Saipan in WWII and had returned here 35 years later to live with his family. Guy owned the island's only charter plane service connecting the Northern Marinas but kindly took time off from work to drive me around the island and explain its history. We stopped first at the telephone exchange where I called home to mom in Michigan to report a safe arrival. Then we stopped at his wife's restaurant where I was treated to a free lunch. Later, at his home in the village of San Antonio I scanned a wall filled with Mr. Gabaldon's medals and awards that competed with space among his souvenirs from his battles against the Japanese. "This movie was based on my life," he replied matter-of-factly as I asked about an advertising poster from the film *From Hell to Eternity* that hung on the wall.

As a young Mexican-American orphan in 1930s Los Angeles, Guy was befriended by a Japanese teacher who took him into his home and taught the boy the Japanese language and their customs. Just 15 years old at the outbreak of war, Guy watched with deep emotion as his adopted family was sent to an internment camp in Wyoming. The day he turned 17 Guy joined the U.S. Marine Corps. Because of his Japanese language skills he was sent to join the invasion of Saipan in June 1944 as scout and observer. He was unemotional as he told me that he had killed

32 Japanese soldiers on the island. I sensed that he needed to dehumanize his victims in his mind, to make them a mere statistic, which was understandable. After all, those Japanese were also out to kill him. I could see he was far prouder to tell me that he had saved many hundreds more from certain death.

Guy had understood the Japanese culture far better than his commanders did. From his first night on the island, Guy went out alone and without permission to search for the enemy. From short-range he shot two Japanese guards outside a cave entrance and then called inside for the rest to surrender. Japanese soldiers were notorious for preferring suicidal attacks over the shame of surrender. By speaking their language, Guy convinced the two soldiers inside that they were surrounded, but would be well treated if they made an honorable surrender. Guy's commander was not initially impressed by the two prisoners taken and threatened him with court-martial for leaving his post. Ignoring orders, the next night Guy again went out alone and returned with 50 more prisoners. This time his commander was persuaded to assign Guy to work as a "lone wolf" operator. He continued to infiltrate the enemy lines at night, crawling alone through battle-torn jungle, whispering friendly words into dark caves inhabited by a desperate enemy.

One night he astounded his commander by single-handedly leading 800 prisoners into the U.S. camp. With rifle slung over his shoulder, the "Pied Piper of Saipan" (as he came to be called) marched these war-ravaged soldiers and civilian laborers into camp as if bringing home a flock of sheep. But sheepish is a word that has never been used to describe the Japanese soldier. Guy had risked death with every step he took. His luck ran out a short time later when a sniper put two bullets into him. He spent the remainder of the war stateside, recovering from his wounds.

Banzai Commerce; American Warfare Becomes Welfare

When I met Guy he worked for and lived side by side with the Japanese investors who had returned to Saipan in force in recent years.

Guy was not thrilled by the recent Japanese invasion after having watched so many of his friends get killed during the war in order to secure this island for America. But his sometimes strained relations with his new neighbors remained mutually respectful, at least on the surface.

In the 1980s era of Japan's economic prosperity, Japanese businessmen bought back much of what they lost during the military struggles of WWII. Saipan was the closest tropical island to the Japanese homeland, so it became a perfect vacation destination for those Japanese tourists who wanted a vacation spot that was closer to Japan in distance and history than was Hawaii. Yet the local economy did not reflect the prosperity that the amount of tourism would suggest. As tourists descended on Saipan like squadrons of camera-toting mercenaries, they were herded to Japanese-owned hotels, ate at Japanese restaurants, took Japanese tour buses to the WWII memorials, and headed home with suitcases stuffed with products purchased at the duty-free shops.

The local Chamorros had been largely excluded from the tourism boom. The labor for building hotels was supplied by contract laborers brought in from the Philippines, most of whom earned less than $1.50 per hour. For this meager amount they were thankful and tried to send a portion of their pay home to their families. Garment factories opened to employ more Asian contract workers, their investors running virtual sweatshops, taking advantage of local corruption and lax laws that permitted them to label their clothing "Made in USA" with the attendant tax breaks.

With the cost of living here so high, most Chamorros could not be enticed to work for those low wages. The decades spent among Westerners have almost completely eroded the spirit-sustaining Chamorro lifestyle of working the land and sea. Not surprisingly, monthly welfare checks and food stamps from the U.S. were preferable to working for nothing. They had unusual priorities these days. Even the most rudimentary native dwelling constructed of tin sheets and lacking indoor plumbing was wired to satellite television. In front of the islander's shacks sat new cars, which were needed, I suppose, because local officials had not set up any form of public transportation.

Gone forever are the days of Micronesian navigators plying the blue seaways in voyaging canoes loaded with trade goods to exchange with their kinsmen in all the far-flung islands of their realm. Gone is the time when each person was an expert sailor, fisherman, or farmer and when each family cultivated extensive gardens. Broad life skills that sustained their culture have been replaced by government office jobs for the fortunate. For the rest, there was a general despondency, widespread alcoholism, Western diet-induced obesity and diabetes, and a miasma that hung over the island as persistent as London fog. Ancient cultures die when they exist on fragile footings that cannot cope with the inevitable modernization of the world. These Micronesians were caught in a Darwinian, "change, adapt, or perish" situation. Although my love of nature runs deep, I admit to being a humanist first. I may not wring my hands over each and every animal species facing extinction, even though their loss is lamentable. Yet I shamelessly mourn the passing of Micronesian culture amidst a still-living people.

On Saipan the U.S. has encouraged the societal transformation to dependency, partly through cultural ignorance and partly because of the island's supposed strategic military importance. Generals and politicians realize a dependent society is a compliant society. When time came for the people of the U.S. Trust Territory of the Pacific to vote on their future political status, most of the other Micronesian Island groups chose independence. On Saipan they chose to join the U.S. Commonwealth. It's not that the Saipanese have developed a kinship with, or patriotic love for America, any more than their tribal neighbors on Guam whose ancestors once hurled stones and spears at Magellan and now tolerate a U.S. military base on their island. Like the Bikinians, many Chamorros are hopelessly addicted to welfare and probably wish we would just go away and send them their checks by mail. Independence would mean at least a partial return to self-sufficiency, but those skills no longer exist. Saipan represented the western edge of

America's Manifest Destiny. Here was the budding Americanization of Eden I had observed in full bloom in Hawaii.

Fresh Breeze for the Micronesian Sailor;
The Okie and the Blue Grotto

Perhaps because my boat was only one of two yachts to visit the island in recent months, one of my new friends there alerted the local cable TV news that there was a person of interest aboard the small sailboat in the harbor. A reporter shouted at me from the pier. As I lifted my head out the forward hatch he asked me for an interview as his assistant bent over his bulky tripod-mounted camera to film my reaction. Declining the invitation on TV would have seemed ungracious, so I ferried him and his camera-laden assistant out to *Atom* in my plastic dinghy, narrowly avoiding dumping the crew and equipment into the water when a passing boat's wake rolled through the anchorage. Sitting with them in the cockpit, I tried not to appear stupid as well as crazy as they peppered me with the standard landlubberly questions: "Why do you sail alone? Aren't you afraid out there? What do you do at night?" Inspiration struck; I shaped my answers to awaken the islander's dormant Micronesian voyaging gene. After each boring rote question I steered the conversation back to the magical essence of seafaring, of setting out under sail on the dancing sea on a quest to see new horizons, to walk on new lands, to know new people. The message was well received. As the tape was aired repeatedly on the local news channel for two days, I was recognized and greeted with friendship by the locals wherever I went. On a small island, just about anything passes as newsworthy.

An American, who was born on Saipan and lived with his Japanese wife in a hillside house overlooking the harbor, owned a homebuilt Wharram-designed catamaran moored next to *Atom*. Living aboard and working on the catamaran was a young American traveler named Colin Absher. Looking now at *Atom*'s shredded, salt-stained guest log I see that Colin signed it: "Visiting from Mustang, Okiehoma. Came seeking fame and fortune!" But for now he was willing to work for $3 an hour as yacht caretaker to get started. Colin had been on the island for one month, the first three weeks of which he had lived with a Chamorro family in their house. He was already speaking long sentences in the native tongue, which he used mostly to amuse the local girls. His real goal, he confided to me, was to go live for a few weeks on one of the empty islets to the north where he could put into practice the survivalist skills he had developed during wilderness vacations back home.

As a prelude to marooning himself on a smaller island, Colin accepted my invitation to join me on a two-day walk across Saipan. Our trek began at the quayside at Tanapag where we planned to follow the coastal road to the mountainous northern end of the island, continue partway down the rugged and roadless windward coast, then backtrack to return to the harbor. Our route followed the Japanese Army's line of retreat after they failed to repel the U.S. invasion of June 1944.

We moved along the narrow road lined with pines and flame trees. The deep blue of the sea was visible on our left, and the vegetation-clad hills rose to our right. We passed through the village of Tanapag and the even smaller village of San Roque, whose half-dozen houses were all but hidden behind the prolific tropical flower gardens. It was a pleasant walk through a pleasant land, but something was missing that I had known when I had walked across the islands of the South Pacific two years earlier. We saw no children playing and few people were visible. Perhaps they stayed inside by the physical comfort of their air conditioners and the mind-numbing companionship of their televisions.

On the eve of the American invasion, over 30,000 Japanese defenders had dug in on Saipan. By the time these soldiers of Nippon had retreated this far along the coast, they had lost 20,000 men. Here, most of the remaining soldiers made a fanatical *banzai* charge at the instigation of General Saito who ordered each man to "take seven lives for the Emperor." With bayonets and swords drawn they momentarily overwhelmed the American forces, driving them back into the sea. The

Japanese pursued them relentlessly, swimming out to the exposed wave-lashed reefs to man their machine guns. After a successful U.S. counter-attack, 4,000 more Japanese lay dead. On one reef, a surrounded Japanese officer was seen beheading his own terrified soldiers until an American put a bullet in him. All these years later the bones of long-lost soldiers continued to wash up on the beach along this bloodied coast.

Farther along the gravel coastal road, a huge construction project was underway. Nearly completed, the Hotel Nikko Saipan thrust skyward with Filipino contract laborers swarming like bees on its multi-storied honeycomb flanks. By the following winter, its suites would be packed with *nouveau riche* Japanese tourists on an excursion to recapture the memories of Empire.

At the island's north end, our road took us along a narrow plain between seaside cliffs and high inland mountains. Stone lions and manicured gardens marked the Korean Peace Memorial. During WWII the Japanese had conscripted their Korean subjects to help defend the Empire of the Sun. Further along, we saw a similar Japanese memorial of bronze plaques and stone Buddhas.

"Man, this pack is heavy," I complained after we stopped to check our position on the road map. Colin smiled and said, "Oh, maybe it's those rocks I put in there when you weren't looking as we were packing up."

"Ha-ha-ha," I said in mock humor. But the joke was on me when I rummaged through my pack and dug out two fist-sized lava rocks. "You bastard," I cried out but couldn't help eventually joining his howls of laughter. I didn't mind at all listening to his complaints of a blistered foot on the return hike the next day. Apparently, some jungle rat had carried off one of his socks as he slept in the cave that night. Despite my straight-faced denials, Colin said I was the only rat he needed to watch out for.

The afternoon sun radiated a stifling heat off the land, enticing us to follow a detour to the "Blue Grotto." For another hour we plodded along the shadeless, switchback dirt road as it snaked its way over the green hills. Occasionally a bus stuffed with tourists burst over a hilltop, passed us, and became instantly lost in a cloud of dust. Towering above us on this part of the island rose an imposing vertical cliff of brown rock speckled with lighter-colored marks of craters from past naval bombardment. A hundred feet above the ground on its pockmarked face lay a seemingly inaccessible cave entrance of the type once inhabited by the Japanese soldiers.

A narrow trail led us down a steep ravine to the Blue Grotto. Descending the final stone stairway, we squeezed past a group of Japanese divers on their way out. At the bottom we stood within a massive open-topped cave whose floor was an out-of-place pond of heaving sea. The waters surged in powerful roaring gushes in tune with the ocean swell beating unseen on the opposite side of the mountain walls. A deep blue iridescent glow streamed in from the underwater passage at the base of the back wall, revealing an underwater tunnel connecting to the churning sea beyond.

In the center of this pulsating pool lay a flat-topped rock standing clear of the water with enough space on it to hold several people. To reach its refuge we timed our leaps between rocks to avoid the boiling waters that pulled at our feet. Safely aboard the rock, Colin donned his mask and snorkel and dived in. The swirling waters pulled him this way and that as he struggled to keep clear of the sharp rocks. When he called out that he was ready to get out, I signaled him to wait until I perceived a calm moment in the surf pattern. Seven to ten larger swells were followed by a set of lesser ones. When I recognized the pattern, I signaled him to swim in on a small surge that brought him within my grasp. Gushing waters nearly tore him away as I grabbed hold of his arm and pulled him up onto the rock.

Colin's long stare my way apparently meant it was my turn to dive in. I hesitated, as I stood hypnotized by the seething power of the water. I recalled Ken Kubo's warnings to me that on days of high surf, people have drowned here when a surge of water dashed them against the rocks or the currents sucked them down into interlocking coral heads. Sensing my reluctance, Colin took full advantage: "You mean you're afraid to jump into this little pool, even after sailing around the world alone? Are you gonna let a poor dirt farmer from Mustang, Okiehoma better you?" he said in mock disgust.

"Just make sure you pick a calm spot when you call me to come out," I said as I dived into the whirlpool. Within a few strokes I was safely into the center of the pool in less turbulence and glad at once that Colin had goaded me to get in. Below me, schools of reef fish wearing zebra stripes flashed against shimmering hues of coral and rock. Underwater passages to the sea glowed in iridescent sapphire, luring me toward them with the promise of hidden beauty beyond. Just as when sailing, I felt humbled by the powerful, barely restrained force of the sea. Without flippers and an air tank, I couldn't descend far enough to reach the passages, so I turned back. When Colin waved at me to come up, I swam to catch the final lift of a big wave that carried me onto the landing rock like a penguin rocketing onto an ice flow.

We took our lunch of biscuits, nuts, and fruit on the flat rock and then, fully rejuvenated, shouldered our packs once again to return to the road above. Further along the windward coast we stopped at a park overlooking Bird Island, a limestone monolith squatting on the edge of the coastal coral reef. The Japanese had given it the more touristic perfect name of Moon Viewing Island.

Cliffs of Lost Souls

At the end of the road we walked into Peace Memorial Park where a Buddhist shrine sat above Suicide Cliff. Thousands of Japanese troops and civilians jumped to their deaths here and at nearby Banzai Cliff rather than accepting the changing fortunes of war. Others, lacking the nerve to jump, huddled in tight groups and detonated hand grenades. What could compel such mass hysteria? Some Japanese believed that the Americans would be as barbarous as themselves in inflicting cruel tortures on captured enemies. In a perverted Bushido code, Japanese soldiers were taught from the top down that all non-Japanese were vermin in need of extermination. Their officers actually encouraged the enlisted men to rape and murder captured civilians. The Japanese on Saipan followed this twisted warrior code that considered the conquered unworthy of life, even if the conquered were themselves. Our philosophers and priests tell us that every life is sacred, but to believe that is to ignore the existence of an evil that can occupy the human soul. And evil surely found a home in Japan's Empire of Death.

On the edge of Banzai Cliff

A few miles to our south lay Purple Heart Ridge and, beyond it, Death Valley: names of places drenched in blood, coined by U.S. infantry in days of terror. We walked towards those landmarks until our trail ended in a tangle of brush that forced our retreat. On another of our detours we traveled the dirt road to Banzai Cliff, which stood hundreds of feet over the surf. Driven by a strong trade wind, the surf pounded furiously at the base of the cliffs, sending sheets of spray high into the air, misting over my camera lens as I leaned warily over the cliff edge for a shot. Next to us a group of elderly Japanese tourists placed offerings of food and *saki* on a marble alter backed by yet another stone Buddha. The oldest of the women knelt in prayer, ringing a brass bell in intervals between her mournful chant. The driver of their bus told Colin and me that the old woman and her relatives were on their first pilgrimage back to the cliffs where her husband had jumped to his death.

Earlier when I had listened to Guy Gabaldon, his face fell to a low somber emotion as he told me how whole families threw themselves from these cliffs into the raging sea below. He recounted a family lined up single-file with youngest children in front. Then each older child shoved the younger sibling in front to their death. The father then pushed the wife over the side before stepping backwards off the cliff so as not to see the bodies of his family racing up at him from below. Through a loudspeaker, interpreters like Guy had pleaded with them not to jump, but that group had selected its fate. Guy did save many others through his reassuring words in Japanese, convincing them that the Americans were not the rabid beasts the Japanese officers had told them they were and that they could safely surrender. Nevertheless, hundreds of people made their final leap, and they did not all die instantly. As they landed on wave-lashed rocks over a hundred feet below, their collective wails of agony could be heard above the pounding surf. American Marines approached by sea in small boats to attempt to save the wounded before they drowned, but most victims were out of reach and near death with bodies shattered beyond repair.

The Marines had learned to expect anything from fanatical Japanese soldiers, but none were prepared for the self-slaughter of civilians that they witnessed. Overwhelmed by the tragedy unfolding in front of them, a distraught, teary-eyed Marine reportedly fired his rifle into the tangled bodies to end their mutual suffering. Those American boys in uniform now fully understood that the planned upcoming invasion of the Japanese homeland would have been an unprecedented holocaust. Revisionist historians so safe and quick to make damning judgments might first consider the millions of lives that were saved when the

Emperor of Japan surrendered after atomic bombs blew apart Hiroshima and Nagasaki.

To Sleep Among the Ghosts of War

It was nearly sunset when Colin and I left this sad, majestic place to find refuge for the night. Near the Peace Memorial, which was truly at peace now that the throngs of tourists had departed for the day, we followed a marked trail that led us to a cave at the base of the mountainside. The fortified cave had been the final command post of the Japanese Army. Laying down our packs at the bunker's entrance, we looked back over the foreground to see the displayed machine guns and artillery canons. Even a tank had been placed with its gun pointing seaward as if ready for battle. It was almost as if we had snuck into a Disney theme park after closing hours.

Inside the bunker we looked out window-sized holes blasted in the walls. As we unrolled our blankets on the rubble-strewn floor, I imagined the ships offshore firing a constant barrage of shells into this mountain fortress. Japanese officers watched the battles raging offshore from this bunker as three of their aircraft carriers were sunk and 430 planes were shot down in what American aviators came to call the "Great Mariana's Turkey Shoot."

General Saito conceded defeat on Saipan not by surrendering but by kneeling towards Japan and pressing his dagger into his stomach, while an aide shot him through the head with a pistol to ensure a swift version of *hara-kiri*. For months after that, Captain Sakeo Oba and his 46 remaining soldiers refused to surrender, continuing their hit-and-run guerrilla warfare. As they hid among the caves, they eluded capture even after 5,000 U.S. troops lined up almost fingertip-to-fingertip, spanning the width of the island, and marched its entire length from south to north. Captain Oba finally surrendered months after the war was over. As cunning and fearless as Captain Oba may have been, I understood that he belonged to an army of raging psychopaths who were necessarily confronted and destroyed by equally brave and infinitely more compassionate Americans such as Guy Gabaldon.

We slept uneasily that night alongside the ghosts in the Last Command Post. I awoke several times to imagined human intruders, ghosts of the mind, or perhaps a lizard climbing over me. I stepped outside to catch my breath in the light of a half moon and gazed over the guns of battle to the peaceful starlit sea. Spirits linger in places such as this, marking the epic and awful struggles of man against man. The tragedy ran straight through me.

In the morning we explored some of the other hidden caves in the area. Vegetation streamed down the mountain face, all but blocking many of the cave entrances. The remains of Japanese troops who had held out until succumbing to starvation or suicide were still to be found in these caves. It was not until seven years after the war that the last Japanese soldier walked out of here, claiming to be unaware the war had ended.

Morning Hike; The Banzai Bus

By the time we returned to the road it was late morning. Six busloads of Japanese tourists were assaulting the command post and the surrounding memorials. Married couples manned the tanks and guns, posing for photos, while their children ran wild through the bunker, cheering in excitement. Hearing a signal tap of a horn, they all retreated to their buses in orderly fashion. In a minute they were off to the next site in their rigidly guided tour. The Saipan theme park was open.

In Saipan and on later travels around Asia, I learned something about the modern stereotypical Japanese middle-class man. He is highly social and takes his vacations as seriously as his work, performing them with the timing and tactics of a military invasion. A Japanese office worker who is locked in all day with his coworkers often spends the evening at restaurants and bars with the same people. More than likely, this man will take his family vacation with his coworkers on a company-sponsored outing. When they arrive at their vacation target, tour buses await to whisk them from one preplanned location to the next with split-second timing. Each hour of each day is scheduled for productive sightseeing, and any deviation from the original plan is intolerable. The following year he will join the same group for another frantic and forgettable tour of another touristic target. How different my own travel goals were to the regimented behavior of these regimented minds! As the next battalion of tourists approached, we retreated on our long march back to Tanapag Harbor.

Atom, My Home; Saipan Songlines

Hours later, I dropped my pack into my dinghy and rowed back to *Atom*. My legs and back ached mildly from the not unpleasant fatigue of muscles well used after being dormant too long. The stationary exercises I performed aboard daily kept me in fair physical condition but lacked the full range of exercise that comes with hiking the mountainous islands. Colin's ability to travel the world with only what he lifted onto his back was impressive. I had the luxury to carry many of the comforts of home with me from port to port. Simple, compact, self-contained *Atom* provided me a retreat like a crab wearing its shell. But it was a shell that permitted me to enter its shelter and then go out to explore the land world again and again. My walk across Saipan brought me closer to the balance I seek, that of a well-traveled body coupled with an opened, informed mind.

My wanderings by foot and by sail had always filled a need in me that seemed inexplicable. In his book *The Songlines*, Bruce Chatwin made a geographical and intellectual wandering in his study of Australian aboriginal culture. He discovered what I have felt my entire life: that humans are built to walk and wander; to sing of what we see in our songs, stories, and poetry; to create a verbal roadmap for ourselves and those of our tribe. The nomadic instinct of man is reflected in our continuing urge to roam the land and sail the seas. Speeding along in our cars and planes or as passengers in a motorboat serves mainly to bring us from one location to another. We arrive somewhere but lose something during the process. The acts of long-distance walking and ocean sailing are what our souls yearn for. They are the two halves that make the whole of us.

Our civilization has attempted to perfect the imperfectible: designing physically comfortable sedentary lives for nomadic beings. When the nomadic hunter-gatherer within us finds himself locked up in the city, his genetic impulse often leaves him no other outlet but violence, drug addiction, and various forms of nihilistic self-destructive behavior. Civilizations display their collective frustrations with modern sedentary society by mass warfare as seen on Saipan and countless other locations since man created agricultural and city-based societies. But if early *Homo sapiens* had been so prone to warfare and violence against himself as the anthropologists would have us believe, then we would have long ago become extinct. Although we may never have been the mythical "noble savage," it seems clear that the preposterous citadels of civilization we have erected too often thwart the noble intent of modern man.

Sailing Past Silent Cannon

A day later I sailed on a borrowed windsurfer a few miles across the harbor to the palm tree-lined motu called Managaha Island. The fresh breeze propelled me over the waves at an exciting speed. As I leaned with back to the wind, my feet gripped the board, which leapt from crest to crest while blurs of coral rushed beneath me. These surfboards with sails are one of the purist expressions of minimalist sailing craft you can find. I instantly knew I must find a way to bring one aboard my boat on our future travels.

On another day I worked alongside Colin replacing the wire mast rigging on the catamaran he maintained. Along the shore around us I was reminded of the near-constant typhoon danger in this region of the ocean. Four large steel ships sat haphazardly along the shoreline like beached whales above the high tide line. They had been tossed up on shore like toy boats during the previous year's super-typhoon Kim, whose 200 m.p.h. winds also knocked down and blew out to sea several hundred of the islanders' timber houses. One man who ventured briefly outside in the height of the storm told me the only way he could see and breathe without choking on wind-driven spray was to use his dive mask and snorkel. These killer storms occur in the western Pacific each year. Their season is much longer than the Atlantic hurricane season, which partly accounts for the scarcity of cruising yachts in this region. In the western North Pacific, the statistically safest month from these cyclones is February. On March 2nd, just ten days after my arrival on the island, the calendar reminded me it was time to move on. Because of my one day of paid labor, I was fortunate to leave the island with a few more dollars than when I had arrived, despite the $25 bite from Customs.

As we sailed downwind out of the harbor, through binoculars I picked out landing craft and tanks stranded on the reef, with waves crashing over the rusty gun turrets as they have for over four decades. If it hadn't been for these coral-encrusted relics and the memorials ashore, Saipan could easily be mistaken for another Pacific paradise instead of what had once been the world's most war-torn island. Over 30,000 Japanese soldiers and civilians died here in a vain and pointless military struggle, which also claimed 4,000 American lives. The land scars are healing, and memories fade as new generations replace the old. As Saipan receded from view, I looked expectantly toward the west. All the far-flung American territories were behind me. Ahead lay a broad stretch of ocean and another distant world.

9 The Longest Night

Pushed along by two fluttering sails and dreams of adventure.

Upon entering the Philippine Sea, I sensed that ahead I faced the most challenging leg of the voyage to date. The 2,000 miles from Saipan to the coast of China would not be the longest passage I'd made. But aside from the threat of an early season typhoon, once I entered the South China Sea, the Pilot book warned of waters thick with shipping, cold winter gales, and fog—altogether a dangerous mix for a solo sailor. My course was set to take me northwest for the first thousand miles to where I'd pass into Luzon Strait between the islands of the Philippines and Taiwan, then west across the South China Sea to Hong Kong.

We made good progress along our course for the first several days with steady trade winds on the starboard beam. A favorable current added another 20 miles to each day's run. My old companion Polaris rose a degree higher in the north sky each night, affirming our advance to higher latitudes. I slept well those first nights, knowing I was bound for the lands of the mysterious East, a place I'd long dreamed of exploring. Yet this was still winter and to the north lay troubled waters. Change was on its way, according to my nervous barometer, whose needle shot up, hinting at an anti-cyclone passing north of me. Hours later, it was confirmed by a wind shift that drew a curtain of rain across our bow. For a day and a night the feeble and shifting wind held me back. The next day we raced along in rising winds as if to make up for lost time.

I had gone forward to the mast to reef the mainsail so many times over the years that I did it blindly, not even bothering to take a flashlight with me on nights so black I couldn't see as far as my hands. On the dark and windy deck I worked by feel of handrails, lifelines, rope, spars, and canvas; by the varying sound of wind in the flapping sail; and by blind muscle memory. I first eased the main sheet, then crawled forward along the narrow side deck between the lifelines and the coach roof. I lowered the mainsail halyard several feet until reaching the next reef grommet. After placing the grommet onto the hook at the mast-to-boom gooseneck fitting, I found the second of three reef lines, its end marked by two overhand knots so that I could identify it by feel, and pulled in the aft end of the loose canvas that flapped violently in the wind. To finish the reef I hoisted the halyard until tight and pulled myself from one handhold to the next along the canted deck back to the cockpit where I hauled in the mainsheet. During this three-minute procedure, *Atom* followed her course, pulled along by the jib only.

A day later we wallowed drunkenly in a calm for a few hours until a new wind filled in from the south, sending me back to my sail-handling jobs. Just as I resigned myself to the discomforts of interrupted sleep during frequent sail changes through the stormy nights, an old stowaway emerged from its hiding place.

My Nemesis Awakes; Cool Seas and Body Chills

Malaria! At first I refused to recognize my old nemesis, as if denial could free me from its febrile embrace. It began as usual with an increasing pain behind my eyeballs, quickly followed by aching muscles, a raw throat, and alternating fever and chills. Ever since a malicious mosquito had introduced us in the jungles of New Guinea during my first circumnavigation three years previously, this drug-resistant strain of malaria had hidden itself in my liver, emerging now and then from its dormant state to lay me low. The fever had almost killed me back then as I lay trembling in a remote grass hut in the western highlands of New Guinea. I had wasted several days not seeking medical attention since I refused to believe I actually had malaria. After all, I was already taking daily anti-malarial medicine supposed to prevent the disease. Coming in and out of delirium, I finally realized I had a drug-resistant strain of Malaria. Eventually, I was carried down the mountain by my native friends. A young man named Kerowa and his family saved my life by getting me to a distant hospital just in time. I've felt a depth of gratitude to them ever since.

This time, knowing the symptoms of a malarial attack all too well, I grabbed the bottle of bitter quinine sulfate tablets from the medicine locker and began to self-medicate. Fortunately, the wind had settled in from the south and remained reasonably steady for the next few days as I lay shivering in my bunk, ears ringing from the quinine doing battle with the blood-cell-bursting parasites coursing through my veins. Occasionally, I hauled myself on deck to scan the horizon, often sighting Japanese fishing boats following their erratic courses. I cursed their right-of-way status that obliged me to alter course to avoid their unpredictable movements. More often, I suspect, the fishing boats passed me unseen, as I lay in my bunk on sweat-soaked sheets, too weak to summon up much interest in preventing a collision.

I brought a bottle of quinine with me everywhere I went for the next couple of years until I found I had finally outlived my hitch-hiking adversary, who apparently died of old age after five hard-fought years, harried along by my bitter-tasting, quinine-laced blood. Many times I've silently thanked the Jesuit priest and apothecary who brought this life-saving extract from the bark of the Peruvian cinchona trees back to Europe to treat the malaria that was endemic there at the time. He had noticed the Peruvian Indians using the bark extract to reduce their shivering from the low temperatures of their high-altitude homelands. The priests' simple reasoning was that since the herbal medicine reduced shivering from cold it might also reduce the mortality of what later was recognized as malaria, since one of its major symptoms was uncontrollable shivering. It turned out he was correct, except that by luck the quinine actually killed the parasite instead of only helping with the shivering. Since the early 17th century, the "Jesuit's bark" has saved the lives of European royalty and Popes, as well as hundreds of thousands of the rest of us around the world. In recent years, less toxic drugs than quinine have been developed, but malaria remains the number one killer in many poor tropical countries of Africa and Asia. A lack of cheap medicine for the poor and an understandable reluctance to fill or drain swamps and poison the mosquito's habitat still claims the lives of more than a million people each year.

Batan Traffic; Exhaustion; Sleepless Miles

Twelve days out of Saipan and partly recovered from my malarial malaise, I sighted the cloud-capped island of Batan, one of the northernmost of the Philippine Islands. It was afternoon when I first discerned its hazy outline from 30 miles away. Upon sighting the island I committed myself to a mad dash against the setting sun, hoping to pass through the channel between Batan and its smaller neighbor, Diogo Island, before darkness fell. The race was lost when the sun dropped behind the island while we were still several miles away. Unwilling to risk negotiating the channel at night, I tacked slowly with shortened sail back towards the east and then hove to until dawn.

That night my weary eyes never closed as I watched ships pass on all sides in a sea of inky blackness. For long hours I peered into the darkness for some sign of lights from the island that I knew to be close, but I saw no sign of it. As we drifted into the sunrise, Batan gradually appeared 15 miles to the west. From compass bearings on the island I could see that tidal currents were carrying us in circles. The west wind was on our nose, so I began a series of short tacks to enter the straits: one hour on port tack, one hour on starboard tack, then repeat and repeat again. Batan rose in stature before me until the towering mountain on the northern flank of the 10-mile-wide island made it appear nearly as tall as it was wide. A scar of a dirt road traced its way up the green and corrugated landscape. My chart indicated a small Filipino settlement on Batan. I yearned to visit this lonely island, but there was no protected anchorage anywhere on its circular coast. As I watched the island throughout the day, I resigned myself to traveling that solitary road to Batan's misty heights in my imagination. By afternoon, a swirling white scarf of cloud wrapping the upper half of the mountain added to its unreachable and mysterious allure.

Eight tacks in eight hours brought us to the center of the straits where we sailed over conflicting tide rips churning the waters on all sides. At this point the obstinate headwind I'd battled all day went calm, leaving me helplessly spinning in the currents. We drifted relentlessly towards the rocky shores of Batan. Each minute that passed brought us closer to destruction. Just as my anxiety rose to the terrifying reality of impending shipwreck, a new current gripped us and pulled us away to safety. Lacking a steadying wind in her sails, *Atom* bounced and rolled in the bumpy seas. We stood at the gates of the South China Sea, which seemed reluctant to let us enter, as if my penance had not yet been great enough.

South China Sea – Gales, Fishing Boats, Fog, Endurance

Just before sunset, after an absence of five long days, the trade wind, referred to as the northeast monsoon in this part of the world, granted a reprieve by filling our sails. We burst free of the straits, and my spirits soared. I shouted with joy and did a little dance in the confines of the cockpit. I laughed loudly, shaking off the previous days' pent-up stress and fatigue. It takes nothing more than a fair wind at the right moment to cause the engine-free sailor to rejoice. For two days I had not dared to sleep because I was constantly in danger of being either swept into Batan's rocky embrace or run down by an unseeing ship. Caught between those sea-going monsters and the perilous rocks reminded me of Odysseus threading a course in the straits of Messina between the rocky shoals of Scylla and the whirlpool of Charybdis. Now, confident that *Atom* could look after herself while surging ahead on the proper course, I cooked a quick meal of pasta and vegetables seasoned with a heaping spoon of black pepper. As soon as I had washed the pot in the saltwater streaming past the cockpit, I returned to my bunk and collapsed into blissful sleep.

An hour later, my kitchen timer alarm roused me to make a scan of the horizon. A ship was passing astern of us, reminding me that we were still in the shipping lanes and that there would be no more of my lubberly penchant for sleeping through the night. From here until I reached my destination, I set my alarm for no more than 20 minutes, which in good visibility was the amount of time before a ship of average speed that was sighted on the horizon could crush us under her bow.

The next dawn, the three stars I shot by sextant provided three lines that intersected on my chart in a tight triangle, indicating we had traveled a satisfying 70 miles during the night. The wind continued to build, bringing with it multiple banks of clouds and finally a flat gray sky. *Atom* rolled and surged over the heaving, sunless sea into a cold and windy night. The next day I dipped a thermometer in the water and found the sea temperature had dropped a shocking 10 degrees Celsius (18F), which was matched by the plummeting air temperatures. For the first time in years, I dug out my thermal long underwear and scarf from the musty bottom of my damp clothes locker.

A gale from the north struck us 150 miles off the coast of China. To compensate for a current setting us to the south I stubbornly held *Atom*'s bow into the storm on a northwest course with triple-reefed main and storm jib. Waves pounded with sledgehammer blows to the windward side of the hull while driving rain and spray obscured my vision. By nightfall the sea had built to an angry state, and I debated whether to heave to, finally deciding I must press on to avoid letting the wind and current set me to leeward of my destination. It seemed a mocking irony that our worst storm should arrive on what could have been the last day of the voyage to China. But *Atom* was no stranger to a bullying sea. She took the punishment better than I did. As the temperature dropped into the 40s, the cold bit deeply into my post-malaria weakness. I crawled in and out of my damp bunk, still wearing my one-piece foul weather suit and rubber boots over my wool sweater and long underwear. In addition to my weakened physical state, my body had acclimated to years of tropical sailing, and now the damp wind cut into me until I could not feel warm enough, despite the amount of clothes I wore.

At the height of the storm, in the middle of the deepest darkness I had ever seen, I sailed through an area thick with what I assumed were Chinese fishing boats. Within a ten-mile expanse I sighted at least thirty boats in my restricted zone of visibility. Wave tops broke into sparkles of bioluminescence, camouflaging the dim lights of the fishing vessels. We repeatedly passed the shadowy hulls of these boats within hailing distance as I sailed zigzag courses nearly out of control, hurtling down the faces of the waves. Although some of the boats were lit, others showed no lights at all, like apparitions of ghost ships materializing out of the fog and spray. They may have been riding out the storm by drifting instead of actually fishing, but even if they had nets in the water, I was confident I could sail harmlessly over them without entanglement because our rudder was attached flush to the aft end of her well-rounded keel and because we dragged no propeller to snag. At least the gale all but eliminated the chance we'd become victims of fair-weather Chinese pirates who frequented these waters, preying on the fishermen and ethnic Chinese refugees fleeing the turmoil and persecution in Vietnam. Even so, I placed my few valuables in a hidden locker. Being weaponless, I trusted that my obvious poverty would protect me even if the foul weather didn't.

Dawn brought a somber gray sky above a sea that had turned from deep blue to the greenish brown of shallow coastal waters. The wind lessened, and I timidly hoisted more sail. There was no land in sight, but my dead reckoning indicated the coast of China lay 30 miles ahead with Hong Kong bearing 80 miles to the southwest. This position was little more than a guess because I had not had a celestial observation in several days. Cloud and fog throughout the days and nights left no sun or stars to guide my way. There was no other option but to sail as the earlier explorers had by following the compass west until we reached sight of the Chinese coast. I did have one navigational advantage besides a more accurate chart, but it was also my biggest threat. The incessant coastal shipping, much of it running to and from Hong Kong, indicated just as well as a radio beacon that I was on the correct path. But unlike a harmless beacon, these ships of commerce could run me over without noticing the event until possibly someone spotted a sailboat mast entangled in her bow anchor as she steamed into port.

Entering Hong Kong by Sail and Oar; A Miracle Wind

Tension built within me as I closed with the fog-hidden coast. I strained to see land, sensing its proximity by the subtle change in wave patterns. Lacking an electronic depth sounder, I hove to and cast my lead line over the side, finding bottom at 20 fathoms. The depth indicated I was close enough to shore, so I turned off the wind to run southwest, parallel to the coast. An hour later, the solitary rock marked on my chart as Pedro Blanco emerged from the mist. I had never been so happy to see a dismal, surf-beaten rock in my life, since it provided me with a much-needed position fix. Now I knew positively that Hong Kong lay another fifty miles down the coast. I hit the coast exactly where I'd intended. Any cautious navigator will aim upwind and upstream from his destination, partly because once he sights land he does not have to guess which way to turn next; it is obvious that turning downwind will bring him to his destination. Even nowadays with a GPS, it makes sense to stay to windward of your destination to prevent other mishaps, such as unexpected leeway from a storm or equipment breakdowns, from sweeping you away from your desired port. In a small boat it will be exhausting or possibly even impossible to beat back against a strong unrelenting wind and current.

Despite the challenging conditions, I was not overly worried about my ability to navigate blindly through fog or dark nights. I had learned to trust my other senses and navigation strategies years earlier. On my first long solo passage from Fort Lauderdale, Florida to New York City, I found myself approaching a completely fog-hidden harbor entrance to New York after ten nonstop days at sea. It would seem a reckless choice to approach shore in fog, but it seemed riskier to wait about offshore, unable to sleep in the shipping lanes converging on New York. To complicate the issue, I had developed a fever with angry red streaks running up my leg from where a fish spine had punctured my foot a few days previously, causing an infection. This was before I had become vegetarian when I caught fish on passage by dragging a lure on a line to a sheet winch. Lacking antibiotics in my medical kit allowed that infection to turn into blood poisoning. One of the bizarre symptoms was a strong nauseating metallic taste in my mouth that made it nearly impossible to eat or drink anything for nearly a week until my body recovered on its own. At first I didn't recognize the connection between the swollen fish spine wound and the sensation that anything that entered my mouth tasted like liquid copper. Assuming my water tank was contaminated, I tested each water jug and sampled different foods until I slowly came to the obvious and scarier conclusion that the problem was within me and not in the water.

In order to find my way into New York Harbor, I had changed course from north to west in order to come upon the coast of New Jersey about twenty miles to the south. As I sailed into shallower water I stood at the bow staring into the fog, attempting to sight land before the keel struck the shoaling bottom. Finally, I detected the sound of surf beating on the shore, which confirmed my position. With relieved confidence, I instantly changed course back to the north and sailed parallel to the unseen Jersey shore, keeping my distance off by watching my depth sounder and listening for the churning surf. I sailed along the low empty finger of land known as Sandy Hook until deeper water and fog horns from unseen ships made it obvious I was in the center of the harbor entrance. I altered course to follow the sounds of ships cautiously and noisily making their way into port. Regulations required I ring my own little brass bell to alert other shipping to my presence, but I soon gave up this futile gesture and concentrated on listening as intensely as a blind man walking through a pit of snakes. A few miles farther on I heard automobile traffic overhead. Yes, overhead! I passed under the Verrazano Narrows bridge between New York's Staten Island and Brooklyn without ever seeing the bridge itself. Fortunately, a few miles ahead the blanket of fog lifted enough that my first sight of land after ten days at sea was the welcoming torch of the Statue of Liberty emerging from a fog-shrouded curtain.

Approaching the coast of China

On my Hong Kong approach, I wanted to avoid arriving in the middle of the night at this busiest shipping port in the world, so I hove to and made short tacks to hold my position behind Pedro Blanco until nightfall. There was no chance to sleep there either, because I needed to monitor our position to avoid drifting onto or losing sight of the rock. Another distraction was the Chinese fishing boats passing on all sides, running along on seemingly random courses. These were all old-style wooden sampans, 30–40-feet long, some still flying their distinctive junk-rigged sails while others had been modernized by cutoff masts and diesel engines. In the gray evening twilight I resumed course towards Hong Kong under reefed sails, expecting the strong northeast monsoon to carry me within sight of Hong Kong's lighthouse on Waglan Island before dawn.

The longest night of my life ensued. I had slept only in brief naps totaling no more than a couple hours over the past several days. On this night there was to be no sleep at all. Just in case I dozed off, I set my alarm to five minutes each time I entered the cabin to shelter from the wind and spray. Even then, as I climbed the companionway steps to scan the darkness, I was frequently surprised to see a ship passing within a stone's throw after I had sighted nothing five minutes earlier. The hours dragged on as I fought to remain conscious. Since I carried no caffeine-laced drinks aboard such as coffee or tea, my only stimulant was a shot of pure adrenaline triggered by fear of collision with another boat or grounding on the nearby rocky shore. I had learned to drink only herbal teas on my passages because I didn't want to be dependent on drug stimulants. When drug-free, I found it easier for my mind to settle down and allow me to catch brief snatches of sleep as conditions allowed. But on this night I learned the limits of endurance and desperately missed having a strong brew to help keep me alert for one more night.

We sailed in an eerie scene of breaking waves burning with bioluminescence and fog-shrouded ships emerging out of the blackness. Sooner than expected, due to a lift from a favorable current, a flashing light cut through the fog at 0300 hours. It was Waglan Island's lighthouse less than a mile away. Unwilling to risk entering the strange and congested harbor at night, I began tacking back and forth across the shipping lanes to maintain my position as I awaited the dawn. The single white light I installed on the mast top while in Hawaii served as my only navigation light to alert other vessels I was there. It was a safe choice for a navigation light in the sense that ships could see me and would probably avoid running into me, but it was not a "legal" light for anything other than marking the boat when at anchor. The International Maritime Organization's *Rules of the Road* states that all sailing vessels at sea must show red, green, and white running lights at night. But that dim and confusing color scheme could easily be ignored or go unnoticed by other vessels, particularly in foul weather. I believed this single white anchor light was a better choice for solo sailing Asian waters, where I could be asleep at the wheel, literally, and the person at the helm of a passing ship might have little knowledge of the rules of the road. The unwritten navigation rules in Asia are that he with the greatest tonnage rules the sea. The idea that a sailing vessel underway has a universal right of way on the open ocean is largely ignored. But if a motor vessel sights a white light at sea, he will likely assume it is the white stern light of another boat. This makes him the overtaking vessel. Common sense as well as the navigation rules requires him to alter course to avoid collision. This theory worked well because my boat was relatively slow compared with commercial ships, and they could easily avoid me even when our courses crossed. As for my impersonating an overtaken vessel, well, survival trumps legal technicalities.

Atom moved like a ping-pong ball as we short-tacked between the obstacles of ships and land. Finally, the density of traffic forced me to alter course to run parallel with the shipping instead of seeming to make a futile attempt at blockading the harbor entrance. We passed near several small islands that were marked on my chart, but they remained unseen in the fog. At dawn my equally foggy brain finally recognized the blurred outline of Hong Kong Island lying one mile ahead. Temperatures of 45 degrees with driving rain during the night had seemed miserable enough. I didn't expect I was now courting disaster so close to my goal.

At the worst possible moment the island's mountains blocked the wind, leaving us sitting becalmed in the center of the shipping channel. "Holy Christ, not now," I mumbled as a ship blasted a warning horn my way. I watched his black hull slide by so close I could almost reach out and touch the rust-streaked side. I laid my oar over the transom and sculled like mad for the edge of the channel. Progress was desperately slow because the choppy waters kept pulling the blade of the oar out of the water, and my strength to twist the figure eight pattern needed for sculling was waning fast. I now wished my boat were half its size and displacement so that I could row her like a dinghy with a pair of standard Western oars.

Usually, a pair of rowing oars was not as efficient as a single sculling oar on a boat this size. Though two oars do provide increased thrust on the pulling stroke, provided the rower is strong enough for the job, lifting oars clear of the water after each stroke makes for lost time and effort. A sculling oar that is twisted instead of lifted provides thrust on both strokes with little wasted effort. In calm water, a person can scull a boat just as fast and perhaps twice as far as he can row it. Obviously, a single sculling oar is less weight and easier to stow on a small boat. Also, the combined length of two outstretched oars, coupled with our beam, meant the total width of my boat would be 25-feet, which would make it difficult to maneuver in Asia's confined and busy harbors. This is probably why sampans have featured sculling oars for uncounted generations.

Once I had sculled away from the center of the channel, I paused to catch my breath and ease my aching forearms. I stripped off my foul weather gear as the heat of the day burned away the fog. Within minutes all my energies were for nothing, as the current dragged me right back into the shipping channel. The calm lasted three hours, during which time I never dropped the oar to sit down because I knew that doing so meant I would slip into unconsciousness and be crushed and drowned by a collision. I longed for the oblivion of sleep. Being so tantalizingly close to my goal and yet having it beyond reach was becoming too much to bear.

As I swayed on my legs with fatigue and fading adrenaline, I watched hopefully as a whisper of new wind drifted down the mountain, tracing its fingerprints on the surface of the bay and ruffled *Atom*'s sails. I laid down the oar, trimmed the sails, and tacked between the ships towards the moorings of Aberdeen Harbour. Tiered layers of high-rise buildings rose higher from the waterfront as I inched my way past the stone breakwater marking the entrance to Aberdeen. The harbor was designated as a typhoon shelter because of its high breakwaters and location wedged between Hong Kong Island and the smaller island of Ap Lei Chau. At the edge of the breakwater, the fickle wind blew its last breath. Again I pulled on my oar, summoning the last of my reserves of strength. Just as I cleared the entrance, the oar dropped from my cramped hands. I released the anchor from its bow roller and then crumpled down into the cockpit seat, head numb and swimming, arms and back screaming for relief. On all sides of me swirled the chaos of moored junks and yachts, fishing boats coming and going, and water-taxi sampans bobbing on the water like big wooden bathtubs powered by sputtering diesel engines.

The English Samaritan; Teeming Humanity

Almost immediately, two taxi sampans came at me from opposites sides, rightly assuming that I needed to be relocated and that they would earn a fat towing fee. Ignoring my presence, one elderly driver silently jumped aboard and lashed his boat to our side. He began hauling up my anchor while the other driver put a line onto our stern and began tugging us backwards. Seeing me rise again to my feet, the drivers began shouting at each other and me in Hong Kong's choppy-sounding Cantonese language, which seemed doubly odd to my ears after so many speechless days at sea. Seeing my predicament and my yellow quarantine flag flying from the starboard spreader, the English skipper of a passing motor yacht stopped alongside. He shooed away the miniature tugboats and threw me a line for a free tow to the Aberdeen Boat Club dock. If I had known Hong Kong waters better, I would have chosen to sail into the quieter and more easily entered anchorage of Deep Water Bay, two miles away. But another sailor had advised me that Aberdeen was the best place to enter. That was true only if you had an engine aboard and were looking for the convenience of being in the center of town with all the city's services at hand and actually had a paid mooring prearranged.

You might think only a fool would attempt to sail into the busy port of Hong Kong without an engine. You might be right. On the other hand, if I had not been dead on my feet from sleep deprivation it would have been as easy to me as jostling my way on foot through a crowded airport terminal. I would come to sail and scull in and out of Aberdeen several more times without incident in the future. The greater part of sailing without the aid of an engine requires little more than patience, good planning, and an occasional physical workout. Yet there are times when it pushes you to the limits of your endurance and possibly beyond. That is the risk. That is also the reward: to test these limits and expand your world.

Exhaustion and a calming relief put my body and mind at peace. Within five minutes of passing my mooring lines to helpful hands on the club's fuel dock, I was deeply asleep in my bunk. Throughout the day I heard nothing of the noisy harbor around me until I awoke sometime in the evening hours, startled by a dream of a ship's bow bearing down on me. As if waking from a coma with amnesia into an unrecognized world, I popped my head through the hatch to see the unexpected sight of a harbor ablaze from the gaudily decorated and brightly lit four-story-high floating restaurants moored nearby. Like bees to the hive, motorized sampans scooted back and forth, ferrying customers from shore. Regaining my sense of place and time, I returned to my bunk until sunrise. That night, minute by restful minute, my body and mind were renewed.

The next morning I sculled *Atom* from the Boat Club—whose single dock was only meant for fueling or disembarking—a short distance to where I saw a fishing junk moored to a quay. With no other spaces available along the wall, I secured my boat alongside the junk. Her Chinese crew paused from dismantling their antique diesel engine, looked at me for a long moment, and then went back to their work. I had been told at the boat club that local craft could freely moor side by side to the quay in order to squeeze as many boats as possible into the already tightly packed harbor. I found out why other yachts were not rafted together in this free corner of the harbor when the crew of another fishing boat bashed into the side of *Atom* without laying out fenders, made fast their heavy mooring lines to our small cleats, and clambered over our deck with oil-soaked shoes to go ashore. I didn't possess enough fenders to protect both sides of the boat, so I rummaged through the boat repair yard next to us and found two old tires to hang alongside. Every few hours a boat would pull out from our raft, and another would arrive in a waterfront game of musical chairs. *Atom* was too small to be placed on the inside of the raft, so I kept busy shifting lines as boats wedged themselves inside of us. This was certainly a rough place to keep a little yacht, but for now it suited my budget and had the added benefit of placing me right in the middle of Aberdeen's fascinating and colorful parade of people and watercraft.

The chaos of Aberdeen Harbour

Around me I watched taxi sampans making continual circuits of the watery alleyways between lines of boats on moorings, stopping to pick up passengers for a quick trip ashore. One young woman sampan driver performed her work with one hand on the tiller and her baby strapped to her back where it could stay out of trouble. Around noon a sampan pulled up to our raft, and the driver uncovered a large iron *wok* above a gas burner. Within a minute the pleasant aroma of fried noodles, vegetables and spices brought fishermen and boat workers marching over our deck to reach the mobile lunch station. I joined the group on the sampan and received some concerned looks and a few chuckles usually reserved for ignorant tourists when I paid for my lunch with a one dollar bill. My query about the exchange rate to the U.S. dollar brought blank stares, but it was apparent they thought I had overpaid.

I launched my kayak to tour the harbor and scout for a safer, less chaotic spot to moor *Atom*. One corner of the harbor held a raft of hundreds of junks that were part of a floating village containing thousands of boat people. Between the 14th and 17th centuries, when Aberdeen was the principal port of Hong Kong (meaning Fragrant Harbor), the locally harvested aromatic sandalwood made it a center of trade. Oddly enough, the "fragrant harbor" was now so polluted with oil and sewage that I took extra care to avoid capsizing when hit on the beam by motorboat wakes.

Generations of families belonging to the Tanka ethnic group have lived on these boats continuously for centuries, going ashore only occasionally because all their needs are met on the water. Sampans circled the water lanes of the village, acting as floating supermarkets and mobile hardware stores. People on the junks merely stood out on their aft deck if they needed anything. Whatever it was, from water to fuel to food, would arrive at their home within minutes. Salted fish hung on lines across the decks to dry. Children leapt from boat to boat to visit their friends. The Tanka boat people I saw were a shrinking population, many having already moved ashore into drab concrete box apartments in high-rise buildings put up by the government to encourage the people to leave the boats "for their own good," as the government put it. I felt in good company here among the Tanka. Shore-bound people and the governments they elect universally consider boat people—whether the

Tanka of Hong Kong or Westerners living on yachts in America—as a tax-avoiding nuisance. Like traveling gypsies who stay too long, we are a harassed and unloved breed. Perhaps we will survive a few more generations. In most places, we probably won't.

Though on this day I found no better spot to moor my boat, in the coming days I learned that to survive in Hong Kong, whether afloat or ashore, you need to adopt the local strategy that no matter how packed a place is, there is always room for one more. In this environment, your personal space does not exist.

Customs, The Right Way!; The Thrill of Adventure Refreshed

A member of the Boat Club had told me that to clear Customs and Immigration, I needed to travel to their office in the main commercial district located on the opposite side of the island. Within 24-hours of leaving the solitude of the ocean, I stepped aboard a packed double-decker bus that crossed through a tunnel under the mountain and suddenly plunged us into the heavily populated northern shore of Central District. I found my way to the Customs office located in a towering office block where a uniformed man behind a glass wall stamped my passport and sent me on my way without any of the fuss and drama I had encountered in the last few ports I'd visited.

Along the north shore of the island, the sprawling business district faced the main harbor with its residential areas backing up against the inland mountain range. A tram carried tourists and residents up to the misty heights above the city to the district known as "The Peak." Real estate on the island is in such demand that generations of construction workers continually nibble at the mountainside to create more level land to build on. The rock they remove is dumped into the water's edge to expand the land out into the harbor, thus creating two buildable lots where there had been none.

At 1 Queen's Road, I stepped between a pair of bronze lions and into the massive and futuristic-shaped Hong Kong and Shanghai Bank where

I exchanged my U.S. dollars for Hong Kong dollars. The lions out front are part of the bank's perceived excellent *feng shui*, and are venerated by locals who rub their hands on the lions' haunches in passing to ensure prosperity. This modular tower was at the time said to be the most expensive building in the world, a true testament to a city built solely on commerce. With its external aluminum trusses it looked as if it might start its engines at any time and lift off the surface of the earth. Although still a colony of Britain during my visit, the business-savvy territory pegged its currency at 7.8 H.K. to 1 U.S. dollar. Even today, with the financial giant of China as its new overlords, the semi-autonomous Hong Kong territory clings to the security of the American-linked dollar.

From the bank I stepped onto a tram, paid a fare equivalent to eight cents U.S., and climbed to the open-topped upper level. Seated there, I watched the revolving hurricane of humanity below me as we passed through the shopping districts of Wan Chai and Causeway Bay. In Wan Chai, everything imaginable or otherwise was sold from small shops stacked on top of and in front of each other in a labyrinth of streets and alleyways. On one block I counted four banks, ten restaurants, a dozen electronics shops, and over thirty clothing stores. Another block held the bars and nightclubs where prostitutes have entertained generations of thirsty and lustful visiting sailors. When local friends later took me out for a night on the town, we found the seedy bars and aging hookers to be a poor remnant of the descriptions I had read of Wan Chai's earlier days when U.S. Navy ships had docked here for R&R during the Vietnam War.

Back along the waterfront of Central District, I boarded the Star Ferry for the ten-minute crossing of Victoria Harbour to Kowloon (meaning "Nine Dragons"). The nine dragons reportedly stem from eight mountain peaks behind Kowloon together with an honorary ninth dragon thrown in to represent the Chinese Emperor. The Kowloon peninsula on the mainland Chinese coast was ceded from China to Britain in 1860, nearly 20 years after the British acquired Hong Kong

Island as a trading center. The powerful foreigners' insatiable demand for land was not appeased for long. Eventually the Brits demanded and got a 99-year lease of an additional 368 square miles of land and several more islands beyond Kowloon. My ferry ride to Kowloon cost only 50 H.K. cents (6 cents U.S.). In 1966, a violent three-day riot broke out among the Chinese population when the ferry's owners announced a plan to double the fare. The riots were quelled, and the fare increased. The fleet of Star Ferries does a brisk business, but with such low fares and penny-pinching, resentful passengers, how, I wondered, could they remain in business. Apparently they have managed to turn a nice profit because they've been in business for the past 90 years.

I entered a not too expensive-looking restaurant that was as noisy and chaotic as a stock exchange: clattering dishes and chopsticks, waiters rushing food out from the kitchen and empty plates back in, diners shouting good-naturedly at their table mates in order to be heard above the din. A grinning waiter approached and handed me a menu. There were over a hundred dishes listed, and fortunately for me most of them had pictures that I could point to. I pointed to one photo, and the waiter rushed off to the kitchen. He returned still grinning, though empty-handed and said, "*Meiyo*" (don't have). I pointed to another dish. "*Meiyo*" again. Another picture, another *meiyo* through taught lips over clenched teeth. I later got used to this common charade in Chinese restaurants that wanted to appear to have a better selection than they actually did. Many dishes on their menus were not only unavailable that day; they never would be available. Before my waiter could grin himself to death, I stumbled upon the daily special and enjoyed a dish of noodles, vegetables, and tofu, while picking around the tiny flecks of unidentifiable meat. For the past several years I had been following a diet low in fats, but I came to find out that almost all common dishes from Chinese kitchens were fried or had pig's fat poured on top.

Even after spending some hours walking the streets of Kowloon, I hadn't really seen the place. From the moment I stepped off the ferry, a wave of people engulfed me. The rushing surf of pedestrians and horn-blaring vehicles flowed like tidal currents around the buildings. Borne along on this wave, I could barely divert my attention long enough to see where I was. When I needed to break pace, I tucked into a doorway. Looking at my map, I noted I had been swept along Nathan Road, past Peking Road and the Tin Hau Temple. On the way back to the waterfront I turned onto side streets whose signs were written in indecipherable Chinese characters. On one of those back streets I discovered sidewalk fortune tellers and tea rooms decorated with hanging bird cages. There was even a traditional Chinese street puppet show backed by an orchestra of screeching, clashing, and banging instruments that sounded like a gang of fighting cats and dogs and mimicked the discordant street life of Hong Kong. Coming here from the solitude of the sea, the entire crushing weight of humanity seemed to me as actors on a crowded stage.

My guidebook mentioned that one corner of Kowloon, called Mongkok, contained the most tightly packed mass of people on earth, with over 165,000 people per square kilometer. The competition for space there hung over the city like a herd of elephants competing to command an anthill. Up to ten people occupy apartments the size of an average American bathroom, sleeping on tiered bunks in shifts. On the roofs of these high-rise tenements, squatters have erected tin and bamboo shacks. Then another family comes along and builds another precarious perch on top of those. Individuality is as lost here as a single drop of water in the sea. Yet these individuals endure and survive. Occasionally they prosper, at least in financial terms compared with the poverty they left behind in Communist China. Above all, Hong Kong people are hardworking. They often hold down two jobs in order to fill their apartments with the needed luxuries of radios, televisions, refrigerators, and air conditioners. It is Asia's version of New York City, except the inhabitants here are packed more tightly, work harder, and live with less fear of crime. That is not to say the average person of Hong Kong is any more courteous than the average New Yorker. A lifetime of push and shove and of queuing up in lines has shaped their temperament and worn their patience to the breaking point.

What I found in Hong Kong was a curious mixture of China and Europe: a meeting ground for the world's communists and capitalists, socialists and libertarians. Forget East meets West; it is a place where the East collided headlong with the West and redefined what a city could be. Hong Kong is the future of feverish capitalistic society; at least until we all go down fighting, firing rockets at an incoming, life-extinguishing comet—or at each other. Until then, we obedient creatures of capitalism know our place as well as worker bees in the Hong Kong hive.

The contrast between the human orgy of free enterprise in Hong Kong and my life on the empty ocean wave left me dazed and dismayed. But it was also a thrilling time to be there, and I was eager to immerse myself in this new world, since I knew that I, at least, had *Atom* as my ticket out.

10 Hong Kong – Locked Gateway to the East

I would rather weather a typhoon than get entangled in the Sargasso Sea of Chinese Bureaucracy.

Soon after I arrived in Hong Kong I found I was unable to obtain a permit to make a river journey into mainland China as I had originally hoped. I had planned to sail down the coast to the Pearl River Delta and sail upriver, working with the tidal currents as far as possible. Then I would hire a sampan to tow me upstream to the river's furthest navigable reaches. At that point I would sail and drift downstream, like an Asian Huck Finn, visiting rural villages and making land excursions at interesting locations. One of those places that captured my imagination was the region around Guilin on the Li River where a spectacular and surreal karstic landscape has formed, leaving rock pinnacles towering over a flat valley where a winding river flows among the rice fields. I had pored over charts and maps that seemed to indicate the area around Guilin could be reached by taking the Pearl River to one of its tributaries that eventually joined the Li River. It was a journey of hundreds of miles inland, and I had no idea how far it was navigable by a boat that draws four feet or if there were any ship-stopping dams or low bridges along the route. But my enthusiasm and confidence in the plan seemed unshakable at the time.

Chinese officialdom had other ideas. At the Chinese Embassy in Hong Kong, I repeated my travel plans over and over to a thoroughly mystified bureaucrat who was used to stamping simple tourist visas. Finally he either understood or gave up trying to understand and told me my request was "too much impossible." When I pressed the matter further, he summoned his boss, who appeared wearing that perfunctory Asian grin commonly worn when one is displeased or stressed, and told me I might be allowed a cruising permit provided I had an official of the

People's Republic aboard for the duration and that I pay about $5,000 per month in permits and fees. This, effectively, was an outright refusal. Their version of a tour guide was a police escort whose job was to tell me all the places I couldn't travel and to monitor my every move. The new crack I had heard about in the Great Wall of China apparently was only big enough for herded tourist groups and the super-rich to gain entry. Beware of any country that uses "People's Republic" in its title, since that is the first clue that it is concerned neither with serving the people nor with being a republic. Chinese officials also had a reputation for being far more serious and strict in their control of the foreign devils than the other countries I'd visited where I had often discreetly ignored inconvenient regulations. It seemed my dream of a river journey in Asia needed some modification. I had not come this far merely to have an urban adventure in Hong Kong. In the back of my mind I knew my great plan was defeated. However, the idea of an exotic river journey in Asia was not dead. I soon began to consider a future trip up the Ganges River in India as a possible alternative.

If Marco Polo Could Do It . . .

Meanwhile, I had a backup plan that would at least get me into some coastal ports in China. While in Hawaii, I had corresponded with Dr. Wayne Moran, who was then in the middle of organizing the building of a three-masted, 76-foot Chinese junk named *Cocachin* for a project he called the Marco Polo Voyage. His intention was to make a voyage retracing the homeward route of Venetian merchant and explorer Marco Polo. Two centuries before Vasco de Gama discovered the sea route to India, Polo was the first European to chronicle an overland journey to China and a sea voyage back to Europe. The young Marco Polo, together with his father and uncle had survived the dangerous journey through hostile foreign lands to reach the fabled Chinese Kingdom of Cathay. While there, Marco's bravery and wit allowed him to rise quickly to the post of chief advisor to the powerful Kublai Khan.

The Polos' trip home in 1292 began in Quanzhou, a few hundred miles north along the coast from Hong Kong, aboard a ship in Kublai Khan's imperial fleet. They hitchhiked a ride in the flotilla tasked with carrying the beautiful 17-year-old Mongol Princess Cocachin, whom Kublai Khan had promised as a bride for King Aghun of Persia. Over 2,000 crewmen manned their impressive fleet of 14 ships. Along the way, hundreds of sailors died from disease and shipwrecks on the hazardous two-year journey around the Straits of Malacca and across the Indian Ocean. By the time they arrived in Hormuz, King Aghun himself had died. The princess found herself widowed before she met her intended husband. However, Princess Cocachin was presented to the king's son Ghazan, and she became Queen of Persia. At the time, of course, there was no Suez Canal linking the Red Sea to the Mediterranean, so the three Venetians carried on overland for another perilous yearlong journey until reaching Venice.

After an absence of 24 years, the long-lost Marco Polo was unrecognizable to his relatives. He had arrived home wearing the rags of a Tartar and astonished his family by revealing from hidden pockets the precious jewels he had collected in China. Venice was at war with the neighboring city-state of Genoa at the time, and before long Polo was captured and imprisoned. But he made good use of his time in captivity, dictating the stories of his travels to a cellmate named Rusticello, who happened to be a professional writer when not employed fighting against Genoa. The book was later released as *The Travels of Marco Polo*, which gave the first detailed account of life in the Far East. Although filled with some fanciful and exaggerated descriptions, likely added by later translators, the book inspired Christopher Columbus and other explorers throughout the ages. The story had certainly fired an obsession within Wayne Moran to retrace the maritime silk route of those earlier explorers.

Dr. Moran explained to me how he first came to Hong Kong in 1980 to purchase an authentic Chinese sailing junk and ended up buying and renovating a 59-foot, three-masted shrimp trawler. Over the next decade he sailed on numerous Chinese junks, learning the details of their construction as well as how they are sailed. He also worked as a marine coordinator in the film industry, participating in documentaries about authentic Chinese sailing vessels and came to be considered an expert in Chinese maritime history and Chinese sailing junk construction.

In a letter Dr. Moran had suggested I sail into Aberdeen Harbour where *Cocachin* was under construction to join their crew for the final stages of fitting out the boat. I could then sail as crew on the expedition to various Chinese ports and then on to Europe. Although I was reluctant to leave *Atom* for the duration of *Cocachin*'s voyage, Dr. Moran's proposal provided a way for me to sidestep the Chinese bureaucracy. I felt extremely hopeful about the Marco Polo Voyage project, and lucky to be there at the right time.

I first spotted *Cocachin* standing out prominently from the smaller, motorized junks crowded around her as I kayaked through Aberdeen Harbour. The high-sided and brightly painted junk had recently been launched from the small Shing Ge Fat shipyard in Aberdeen. Her three solid timber masts had been stepped a few weeks before, but the rigging and sails were not yet in place. To my Western eye, this near replica of a Fuzhou pole junk design dating back at least 700 years was like a fantasy out of a Disney animation. On each side of her exaggerated flared bow wings, bulging painted eyes gazed out as if to scan the horizon. The rounded hull planking led aft to a high stern where her ample transom was decorated with painted celestial beings and mythical creatures in what the Chinese called "*Fa Mei Koo,*" (flowered buttocks). The overall impression was beautiful and bizarre, like a hybrid between a goose and a tattooed fish.

A Jagger Doppelganger; "Salt Water Girls"

I climbed aboard and met Wayne and his wife Teresa, both 38-year-old British doctors, and their three children, aged between one and nine years. Teresa was a petite woman bursting with energy. With one arm she held the baby resting on her hip while attempting to keep track of her other two children who were running about like kids let loose on a theme park pirate ship. Wayne had a swarthy Mick Jagger look to him but spoke with a more upper-class BBC accent.

There was a flurry of activity as paid Chinese shipyard workers and two young British volunteers worked on completing the deck and interior construction. Mechanics, known in China as "*O Chew*" (meaning "black hand" for the telltale oil-covered hands of their trade) labored deep in the bilge to install a newly donated diesel engine. Wayne led me on a tour of the boat, pausing to explain details of its construction and projects that remained unfinished. Pausing briefly on the raised poop deck, Wayne explained, "After years of researching authentic Chinese vessels of the era, I put together construction blueprints and a three-dimensional, computerized hull design. The builder here studied my plans, took the dimensions to cut the lumber, and then finished the construction by memory, using only his vision of my plans he carried in his head, to guide his carpenters."

In traditional Chinese boat building the shipwright in charge was the essential "eye" of the project, guiding his crew with astonishing accuracy as they shaped and fit each piece of lumber to the exact dimensions in his mental blueprint.

Wayne's enthusiasm and grand plans for the Marco Polo Voyage enthralled me just as they had everyone else involved. That same day I joined the other volunteers assisting with fitting out the rough workboat-style interior cabinetry, adding basic electrics and plumbing, and finishing installation of rigging and sails. Aside from the compromise of some added modern touches, coming from my small fiberglass boat to this massive ship of wood, iron, and bronze was like passing into another time and place.

Wayne's plan was to get *Cocachin* ready in the next several weeks to make a shakedown trip along the coast of China. Since he had exhausted his own funds, these first trips to Chinese ports were essential to generate publicity and sponsors to fund the voyage to the Persian Gulf and then on to Europe. Wayne lived on the edge, daring the winds of finance to carry him towards his goal. I guess any of us sailing the seven seas without enough money to carry us to the end of our journey share a similar flair for a daring venture.

Cocachin being prepared to launch

Over the next few weeks our hammering, painting, and shouting of instructions back and forth added to the already noisy and bustling waterfront. We broke for lunch each day when the sampan lunch boat pulled alongside and the old, black-toothed Chinese man in gray pajamas handed up steaming bowls of noodles, soup, rice, and fish. When I asked for tofu instead of fish, the old man shouted in Chinese, "No *doufu*, only fish la! Maybe the *Gweilo* likes salt water girl la? I send you one, la!" The Chinese mechanics with us grinned as one of them translated the message for me. *Gweilo* I knew was Cantonese for "foreign devil," though it was also used in the slightly less pejorative sense of "ghost man" due to the pale white skin of many expats who came here. Cantonese comes across like bursts of gunfire to sensitive Western ears.

Sentences commonly end with "ah" or "la" or some other crutch word, kind of like a Canadian's unconscious verbal tic "eh," except "la" sometimes denotes the speaker's sense of pity or derision. I had been studying Cantonese with phrase book and dictionary since before arriving in Hong Kong, but it required months of immersion here before I got beyond the level of asking for basic directions or common shopping phrases such as negotiating a price at the market. Try as I did, I never mastered the nuances of tone and dialect that are essential to fluency.

I later learned the old noodle vendor comedian had referenced the "ham-shui-mui" (salt water girls) who were the local prostitutes among the Tanka boat people. These girls captained their own crewless little covered sampans, twisting their *yulohs* (sculling oars) and their hips to scoot the one-woman brothels around the harbor until finding a lonely foreign sailor to pull under the canopy for another kind of twist.

Over several days of working alongside Wayne and evenings spent discussing the practicalities of the trip ahead with him, I must have made a positive impression because he called me into the combined main cabin and galley and stated, "I want you to be our navigator and first mate on the first leg of the voyage."

This was a great opportunity for me. Honored and thrilled, I accepted immediately. Although I could understand being chosen as navigator (no one else aboard had anything near my experience in navigating), I was apprehensive about taking on the responsibilities of first mate because I had never sailed on a junk or any sailboat of this tonnage and complex sail plan.

Wayne set down on the table a copy of an ancient Chinese version of a wooden cross staff to measure star angles, a bronze bowl with Chinese characters engraved around the perimeter that may have been a "south finder" open-topped water compass that had lost its needle, and some other unrecognizable instruments. He also unfolded a narrow and long copy of an archaic pictorial chart that supposedly depicted the route from China to Persia. Instead of the Western charting method, which depicts an expansive top-down view of the world, it was drawn from the perspective of what the sailor aboard would see on that particular route. Straying off the map would be like trying to navigate in Boston with a New York City subway guide. At first glance, I didn't recognize anything on it. Wayne asked me, "Can you learn to use these?" Seeing my dropped jaw and widened eyes, he added, "We need to test these navigation methods for our research, but don't worry. We'll have modern charts, satellite navigation, and a radio direction finder as well."

"This voyage is really a great detective story. Marco Polo left no original log of his journey, so we have to piece the route together out of his disjointed descriptions of the places and people he met. Many of the place names he recounted were rough phonetic translations given to him by Arab or Chinese sailors and are not always obvious to us. For example, I believe his description of 'Java the Less' refers to the island of Sumatra. Some of the local inhabitants there may recall verbal histories of the lost kingdoms Polo described. Theresa and I want to discover what Polo saw, unravel the mysteries of the people, places, and animals he reported. I'm very focused on the sailing techniques, while Theresa is mostly interested in researching the spice trade and herbal medicines. By following this map and using these navigational techniques, I believe we can finally solve the puzzle of the exact route they traveled, which islands and ports they called at, and how things have changed in those places since the thirteenth century."

To get ready for the task, I set out to learn everything I could about sailing and navigating boats of this design, paying particular attention to how they were rigged and sailed. Four of us worked for a week straight to set up her mainsail by lacing bamboo battens and wooden yards to the heavy canvas. Everything was on an enormous scale compared with my boat. On *Atom* I could hoist the mainsail alone in less than a minute. On *Cocachin* the combined sail, yards, and bamboo battens weighed over one ton and required four men turning spokes on a capstan drum for 20 minutes to raise and trim the sail. And that was on a calm day in harbor. It would take an even greater effort at sea.

Manila; Slackers, Pole Dancers, and the Next Forgettable Man

One corner of Aberdeen held a modern yacht marina where I often walked the docks to meet other visiting and local sailors. On the dock there I met Mike Simpson, owner of Simpson Marine, the main yacht sales and maintenance business in the territory. Because the yachting community in Hong Kong was like a small village, where everyone was privy to the details of everyone else's life, Mike already knew about my travels on *Atom*. He told me he had an urgent job for me if I was available. My savings were rapidly evaporating in the city, so I listened with interest to his proposal. "I have a local English customer who joined the Hong Kong to Manila Race on his Beneteau 51 last month," Mike explained. "Just before arriving in Manila they had a rigging failure and lost the top section of the mast. I flew down two of my repair crew to get the mast repaired and sail the boat back to Hong Kong. They've been there for a month now. They have plenty of excuses for the delay, but the owner is riding me to get his boat back. Do you think you could fly down there to take charge of the boat and expedite repairs and the return delivery trip?"

To me a paid sailing trip was always preferable to a job ashore. That this was a somewhat crippled racing boat, whose handling characteristics were unfamiliar to me, only served to encourage me to take on the challenge. I let Wayne know I needed about ten days off and that I would continue with the *Cocachin* project as soon as I returned.

I left *Atom* nestled between sampans on a rented mooring in Aberdeen and boarded a flight across the South China Sea to Manila. From the open windows of the non-air-conditioned taxi that took me across town to the yacht club on the waterfront, my first impressions of Manila were of a hot, congested, and chaotic city still wearing the decay of an old Spanish colonial capital. It was perfectly charming. Even better, after exploring the city over the next couple days I found everything there was cheaper than in Hong Kong and the Filipinos extraordinarily friendly for inhabitants of an impoverished capital city.

The guard at the gate to the Manila Yacht Club let me into the club grounds containing an open dining area and clubhouse. Inside the breakwater that protected the mooring area from the waves that can kick up on the 20-mile-wide bay, were about 100 sailboats and small motor yachts on tightly spaced moorings. I found the stranded Beneteau at one of the few slips along the single dock, reserved for boats being repaired. It was afternoon when I stepped aboard and pushed aside the trail of empty San Miguel beer bottles, tools, and clothing that led me to the bunks where the two crewmen from Simpson Marine were apparently sleeping off a late night. My crew groggily came to their feet and gave me that lukewarm English greeting of a handshake, nod, and grunt, before wandering off to the club in search of something to take the edge off their hangovers.

My young British crew, whom I'll refer to as Ian and Josh, on the off chance they may be leading different lives these days, filled me in on their time here in Manila for the past month. "Everything is great," Ian answered when I asked how things were going. "This town is bloody amazing." Josh added, "The bars are hot and hookers are only $20 for a whole night. The owner is picking up our tab, so what's not to like, right?"

"I meant, how is it going getting the boat ready to sail back to Hong Kong?"

"We can't go for a while, the engine's crapped out, mast repairs are still underway, and the sails need to be modified to fit the shortened mast," Ian replied with unworried resignation. Quiet Ian was about my age, and his gregarious sidekick Josh was just 19 years old. Their mood darkened when I told them I had been sent by the owner to take over organizing the repairs and captain the boat back to Hong Kong with them as my crew. Since I had never been into yacht racing, I was nobody to them. They had come out to Hong Kong from England where they had considered themselves hotshot yacht racing crew and repair technicians. Ian assumed he would be chosen captain and laughed out loud when I told him we needed to depart within three days.

"No frigging way to finish all this in three days," the younger Josh said. "Besides, I've got a girlfriend here I'm not ready to say goodbye to."

"She's not your girlfriend if you have to pay her, you twit," Ian admonished.

"Listen, guys," I said. "The owner is pissed, and he's not wiring another dollar here. He gave me just enough money to finish repairs, so you can either jump a plane back to Hong Kong today or help me get this boat ready to sail."

"The owner is pissed you say, ha-ha-ha," Josh guffawed. I then remembered the term pissed meant drunk to the English.

"That's Yank-speak. He means he's angry, you idiot," Ian corrected. "No reason he should be that I can see. It's not easy to get these blighters to work in this country."

Our meeting started off badly. Later our relations only got worse. But for the moment, the boys went back to work prepping the boat. We got the diesel mechanic to return and install the engine's broken alternator. All three of us spent two days fitting a new mast cap and attaching shortened rigging to the end of the broken mast. The local sailmaker never did get around to shortening the luff of the roller furling genoa so I decided to tie a knot in the sail near the head to shorten it enough to fit the reduced length of the roller furling tube.

Each evening after work my crew disappeared in a taxi to tour the girlie bars of Ermita, Manila's red-light district. They'd come back to the boat in the early hours, roaring drunk with their giggling girlfriends on their arms. Telling me I was missing out on something good, the guys insisted I join them for a romp on the town our last night in Manila. Since I didn't drink alcohol at the time and was too uptight to enjoy the paid companionship of some unknown hooker, my crew considered me a dull chaperone. We all stared up through the smoke and flashing colored lights at the bikini-clad girls dancing that half-hearted seductive twist and twirl around the poles on the raised walkway. My crewmates picked out two slender beauties to take back to the boat for the night. I felt a long distance sailor's loneliness: the need for the touch of a woman's heart and body. Before I reached for my wallet to seek that comfort, I remembered there would be no heart offered with the body. I had seen how the piercing, sober light of day transformed a beguiling beauty into a tired, pallid sex merchant, abandoned by makeup and allure. By morning she would want only to be paid, wander home, eat a meal and sleep until evening. She would awaken, put on her dress and heavy makeup, and go offer herself to the next forgettable man.

On the fourth morning after I arrived in Manila, my crew escorted their disheveled ladies to the front gate, and we got underway. I had hired as extra crew one of the young men, named Joy Hugo, who worked on boats at the yacht club. I knew that if the electric autopilot failed we would be hand-steering around the clock, and that would be much easier to do by splitting the watch between four persons. Additionally, having at least one unquestioningly loyal hand aboard would increase my chances of nursing this handicapped boat back to Hong Kong.

Powerless; Near Mutiny

Our nearly new Beneteau 51-foot racer presented a shabby sight as we sailed across the bay in light winds with a tangled knot of sail at the top of the jib and two reefs in the mainsail. That was all the sail we could carry with our shortened rig. Darkness fell as we sailed past Corregidor Island near the entrance to Manila Bay. Our fair wind died away to nothing in the wind shadow behind the mountains of Batan Peninsula. We restarted the engine and motored into the South China Sea, setting a course northwest for 600 miles.

Several hours later, both the boat's batteries went flat, and the engine died—sorry work by the Manila mechanic was back to haunt us. No one aboard had the skills or parts to get the iron beast rumbling again. Because this was a stripped down, lightweight racing boat, we had no backup generator, solar panels, or wind charger to recharge the batteries.

With no way to charge the batteries, we had no power to run the autopilot, lights, satellite navigation, wind instruments, or depth sounder. Worse yet, at least from the crew's point of view, the propane stove wouldn't fire up, and the freezer was rapidly getting warm, which meant their meats would soon go bad. For Ian and Josh the prospect of drinking warm beer was a major crisis. As we drifted in the currents, the crew and I jockeyed over our course of action. Or to put it directly, Ian and Josh demanded we turn and sail back to Manila, I refused, and Joy stood silent on the issue.

These sailing jocks began to whine like children. "There's no bleedin way we can go on with dead batteries. We have to sail back to Manila for repairs," Ian and Josh pleaded over and over while I pretended to weigh the merits of their plan. Now that I had finally gotten these two out of the brothels of Manila there was no way in hell I was going back. I needed to be diplomatic, which was damn tough for a man used to sailing alone. There is no dissent, no complaint, no arguing on a solo sailor's boat. Ian and Josh continued bleating like angry sheep. I stubbornly stood my ground, which is exactly what a crew can expect from their captain, be he right or wrong.

Finally, I told them the decision to carry on was final. "We can't turn back when the boat can still sail, guys. I know it will be a struggle, but there's no reason we can't finish this delivery. The owner hired me to bring the boat back without delay, and I promised him I would. Don't worry. I have my sextant for navigation. We have flashlights, and I can bypass the solenoid to get the stove working. It's not so bad. Hell, I sailed across the whole Pacific with no engine and the first half of the way without even any electrics."

"That's just bloody stupid!" Josh shouted. After scolding brought no response, Josh and Ian switched back to pleading. When Joy voted to carry on with my plan, the English boys glared at us in disbelief. That made it two against two now. There was tense silence as slow seconds passed. We each stood in our corners of the cockpit about to throw insults and fists like Irish pub drunks at closing time. I looked up and pointed to a new wind fluttering the untrimmed sails. With incredible relief, Joy and I trimmed the sails and set course for Hong Kong, as Ian and Josh went below to grumble and plot their next move. I leaned through the companionway hatch and told them I was setting the deck watch into four hours on and four off with Joy and myself on first watch.

The oversized steering wheel on this race boat was easy enough to handle, though turning it grew tiresome as the hours went by. The boat balanced surprisingly well and sailed fast enough with her reduced rig in the increasing beam winds of the northeast monsoon. I showed Joy the technique of steering by the angle of the waves, watching the sails for correct trim, and how to follow a guide star off the bow. We confirmed our course by occasional checks of the compass by flashlight. Four hours later, we had made good progress, covering about 25 miles when I called up the other watch to take over.

Within an hour of crawling into my bunk I awoke to the feeling that we had made a course change. A moment later the boat heeled onto the opposite tack, and I knew my mutinous English friends had turned the boat back toward Manila. I decided not to rush out to confront them. Instead, I rested in my bunk and waited. When our turn at watch came up, I awoke Joy, and we relieved the deck watch without speaking a word. After the mutineers got settled into their bunks, I tacked the boat back towards Hong Kong. I was certain I could play this crazy game longer than my opponents. On the next watch they held my course to Hong Kong and quit grumbling about turning back.

The wind held fair for the next four days. We close reached with winds just forward of the beam, maintaining six knots or better most of the time as we rose and fell to the high swell, occasionally slamming down hard into the trough between sets of the larger waves. We approached Hong Kong a couple hours after sunset on our fifth day out of Manila. I normally don't enter a port at night because of the obvious dangers, but having previously entered in daylight, I knew the courses and hazards well, had plenty of alert eyes on deck, and was unusually eager for this passage to be over. We had no power to call for a tow into the marina because of our dead batteries. "I'll shoot off a signal flare to alert a tugboat," Ian announced.

"We don't need all that drama, " I told him as I eased the flare pistol from his hand. Our good wind held as I maneuvered the boat under reduced sail into the typhoon shelter of Aberdeen. My crew waved over a passing sampan. We cast him a towline and minutes later glided into a slip at the marina. Ian and Josh were suddenly friendly towards me again now that we were back in port. Were they impressed with their captain's abilities after all? More likely, they did not want me to report negatively on their behavior to our mutual employer.

"Glad to see you back so soon," Mike Simpson said as he greeted me the next morning in his office. "How did the trip go?"

"Fine. No serious problems. Just dead batteries and a broken alternator," I told him as I collected my $900 dollar payment and another $200 and a plane ticket back to Manila for Joy. There was no need to upset him with all the details. Ian and Josh continued to work at Simpson Marine for a few more months before heading home to dreary England. My experience on my engineless Pacific crossing had paid off by giving me the skills and confidence needed to bring that crippled racing boat home.

Diplomacy and Survival When the Captain's Word is Law

Working as yacht delivery skipper has its ups and downs but is certainly better than being among the paid crew serfdom. I had worked my way up from that under-appreciated lowly caste in my early years of sailing. Soon after sailing *Atom* on our first trip from my home port in Detroit to the Bahamas, I sailed into the yachting Mecca of Fort Lauderdale, Florida to look for yacht-related employment. After signing up with a crew-finding service I was sent out to join a locally based sailboat as deckhand on a round-trip from Lauderdale to St. Petersburg, midway up the west coast of Florida. It was about a four-day trip each way with several days of unpaid layover at a St. Pete boatyard. The purpose of the trip was to have the boatyard saw off the bottom 12-inches of her lead keel, slice it up into smaller pieces and fiberglass them back into the inside of the bilge in order to reduce the 55-foot boat's unusually deep 8-foot draft. As it was, the boat could only leave or return to the dock on high tide. This modification would make it considerably easier to navigate shoal waters at the expense of raising her center of gravity, which would slightly reduce her ability to carry as much sail in strong winds—a reasonable tradeoff.

Our crew initially consisted of myself and another young sailor named Greg as the deckhands, the middle-aged Portuguese captain, and his wife. Minutes before our high-tide departure, a chubby young woman came swishing down the dock on short pudgy legs with her seabag over her shoulder. As I reached a hand down to help her aboard, she introduced herself as Miriam, our cook.

Our captain was full of imperial poise and dignity. His wife had learned to remain silent in his presence, and it was some time before I discovered she wasn't a mute. The captain's bald head and serious manner of speaking caused Greg to give him the nickname Kojak, after the detective in that 1970s TV crime drama. But our Kojak, I learned in the coming days, was a man of bluster, with limited practical sailing experience and a knack for making bad decisions. In my experience, a stern and officious manner is frequently a cover for fear or incompetence or both. The yacht he captained was owned by a Canadian corporation, which used it for executive vacations, hiring Kojak as their full-time caretaker and captain.

As we motored down the river and passed the breakwaters into the Atlantic, our captain literally laid out the rules of the boat by placing a typed three-page list in our hands. Crew would receive $50 per day and their meals while underway. The cook would serve all meals according to his detailed menu and timetable. To prevent a scalding from an errant pot, the cook was forbidden to approach the stove unless wearing full foul weather gear, including rubber boots. Miriam twisted up her perpetually pouting lips as if ready to protest. His majesty held her back with a raised finger, then turned to give further directions to Greg and me. "You two will do all the sail handling, under my direction, of course. And you will hand-steer, four hours on, four hours off, around the clock." His dour wife apparently had no duties at all, and during the trip she rarely left the confines of the aft cabin.

As I glanced over his shoulder at the windvane self-steering mechanism bolted onto the transom, I asked, "Aren't we going to use the windvane at all?"

"No. You'll keep a more alert watch if you hand steer," he said with a tone of finality. There was some truth in that, but it was absurd to have the two of us laboriously hand-steering four hours on and off, throughout the days and nights ahead when there were five people aboard to share that tedious task. And why, I wondered, was a windvane installed but not to be used when steering the boat was exactly what it was meant to do? Perhaps his preference for hand-steering may have been to cover for his inability to understand how the newly installed windvane operated.

Our skipper laid a course to round Key West but, for reasons known only to him, kept us far enough offshore that we were bucking into the strong current of the Gulf Stream. As Greg steered into the fresh southeast wind that first night, I squeezed into my bunk in the forward shoebox of the crew's quarters. Our tiny cabin was at the very front of the boat where a more sensible designer would have placed the chain locker and sail stowage compartments followed by the forward head. It was located so close to the pointed bow where the motion was worst, that my body was frequently airborne as the bow plunged into the head seas. After two days, I was seriously fatigued from alternating from swinging the steering wheel while fixating on the compass and bracing myself in my bunk as if in a perpetual barrel ride over Niagara Falls. Greg took it about as well as I did, with grim, quiet determination as we counted the days, hours, and minutes to landfall.

When we finally turned downwind, our gallant skipper announced it was time to fly the spinnaker sail. Greg and I managed to get the huge billowing nylon sail and its aluminum pole rigged and drawing, despite our commander's mistaken orders on course adjustments and which lines to set first. When the time came to turn our course more upwind and drop the spinnaker, Kojak ordered Greg to climb onto the boom and remove the spinnaker pole fitting from its bracket on the mast. The 15-foot-long pole was under tremendous pressure from the wind filling the sail attached to its outer end. I suggested to the captain that we should first either turn downwind and ease out the control line of the pole or gybe the mainsail over to provide a wind shadow to lessen the pressure on the pole. My proposal was dismissed with an imperial wave of the hand. Since the captain insisted it be done his way, Greg climbed up and attempted to lift the pole from its bracket. It wouldn't budge. "Push harder!" Kojak ordered. After a mighty shove, the pole popped up and shot back, punching a nice hole in the mainsail and nearly mangling Greg's hand. Kojak nearly fell down from fright as the plunging pole missed his head by a few inches. We wrestled the wildly flogging sail to the deck, stowed the pole, and patched the mainsail. That was the last time the spinnaker was used or mentioned.

In some respects, the cook was even less fortunate than us miserable deckhands. Our skipper demanded hearty cooked meals: always a thick fried steak and potatoes with vegetable side dishes for dinner, no matter the heat of day or angle of the boat's heel. During one meal prep, Miriam finally stripped off her plastic rain pants, jacket and boots. Streaming sweat, she turned to Kojak who was sitting at the table next to a fan, sipping his coffee, and announced, "I'm not wearing this crap any longer. It's too dammed hot to cook in this gear!" To everyone's relief, they compromised by agreeing she would wear only the partly-zipped raincoat over her normal clothes, without the boots and pants. As I rested on the off-watch the last night before arriving in St. Pete, poor pudgy Miriam, reeking of fried steak, onions, and sweat, crawled on top of me in my narrow bunk, and cooed into my ear: "I found a jug of insecticide in the pantry locker. I'm going to put it in the bastard's food." She sounded serious and was obviously becoming unhinged. The look of anger and then lust on her face made me squirm out from under her considerable weight.

I tried to console her as we lay there squished side by side with noses almost touching: "Don't worry about him. The trip will be over soon enough." Then I turned over and hinted that she should return to her bunk so that I could get some sleep. Apparently, she didn't appreciate my advice or my refusal to sleep together, because the next morning the coffee she handed me tasted as if it had been laced with a spoonful of salt. Maybe confusing the salt for sugar was an honest mistake? At least it wasn't poison, I hoped, as I dumped the brew over the side. Just as she had stood up to the captain, perhaps Miriam felt it was her task to teach me some humility around a needy woman.

As the captain navigated his way into the harbor of St. Pete on a clear, calm night, he ran us aground on a clearly charted sandbar. Instead of dropping an anchor and waiting for the tide to rise, he ordered Greg and me to launch the inflatable dinghy and carry out a 60-pound anchor on the end of a 200-foot-long rode. Then we pulled ourselves back aboard and ground the rode in on the cockpit sheet winch to attempt to pull the boat backwards into deeper water. By the time the anchor was set and tensioned, the tide had dropped further, heeling the boat and leaving her hopelessly stuck. I mentioned to Kojak we could wait for the next tide to float the boat. Instead, we were directed to continue grinding in the rode by hand. Since the boat was immovable, we only succeeded, after much effort, in winching the anchor back to the boat. We were directed to take it out again and repeat the procedure, plowing another slow furrow into the sand. We felt like harnessed mules struggling to plow a field of hard-packed soil. With our young strong backs nearly broken, our skipper finally concluded we should wait for the morning tide to lift the boat free. Greg and I climbed exhausted into our bunks, which slowly canted over and then floated back upright with the cycle of the tide.

The next day we moved into the marina where a travel-lift hauled the boat out of the water and set it on blocks and jackstands. Boatyard workers began sawing off the excess keel while Greg and I washed the boat, stowed the seagoing gear, and repaired the many items that had broken down on the trip. The next morning we expected a day off to visit the town, but the captain told us to help him with a "little job." It turned out the yard workers were only contracted to cut the keel, and it was up to Greg and me to hoist the heavy lead blocks up, carry them into the bilge, and assist with fiberglassing them into position. I reminded the captain that according to his list of duties we weren't being paid while in port and that he should cough up the extra $50 a day if he wanted us hauling ballast. The demand infuriated him, but he reluctantly agreed.

Our return trip to Lauderdale was slightly less awful, not only because we were no longer hopeful of anything other than a hard and stressful passage, and therefore could not be let down any further, but also because we caught a lift from the Gulf Stream current once we rounded Key West, which gave our speed a welcome boost. I was by now lacking any faith that our captain and his massive ego could get us safely home.

As I steered us homeward through a black night off the Florida Keys, Kojak poked his head up out of the companionway and told me the course was now changed from 80 degrees to 30 degrees, or from nearly east to closer to north, and then returned to his soft bed in the aft cabin. I thought our course change premature because I knew the reefs off the low islets of the Keys lay a few short miles to the north. But what could I do? He was still the captain and navigator, and he had not invited me to look at his charts. With an uneasy feeling, I altered course as directed. In a few minutes I rushed below to call Greg to take the wheel while I went to the navigation table and quietly checked the chart. The last thing a professional captain appreciates is having some unlettered deck swabbie questioning his navigation.

This was back in the days when Satnav first became available on yachts. The $4,000 Satnav box, not much smaller than a microwave oven, tracked just a couple of satellites that provided a position fix about once every 90 minutes as a satellite came into view above the horizon. I turned on the hallowed magical machine for the first time, and luckily it latched on to a satellite within a few minutes. I copied down the position numbers. When I transferred them to our chart I saw that Kojak had misread one digit of longitude, placing us almost 60 miles east of our true position. Worst of all, just as I had suspected, we were headed directly for the reefs only a few miles ahead. If we struck them at this speed with these high waves running we all would most likely drown. I debated with myself just a moment on how to break the news to our master before knocking on his door. When he came out, I told him in as meek a fashion as I could muster, that the machine must have been in error earlier because now it said we were heading for the reefs. He studied the numbers and the chart position and then said, "Of course. Change course back to 80 degrees."

When Kojak wasn't telling us "no," he always said "of course." Over the years, whenever Greg and I met again, we greeted each other with "Of course!" That experience made me reluctant to sail again as crew on another captain's vessel. But it did not change my basic belief in the strict hierarchy in which the captain's word is law. Crew are there to follow orders, no matter how they feel about them. A more democratic approach—in which each person aboard is consulted on his or her opinions and feelings—sounds wonderfully progressive. Occasionally that can work if all aboard are of the same mind and experience level. But more often it invites chaos. Kojak had put a strain on my belief in the unassailable captain. That belief would soon be put to the test again when we got underway on *Cocachin*.

11 Marco Polo Schemes

*Sailing a thousand miles downwind is preferable
to one hundred miles against the wind.*

Once I had returned from the Manila to Hong Kong delivery, I resumed my volunteer work on the junk *Cocachin*. Over the past months some of *Cocachin*'s crew had lost interest due to delays in fitting out and had drifted away as other new faces joined us. Currently our crew, all in their twenties, consisted of a lead deckhand from England named Rex; our English cook, Kate; and a Canadian named Wendy, who joined as the Moran children's nanny and home-school teacher. There were also two more apprentice deckhands, Choi and Yin, teenagers on loan from a Hong Kong maritime academy. These Chinese boys were somewhat mystified to find themselves on an extinct class of sailing junk when they expected the academy to prepare them for the modern merchant marine service. They had never been aboard a sailing vessel before and were at first understandably bewildered. Even so, they worked as hard as any of us and learned the ropes quickly. Because their English was limited, working alongside them gave me another opportunity to learn Cantonese. Wayne Moran already spoke passable Cantonese after living in the colony for nine years. His fluency in the language enabled him to work effectively with the Chinese-speaking carpenters and shipwrights on this project as well as the Hong Kong and mainland Chinese bureaucrats in charge of the stacks of licenses and permits required for a project of this scale.

Cocachin was modeled after ships built during the pinnacle of Chinese junk design, before Europeans arrived in very different-looking vessels at the end of the 15th century. Her transverse watertight bulkheads divided the boat into sections much like the segmented joints of bamboo. These partitions not only strengthened the hull and deck but also provided reserve buoyancy in case of flooding. The *Titanic* had a similar design but was flawed by not having the bulkheads carried all the way up to the deck, allowing the weight of water in the forward sections to lower the bow and spill water over the tops of the bulkheads, flooding one section after the other until she went down in the icy waters of the North Atlantic. In theory, *Cocachin* would not sink so easily.

On *Cocachin*'s deck, the anchors and sails were hoisted by manually turning 4-foot-long spoke handles on archaic but functional wooden capstan windlass drums resting in heavy timber chocks. Steering with the boat's ten-foot tiller was also laborious. To control the heavy, barn door-style rudder when under sail in anything but the lightest winds, required two men working in unison to heave the rope and block tackle attached to either side of the tiller. This wooden rudder could be raised and lowered by other tackle to balance helm and leeway for different sail angles and wind strength combinations. Her three sails were set on individual masts. The Chinese had developed sails set fore and aft, which enabled them to sail to windward, long before Europeans, who at that time still used galley oars and crude square sails incapable of sailing upwind. Although the junk sails were simpler to operate than the equivalent sails on an old European square-rigger, they still required a coordinated and strenuous effort by the crew to handle them because of their enormous size and weight.

Even today, some Western cruising yacht owners, looking for a distinctive and simple rig, have opted for one of several versions of the junk rig. As set up on *Cocachin*, the rig could be described in Western terms as a fully battened standing lug, where the sails ride on one side of the mast with their ends extending forward of the masts by several feet. Every few feet from the foot of the sails to their heads were horizontal bamboo battens, each of which was brailed to the mast with rope. When the vessel is underway, the sail presses against the mast on one tack. On the other tack the brails hold the sail from bowing excessively away from the mast. By the standards of a Bermudan-rigged sloop like *Atom*, the junk rig, even in its modern versions, is not particularly efficient for sailing to windward and is frustratingly slow in light winds. Yet the junk rig remains a desirable alternative for those sailors who value its other benefits such as ease of reefing.

Another Troubled Engine; Ten Miles of Motion Versus One Mile to Windward

What was not at all traditional on *Cocachin*—the diesel inboard engine coupled to a donated hydrojet propulsion system—would become one of her most troublesome features. In theory, the water-jet drive was easier to install and perhaps created less drag than conventional propellers. In practice, we later learned that the amount of thrust was pitifully small, partly due to the less-than-ideal angle of the water-jet exhaust, and we were obliged to sail our awkward vessel as if she were engineless. If it had been up to me, the voyage would have been completed in a historically accurate way by having no engine aboard at all. Each time a historical reenactment voyage is organized, one of the main decisions made is how closely to follow the equipment used on the original voyage, from the craft itself to the clothing and food for the crew. The closer to original they can make it, the more relevant and interesting will be the results. But sailing an engineless boat whose size restricts her ability to maneuver would be an unacceptable risk for most of the crew as well as the sponsors. The water-jet design defect was a huge disappointment for Wayne and became a constant worry for him as he devoted much time and resources to various attempts to get the propulsion system working. One problem with technology is that as it serves you it often enslaves you. Our captain and many of the crew, as well as the scientific guests who planned to join the expedition, were understandably unable to accept the liabilities and logistics of sailing the vessel in a purely traditional manner.

After we had completed a couple of test sails on *Cocachin* in local waters, we felt ready to depart for a voyage up the coast of China towards Shanghai. We motored the junk out of Aberdeen at full throttle, which allowed us to crawl along at barely three knots in the calm waters of the harbor. Once we entered more open waters, we shut down the engine, and all hands worked the manual windlasses for most of an hour to hoist and trim the three tanbark sails. Traditionally, a junk's natural fiber sails were sometimes treated for rot by dying them in pig's blood. On *Cocachin*, the pigs' lives were spared because the sailcloth was of a stronger and longer-lasting synthetic blend made to look and feel like heavy canvas.

Cocachin under sail in Hong Kong

Under full sail, the junk was a magnificent sight, heeling sharply and making way smoothly through the breaking seas as we sheeted in the sails and brought her bow close to the wind. All that seeming chaos of heavy sailcloth, timber yards, and bamboo battens aloft worked together synchronously, harnessing the wind to drive this ungainly, 75-ton vessel through the seas. For a better view, Wayne, Rex, and I climbed the mainsail by using the bamboo battens and rope brails as foot and handholds and then eased our way cautiously out along the sail near the upper yard. We stayed just long enough to take in the stunning view of the ship rolling below us and then climbed down before a wind shift or inattentive helmsperson caused an accidental gybe of the sail, flinging us into the sea like flies on a horse's swishing tail.

The northeast monsoon of spring was still in force as we lumbered along, tacking our way up the China coast towards Shanghai. Progress was slow at best. Despite the promising wind tunnel tests Wayne had commissioned on a scale model of *Cocachin* in Europe, in the real world she performed miserably when pressed to windward. Although in ideal conditions we could hold a course 60 degrees off the wind, the leeway caused by her shallow keel combined with the wind-driven current to set us back so far that we sailed ten miles for every mile we gained to windward. And that was on a good day while carrying full sail in a moderate wind. On a smaller junk-rigged yacht, tacking is sometimes accomplished by swinging the bow through the wind as on a modern Western rig, but on *Cocachin*, with her slow speed and high windage, that maneuver was rarely possible, so we usually "wore ship" (turned downwind and gybed the sails over to the other tack). I was not as disappointed in her performance as Wayne because I had expected nothing more. It was well known that the ships of ancient design had serious limitations when sailing to windward.

With the winds increasing on the second day out, we reefed the sails to reduce heeling and leeway. The chaos of reefing, with wildly swinging yards and sheets, kept us alert and busy. Meanwhile, as navigator, I took compass bearings off prominent points on headlands along the coast and found we were barely holding our ground, making almost no progress to windward—disappointing to all aboard, but I was not surprised: ancient Chinese junks did not generally attempt passages to windward. They waited for the right seasonal winds to carry them to their destinations and then waited again for the season to change and the monsoon winds to reverse before coming home. We should have been sailing southwest at this time during the spring season, not fighting our way northeast against the monsoon. Even so, the attempt to sail to windward, though largely futile, was a useful and necessary step in discovering the boat's limitations.

The Court Eunuch Admiral; Wayne's Nightmare

Despite their limitations, junks were in many ways far superior to ancient European vessels. Less than a century after Marco Polo sailed with his fleet of Imperial junks to the Persian Gulf, the Mongol rulers of China were overthrown, and a native emperor of the Ming Dynasty unified China. The Mings were eager to assert their dominance and trade beyond China. They appointed their capable court eunuch, Zheng He, to be Admiral of the Imperial fleet. Generations before Columbus arrived in the New World, the masterful navigator Zheng He had already made seven epic voyages from China into the Pacific and Indian Oceans, reaching beyond the Persian Gulf to the east coast of Africa. Some suggest he may even have rounded the Cape of Good Hope and sailed some distance into the Atlantic. His flotillas contained upwards of 200 ships, some up to an astonishing 400 feet long, sailed by crews of over 20,000 men. This record dwarfs Columbus's first fleet of three ships, each much less than 100 feet long.

Not only were Zheng He's grand expeditions meant to impress the barbarian rulers with the might of the Middle Kingdom; the ships also carried vast amounts of treasure in the form of gold, silver, silks, porcelain, and other valuable products from China. Such items were given as gifts to the kings of over a dozen countries where Zheng He's fleets anchored. You can imagine the stunned local rulers waking up one day to see Zheng He's magnificent fleet of ships completely filling their harbor and hundreds of Chinese diplomats and soldiers coming ashore to present their gifts. In return, those awestruck rulers were "encouraged" to recognize the Middle Kingdom's dominion over "all under heaven" and provide tribute and gifts of suitable value and rarity to the Dragon Throne's Son of Heaven. It was this naval shock and awe that no doubt avoided armed revolts of natives like those encountered by the relatively small and weak European fleets on their voyages of discovery. Besides new medicinal plants and spices, the Zheng He's ships brought home to Nanking such exotica as lions and zebras. Even giraffes were delivered to the Celestial Zoo for the amusement of the emperor.

Just before our departure from Hong Kong, we were joined by Vlad, our final addition to the crew. Vlad was a young aspiring Canadian filmmaker who came aboard lugging several bags of expensive camera equipment with the plan to document the voyage. Although Wayne had invited him for that purpose, once Vlad began setting up his camera for filming on our first day underway, Wayne gruffly told him, "Put that camera equipment away, can't you see we're busy and there's no time for filming now?" That seemed odd to me, but I figured Wayne was just nervous about getting underway, without what he considered a disruption for filming. Vlad dutifully stowed the camera and helped to work the boat with the rest of us on deck. My suspicion that something was not right between Vlad and Wayne was confirmed over the next week as Wayne chased and hounded Vlad around the deck each day, demanding loudly "Put that camera away!" Wayne had invited Vlad here to make a documentary. Now that he was here, Wayne inexplicably would not permit any filming. For some unknown reason, Wayne had changed his mind about making the film but was not ready to say what the problem was. It seemed he was looking for a way to annoy Vlad to the point where he would willingly give up and return home.

I later learned Wayne had sold the rights for a book to be written on the voyage and had received a cash advance from Bantam Press. Perhaps his publishers had a clause pertaining to movie rights, or possibly Wayne was looking for a better film deal elsewhere. Or maybe Wayne was coming to suspect that the voyage was doomed and did not want a film out there advertising that fact. In any case, at the time we were all mystified by Wayne's behavior and felt sympathy for Vlad's predicament. I knew that Wayne was constantly working on hunting down sponsors and companies to donate money and equipment for the boat. What we didn't know then was that Wayne had invested all of his personal savings, over $200,000 U.S. in the project. After a year of delays in building and fitting out, he was now on the edge of bankruptcy, trying desperately to keep ahead of his creditors. The Marco Polo Voyage deadlines were being missed, and his sponsors required constant reassuring.

All these stresses were understandably weighing heavily on Wayne at the time. Little by little they piled up to the point where they were affecting his behavior. He began to spend long hours in his cabin. When Wayne came on deck, on some days he seemed drugged or in a fit of manic depression. He sat silently for extended periods, then had unreasonable outbursts of temper directed at everyone around him, which seemed so out of character from what I had known of him before we got underway. Theresa was quietly nervous and upset with Wayne's behavior but kept their troubles mostly to herself while doing her best to shield the children from their father's problems. A few of us were mostly exempted from his abuse, possibly because he realized we were indispensable at this point, but Vlad and the Chinese boat boys caught hell over and over again. One evening Wayne sat with me at the galley table, his eyes red and watery and his speech slurred from alcohol and, I suspected, self-prescribed medication, as he confided to me: "I don't know how I'm going to make this whole thing work. The bank is all over me for money and may confiscate the boat when we return to Hong Kong if I don't find more sponsors immediately. I'm not going back to being a doctor; I hate sick people. I mean, they're always complaining." Wayne looked aside with a thousand mile stare, unaware of the humorous irony of a doctor so averse to treating the ill. Wayne's daring vision, his heart's pride and joy, now lay in financial and personal ruins. He was struggling to hold body and soul and ship together. The expedition seemed doomed and returning to a career in medicine looked doubtful. His dream had turned into a nightmare that was going to darken further before the journey was over.

After two days we gave up our futile attempt to beat against the relentless monsoon winds. We eased her sheets and altered course to run free with the wind behind us. *Cocachin* had been made for downwind sailing. You could hear the relief in her creaking timbers as she seemed to revel in plowing her course ahead with winged-out sails. In a day we had sailed past Hong Kong and were carrying on towards Macau.

With our hydrojet ineffective against wind and current, Wayne arranged by VHF radio for a tugboat to meet us outside the Macau harbor entrance to tow us into the anchorage. The powerful ocean-going tug approached us as we were hastily lowering the sails. The tug crewman threw a monkey's fist messenger line onto our deck, which we grabbed to haul in the tug's heavier towline. Wayne began winding and lashing the towline to the base of the main mast. There was a confusing tangle of lines and halyards with Wayne standing in the middle. Vlad and the Chinese boys moved in to assist Wayne in untangling the mess. I looked up and noticed the tugboat was moving forward and the towline beginning to come under tension. "Get back!" I shouted as I pulled Vlad and the boys free of the ropes. I looked on in horror to see Wayne had somehow gotten himself wound up in the towline. At the last possible second, he lifted the lines over his head and ducked below them as they came screeching taught against the mast. One fatal second separated Wayne from being pinned to the mast like Captain Ahab fatally entangled by the lines of his own harpoons in the flesh of *Moby Dick*. The incident reminded me how inherently dangerous big boats are. Most people assume it is far more risky to cross oceans on a small boat. In fact, it is the bigger boat, with its lethal swinging spars and highly loaded lines for sails, anchors, and towlines, that is more likely to maim or kill you.

For over 400 years the tiny enclave of Portugal on the Pearl River Delta has been a trading port similar to the larger British colony in Hong Kong. Macau was to be handed back to Communist China in 1999, two years after the Hong Kong handover, when its land lease expired. Meanwhile, the economically significant trading and manufacturing center worked hard to make a profit before "the handover." Beyond marking an end of a political era, the term "handover" was used in a solemn and sparing way by the locals and resident expats in both these colonies as if discussing their mutual execution dates. For now, Macau also profited as a tourist destination due primarily to legalized gambling at its increasingly popular casinos.

I took a morning stroll across the length of the territory from the harbor to the border gate to communist China. The ornate border archway contained an inscription from 1849 in Portuguese: "Honor your motherland, for your motherland looks over you," which, I suppose, refers to the border skirmishes that had taken place there between Portuguese and Chinese troops in previous centuries. On my walk across Macau, I marveled at the juxtaposition of ancient stone cathedrals squatting next to modern apartment blocks, the old castle-like fortress on Persimmon Hill with its now broken view of the sea through high-rise office buildings, a mini-state as densely populated as Hong Kong and still under construction after four centuries.

Though small in size, Macau physically grew perceptibly bigger by the day. Land reclamation, they called it. As hardhat brutes waved their arms and unrolled their diagrams, dynamite and machines bit into the mountain, and dump trucks hauled the rocks and trees away. The insatiable excavators had already nearly leveled the mountains of two neighboring islands and plowed the earth into the shallow sea. Over the years they had transformed the main one-square-mile island into a peninsula of eight square miles. As happened in Hong Kong, landowners in Macau should be prepared to see their waterfront property of today located one block or one mile inland sometime in the near future. They have big plans, those builders. Out with the rocks and trees. Dump them in the sea. In with the towers of concrete, glass, and steel sleaze. Dig deeper, build higher. Go wall-to-wall and block the sun from the sky. Tear down the old and build anew. Those builders won't be denied. They need to build as much as I need to roam as far from them as I can get.

From my inland tour I turned to explore the waterfront. I had brought my Hawaiian kayak with me aboard *Cocachin,* which I now used to paddle around the harbor and the two islands south of the peninsula.

Paddling Macau, Drifting Back to . . . Minnesota!

I took my time, dipping the double-bladed kayak paddle at a leisurely pace. My mind started to disengage from the stresses of the junk voyage and untether from the locale. I mentally noted this speck of a country was only about half the size of my grandparents' farm in northwestern Minnesota, where I had spent considerable time in my early teens. My exasperated parents had wisely loaned out their headstrong and troublesome only child to assist with the hard labor of the hay and wheat harvests. More exciting to me, while there I accompanied my grandparents to a steer auction and somehow managed to talk them into buying me a kicking chestnut stallion. We brought the as yet unbroken and headstrong stallion back to the farm where my uncle taught me how to break the horse and use him to herd cattle. After a deranged bull gored my horse in his shoulder, my grandfather had me help him pen and tie up the mad bull while he cut his deadly horns off with a handsaw. I hadn't expected the horn cuts to suddenly spray blood in my face. I held fast to the ropes in my grip as the bull cried out in pain and jerked around trying to knock down the stall. The bull and the horse both soon healed. I developed a close bond with that stallion, even though early on he tried some tricks to be rid of me. The character-building experience on the wide-open plains cultivated within me a love of great open spaces and a vigorous outdoor life. Strangely enough, that summer on the farm helped steer a boy from the suburbs of Detroit towards two decades of travel on the sea.

Breaking a working horse is something like training an inexperienced crew on a sailboat headed for troubled waters. First, you need to gain their trust and respect by a combination of kindness and a display of firm control and competence. When I first successfully cinched the saddle's girth strap and pulled myself onto my horse's back, we didn't go far before the saddle came loose and rotated downwards until I was dumped headfirst onto the ground. I told my sour Scandinavian grandfather, Gunnar Bodell, of the problem. He nodded his capped, bald head and climbed down from his tractor to assist me. My grandfather spoke sparingly, as if words cost him a dollar each. Physically he resembled the stern-faced man holding a pitchfork in Wood's famous *American Gothic* painting of the Midwestern farmer and his spinster daughter. Grandpa wordlessly threw the saddle over the stallion's back, cinched the girth strap, waited a few seconds, and then sharply raised his knee to strike the horse's belly. As the surprised horse let out a gasp of air, grandpa Gunnar pulled the girth strap several inches tighter. "That'll do it," was his three-dollar reply as he walked back to his tractor.

It seemed my clever horse had tricked me by sucking in a deep breath and extending his belly as I cinched the saddle so that later he could exhale and roll me from his back. Like a captain getting to know the habits of a new crewmember, that horse and I eventually grew to respect each other. We learned our respective positions in the relationship and how to work together as a team. At 14, I was too young to borrow my grandparents' car, so I rode that horse all over the county, including repeated visits to one neighboring farm where I tasted my first bottle of Grain Belt beer and shared a first kiss with a farmer's friendly daughter. My adolescent passions were cooled somewhat when the girl later informed me in the backseat of my older cousin's '58 Chevy at the drive-in movie that she was my second cousin. I learned I would have to ride far and wide to meet an unrelated girl in that kin-filled county.

At one point I was so infatuated with the cowboy life, coupled with dreams inspired by works such as Jack London's *Call of the Wild*, that I pored over maps from Minnesota to the Yukon, seriously considering a solo horseback trip from the farm all the way to the Klondike goldfields. The difficult logistics and practicalities of that plan eventually turned my quest from a horse trip to a boat journey. Like galloping on horseback at dizzying speed through fields of waving wheat until those grain silos dropped below the horizon behind me, riding *Atom* across the seas towards a setting sun was for me all about solo exploration and the physical effort of harnessing nature to take me to new places.

Shenzen Bound; Mao Saves Face, Millions Die

While in Macau, Wayne arranged for the local boatyard to haul *Cocachin*. Portuguese mechanics came aboard and worked for two days modifying the hydrojet in hopes of better performance. Some of us in the crew assisted the boatyard workers in hammering in new caulking, then tarring and painting the seams between the hull planks in areas that were leaking. Tensions aboard eased now that we were ashore and could come and go from the boat, while Wayne engaged his energies in directing the boatyard workers. One evening, our captain led the entire crew out to dinner at a pricey Macanese restaurant. It was a treat I knew he could ill afford, but his thoughtful gesture softened some hard feelings among the grumbling crew. Our table was loaded with local seafoods and vegetables, coconut curries, Portuguese bread, wine, and cheese, all cooked in a fusion of cuisines from China and Portugal. Late that evening we strolled home along the worn cobblestone streets of the old town, passing between rows of centuries-old stone buildings. Any bad feelings among us were temporarily erased by a night on the town and bellies full of hearty Portuguese food and wine.

With slightly increased engine performance, we motored our way somewhat apprehensively out of Macau Harbor, headed for Shenzhen, a Chinese port city located just a day's sail away. A couple hours after the sails were fully set and trimmed, it was time to begin orchestrating dropping them to prepare for entering port. As we tied up along the commercial quay in Shenzhen, *Cocachin* was swarmed with curious police officials and reporters whom Wayne had earlier alerted to our planned arrival. Through months of prior negotiations with Chinese officials, Wayne had secured permission for his historic vessel to visit here and several other selected ports in China. At the time, Shenzen was growing fast, having recently been designated a Special Economic Zone by the communist government whose officials were hoping to compete financially with Hong Kong, although in a very restricted way. Within a few years, this once-forgotten, poorer sister city of Hong Kong would become one of China's main manufacturing and economic centers.

Going aloft in Chinese waters

After an hour of seemingly intense discussions with the police, Wayne collected our passports and left with the police to get our documents stamped by the chief of customs and immigration. In his absence, Theresa and the children entertained the reporters with stories of retracing the route of Marco Polo, to whom they had never been introduced in their communist schooling. One elderly official left us an English translation of the *Little Red Book*—a collection of Chairman Mao Zedong's thoughts on everything from agriculture to how to defeat the "reactionary paper tiger of Western Imperialism." The text is second only to the Bible in circulation, with over a billion copies printed since the 1960s. The book helped fuel the cult of Mao up until the end of the disastrous Cultural Revolution.

Travel well and long and you are forced to open your eyes. Spend enough time at a place and the depth of its history settles upon your mind and emotions. The story of China's disastrous turn towards Mao had that effect on me.

That once sacred text of Mao was so widely distributed in China that printers were forced to cancel most other works. Soldiers and illiterate farmers alike were required to publicly recite passages from the pocket-sized ideological weapon of political struggle. To damage a copy of the *Little Red Book* was to risk imprisonment. Recent generations of communists around the world have read Mao's writings, apparently oblivious to the uncomfortable fact that he was responsible for the largest acts of genocide in human history.

Mao's Great Leap Forward program, begun in 1958, in which he collectivized farms and sacrificed food production to increase industrialization, caused up to 45 million Chinese deaths. Mao casually observed at the time, "When there is not enough to eat, people starve to death. It is better to let half of the people die so that the other half can eat their fill." His politically induced famine was reinforced by mass executions of anyone considered to have criticized the program or not to have contributed enough to its success. The Communist party's militias murdered millions of peasants through starvation and even by beating them with sticks or burying them alive. Perhaps over a million more committed suicide rather than submitting to the continued torture. Others survived by eating the dead. With people starving to death throughout the country, the Great Denier Mao, in order to save face internationally, continued to export to Africa and Cuba the dwindling grain supply that could have saved millions of lives at home. After the Great Leap Forward plunged the country backwards and temporarily lessened Mao's popularity, he changed course by launching the idiotic Cultural Revolution. Although somewhat less lethal, that program further devastated people's lives. Mindless recriminations against "bourgeois elements" set neighbor against neighbor and sons against their fathers. Mao's program predictably resulted in unprecedented cultural devastation as members of the Red Guard destroyed shrines and temples and arbitrarily tortured tens of thousands of innocent people in their program of violent class struggle to purify the communist state. Many Chinese prefer not to discuss openly or obsess over past crimes as we do in the West. But editing history is dangerous work. When the outrageous crimes of Maoism are quietly ignored, variations of the same theme are likely to be repeated. With a seemingly unlimited capacity for ignorance and historic sophistry, in 2013 those in China who wished to resurrect their perceived glorious leader, reissued a newly edited *Little Red Book*.

A people who abandon an established religion, such as Buddhism or Christianity, will create another to take its place. The vacuum of the mind will construct its religion around prophets or politics. New religions—whether the seemingly benign government mind control of liberal socialism, a death cult in Waco, Texas, Communism, Fascism, or the latest evil of a resurgent Islamic Caliphate—are typically the most dangerous because the heated zealotry they inspire has not yet undergone the cooling effects of time. What they have in common is that they are all at war with individual freedom to some extent. A culture whose religion strikes the right balance between the freedom of the individual and the common social good must remain forever vigilant in order not to fall from the cultural high wire their society has erected.

Thousands of generations of humans have painstakingly built up our civilization to a point where we can comfortably sit back and criticize our neighbors for minor differences of opinion, while the barbarians rush through the gates to wreak their havoc. To my simple mind it seems that a civilization is raised like a family—teach the children with compassionate discipline, give them a sense of purpose, a direction to travel, align their moral compass. Then the hard part comes as they begin to mature, when you must decide to intervene or step back and risk having them tear your world apart.

Although while aboard *Cocachin* I only had time to skim through
Mao's moronic manifesto, I did read it thoroughly a few years later when
I captained a transatlantic delivery and found out too late the only two
books aboard were the Yanmar engine manual in seven languages—and
the damned *Little Red Book*. Perhaps that liberal-minded yacht owner had
placed the book aboard with the same goal as the missionary
organization that endeavored to place a copy of Gideon's Bible in every
American hotel room. If you were locked in a hotel room without
television for a month, you would emerge well versed from Genesis to
Revelation. Just as surely by the time that delivery trip was over I could
have overhauled the engine in at least three languages and quoted Mao
as well as the Pope quotes scripture.

Sudden Anger; Safe in Hong Kong

When Wayne returned with our passports from the immigration
office, he looked harried and frustrated. For reasons unexplained, he
told the crew we would be departing the next morning for another
unnamed Chinese port. Throughout that day and night we remained
under surveillance by several guards who gazed down at us from the
quay. Their presence obviously agitated Wayne further. The following
morning Wayne accompanied a government official back to the
immigration office to clear out for our next port. When he returned we
began preparing *Cocachin* for departure. Just then a uniformed official
came rushing down the quay waving his hands. He jumped onto the
deck and asked Wayne to delay departure because some neglected
department head felt one more stamp was needed for our clearance
papers. You might think that Wayne, with his vast experience with the
Chinese bureaucracy and fluency in the culture and language, would
handle this minor request with diplomatic ease. So what did he actually
do? He pointed his finger an inch from the man's nose and screamed in
Chinese something along the lines of: "Get off my boat this instant. This

is British property. I know what you are up to, and I will not tolerate your trickery."

As Wayne verbally pinned the poor short man against the bulwarks, for the first time I felt sympathy for a bureaucrat. The stunned official retreated backwards onto the dock as if in a one-sided sword fight with our captain whose finger was a swinging blade. Meanwhile, Wayne ordered us to start the engine and cast off the dock lines. Wayne pushed the engine throttle lever to full ahead. *Cocachin* pulled hesitantly away from the dock still dragging her mooring lines through the water. Dozens of onlookers gaped at us from the shore. Addressing no one in particular, Wayne continued his string of insults and accusations of bribery and trickery against the port officials as he set a course to bring us back into Hong Kong waters. "All hands hoist sail and make it smart!" Wayne shouted from the helm. The sails got set in record time. Sensing our hasty departure was not the end of the incident, I picked up the binoculars and scanned the shoreline behind us. Within a few minutes I spotted a boat speeding towards us from shore. I'll admit to a rising panic as I went directly to the navigation room and made a "Security" call on the VHF radio to the Royal Hong Kong Marine Police, reporting to them that we required a police escort because of a possible pirate attack. I told them that we were we still a few miles outside Hong Kong's territorial waters and that we would attempt to meet them at their sea border. I knew my ruse risked dragging all of us into an international incident, but desperate moments call for creative thinking. I couldn't just tell them the truth, that we had run away from port officials in Shenzen for no apparent reason and were now being pursued by a Chinese government patrol boat. I was on Wayne's side in at least one respect—I certainly did not want to sit in a Chinese prison cell that night. Wayne had reached his breaking point and had caught the Chinese obstructers off guard, much as my wily grandfather had kneed my uncooperative horse in the gut. And just as my horse capitulated, the Chinese police later let Wayne back in the country.

With *Cocachin*'s jetdrive at full thrust and all her sails hoisted and trimmed to take best advantage of the fair wind, we watched nervously astern as the Chinese police boat gained on us. As they got closer I could make out their waving arms trying to get our attention. Closer yet, I saw armed and uniformed police or navy personnel on the foredeck. As they pulled alongside, demanding we turn back to Shenzen, Wayne continued to harangue them as he peeled their clinging hands off the side of our boat. Wayne had gone stark raving mad at what seemed the worst possible time.

An eternity went by until a few minutes later we crossed into Hong Kong waters with our pursuers still alongside and attempting to force their way aboard. By a great stroke of luck, a Hong Kong gunboat that was four times the size of the Chinese police boat, was on patrol in the area. They approached and turned on their piercing siren. The tables were turned, and our pursuers were now the ones in danger of arrest as they found themselves on the wrong side of the border. The Chinese police fell silent and turned their boat back for home. We all breathed an immense sigh of relief. I got on the radio and thanked the Hong Kong Police and told them we would continue on our own and that nothing more was needed. They never asked me why my "pirates" were actually government officers, the difference between them being not that great. Wayne certainly displayed the spirit of Magellan with his bold and decisive action. Perhaps he knew something we didn't and was justified in his behavior. Unfortunately, at the time it seemed to the rest of us to be a completely unnecessary and foolhardy action—risking imprisonment or death to avoid inking another piece of paper.

Darkness of the Mind; Mutiny; The Phoenix Rises Again

No sooner had the first crisis passed when another one erupted. Wayne and Vlad had gotten into a loud argument on the main deck. Out came Wayne's verbal assault and sword-like finger. After some back-and-forth accusations and denials, Wayne ordered Vlad to get off the boat immediately. Wayne got on the radio and called for a sampan taxi to come out to us several miles off Lantau Island, which is located a few miles west of Hong Kong. Vlad soon had his bags packed and on deck. He was not alone climbing into the sampan. A shipboard romance had sprung up between him and the nanny Wendy. She was more than ready to get off this troubled boat and join him to return to Canada. The boat could still sail without a nanny, of course, but Wendy had cheerfully lent a hand working on deck and in the galley as needed. She would be missed by all of us. The entire crew had also become good friends with the easy-going filmmaker turned deckhand. Their absence left us shorthanded and depressed at the voyage's future prospects.

Wayne had me set a course for offshore, giving me no particular destination, and retreated to his cabin in a sour mood. Rex and I had a conversation that neither of us wanted to have. Wayne's troubles were affecting him to the point where we seriously questioned his judgment, let alone his terrible treatment of those around him. I was torn between my loyalty to the captain and an unacceptable situation. Life aboard degenerated into a scene reminiscent of the plotting in *Mutiny on the Bounty*. Rex agreed to back me up when I suggested we take control of the boat and bring her back to Aberdeen. I informed the rest of the crew and found no dissenters among them. Sadly, the voyage for us was over. I knocked on Wayne's cabin door. He came out with that glazed, red-eyed, medicated stare I had seen on him too many times before. With Rex standing a few feet behind me, I explained to Wayne, politely but firmly, our decision to return the boat to Hong Kong. Theresa stood in the doorway behind Wayne with tears in her eyes, silently giving her support by a nod of her head. "What's happened to my loyal officers?" Wayne said with raised arm in a final theatrical flourish. We all stood for a time in embarrassed silence. I felt like a scoundrel or worse. Wayne cast his head down, defeated, and slowly stepped back into his cabin. I sensed he was relieved to have the decision to end the voyage taken away from him.

Wayne remained below deck until the next morning when we arrived back at the entrance to the Aberdeen typhoon shelter. He emerged on deck looking and acting like a new man after an uninterrupted night's rest, finally free of the need to make difficult decisions. Without a word about our uprising spoken between us, Wayne took the tiller and guided us back into her old slip in front of Shing Ge Fat boatyard. The mood aboard lightened as Wayne resumed control of his vessel. I was grateful to have Wayne back and the unpleasant drama left in the past. The crew prepared to depart *Cocachin* for the last time.

I don't want to give the impression that Wayne was incompetent or had a serious personality defect, but only that his obsession to succeed in realizing his ambitious dream had trapped him in a series of overwhelming events—just as it could have done to any of us who sit in judgment. Wayne had spent the better part of 10 years planning and working to retrace the maritime silk route from China to the Middle East. It had been his life's main mission and his highest aspiration. He reached high, and he wasn't finished.

Most expeditions of this size don't get beyond the planning stages. Though we never spoke of the unfortunate incidents on that abbreviated voyage, I did remain in touch with Wayne, and I was happy to learn the next year that he had pushed aside his personal demons to regain control of his life and the Marco Polo Voyage. Looking back, I believe that our first ill-fated shakedown cruise on *Cocachin* was a turning point for him. With new sponsors, a new crew, and new resolve, Wayne successfully captained *Cocachin* up the coast to Shanghai and back to Hong Kong on a voyage lasting just over 100 days. This time they embarked with the favorable winds of the southwest monsoon behind them. Unfortunately, it was also the height of the typhoon season. Along the way they weathered at least two near hits from typhoons, were held under armed guard at the port of Quanzhou after putting in for repairs without advanced permission, received bullet holes in their sails when passing too closely to a Taiwan military base located on an island near the coast of China, and were boarded by Chinese pirates who turned out to be more intrigued by the ship's design than in pilfering and who eventually left her odd foreign crew unmolested. That year Wayne was awarded the coveted Rolex Award for Enterprise, and his Marco Polo Voyage expedition received endorsements from the Royal Geographical Society and UNESCO.

Wayne described as follows what happened after their return from Shanghai: "The first Gulf War was in full swing by the time we returned to Hong Kong. The sponsors all refused to continue to sponsor an expedition sailing to where there was a war on. I spent several years trying to revive the expedition but never succeeded. *Cocachin* was eventually sold and has sadly been radically altered with a fixed steel rudder and a horrific wheelhouse on the poop deck as well as the masts being replaced as the owners were informed that she would tip over in a typhoon! This was in-spite of the fact that in the eight years that I owned her she had seen many typhoons and was never even close to being 'blown over'! I subsequently returned to my medical profession with the idea that someday I would pick up where I left off and find a shipyard that would be able to build another authentic sailing junk."

During the years since, for a time Wayne ran a Hong Kong medical clinic for addiction. His program was noted internationally for its successful and innovative approach, using techniques Wayne may have learned in his own past struggles with addiction. In 2010, he partnered with a shipyard in Zhoushan City in central coastal China. Plans were for Wayne's new company to have a 30-meter (98-foot) sailing junk built as well as smaller junks from 4–11m (13–36 feet) that could be fit into shipping containers and sold to the recreational public worldwide.

Over the years, I kept in touch with a few of the crew members. Vlad and Wendy stayed together for a time in Toronto. Sadly, a heart-broken Vlad told me that an illness had taken her away too young. Vlad went on to complete a circular cruise of the Atlantic on his own sailboat and continues to produce films in Canada. Rex Warner went on to lead his own expedition the next year, commemorating the 500th anniversary of Bartolomeu Dias rounding the Cape of Good Hope. On that voyage the crew endured two dismastings of the 50-year-old wooden yacht, which resulted in an unbroken stint of 104 days at sea, an attempted murder, and some ferocious storms that almost sank the boat. Undaunted, Rex later organized and led The Voyage of the Dragon Kings, in essence finishing what Wayne Moran started, by sailing the 60-foot junk *Fortunate Cloud* from Hong Kong to Oman.

I've often thought about the adventures I missed by not rejoining the Marco Polo Voyage on its second and more successful trip. A solo voyage was in some ways easier to achieve than participating in a fully crewed expedition, whose outcome is in the hands of too many others. In any case, events soon unfolded that carried me in a far different direction than I could have imagined. Serendipity was again my polar star.

12 Taiwan Interlude

A sea-going soloist rejoins the discordant world of industry.

I stepped off the elevator to my sixth-floor penthouse apartment in the hilly upscale Peitou suburb of Taipei, Taiwan. I had slogged out another 10-hour workday, running among the four Hans Christian Yacht building factories scattered outside the capital city. Later that evening I needed to work in the downstairs office on construction flow charts and materials lists. As I ate my dinner alone, I gazed out over the surrounding mountains and valley where here and there the heat from geothermal vents caused puffs of steam to rise from the rivers in the chill winter air of northern Taiwan. My focus settled directly across the street on a bare concrete building foundation. For nine months I had endured living next to the noise and dust of the construction of a proposed combination of temple and office complex. The Taiwanese are certainly accommodating people. But the idea of that odd union of meditative monks and harried office workers seemed as unlikely as a church and strip club sharing the same building back home. Just weeks before the building's completion, work halted for a month. My suspicion that something was amiss was confirmed during the next three months as I watched, stupefied, as they noisily raised even bigger clouds of dust by tearing down the entire five-story structure. The rumor was that a building inspector eventually discovered that the foundation had been placed too close to the unstable riverbed in an earthquake-prone area.

The colossal blunder of the vanishing building matched my own rise and fall in Taiwan. It turned out my life here was built on a shaky foundation, and I would soon be departing. I had begun my work here a year previously, filled with an irrepressible enthusiasm for the job and a fascination with learning a new language and culture. In the beginning I had enjoyed the good will between myself and the factory owners, managers, workers, and my own office staff. But changing economics, greed, and deceit slowly poisoned the atmosphere. Ultimately, the result was a paralyzing lack of cooperation between the Chinese factory management and the American owners of Hans Christian Yachts who contracted these factories to build their traditional-style sailing yachts. As production inspector, I was the conduit for communications between them as well as being in charge of maintaining or improving the construction standards. I was trapped in the middle of an unwinnable war. But at the beginning of my time in Taiwan these troubles were still in the future, and I was happily ignorant of the stressful times to come.

My link to Taiwan was forged the day I happened to meet John Edwards on the marina docks in Aberdeen, Hong Kong. As I passed by his 48-foot Hans Christian sailing yacht, I paused to give the boat an admiring glance. Though her hull and deck were of modern fiberglass construction, her sweeping bowsprit, canoe-shaped stern, and ample use of teak trim and bronze fittings bespoke an elegant, yet traditional, design. It was more boat than I would ever care to own, but I admired her as a sea-going piece of art. The boat's owner then stepped up into the cockpit and called out to me by name: "Mr. Baldwin! I've heard you were here. I read your circumnavigation article in *Cruising World* magazine. Congratulations and welcome to Hong Kong. Step aboard—I have a job proposal you may be interested in."

I had just returned from our abbreviated saga on the Marco Polo Voyage and was considering my next step in exploring Asia when Mr. Edwards told me that he needed a new production inspector for his yacht building factories in Taiwan. He proposed flying me to the island for a one-week job trial and training. My initial tasks would be to get familiar with the production process and to make a complete survey report on a soon-to-be-completed Hans Christian 38. My savings were almost gone. Taking a job in the yacht building industry for a year or two meant I could build up my cruising kitty as well as take a big step forward with my boatbuilding skills. When I returned with my survey report to the Hans Christian office in Hong Kong, Mr. Edwards was impressed enough that we then worked out the details of his job offer.

He would provide me with a furnished apartment, a car, and a fully staffed office. My pay would start at the then fantastic sum of $2,400 U.S. deposited into my U.S. bank account each month. The company would pay all my taxes and living expenses.

Factoring in the perks, it was more than double what I could earn at a similar job back in the States. This shoestring sailor had hit the jackpot. Back home, where I would have competed with more experienced boatbuilders and inspectors, my lack of formal education and experience in the field meant that I would not have been considered qualified for the job. But Mr. Edwards believed my limited experience coupled with the skills I had picked up on a solo circumnavigation and a solo voyage to Asia to be sufficient qualifications. He was willing to take a chance on me. He also knew that there was a shortage of qualified inspectors willing to accept and stick with this challenging overseas position.

The growing spirit of independence I gained during my first solo circumnavigation made me a less than ideal team player. Certainly it meant that I would never again be satisfied to struggle for work in a highly competitive market. Competition drives innovation, but for me it is overrated. There will always be enough competitors and innovators to move society forward. I had decided to make my own path rather than engaging in an adult version of King of the Hill that friends and I had played on dirt piles as children. Rather than joining a race to beat my competitors, I preferred to go my own way, even to the opposite ends of the earth, to discover the opportunities awaiting me there. Just as when I had worked in the boatyard in New Guinea two years previously, I found that getting a foot in the door here was easy enough, but I knew that to keep this challenging job meant I needed to prove my worth by quickly gaining the experience and competency on the job, which I currently lacked.

Leaving *Atom* on a double mooring among the tightly packed mass of junks in Aberdeen Harbour, I boarded a China Airlines flight to Taiwan. I would have preferred to sail my boat to Taiwan. Since 2010, several new marinas have opened up around the island. But in the late 1980s, it was nearly impossible to keep a sailboat in Taiwan waters. The government then was obsessed about possible communist invasion from mainland China and viewed yachts as a security threat. Most Chinese also considered yachting a frivolous foreign activity that was utterly without merit. It was all right to build them here for export, but local use was highly discouraged and, for the most part, illegal. Sometime later during my stay on the island, I was amused to read a sign posted along Taiwan's coastal highway in front of a small military post, which read in Chinese and English: "No photographing, sketching, or describing."

Know the History, Know the Culture

The current government of Taiwan had ruled most of a fractured China under Chiang Kai-shek's Nationalist Party until they were defeated by Mao's communists in 1949. The Nationalists then retreated to Taiwan. But instead of declaring an independent state of Taiwan, the leaders there believed they remained the sole legitimate government on the mainland, just as the mainland government considered Taiwan a renegade province to be brought under communist control. For over twenty years, most countries continued to recognize Taiwan as the official China until the political realities of communist China's growing power and influence caused most countries to reverse their support, leaving Taiwan something of an international orphan. Most world political leaders and businesses continued to support Taiwan, while simultaneously recognizing communist China as the legitimate ruler of the mainland.

A constant reminder of the Nationalist Party regime's influence was the Taiwanese *Minguo* calendar, which is used instead of our Christian-based Gregorian calendar for official documents. My first experience with this was when I noticed my Taiwan driver's license had an issue date of 78. In Taiwan, year one began with the founding of the Republic in 1912, which means you must subtract 1911 from the Western calendar to find the correct current date. At first it seemed absurd to me that a modern country would continue to use a calendar incompatible with the rest of the world. It's as if we in the U.S. had declared year one began with our Declaration of Independence—now *that* would be some independent declaration! But at least Taiwan does not expect the rest of the world to follow its calendar, and after some reflection, you have to admit a dynastic-based calendar has more meaning to the local population than one that is religious-based.

As our plane landed at Chiang Kai-Shek Airport outside the capital city of Taipei, I watched the alarming spectacle of passengers leaping from their seats to grab their overhead luggage and rush towards the exit at the precise moment the plane's wheels hit the tarmac. When this had happened on my previous flight to Taiwan, I looked out the window expecting to see an engine on fire. As before, the stewardesses gallantly tried to hold their place in the isles, begging people to remain seated until the plane taxied to the arrival terminal, but they were ignored, pushed aside, and all but trampled underfoot. This same touchdown bedlam was repeated on every airplane landing I made in Chinese cities. Each time I remained in my seat until the exit rush was over, when I would make my way unruffled and dead last to the door. Of course, there was no fire or other emergency beyond the Chinese compulsion always to be at the front of the line. It was the same story on buses or the subway, where incomers did not give you a fair chance to get out the doors before they shoved their way in.

In my travels, I noticed that the British will in every case form a silent military-like queue. The Americans will also generally stand in line and loudly enforce against line jumpers. In the French islands, locals prefer to form a good-natured jostling mob. But the Chinese aggressively use headbutts, elbows, and shoulder thrusts as if they were in the final lunge at the one-yard line in American football or participating in an English rugby scrum. In fact, the chief complaint of the Brits in Hong Kong was that "the Chinese don't know how to queue."

A sociologist might describe the lack of queuing in China as a legacy of over-crowding, poverty, and a Confucianist emphasis on the family unit over the proper treatment of strangers. A casual observer would consider it rude and counterproductive. Our other stereotypes of the Chinese with at least a partial basis in fact include a strong sense of collectivism that labels anyone whose behavior deviates from the norm as an outsider. Being an outsider is to be shunned, or worse, to be criticized. Individualism is as undesirable to them as it is inexplicable. They also have an affinity for holding a life-long grudge against those who may have wronged them (no matter how slightly); notably lack a sense of humor behind their chronic smiles; are prone to a wide range of superstitions; and are apparently obliviousness to pollution. The traditional Chinese dwelling was built behind a wall and enclosed courtyards containing several adjoining buildings, which housed multiple generations of the family. They kept their homes and courtyards scrupulously clean by dumping their trash on the street, much as in medieval Europe. In recent years the actions that formed these stereotypes have been slowly disappearing as Taiwan and China modernize and become more exposed to the sensitivities of the global community.

Before we Westerners overly indulge ourselves in our perceived superiority, it's wise to consider that the Chinese have traditionally viewed us with some legitimacy as demanding, impolite, overly emotional, quick to inflict public embarrassment on each other, and prone to inexplicable violence. We walk through the filth of the streets and public toilets and then refuse to remove our shoes when entering their homes. We have sex with near-total strangers if we like their looks. We treat our pets better than some family members, even going so far as to create something as unimaginable as "pet food." From the traditional Chinese point of view, we also abandon our families and show little respect for elders and ancestors. The list of our misdeeds could go on for pages. Living between these two worlds taught me about the fluidity and seeming randomness of the cultural traits that my American childhood had instilled in me.

To the Westerner, many Chinese habits and methods seem bizarre as if all our hard-learned arbitrary habits and rules of etiquette were reshuffled and dealt out again. For example, the Chinese read a book from left to right and back to front, beginning at what seems to us the last page. They count their age the way we count centuries; a person 20-years-old is considered to be 21 (or in his 21st year). I observed it all, sometimes without understanding, but appreciating the effect it had of opening my eyes to hidden elements of cultural bias that we all carry.

My job required me daily to tour at least two of the company's four factories to document every phase of construction as well as to explain the details of each yacht order to the factory managers. Between the four factories, at any one time there were around a dozen boats, ranging from 33 to 52 feet in length, in various stages of construction. It typically required three months from the time a hull and deck were laid up in the molds until the completed yacht was loaded as deck cargo on ships bound to dealers in the U.S. and Europe.

Nowadays, almost all yachts have a full interior fiberglass pan or liner, which greatly speeds up production and reduces assembly costs. This gives many modern boat designs the sterile ambience of the inside of an airliner. In contrast, I appreciated that our boats were still hand-built, piece-by-piece. On deck, the double-ender design incorporated high, teak-trimmed bulwarks; heavy, teak-planked decks; ornate butterfly hatches; and generously sized bronze hardware. Down below, the solid teak-strip stavings covering each bulkhead, real granite countertops, and finely upholstered settee and bunk cushions created an irresistible sumptuousness that few potential yacht owners could resist falling in love with. However, purchasing and maintaining these yachts as they aged required owners with pockets as deep as their love of a classic design.

Chinese Face Saving Versus American Hard Nose

Most of our boats were built to order from dealers in the U.S. who had taken deposits from their buyers. Although some boats with standard configuration were built on spec, many of them were ordered with a customized interior layout and multiple options on colors and equipment. Supervising the construction of these heavy-displacement cruising yachts and working alongside the Chinese craftsmen who created them gave me new insight into the union of Eastern and Western boatbuilding techniques. The famous first solo circumnavigator, Captain Joshua Slocum, remarked on Chinese boatbuilding in the late 1800s: "Though peculiar and slow in their methods, they are excellent mechanics, as anyone may see by examining their native craft. In the European-controlled shipyards they grow to be more efficient, and there a gang of Chinese boatbuilders will do a better job on a copper-fastened teak lapstrake boat than is done anywhere in the U.S."

A hundred years later, with power tools, new technologies, and several more generations of boatbuilding experience behind them, the Chinese are neither slow nor particularly peculiar in their methods. They are simply master craftsmen. In the Hans Christian factories they had succeeded in producing outstanding traditionally styled, modern seaworthy vessels that have taken many of their owners safely and comfortably across the oceans. Yet, as skilled as they were, none of the Chinese builders, managers, or factory owners were sailors. Almost none of them had even stepped aboard a floating sailboat. They lacked a full understanding of why the boat is designed and assembled the way it is. Through repetition, they knew how to build a particular boat, but if you asked them to make a modification to the construction, they were often at a loss as to how those changes could best be integrated into the whole in order to maintain seaworthy integrity of all the various systems on a sailboat.

As changes in the production process were issued from HC headquarters, it was my task to ensure they were done right. Here is where I was introduced to the cultural differences between factories in the East and West. In the West, from my vantage point as a one-time, lowly assembly line worker, if a manager wanted to introduce a simple change in a product, he worked out the details, he issued the orders, and the workers complied. In the Taiwan factory change was rarely that simple. There was an inherent reluctance to take responsibility for a decision. Simple questions and requests were taken as a personal challenge that might invite undesirable conflict. Every issue seemed to require a committee meeting to sort out. If the boss did not want his workers to walk out he had to ensure none of them lost face. A worker might interpret ordering a change to his methods as his work being considered unsatisfactory. Rather than lose face, he would simply quit the job. And just as in corporate meetings held around the world, half the people were there merely to take sides with whomever had spoken most recently.

"Could you please change this cheap brass fitting to the more corrosion-resistant bronze?" I asked a manager one day.

"No, that's not possible," was his reply. When I persisted, he called a meeting of workers to discuss the proposal. Even the cleaning woman was present and had something to say. Finally, they all agreed that the change could not be made because "we have always done it this way." I walked away deeply discouraged. Surprisingly, two days later I found they had made the requested change. That drama was repeated over and over again with other issues large and small. The manager would fight me over every suggestion or just quietly ignore me. Then after I had left for the day, more often than not, he would make the change I had requested. Despite a growing understanding of the workplace culture, I never did get used to this strange process. On the other hand, the merits of gaining consensus are summed up in the Chinese expression: "Three shoemakers are wiser than one emperor's adviser."

Mr. Edwards had joined me for my return trip to Taiwan, where he introduced me to our all-Chinese office staff, including chief secretary Josephine; Debbie the draftswoman in charge of construction drawings; and Tony Chen, the current production inspector. They all also had Chinese names, but it had become fashionable for young Chinese in the cities to adopt a Western first name. For them it was less trouble working with foreigners if they could actually pronounce and remember your name.

In my private office, Mr. Edwards sat down across from my desk and gave me the worst advice possible. "In this job you cannot become friends with the factory owners and managers. To get their respect you must be forceful in your demands that the yachts get built our way. They will smile and lie to your face, so don't believe anything they tell you. Verify everything and don't let them trick you. Because our current inspector is a local Chinese, they are walking all over him, and he has become ineffective in his job. I need you to push them hard in order for us to regain control. Oh, and don't try to sleep with any of the girls in our office."

Mr. Edwards's hard-nosed attitude and his advice not to trust or befriend anyone surprised me at the time. But what did I know? He was the boss—the expert who had built yachts successfully here for fifteen years. Of the turbulent relationships between Edwards, the designers, and the builders over those years, I was wholly unaware. He had recently sold controlling interest in the company to a Mr. White who ran the stateside operation. Meanwhile, Edwards remained in position as a consultant and overall manager of the Asian operations. When Edwards had been working as an educator in California in the early 1970's, he had noticed the rapidly increasing trend of Americans buying sailing yachts that were designed for offshore passagemaking, such as the successful Westsail 32. He believed that with the right design and marketing, he could cash in on the higher end of that market with a line of boats built to a high standard at low cost in Asia.

Edwards presented himself to me as my mentor, and I trusted him for guidance. He was a proud and intense man in his mid-60s whose sharp intellect, gilded tongue, and apparent honest demeanor had given him some success along a bumpy road, at least thus far. At the time he treated me with respect. For the next several months, his honeyed words and cat-like smile hid the other side of his true character. Later I learned that his bigoted, obstinate point of view was opposite of the way I should have approached my job. Too late, it became obvious that I could have gotten more done with less conflict if I had shown more respect to their cultural code.

On my first week, I tagged along with Tony Chen as we made the rounds of the factories. Speaking good English, Tony explained the inspection process to me. He did not say much about why he was leaving the company or his relationship with Edwards, but his brow lowered and his lips tightened whenever the subject came up.

Watch That Tone of Voice . . .

Learning to speak Chinese with the factory managers and workers was the toughest part of the job, and there I also ultimately failed. Actually, after my several months of study I had an extensive vocabulary in standard Mandarin, sprinkled with the predominant Taiwanese dialect spoken by the factory workers. My study of Cantonese in Hong Kong was of little benefit here because of its major differences from Mandarin. The result of learning two Chinese languages almost simultaneously sometimes meant that my sentences were a chaotic mixture of both. Nevertheless, I spoke my pidgin Chinese with pride to anyone who could bear to listen. But understanding spoken Chinese requires the speaker to maintain complete tonal accuracy on every word so that it is not confused with three, four, or even five other identical words of different meanings. For example, in Mandarin the word an English speaker might pronounce as a flat *ma*, has four possible meanings. Depending on if the tone is high, rising, falling/rising, or falling, *ma* could mean horse, scold, hemp, or mother. Putting together a sentence could easily have me unintentionally scolding someone's mother or calling her a horse.

When it comes to learning languages, I have an unfortunate handicap. I work hard at my studies, rapidly memorize a few hundred words and phrases, and then become stuck at the conversational level of a native three-year-old. Like a three-year-old, I have absolutely no shame of mispronunciation. The part of my brain that recognizes subtle tonality somehow got miswired. Since the same parts of the brain handle language and music, this might explain why after hundreds of hours of studying and playing guitar, I remain a miserable musician. Being nearly deaf to many of the tonal nuances of Chinese languages ultimately defeated me. Besides, most Chinese people I encountered had never heard the foreign white devils speak Chinese, and simply could not believe they were now hearing one do so. Although I could speak hundreds of words—a few even with the correct tone—the Chinese frequently responded to my croaks with open-mouthed stares of the type you might use if your pet cat suddenly said "Good Morning" to you. In my travels around the world I eventually learned to speak a good chunk of about ten languages, but in most of them I remained not much more learned or intelligible than a drunken parrot. I remain strangely and happily unashamed of my flawed language skills and continue to torture the ears of my tolerant foreign friends.

I mentioned our tendency to think the Chinese lack a sense of humor, but that's not entirely true. On my second week on the job I noticed a table full of dishes containing rice and other prepared foods that had been set up next to the office. A worker there who saw me looking it over, said, "Please, eat, eat!" and then walked quickly away.

As I was sampling the rice and vegetable dishes I looked up to see through the window the office manager and secretaries staring horrified at me as if I had just urinated over their nicely set table. The manager rushed out and shouted at me, "No, no eat before the ancestors!" and grabbed the bowl from my hand. It turned out the food had been set out on an auspicious day to make offerings to either Buddha or the ancestors so that they could partake of the essence of the offering. At the end of the day, the office staff would eat the leftovers. I noticed the factory workers were by now staring my way with toothy grins on their faces. No doubt they were saying to themselves, "Oh, how stupid is this white devil. Very funny."

Humanity as One; Sharp Elbows; Yellow Fire Sister

For the most part, the Taiwanese are a generous and amicable people, and I made many friends among the locals while living there. A common theme was their amazement that for the past several years I had traveled so far alone. It was incomprehensible to them that you could leave your family and just sail away. One of their worst fears is of being separated from family. Strong family ties may constrain individualism and the pursuit of happiness, but they do have an overall positive impact on society. There was very little crime and virtually no homelessness on the island from what I could tell. I never felt unsafe even when I strayed into the poorer sections of the city. Times change, though, and just like almost every other part of the world, Taiwan is not as safe as it used to be. A main reason there was so little crime there is because being caught in a criminal act would severely ostracize the person from family and friends and embarrass them all unbearably. They do not want to be out of the mainstream. The tendency is to be content to act and think exactly as those around them. That does not mean they have no vices. Married men who are successful in their business, I observed, have a penchant to drink themselves into oblivion from time to time and almost universally keep a girlfriend on the side. Gambling is the national pastime and, for too many, an addiction. The owner of one of our factories routinely put down large sums of money in the numbers lottery by placing his bets on what he hoped was the lucky hull identification number of each completed yacht.

However, many Taiwanese simply could not afford to gamble. Though the government had adopted business-friendly policies that had grown Taiwan into one of the mighty Asian economic tigers of manufacturing, the nearly full employment statistics hid the fact that too many jobs paid less than the cost of living. One of these low-paid and probably unneeded jobs that I observed was on the public buses. The whistle girls' job was to hang their pretty heads out of the rear bus windows and blow their whistles like trumpets if the driver were about to turn a corner too tightly or if a vehicle were attempting to pass in the congested downtown streets.

Adding to the challenge of driving a bus in the crowded city traffic were the countless small motorbikes jamming the streets. Helmetless riders zoomed in and out of traffic with little regard for traffic signals. If you think you can get through, you go for it, even if that requires an occasional detour onto the sidewalk. The motorcycle serves as the family SUV, often carrying both parents and children squished together in one unstable, top-heavy mass. As with the teenaged car culture in the U.S., in Taiwan the motorcycle is a young person's ticket to a fleeting freedom from extended families, which frequently contain ten persons or more per apartment. Each evening, the streets were brimming with young couples—the boy zigzagging through traffic with his girl sitting sidesaddle behind him in her wind-whipped dress. Many were off to see a movie or visit friends at the newly popular coffee houses. For the truly amorous, hundreds of discreet hostels around town rented their rooms by the hour.

However, for the most part, my younger Chinese friends did not seem comfortable being alone with their girlfriends or boyfriends. When I joined my local friends for a bus trip to a popular beach across the island one weekend, I noticed the couples barely interacted directly. There was much happy chattering among the group, but there was no handholding or kissing. I asked one friend if the girl next to him was his girlfriend. "No!" she interjected immediately.

Then the boy whispered in my ear, "Yes, she is, but she's ashamed to say so."

The beach was packed with families and friends sitting under umbrellas on the sand or milling around in ankle-deep water. In a small nation surrounded by water, for the most part the Chinese inexplicably were non-swimmers and seemed overly fearful of the water. Parents did not teach their children to swim. Instead they might chase them out of the water with bamboo switches and shouted warnings about unseen dangers. On this day a few brave people ventured out to waist-deep waters, but beyond that the sea was empty. As I waded out to enjoy swimming in open waters, I was immediately alerted to come back by the frantically waving arms and blowing whistle of the lifeguard. Apparently, swimming in waters over your head was not just crazy—it was forbidden.

As we got on separate trains to head home, my friends who were couples simply divided and went their way without even saying "goodbye" to each other. When I asked my secretary why this was so, she told me, "There's no reason to get so emotional. They know they'll see each other again soon."

When Debbie, our company draftswoman, became engaged to her boyfriend she asked me if I wanted to come along on their honeymoon to the mountain resort at Sun Moon Lake. I was flattered but mystified. I replied, "No, you two need that time alone."

"Why would we want to go alone? " she asked me in an equally surprised tone. "We're inviting all our best friends. It's more fun that way." I stayed away from that honeymoon, partly because by that time I was involved in my own budding romance.

A mutual friend introduced me to Huo-Mei Huang (which I liked to translate literally as "Yellow Fire Sister"). Mei was in her mid-twenties (I was 29 at the time) and worked nearby as an accountant and assistant office manager for a tool exporting company. Her college education and frequent business contact with foreigners made her English unusually good. Because she rented a house, which she sublet and shared with expats in Taiwan on work contracts, she gained a partial understanding and acceptance of Western culture. When I asked Mei if she'd like to show me some local attractions, she willingly agreed. Together we made the usual tours of the capital sites, including the National Museum, which contained the priceless Chinese artifacts lifted from the mainland by Chiang Kai-Shek's retreating army. Later, we hiked the mountain trails on the edge of the city. I noticed Mei was like many city girls in Taiwan who had a vampire-like aversion to direct sunlight touching their skin. She dressed to stay well-covered from the sun and carried an umbrella on particularly sunny days outdoors. When asked about this she said, "If I get a tan my friends will tease me that I look like a farm laborer."

With Mei in the mountains

Many Chinese in the city did not often cook for themselves. Like them, Mei and I ate out at evening street food markets where we sat at sidewalk tables under bright signs advertising the foods available. Here you could find grilled meats marinated in soy and sesame oil, hot bowls of noodles, local seafoods, fresh dumplings, and a hundred more unidentifiable items. One dish I grew to tolerate in my unending quest to eat vegetarian was *chou doufu* (stinky tofu), which is a fermented deep-fried tofu whose stench of rotting eggs is considered too malodorous to the delicate foreign palate. Up close, the chili sauce and sour pickled vegetables that are spread over the offensive blocks of tofu render it slightly less overwhelming.

At Snake Alley night market we watched a blind man giving a customer seated on a sidewalk chair an invigorating head and neck massage. There too I watched, hypnotized, as a sweaty man in T-shirt and shorts pulled a 6-foot snake from a basket and hung it live from its head on a suspended hook. Gripping its tail with one hand, he slit the length of its belly with a knife in the other hand. He collected the dripping blood in a cup and pulled out the snake's gall bladder. He placed the cup of blood mixed with snake bile and rice liquor on a table were it was gulped down by a man presumably in search of increased sexual potency. The snake's meat was also considered an aphrodisiac and was served to couples at nearby tables. Houses of prostitution were located nearby as the dessert course for diners who had forgotten to bring their wives along.

With Mei and another local friend as guides, we visited one particularly memorable mountain village an hour's drive inland from the city. In a steep green valley between the mountains, a footpath led us over an arched stone bridge above a babbling rocky stream and past a cluster of small stone-walled homes laced with moss and set organically into the mountainside. My friend stepped up to a porch and tapped on the door. "I know a man that lives here you will enjoy to meet," he told me.

We were invited inside by Chih-Cheng, a man perhaps in his forties with shoulder-length hair and a thin beard graying around the fringes. He seemed pleased to have visitors and told me through our interpreter-friend that he had moved from the city some years before to this village "to find a more peaceful atmosphere living among other artists and simple country people." As we sat on low stools in the sparsely furnished two-room cottage, sipping tea from glazed earthenware, Chih-Cheng showed us some paintings he had made of local nature scenes bordered by blocks of fine calligraphy. He explained: "My sole ambition is to practice my poetry and painting as you see here."

The popular marriage of Chinese calligraphy, painting, and poetry is based on the scholar-artist's ability to meld his words and images to create a lively interaction in the mind of the viewer. Lying within the many delicate and precise brush strokes of each character is more than a mere representation of a word; the characters offer an opportunity for the writer-artist to convey his spiritual energy and mood, as do the images in a painting.

I had seen my Taiwanese friends' children struggling with hours of homework on weekends or after school in order to learn how to write the thousands of individual characters that make up their written language. Over and over they copied rows of characters on worksheets until each was memorized. Because they have no alphabet, each word has its own distinctive form. Even using a simplified modern version of written Chinese, a well-read person has a visual vocabulary of over 5,000 characters. We Westerners, used to the advantages of a simple alphabet, can only marvel at the ability of the Chinese to achieve this seemingly unattainable expertise.

Sea of Ghosts

The simmering heat and humidity of summer in Taiwan sapped the energy from the workers in our non-air-conditioned factories, but production slowed only slightly as we wiped the sweat from our brows and carried on to meet our shipping deadlines. I escaped the heat whenever possible by borrowing a friend's windsurfer that he kept at a beach along the island's north coast. Here I reconnected with the sea by sailing my board out beyond the coastal reefs—all worries temporarily left behind as I skipped across the waves, intently focused on balancing board and sail between wind and water.

The normally busy beach here became nearly empty during the seventh lunar month (called "ghost month"), when locals consider it particularly dangerous to be in the water. During ghost month the dead come back to visit the living, including petulant spirits from the underworld who may pull you under water to drown. I had seen a man apparently drown in knee-deep water just the week before ghost month. He had simply collapsed, possibly due to a heart attack, and could not be revived with CPR after he had been dragged up onto the beach. I watched helplessly as his lifeless body was carried up to the road and lifted into an ambulance. The beach was deemed unlucky for a time after this and remained utterly deserted the rest of the day.

The ghosts nearly claimed me as well when I went out to windsurf on a high-wind day as a typhoon passed some distance offshore. I was not quite foolish enough to windsurf during a direct hit from a typhoon, but this moderate-sized storm was forecast to bring only 30-knot winds to the coast, which I felt I was well able to handle. What I hadn't fully appreciated was the breaking surf from storm swells that rapidly grew larger during the day. At first these typhoon-driven swells filled me with excitement as I rode over their swollen backs. As they grew larger through the day, I enjoyed the most thrilling high-speed ride of my life. But when I tried to return to shore in late afternoon, the breaking surf and gusting winds knocked me down. Now trapped within the surf zone, I found I could not regain my footing on the board. After floundering about in the chaos of breaking waves and rip tides and swallowing a few mouthfuls of saltwater, I felt a rising panic creep over me. I was a fairly strong swimmer and wore no lifejacket. Realizing my only chance to make shore was to swim underwater, I dove under the next breaking wave whose force momentarily drove me down and pinned me to the shallowing gravel-and-sand bottom. Once it passed, I made a few strokes shoreward against the force of the undertow, popped up for a breath of spray-filled air, and then repeated the procedure. As I neared the end of my strength, my feet touched bottom, and I waded up to the beach where I fell flat onto the sand to rest aching muscles and calm my nerves. The windsurfer eventually washed up near me. Besides escaping the clutches of evil spirits, I gained a greater respect for the power of the sea in its most furious state. I now also better knew my own limitations.

Hong Bao, Chicken Heads, and Cryptic People Skills

As the Chinese Lunar New Year approached, our factory workers looked forward to receiving their annual *hong bao*, a fat red envelope of cash. It was customary for workers throughout the country to get this end-of-year bonus from their employers, equivalent to one to four months' salary, depending on the individual company's profits. At our factories, profits were down, and the workers feared losing a good portion of their *hong bao*, or even losing their jobs. Around this time, a factory manager with whom I was still on good terms invited me to join the yearly, catered company banquet celebrating *Weiya* (for the earth god in charge of wealth) and to show his 30-some workers his appreciation for their hard work. Dozens of dishes of food were laid out on the table so that people could serve themselves. "Ah, no chicken heads this year," someone cried in relief as the rest smiled or chuckled. It was later explained to me that because it would be rude to fire a worker directly, one tactic used by bosses was to ask the waiter to serve a whole cooked chicken with the head still on and to place the dish with the head pointed at the unfortunate person to be terminated. No words needed to be said between them. When the worker saw the chicken head pointing at him, the message was clear; he did not return to work after that fateful dinner. Likewise, if the employer did not give out a red envelope at New Year, that employee knew he was expected to quit the job without discussion. Here was an example of the widespread Chinese belief that a problem or unpleasantness, if ignored, will go away on its own.

Being raised in a society that is more direct and confrontational and having lived alone for so many years left me disadvantaged when it came to reading people's unspoken feelings. For me, intuiting the feelings of those around me is like being on a perpetual first date, but it is a commonly practiced art form in Taiwan. The nuanced and intuitive nature of personal and working relationships in Taiwan came home to me when my normally pleasant secretary became increasingly glum and brusque. It was soon obvious that her ire was directed towards me. "What seems to be bothering you lately?" I asked.

"Nothing" was the curt reply. Apparently it was up to me to guess the source of the problem and remedy it. When I pressed the issue, the most I got from her was a cryptic "You should know. I shouldn't have to tell you." I guessed it must be that she had not had a raise in pay recently. I talked to Mr. White about the matter, and he agreed she would get an increase of 400 NT (New Taiwan dollars) per month. When I told Josephine the good news, her mood only darkened further.

"What could possibly be wrong with getting a raise?" I asked.

"Everyone knows four is an unlucky number," she sneered as if I were an imbecile. I had forgotten that because in Chinese the number four is pronounced similar to the word for death, it is to be avoided much as generations of superstitious Americans disliked the number 13 or the accursed 666. We raised her salary by 500 NT, but even that news did not improve her mood.

One day, finally exasperated, I sat down next to her desk and explained that because I was from a culture of insensitive and verbally expressive brutes, I simply could not guess what was bothering her. Eventually I coaxed her into telling me: "You don't answer the telephone for me like you used to, even when you know I'm busy."

Aha! Now I understood—it was about the *wei-wei* game. When I began working there I often took the opportunity to practice Chinese by answering the office phone if Josephine did not grab it first. I quickly learned the format: answer by saying "*Wei*" (pronounced "way"), which is equivalent to "Hello" but only used for phone conversations. The caller replies with *wei*, and because of shyness, hopes that stating a name won't be needed. If you don't recognize their voice, you repeat *wei* to each other a few more times in hopes of making recognition instead of rudely asking them to state their name. If all this *wei-wei*-ing fails, then at some point you may state your names. Although I got used to the strange *wei-wei* game, what eventually caused me to give up answering the phone was that many callers preferred to hang up on me abruptly once they realized they had a real live *gweilo* on the phone speaking a barely recognizable Mandarin. There was never any explanation other than a sudden dial tone. I took this as rudeness, like a phoned-in slap in the face. But to them it was just the easy way to avoid further embarrassment in a culture that considers embarrassment the highest form of punishment. In a few minutes they would call back and hope to get Josephine on the line instead. After I explained the details to Josephine she finally understood, and her mood returned to normal. All the days of unpleasantness could have been avoided if she had told me right away what was bothering her. From her perspective the communication breakdown was unavoidable as long as I remained so stubbornly unperceptive to the meaning behind her moods.

First, Do No Harm; Lucky Ticket No. 329

Another example of my cultural ignorance occurred when I went to see a dentist after one of my fillings fell out. From the street I opened the door directly into a room containing about ten chairs in a close row, filled with white-robed dentists grinding and pulling teeth from groaning patients. I sat on the bench against the wall and tried in vain to avoid looking at what was soon coming my way. There was no waiting room to shield the next victim from the coming ordeal. When my turn came to occupy the seat, my thick-spectacled little doctor leaned in and asked in English, "Which tooth we pull?"

"No. No." I pointed to the hole in my tooth and asked, "Just replace this missing filling please." When the drilling and filling were complete, I asked, "Can someone here clean my teeth?"

"What you say? Clean your teeth!" he replied after giving me that long slack-jawed stare of amazement I had become accustomed to during communications in Taiwan. When I nodded and repeated I'd like my teeth cleaned, he laid into me and told me what he really thought: "Maybe you like I wash feet and polish shoes too, ha!"

As I tried to explain that my past dentists or their assistants always cleaned my teeth with dental pick and polishing wheel, he cut me off and explained that Chinese dentists have more self-respect. In other words, dentists in Taiwan expect you to clean your own damned teeth. Maybe he misunderstood my request for a cleaning to mean I wanted him simply to brush my teeth with a toothbrush. In any case, he told the dentist working next to him what I had said, who passed the message down the line. Soon there was chuckling and smiles coming from everyone, including some of the pained patients. I felt like fresh meat on Alcatraz who had just asked the prison barber for a pedicure.

My visit to the dentist should have prepared me for a later visit to the main Taipei Hospital, where I went seeking diagnosis and treatment for lingering unexplained fever and nausea. But the hospital visit was stranger and more stressful than I could have imagined. My long ordeal there began with pushing my way through the packed lobby to register at the front desk. I was given an I.D. card and sent across the lobby to pay for registration. Then I went back to the first counter to make an appointment to see a doctor. "Go to fourth floor," the overworked lady instructed me. The main elevator was broken, so I joined the mash of patients and medical staff moving like Hajj pilgrims circling the Kaaba in Mecca. Those too ill to walk were carried up and down the stairs in their wheelchairs by their relatives and orderlies.

On the fourth floor I received a ticket numbered 329 and looked up to see they were now serving number 245. Not bad, I thought, considering the crush of people in the large waiting room. Within an hour I was called in to see the doctor. I explained about my fever and nausea. After a quick check of my vital signs, he asked me if the mole on my neck ever bothered me. "Not that I know of," I replied. Watching him stare at it with his magnifier, his power of suggestion must have taken hold and I added, "I guess it does itch occasionally."

He scribbled a note in Chinese and handed it to me with the urgent instruction, "Please go now to cancer treatment center on sixth floor."

Cancer! Christ, I was only 30 years old and thought cancer was the least of my worries. He had me so anxious we both forgot about the original complaint that had brought me there.

I rejoined the zombie mass of humanity moving up the stairs. We made way for another man being bounced down the stairs in a wheel chair. It seemed the hospital was laid out with the most serious illnesses treated on the upper floors, which was disconcerting for us cancer patients facing six flights.

On the sixth floor I waited again until called into a room. Two doctors read my note and called in two more doctors. The four of them held a serious discussion in Chinese and called in a photographer who took several pictures of my neck. "We will remove that suspicious mole," one announced. It was half the size of the tip of an eraser, so it should have been an easy procedure. A Western dermatologist could have made a quick snip and sent it to the pathologist and called me back on the off chance it was indeed cancerous and he needed to cut deeper. But here the procedure was backwards. The doctors placed a sheet over my head, gave me an injection of a local anesthetic, and proceeded to cut out the mole and a good chunk of surrounding flesh and close the wound with eight stitches. Their technique was to assume the worst, cut deeply to remove any possible cancerous tissue, and then assume no further treatment would be needed, regardless of the pathologist's report. I have no way of knowing for sure, but I felt as if I were getting special treatment. Perhaps these doctors had encountered ill foreigners before, knew how demanding they could be, and decided to get me out of there once and for all.

I was sent back with the other walking wounded to the second-floor pharmacy with a prescription to fill. Arriving exhausted, I plucked number 364 from the dispenser. Looking up over the heads of hundreds of people, I saw they were now serving number 456. I took that to mean the numbers were going up to 999 and then restarting at zero. I threw my ticket on the floor and walked out. Over the next few days my fever resolved on its own, just as Josephine had told me it would. I returned to the hospital a week later to find my pathology report was negative. The harmless mole had been an innocent victim of an overactive imagination. Now I understood why traditional Chinese medicine seems to be based on doing as little as possible—take some herbs and give the body's natural healing powers a chance to recover from the imbalance—since a visit to the doctor would certainly be unpleasant and possibly perilous.

The Family Rebel and the Gweilo

When the entire manufacturing sector of the country shut down for two weeks during the Chinese New Year, Mei and I took my car for a tour around the 250-mile-long by 90-mile-wide island. Along the way, Mei planned to visit her family during the holiday, many of whom still lived at their rice farm in a rural area of Hsinchu Province in northwestern Taiwan. I felt honored when she invited me to the family reunion. Only later did I find out that Mei's deeply traditional-minded mother had forbidden her to bring home a *gweilo* boyfriend.

Her family considered Mei something of a headstrong rebel. Dating a *gweilo* was perhaps a new low, but long before that she had pleaded with her father to let her leave the farm and go to high school and then business college in Taipei. Money for school was tight in the family, and her older brother was already causing enough education bills for them. A mere daughter, who was expected to leave the family for another family when she married, was not considered worthy of such investment. But her father had a soft spot in his heart for Mei, and so, against all the family elders' wishes, he worked a second construction job in the nearest town to send his daughter to school. Sadly, Mei's father died from a fall at a construction site a few years after she had finished college.

A longing to escape the hard physical work and scant rewards of farm life to live in the city is an almost universal phenomenon. It was even more understandable when Mei described how she had worked from an early age at the backbreaking task of planting and harvesting rice by hand. There were times when even rice was in short supply. Property taxes had to be paid to the government in bushels of rice. If there was not enough rice left over, the family ate mostly sweet potatoes. Besides the rice crop, Mei helped care for and feed the ducks and pigs, and she gathered wood for the cooking stove. In the years before electricity lines reached their farm, after the long walk home from school, she did her homework by candlelight. On some nights she joined her siblings doing piecework, assembling parts that had been dropped off by a factory. After an exhausting day, the young children shared a single crowded bed and dreamed of the day they could live in the city.

Mei shared with me a vivid childhood memory of when her grandfather had died. According to custom, his body was kept in a sealed casket in the house for over a month as they waited for an auspicious day on the Chinese calendar before burial could take place. During that time the family performed complicated rituals of prayers, made offerings, and avoided numerous taboos. She recalled a professional mourner the family had hired. The strange man clad in a white sheet threw himself on the floor before the coffin, wailing like a weepy Klansman. The coffin had to be accompanied around the clock by at least one of the family members in order to guard against evil spirits. If the family had been wealthy, then the funeral procession would have resembled the colorful and noisy parades I had seen winding their way through the streets of Taipei, containing up to a hundred rented pickup trucks. The lead truck always carried a larger than life-sized picture of the deceased. Following them, the other trucks held bands that played grating, unharmonious music and set off fireworks. Some processions even contained trucks filled with dancing girls and strippers, presumably to send the man off to the afterlife just as he had envisioned it should be.

When we arrived at Mei's mother's house, I still had no idea I was unwelcome. But Mei had a secret plan. She knew that during the New Year festivities there was a type of amnesty practiced among family members. Disagreements could not be mentioned because they might portend a coming New Year filled with arguments. At this time almost any indignity would be tolerated, perhaps even bringing home a *gweilo* boyfriend.

As we stepped out of my car, Mei's mother and numerous relatives filed out of the house. They stood staring at me with open mouths, unsure whether to flee or freeze, as if a rabid dog had just arrived on their doorstep. In true New Year's tradition, they soon recovered their composure and greeted me with forced smiles of the type reserved for a tax collector on their doorstep.

Inside the house, Mei's mother had prepared a feast for the relatives who had come from near and far for the annual reunion. My oddness was confirmed to them when I sampled the vegetables but avoided the meat dishes. "Is he a monk of some type?" Mei's uncle asked her. Mei translated my wordy explanation that although I was not a monk and did not follow Buddhism or any other organized doctrine, my philosophy and habits did intersect what I consider the best of all religious teachings. In this way, I was also on a Buddha-like quest to develop a merciful and compassionate heart by not killing or causing the killing of any animals unnecessarily. The family seemed to understand and approve of my choice.

That day reminded me of my earlier visit to a vegetarian restaurant in Taipei. Inside the restaurant several robed, bald-headed monks were eating at the tables around me. On the menu were pictures of each dish. Aside from the obvious vegetable dishes I noticed many that looked exactly like meat. A local friend with me translated the menu, which included dozens of dishes of soybean product such as tofu, all formulated, labeled, and disguised to look like chicken, pork, beef, and seafood. The convivial owner of the restaurant came over to me and introduced himself. I asked him, "Why do all these dishes look like meat when vegetarians are trying to avoid meat?"

He laughed at my silly question and said that the monks had been restricted from eating meat. They would love to eat meat if they could, so they appreciated the artful way he disguised his tofu to look like meat. That seemed mildly blasphemous to me at the time, but I had to admit his food was delicious, whatever it looked like.

Similar to the ten commandments of the Bible, but half the number and twice as memorable, the five precepts of Buddhism are as follows: do not kill, lie, steal, commit harmful sexual misconduct, or indulge in intoxicants. The first precept is sometimes interpreted to include animals, which is why some Buddhists are vegetarian. According to the collection of teachings on the moral and spiritual path of Buddha in the book of *Dhammapada*, it can be argued that the Buddha's injunction not to harm any "sentient beings" extends to the world of non-human animals. In it the Buddha states: "All beings tremble before danger, all fear death. When a man considers this, he does not kill or cause to kill."

I wanted to believe that monks were something more than men, that by conquering their desires they could teach us the importance of self-restraint. But they were who they were, normal men, most of whom were part-time monks taking a few months out of their secular life for a brief spiritual quest, not life-long masters from the Shaolin temple. It was none of their concern if I put them on a pedestal. It was equally unimportant to them if I pulled them off that pedestal.

On New Year's day in Hsinchu, Mei and I accompanied her family to the local temple where we joined many happy villagers rushing up to burn vast sums of money in the temple fire pit near the front gate. Actually, the millions of dollars we burned were counterfeit. This "spirit money" was printed, sold, and burned in great quantities as an offering for the deceased relatives to use in the afterlife. The smoke of a thousand incense sticks hung in the air as strings of firecrackers exploded one after the other to scare away evil spirits.

I felt as out of place at this bonfire of cash as I did when I had entered another temple while sightseeing alone a few months earlier in Taipei. Just after I entered the temple gates and stood in the courtyard admiring the ornate architecture of the two temple spires and soaking up the peacefulness of the setting, the earth began to shake. I looked up to see the two narrow temples tremble and then sway alarmingly from side to side as if they were about to lean over and touch each other. Some plaster crumbled and fell in pieces around my feet. I stood frozen until several eternal seconds later the earthquake ended. I looked across the courtyard to see a group of monks staring at me, the only foreigner there, as if I had something to do with the event. I turned and walked out before the ill omen of my presence could cause any more damage. Minor earthquakes are fairly common in Taiwan, but this was the biggest shakeup the city had seen in a few years. Another smaller quake happened several days later around 4:00 a.m. while I was asleep in my apartment. It was almost like being aboard *Atom* at sea as my bed swayed beneath me. Avoiding the elevator, I ran down six floors to join my pajama-clad neighbors in the street. In 1999, an island-wide earthquake registering 7.3 on the Richter scale caused widespread damage and thousands of deaths as buildings and temples collapsed.

During the two days we stayed with Mei's family, I helped the men repair a fence and some farm equipment and even lent a hand with the women in the kitchen. Mei later said her mother told her as we were leaving, "He's not so bad, a very helpful young man . . . but don't bring him back."

Mountains; A Single Bed and Love

After what I considered a successful visit, Mei and I departed Hsinchu to continue our trip around the island. A tip for future travelers: avoid making your island-crossing trip during the New Year holiday. Most businesses, including gas stations and restaurants, are closed, the few hotels are full, and the roads are packed with traffic and sightseers. But the island is truly beautiful despite these inconveniences. As we headed east across the corrugated mountains, the thick line of traffic on the two-lane undivided highway allowed us to take in the scenery at a crawl. The road tunneled through the mountains and hung along cliff edges in a marvel of stonework engineering. We detoured off the main road to ascend Hohuan Mountain. But even on this dead-end track, the traffic barely thinned.

An ant-trail of students bound for the 11,000-foot elevation mountaintop carrying flags and wearing dust masks easily passed us on the dirt road. I parked the car, and we joined the student marchers, most of whom were there for their first sight of snow. Just below the summit Mei experienced her first snowball fight, which I started in the ankle-deep snow and freezing temperatures.

Back on the road we followed the Taroko Gorge where the road tunneled into the hillside. Cement arches created an open view out the side of the tunnel, framed by a waterfall spilling down its face. Damage from the big earthquake of 1999, followed by typhoon flooding, permanently closed the Central Cross-Island Highway on which we drove, but alternate routes still provided access to the mountain.

We stopped for tea at an outdoor restaurant in a small mountain village. Seated next to us was a group of local men who Mei informed me belonged to one of the island's aboriginal tribes. One bronze-skinned and weather-beaten man smoked tobacco from a bamboo bong while a monkey perched on his knee. In a flash the monkey leapt across two tables to land on my back. The rascal wrapped one arm tightly across my eyes. With the other hand he grabbed the pan-fried rice flour bun from my plate and shoved it into his mouth. As I ripped the beast from my back he screeched insanely at me while his owner and friends laughed with delight. The monkey then latched onto Mei's leg, causing her to scream, "Honey, get it off!" After I pulled the creature free from her, even Mei laughed out loud, which was a rare event, which soon had me joining in as well.

A mountain man and his monkey

That evening we drove until after dark looking for a town big enough for a hotel. We finally entered a hotel lobby where a crowd of people were coming and going, only to find it was fully booked. Down the street we went until we found another hotel that said they had one room remaining, if we didn't mind a single bed. We took it and were glad to have it even though it was a typical country hotel during the holidays: crowded, understaffed, and overpriced, with unheated rooms that were cold and damp and lacked bathrooms. Down the hallway was a single shared bathtub next to a toilet that was broken and overflowing with sewage. In Mei's ever-positive outlook, she observed it was "Not too bad, for the mountains."

The next day we drove through the last of the tunnels to the island's windward coast. The narrow road clung to the sheer cliffs of the weather-beaten eastern shore. In the coastal city of Hualien, I splurged on a four-star hotel for the wallet-thinning price of about $100 U.S., where the room actually had clean sheets and a modern attached bathroom. Mei was in heaven, and I was right there with her. The following day we completed our romp around the north half of the island and returned to Taipei in preparation for returning to our jobs. After seeing more of the island and more of Mei, I was more in love with both. But my year away from *Atom* would soon come to an end.

13 Afloat in Fragrant Harbor

Rich Man, Poor Man, Sailor, Spy, Lover, Thief

As the jumbo-jet from Taiwan descended through black clouds towards Hong Kong in an approaching tropical storm, the plane lurched and twisted as if she were about to come apart. Like a sailboat caught in a storm, she pitched, yawed, rolled, and bounced so violently I wished instead that I were facing a typhoon alone at sea in my little boat. The fuselage creaked with sickening structural noises as the wings flexed under the stress. Some overhead compartments opened up and rained down their contents on our heads. To make matters worse, we were landing at Hong Kong's notorious old Kai Tak Airport located on the edge of the harbor in the center of the city. To hit that short strip of tarmac, hidden within the mountains and high-rise buildings, required a rapid, accurate descent through the storm clouds and shifting winds into the concrete canyon of the city. Kai Tak had seen numerous fatal crashes over its 73-year history. For passengers the ride in was known as "The Kai Tak Heart Attack." For pilots it was a white-knuckle airstrip on a good day. Today it was our worst nightmare: a sobering view into our own fragile existence. I was acutely aware that the previous year a jet had slid off the runway into the harbor, killing seven people.

When we broke through the cloudbank and caught sight of the city close below us, the pilot lined up the plane's nose directly on the orange and white checkerboard painted on a mountainside. At the last possible moment, just a few hundred feet above the ground, he spun the plane into a 45-degree bank to drop between apartment buildings. On my previous flight in here it seemed our wing tips nearly pulled the laundry off the bamboo poles extending from the Kowloon apartment windows. On this rainy day I looked horizontally out my window to see a flash of a scene of families eating dinner or watching TV in their flats. The mild anxiety I had experienced during previous fair-weather flights into Kai

Tak, now turned to a cold sweat and a pegged Fear Meter. I was strapped into a flying cattle car where my life lay completely in the hands of strangers. Suddenly I wanted to go back to the comfort of facing the dangers of a solo ocean crossing, where I retain some control of my fate. The plane's tires screeched as they hit the tarmac at an angle in the cross wind. The plane bounced once and straightened her track. Suddenly we were safe. A rush of relief ran through my body as the other passengers rushed for the door. They always ran for the exit when landing here, but this time they seemed even more determined than usual to be first off the plane.

Corporate Spy

I was back in the colony for a two-week vacation before setting out for Thailand to begin a new job. Towards the end of my first year working in Taiwan, the Hans Christian company owners had ordered me to take covert notes on each item that went into their yachts' construction and to learn the process of how it all came together in that complex combination of machine and art that is an ocean sailing yacht. I had been studying the construction details since day one on the job, but now I needed to be able to direct the construction rather than merely observe. My boss's plans were to shift production out of Taiwan, where rising wages, a new tax, and shifting exchange rates had reduced the profits they had enjoyed since the late 1970s. After considering the merits of other countries in Southeast Asia such as the Philippines, the company decided to relocate all production to Thailand. However, they did not trust the Chinese factory owners they had contracted with not to sabotage their plan. In this poisoned atmosphere, I attempted to learn every detail of construction, including materials sourcing, in order to become production manager at the new factory in Thailand.

Looking back, I realize that greed and pride in my rising position within the company had corrupted my better nature, squelching my dismay at the deceitful way the production transfer was being carried out. Though it was contractually legal, I felt as if I were stealing on behalf of Hans Christian from the factory's owners and its workers. The Chinese call it "breaking the rice bowl" because it endangers their livelihood. I had doubts as to the ultimate success of such a rapid and complex mission, given the unsavory characters involved, but I reluctantly agreed to a 6-month contract at the new factory in Thailand. It should have been enough time to get production organized. After that, I intended to jump ship from the boatbuilding business once and for all. I was sick of the lies, strong-arm tactics, and intrigues in this work, and I badly wanted to go back to being my own master aboard my own boat.

My spy work in Taiwan did not go long unnoticed by the factory managers and owners who came to consider me a tool of their hated American partners' betrayal. They realized that the shifting sands of global economics left the Taiwan yacht building business on shaky ground. If they could not modernize production and drastically cut costs, they would fold. But all that was now behind me and out of my hands as I looked forward to a sailing vacation aboard *Atom* in Hong Kong.

Her Sun, My Soul

The one thing I was not eager to leave behind in Taiwan was my relationship with Mei. We had grown close over the past few months. She was a warm sun to my chilled soul. When Mei learned my job in Taiwan was ending, she told me, "You can stay at my apartment and find a job as inspector at another factory, or even teach English."

But I was already committed to my path. Beyond that, the other truth was that I was mentally exhausted from my impossible position representing a company in turmoil. After concluding my responsibilities in Thailand I had to go back to the life I knew best—a life of balance and purpose. "Mei, come with me for a vacation in Hong Kong," I asked. "I'll take you sailing, and we can decide about the future there." To my relief, she eagerly accepted.

The first thing I did after catching a sampan taxi back to my boat on her mooring in Aberdeen was to gather provisions to last two people for a couple weeks of sailing. The glancing blow from that early season tropical storm passed by us the next day, leaving behind fair weather as I sailed out of the grinding maw of urban Aberdeen to anchor a few miles away in front of the public park at Deep Water Bay. From here we could enjoy relative serenity and still have access to the city by taking the dinghy ashore to catch a bus. I could also return to Aberdeen by kayak, if needed.

When I had first arrived in Hong Kong a year earlier, I hadn't realized that the combined Hong Kong territories comprised a compact yet surprisingly varied cruising area. Within a day's sail of each other were several inhabited and uninhabited islands. The labyrinthine stretch of the mainland known as the New Territories held a maze of harbors, including parks and isolated empty anchorages as well as simple fishing villages, modern developed ports, and tourist destinations. Most tourists and even many locals never catch a whiff of the old rural Hong Kong, where the English translation of Hong Kong as "Fragrant Harbor" still held true.

I met Mei at the airport the following day, and we took a taxi to the ferry terminal to cross Victoria Harbour to Hong Kong Island. From there a bus brought us back to the serenity of Deep Water Bay. Mei had never been on a sailboat before and showed no disappointment at the tight accommodations. In fact, she was excited to learn about this strange life afloat that I had been describing to her. The advantage of having a guest aboard who had never set foot on a boat before is that she had few preconceived notions about what a boat should have in the way of equipment and accommodations. "No engine?" No problem, it's a sailboat. We have sails and an oar. "No toilet?" No, we use a bucket. "What about hot water and a shower?" We have a footpump for water at the sink and a solar shower bag to hang up in the cockpit.

These springtime nights on the water had a comfortable chill in the air. We spent our first night there wrapped around each other for warmth under a single sheet. As her long silky black hair fell around my face, the yellow light from the oil lantern made her pale skin glow like alabaster. With each embrace I felt born anew as a child in her arms. The hectic world of five million people beyond our floating cocoon did not exist. The moments hung in eternity.

A fishing village on Hong Kong's quiet side

In the morning I awoke early to prepare the boat for our sail around Hong Kong Island to explore the anchorages of the New Territories. Mei got her first lesson in hoisting the sails and trimming the sheets. She even steered a fairly steady compass course after a few minutes of instruction. "This is so nice!" she exclaimed, as we heeled slightly to the light wind spilling down the mountainside. I felt the wave of her newfound wonder at the magic of sailing. We continued sailing past a few potential anchorages and rounded the southern tip of the island where the boat began to lift and drop in rhythm with the ocean swell. To my great relief, Mei continued to show no signs of seasickness. By mid-afternoon we had arrived at a mile-wide protected harbor at Pak Sha Wan, known to local Brits as Hebe Haven. The harbor held perhaps a hundred local sailboats and sampans on moorings, but it was relatively uncrowded by Hong Kong harbor standards. Mei and I rowed our dinghy ashore for dinner at a seafood restaurant in the village by the quay where we overlooked *Atom* lying serenely at anchor.

The following morning I untangled myself from Mei's embrace and prepared her a cup of tea and rice soup, which I knew she enjoyed at home. I noticed there was no wind. We needed wind to move on to our next anchorage, so we stayed another day in Hebe Haven. That morning we cleaned and organized the boat. In the afternoon I showed Mei how to use the kerosene stove to boil water, which we added to the solar shower bag so that we could enjoy a piping hot shower in the cockpit under the cloudy sky. We went ashore to the market and returned to the boat where I prepared for Mei one of my favorite recipes—a vegetable and tofu soup with local bread. Into the soup I added garlic and two handfuls of the spinach-like green leafy vegetable known as "empty heart" because of its hollow tender stems. Mei ate some of my specialty but let me know she would have preferred seafood, or at least fried vegetables with rice, to which she was accustomed. For the Chinese, anything fried is good, and rice twice a day, every day, is not too much.

Cliffs; The Fear; A Saving Zephyr

When we awoke early the next morning I noted a light wind had returned. It was barely enough to ripple the bay but was adequate to fill our sails. Off we went on our 30-mile passage towards the little island park of Ping Chau near the Chinese mainland. At first the light wind carried us easily along the deeply indented and craggy coast of Sai Kung Peninsula. A few miles after we rounded the windward side of the peninsula and altered course to the north, the wind went calm. We were a safe mile offshore, and I expected we'd be fine where we were until the wind returned. Mei went below for a nap as I stood wind-watch. I kept the sails up and sheeted tightly to be ready for the wind and to dampen the rolling in the open water swell. We were on a deserted section of coast with only an occasional fishing boat or private sampan passing by.

Very soon I detected a current carrying us towards the shore. The chart indicated deep water extending up to the bold cliff face, and I noted that anchoring here would not be an option. As our safe one-mile distance offshore rapidly dwindled to a hundred yards, I focused on the swell breaking violently against the rocks. My anxiety grew with the increasing realization that we were in real danger of being crushed against the cliff. I laid my sculling oar in the water to scull us back offshore, but the turbulent water made any progress impossible. There was nothing Mei could do to help us at this point, so I decided not to alarm her. She continued her unworried sleep. I noticed a sampan motoring past a mile in the distance and considered firing off a flare to get his attention and then requesting a tow away from the rocks. But my sailor's pride would not allow so quick a surrender. A few minutes later the sampan was gone, and I had missed my chance of rescue. We were now only a few boat lengths from shore. I thought about launching the dinghy or kayak to attempt to tow *Atom* offshore or use my sculling oar as a pole to push her off the rocks, but neither of these seemed workable in the churning waters.

I was at the point where I must awaken Mei with the shockingly bad news that we had to prepare the dinghy and a grab bag of survival gear to abandon ship. I leaned in the companionway to call her name. My heart ached, seeing her lie there so innocently trusting of my ability to deliver her safely to port. The words would not come from my mouth. She had trusted me with her safety, and I was now very close to failing her in a big way. I must wait and hold my nerves in check until the last possible moment. The same icy fear that I had felt when our plane approached Kai Tak Airport in the storm ran through my veins again. Seconds before we would make impact, a faint zephyr lifted the limp sails. I gripped the tiller and held my breath. We seemed frozen in place, not getting noticeably closer or farther from destruction. During the next few critical minutes, *Atom* displayed the best of her abilities to sail a steady course through choppy waters in the lightest of winds. As we pulled into the safety of open water I fought back tears of relief. When Mei awoke awhile later, I said nothing about the close brush with disaster. At least I could protect her from needless worry. Perhaps I wanted to protect my own reputation with her as well. The incident has remained locked up until my telling in this book. Perhaps I can be forgiven.

We arrived just before sunset at Ping Chau. The mile-long island sits with its horseshoe bay facing directly at the mountainous coast of China two miles away, and its back to Hong Kong at the far eastern extremity of Her Majesty's territory. The once busy island had been a home to fishermen and their families as well as to smugglers. In the years of British rule, Ping Chau had been viewed as a tantalizing sanctuary to mainland Chinese eager to escape the shackles of communism. Many desperate people had attempted the swim to freedom, particularly during the oppression of the Cultural Revolution of the 1960–70s. In recent years the overfished waters around the island caused it to be mostly abandoned for better jobs and entertainment in the city. The isle was now forgotten except as a destination for occasional weekend sightseers.

We dinghied ashore to the crescent-shaped beach and walked inland along paths overgrown with the flowering vegetation of spring. The few decaying wooden or concrete houses were mostly abandoned. Outside one house, Mei stopped to chat with an elderly Chinese woman who was planting vegetables in her garden. She told Mei she had spent her entire life on this island. Her fisherman husband had died two decades ago. Soon after that, her children went off to work in a garment factory. They probably lived in one of those countless shoebox-sized apartments in the squalor of Kowloon. "I'll stay here with my good memories until I die," she concluded.

Mei Huang

Open Paths, Open Hearts

After a few days of swimming, kayaking, and playing aboard *Atom*, and roaming around Ping Chau, we sailed to other islands and mainland harbors around the territory. No new traumatic events occurred on our brief excursions other than the normal thrills of avoiding the mix of shipping, fishing boats, pleasure junks, and the unseeing high-speed ferry boats that rush between the islands and over to the gambling casinos of Macau. Too soon, we ran out of days, and Mei needed to catch her flight back to Taiwan. We spent our last night together at anchor back in Deep Water Bay. Mei and I looked at each other more seriously now. Our futures were diverging, but our hearts were still one. We loved while we had each other, capturing the moments as we sailed into the unknown. Up until now we had skirted this moment of decision.

Mei admitted to me that she wasn't ready to quit her job and leave her familiar life to join an uncertain life with a cruising sailor. And I didn't press the issue because my path was too uncertain. Mei reminded me: "You've been working hard and saved up some money. You can come back to Taiwan. We have an expression in Chinese: 'If money can resolve your problem then it is not a serious problem.'" What wisdom! Money is only an instrument of available choices, a tool to engineer an outcome. If I wanted to see it her way then we could be together whenever we chose.

True, I had more money now than I had ever had in my life. I had arrived in Hong Kong a year earlier, close to broke and lonelier than I had realized. But money would not solve this particular problem. I faced another fork in life's road—and it was a road I'd been down before. In this time and place we both felt the powerful currents of our own life plans. Up to now I had turned a blind eye to what my life choices would do to our romance and the chance of securing my soul mate. My difficulty lay in committing to something or someone other than myself. Much worse than stealing production secrets in Taiwan, I had stolen a girl's heart. I resolved to give her the chance to find a man who would provide for her needs, instead of getting tied up with an adventurer whose course was not set and whose prospects were as risky as the seas themselves. I needed to let her go before I could take the measure of our love. Years later, Mei's chance encounter with a Taiwan fortuneteller and finding an address on the envelope of a previously lost letter would lead to our reunion. For now, our fortunes were unknowable, and we were about to part.

A misty rain fell during the night as a fog wrapped the bay and settled around the boat. Mei lay asleep as I awoke before dawn to gaze through the cabin window at the surreal faint glow of a line of streetlights along the fog-hidden shore. Under a milky, gray dawn, the sky wept over the umbrella she held as I rowed her ashore for the last time. The long gaze, the final kiss, a few words, and then the empty resignation of hearts joined in love, now ripped apart by divergent courses.

I returned alone from the airport to my boat and found a poem Mei had written to me in Chinese. With her help, I later translated it to English:

> *Waves lap the hull like ten thousand raindrops*
> *As street lamps on shore dimly light the anchored sailboat*
> *And curling wisps of fog make the night turn vague.*
> *All of God's creation sleeps soundly under silent moonlight;*
> *You and I embrace as we sleep down below.*
> *Such a scene is like Mandarin ducks playing in the water.*
> *And I, my lover, wish that you may always remember this sentiment*
> *And harbor our final moments in the depth of your heart for all your life.*

A day later, I sailed *Atom* to a new mooring location in Hebe Haven, where she would remain during my work contract in Thailand. The weather had cleared and brightened, but all I felt under the perfect sky was a dark, cold embrace of silence. It was as if a newfound loneliness had slowed my internal clock. For the next few days until I left for

Thailand, the bright moon we had loved under was missing, and the sunrise lost its promise.

A long silky black hair on my pillow triggered lingering memories of hand-holding on walks through the parks; her place in my arms; the saline taste of the sea on her skin; those deep, dark pools of eyes framed by black hair swirling in the air currents as she stood on deck between the sails in a moment of bliss. I imagined her remembering me when a fresh wind blows in from the sea. She would pause and feel her body rise to the ocean swell, the boat heel to the wind as she pressed into my arms. Oceans would pass beneath our keel before fate brought Mei back to her sea gypsy several years later.

14 The Kingdom of *Mai Pen Rai*

To survive life's tempests, a legacy must be built like a boat, with structural integrity.

Thailand was Taiwan without the stress. In the kingdom, *mai pen rai* was the byword. The expression can be translated as "you're welcome" when commonly used as a reply to "thank you." It also carries the wider meaning of "Don't worry, everything is okay." Like Chinese, Thai is a complex tonal language, although just like the people it's more forgiving. Each syllable in *mai pen rai* is pronounced with a soft falling tone that reassures and calms those caught in a stressful situation. Rush or harden the pronunciation and the charm is gone. It can also mean "never mind," though not in the harsh, demanding tone we sometimes use in the West, but always in the Buddhist tradition of acceptance of things as they are, of the impermanence of everything, including your worries.

Mai pen rai was an expression I got used to hearing on my job as production manager at the small family-run Thai shipyard that contracted to build the first of the Hans Christian Yachts from hull and deck molds we had shipped out of Taiwan. I was initially dismayed to hear the yard there had never built a yacht. The closest thing to a sailboat they had experience with was welding together a steel tugboat. There would be a steep learning curve for all of us.

"We must have all these pages of additional materials sourced and delivered by next week," I reminded the pretty Thai factory manager who had recently taken over the shipyard operation from her retired father.

"*Mai pen rai,*" she replied each time I asked. The expression was so soft and sweet as it flowed off her lips like a line from a lullaby that it nearly succeeded in easing my anxiety. But I had a formidable job to do and no amount of *mai pen rai* alone would get it done. Nevertheless, things did eventually get done—never quite on the company's schedule but soon enough for the Thais involved. For us demanding *farang* (foreigners of European descent), well, it was time that we learned the patience of the East.

A group of four Chinese shipwrights, who had worked in our Taiwan factory, accompanied me to Thailand. Each of these men specialized in a different area of production, including fiberglass lay-up, cabinetry, hardware assembly, and the laying of teak decks. Without them, the entire project would have been impossible, and they knew it. They were understandably reluctant to leave their families for a six-month overseas contract. Doubling their wages won them over. Working together, we trained the Thai workers, striving to duplicate the high level of fit and finish for which the Taiwan factories were famous. The total language barrier between my Taiwanese-speaking workers and the Thai-speaking apprentices caused endless delays. I attempted to be in several places at once yet to remain constantly available to translate from Chinese to English. The manager or my secretary then translated my English translation into Thai. Quite a bit got lost along the way. From the start, every step we took seemed to take forever. The unremitting heat and sultry summer rains of the southwest monsoon deepened our frustration as the sweat poured from our bodies and sapped our energy. Studying Thai, my second full-time job over the next several months, brought a similar semi-literate result as had my study of Mandarin.

Once each morning, the shipyard played the Thai national anthem over a scratchy-sounding speaker in our workshop. Like school children, we all stopped what we were doing and stood at attention. The Thai monarchy is revered throughout the land. In the town where I lived, outdoor loudspeakers, which might have doubled as air raid sirens, blasted out the national anthem twice a day in a Thai version of a mosque's insistent call to prayer. Those within earshot stood immobile as if God's own hand had frozen them into pillars of salt. To disparage the Thai King or royal family in any way is strictly forbidden and could even land a person in jail. In recent years, a royal-related story has gone around the Internet. It may be an urban legend but demonstrates the point. Supposedly, a *farang* tourist became outraged over an airport departure tax and threw his Thai baht (the local currency bearing the King's face) on the floor and began stomping it with his foot. The idiot was warned, but when he continued the tirade, he was hauled off to jail and charged with lese majesty.

The shipyard was located in a rural area some fifty miles north of Bangkok on the Chao Phraya River, which is the chief river of transport in the country. Like an Oriental Mississippi, the watery commercial highway is joined by other major rivers as it meanders hundreds of miles through the countryside. Thick with silt and vegetation from monsoon rains, the river runs wide and deep through the center of Bangkok to disgorge into the Gulf of Thailand. This River of Kings had several of its serpentine coils straightened by massive earth-moving canal projects ordered by generations of Thai Kings attempting to shorten the shipping route between their capital city and Thailand's rice-growing alluvial plains.

Bangkok – Danger on Wheels and Lust for Life

Instead of using a car as I had done in Taiwan, here I readily agreed when the Hans Christian company suggested they economize by providing me with a motorcycle. In Thailand, motorcycles were even more ubiquitous than they were in Taiwan. The small family motorcycle here was much more common on the roads than a family car and was often employed to carry a family of three on precarious trips through the cities or at highway speeds on rural roads. My bike was the same type as most locals rode—a lightweight 125cc two-cycle machine that announced its presence with the smoky roar of a chainsaw.

I rarely saw Bangkok when the streets were not in near-total gridlock. A 15-mile errand across town usually took 2-3 hours by bike and up to 4 hours by car. There was no discernible "rush hour." Instead, drivers could expect a daily 18-hour crush. If it rained, as it frequently did in the summer monsoon, I had the choice of riding soaking wet or wearing rain gear and riding in my own steam bath. On calm, rainless days, a blanket of smog draped itself over the city. After each trip across Bangkok, my face looked as if I had applied black soot makeup. As in many cities of the East, motorbikes here could claim no traffic lane as cars did. Instead, they flowed between traffic like water running around boulders in a streambed. Impatient motorcyclists treated the sidewalks here as detour routes. When traffic moved at all, it was a clamoring, noisy, and dangerous spectacle. Even though traffic congestion in Bangkok meant that speeds rarely exceeded 25 MPH, cars could be lethal to us bikers.

One of the many victims of car versus bike was an American businessman, named Tom, whom I had met while sourcing materials for the factory. He also commuted by motorbike through the city each day. Tom was about 40 years old and had been a resident of Bangkok for three years. One day, a couple weeks after we had first met, a car unexpectedly turned through the intersection in front of him, knocking him unconscious. He was rushed to the hospital where he slipped into a coma. When I heard of his accident I recalled he had told me he had no family or steady girlfriend here, so I hurried to check on him. The scene was tragic. He was semi-conscious now, three days after the accident, restrained to his bed as his arms attempted to flail about. Tom never wore a helmet. Now his severe head injury left him unable to speak coherently. His doctor told me he doubted if Tom would ever fully recover mentally or physically.

Tom had a powerful build and a more powerful lust for the sultry offerings of Bangkok. A week earlier, he had insisted on introducing me to the nightlife of Bangkok's notorious Patpong district, where he put on a manly display of drunken lechery alongside the other creepy *farang* sex tourists as we dashed from one noisy club to the next. "Nice girls," he said to me with a crazy grin as he grabbed two bikini-clad dancers in his hairy and muscular arms.

A few days before the accident, Tom had called to invite me to meet him at a street food stall downtown. As he finished a Singha beer and a skewered grilled beef *satay*, he said, "If you've had enough of that damn tofu *satay* thing, follow me on your bike, and I'll show you where to get a great Thai massage." Ever naïve, I thought we were heading for a world-famous, semi-violent Thai therapeutic massage. I had survived one of those massage pummelings before and looked forward to a rematch. When we entered the building I was taken aback. Around a hundred women and girls were on display behind glass walls, lounging on sofas or standing like barely animated mannequins wearing heavy makeup and short, silky thin dresses. Each girl wore a large numbered button pinned on her chest. Tom explained to me that this particular establishment combined the muscle stretching and elbow ramming of a traditional massage with a bath and total body oiling. He went on to describe how the girl pours massage oil over her naked body, then slithers and wraps herself against you like an over-friendly house cat. The finish, Tom explained excitedly, was a "seriously happy ending."

Tom called out his number to the watchful pimp who took his money and brought the teenaged girl out of her glass cage as if he were a pet store worker leading a puppy to a new owner. She shuffled flat-footed and emotionless with Tom following her up the stairs. I stood there uncomfortably next to the pimp, acting as if I couldn't decide on a worthy number. The women—teen-aged girls mostly—reminded me of colorful caged birds or stray cats and kittens waiting to be adopted from the animal shelter. They were the face of poverty and cultural pressures forcing them into enslavement. To service the aging *farang* serpents who had invaded paradise, they closed off their minds and oiled their bodies.

The round-bellied, square-headed Thai pimp counted his money and puffed on a cigarette as he eyed me suspiciously. When he finally turned away to greet a better dressed elder *farang* coming through the door, I sat down to wait. Half an hour later, Tom returned and said, "You got through that pretty fast! Got to love this town, eh?" As I followed him out the door past a group of incoming drunken Asian businessmen, he asked me a bit too loudly, "Care to see Bangkok's best live sex show?" I know a place where this girl does a crazy act with ping-pong balls."

"Thanks, Tom, but I've got a long ride home and need to get to work early." I sounded prudish. The simmer of love in my heart for a girl I had left in Taiwan was too fresh, and the caged girls here were too emotionally distant to arouse my own lustful thoughts. I was reminded how much I missed my girl now that she was gone.

After that display of his craving for young girls, when I arrived at the hospital, I was surprised to see three slender teenaged Thai *kathoey* (also called "lady boys") sitting on the side of Tom's bed. Though not in full female costume, their facial makeup as well as their exaggerated effeminate mannerisms left no doubt as to their sociosexual proclivity. In 1980s Thailand, the *kathoey* were considered a legitimate third gender, and widely accepted, whereas the equivalent class in America was generally shunned. As one of the boys leaned over to wipe the drool dripping down Tom's chin, he said, "Tom's our roommate. We stay at his apartment. If he doesn't get well soon, I don't know where we'll go." Was this another side of Tom's apparently wide-ranging sexual appetite that he had kept to himself? Perhaps he had assumed I would judge him harshly and disapprove. Now he was beyond worrying about anyone's disapproval. When I went back to check on him a week later, I was told a relative had arrived and had arranged for Tom's return to a U.S. medical facility.

The Thai people's acceptance of teenaged girl or boy prostitutes and of the *kathoey* who openly solicited the sex tourists who flock here to embrace them is based on a cultural and social tolerance that is rarely equaled in the world. Most Thais believe in karma, a belief that allows them to regard prostitutes and *kathoey* as having committed transgressions in their past lives and as deserving pity and acceptance rather than condemnation.

Settling In, Thai Style

My employers paid not only for my motorcycle but also for my accommodations in a recently constructed cement house divided into two apartments, located halfway between Bangkok and the shipyard. I hired a single woman in her early twenties, named Charunee, who lived in the same small town, to act as my secretary and general assistant. Six mornings a week I rode my bike to her apartment to give her a ride to our shipyard office. Charunee spoke basic English and helped tutor me in Thai. Treating me like an overgrown school child learning the English alphabet (A is for apple, B is for ball), Charunee had me repeating and eventually memorizing the 44 main characters of Thai script with the following mnemonic song:

Ko oei ko kai (K is for *kai* "chicken")
Kho khai nai lao (KH is for *khai* "egg")

And so on I'd go through the alphabet, over and over again, until rendering myself tongue-Thai-ed.

Charunee loved to sprinkle her English with common Thai expressions, partly because of my rapidly growing vocabulary and because she knew they brought a smile to my face. When she wasn't easing my concerns with *"mai pen rai,"* I often heard *"sabai sabai,"* which is Thai for "very good" or "everything is fine." In Thai, repeating some words twice takes the place of using the intensifier "very." In Thai, sickness is *mai sabai*, or not *sabai*. Thais strive to live in a well-balanced state of body and mind. Westerners tend to misinterpret this as slowness, carelessness, or laziness. Some of their slowness may be due to the climate, but mainly it is the need to avoid the ill effects of stress. Keeping the mind and body relaxed is their key to happiness and health.

Other local customs I picked up from my Thai friends included performing the *wai* instead of shaking hands when meeting people. Why invade a person's private space or spread germs by touching strangers? Instead, the head is bowed or nodded slightly with hands pressed together as in prayer. Hands are held at chest level for those you feel are your social equals and up to your nose when greeting those deserving higher respect or fear, such as monks, bosses, and maybe mothers-in-law. Children rate only a passing nod. And please, fellow *farang*, do not touch Thai people on their head. The head is sacred. Thais may lower their heads in respect when they pass in front of you. It was such a thoughtful gesture that I often felt compelled to say "thank you" as they scurried past. On the other hand, the feet, being the spiritual and physical low point of the body, are the opposite of sacred and must not be pointed at people. Particular care should be made to avoid displaying the bottom of your ungodly feet to someone when you are sitting.

The Kingdom of *mai pen rai* is non-confrontational; shameful arguments or criticism are diligently avoided. To display anger or impatience is considered a psychological handicap. This goes a long way in explaining their uncomplaining acceptance of Bangkok's unending traffic jam. Visitors should keep in mind that the beguiling, ever-present Thai smile is used to mean anything from happiness to embarrassment, from uncertainty to fierce anger. A *farang*'s directness and emotional outbursts are sure to be exasperatingly unproductive. The Thais praise *jai yen* (cool heart) by their perpetual display of patience and acceptance.

While in the Kingdom, I deeply regretted that my job left me no time for a vacation to the inland mountain regions of the country. Too much time spent in a capital city, whether Bangkok, Manila, or Washington, DC, inevitably leaves me depressed. The green heart of a country is where you will have an authentic cultural experience. My work also kept me from visiting the famous coastal and island resort areas such as Phuket Island. Perhaps that was just as well because a visit to the coast without my boat would leave me as lost as a tourist without a hotel.

First Hull, Then Hubris Precedes the Fall

Once we completed construction of the first yacht, I did at least make a trip down the River of Kings. The newly born yacht was launched during a blessing ceremony performed by an elderly, saffron-robed monk. Suitably blessed, the boat was bound up for shipping in a mostly submerged wooden cradle, and we motored her downstream.

Dragging the bulky cradle through the water cut our speed in half, giving me ample time to observe the life on the river. We drifted slowly past ornate riverfront *wats* (temples) into the heart of Bangkok where ferries replaced bridges. Smaller, "long-tail" water taxis filled with commuters rapidly crisscrossed the river. These narrow, open boats, called *hang yao*, are like extremely long canoes with a raised, elongated bow. They are propelled by a standard automotive engine mounted on a swivel bracket driving a prop hanging from the end of a long shaft. Because the engine can swivel side to side, the rudderless boats are steered by turning the entire engine for thrust vectoring. There is no transmission, therefore no reverse. Neutral is achieved by tilting the engine forward until the lethal propeller comes out of the water. The design is ingeniously simple, cheap, practical, and utterly crazy-looking.

Receiving the monk's blessing

We passed narrow side canals, called *klongs*, which forked off the main river like Venetian avenues. City commuters often use the water-taxis on these earth-stained, sewage-filled canals to avoid the traffic-choked streets. Some *klongs* held floating markets where tourists gawked at the locals doing their shopping among the nestled watercraft. Further downstream we arrived at the shipping port. We grappled with the cables lowered by a crane and then disembarked to a water taxi as the yacht was hoisted onto the deck of a ship for transport to a U.S. dealer half a world away.

I didn't realize at that time that despite the success of the launch of our first boat, the production cost overruns, the falling number of customer orders, and Edwards's inept management of people had created a perfect storm that would soon force a halt to production. Days after the first boat was delivered and the next one was being laid up in the mold, I had a nighttime visit at my apartment from Edwards. He started right off by laying into me with angry complaints about insignificant or contrived issues. This was the first time he had spoken to me so accusingly, but I knew what was coming. I stopped him mid-sentence by placing my hand in front of his lips. "I quit," I said.

For a moment he was struck speechless. "Yes, I think that would be best," he replied as I led him to the door. I was so fed up from dealing with that destructive egomaniac that it came as a relief to discover I was no longer needed.

Over the past two years I had silently watched Edwards disrupt lives by making hollow promises to new employees and then firing them instantly when he thought it was to his advantage. That was not so unusual for some business owners. But what made it even more malicious was how, instead of politely telling them that the job situation had changed and that he regretted having to let them go, he preferred to verbally abuse them with undue criticism and false accusations. In that way he could claim the firing was a fault of their own and not related to his own poor business judgment. He also knowingly drew up unfair contracts with designers, builders, and suppliers. Quality suffered as builders and supplies cut corners in an attempt to maintain a profit. When the pleasant young Thai lady in charge of the shipyard tried to explain why the contract terms were impossible to meet, Edwards shook his contract in front of her face and threatened to file lawsuits and to withhold payments due to her.

I had shamefully and stupidly stood by as one of Edwards's stooges. Mr. White, who had bought the company from Edwards several years earlier and had kept him in charge of building operations, was probably unaware of many of his manipulative dealings. The few personal visits and phone discussions I had had with Mr. White showed a man of integrity who treated people fairly. Finally, he too became another victim of Edwards as the business crumbled around them.

With his boatbuilding business failing, Edwards's questionable ethics sank to new lows. He alternately falsely praised or ranted against people around him. In the end, there was no wrong or right beyond what was right for him. His pontifications were worse than a conniving snake oil salesman, and his promises were as empty as his soul. He imagined himself the King of Boatbuilding. He was the Savoy of Stupidity, the master of the smiling lie. He belonged to that sub-class of elites recognizable by their large vocabularies and small-mindedness. For Edwards, the truth was much too troublesome. Unfortunately, it had taken me a full year to realize that it was he who was the lying scoundrel who needed to be watched, rather than the factory owners whom he had warned me against. It was ironic to think that the high end of a high-end market was based on such low scruples.

I don't believe that Edwards had set out to become the hated man that he turned into. His vision had been to create a functioning work of art that a sailor could love, depend on, and be proud to own. In that, he succeeded, for a time. Somewhere along the way, his struggles with a competitive market had infected his dream to the point of destruction. As Henry David Thoreau states in his book *Walden*, "But I have since learned that trade curses everything it handles; and though you trade in messages from heaven, the whole curse of trade attaches to the business."

Despite Thoreau's eloquent rejection of capitalist transactions, he was a business babe in the woods. We know that greed and dishonesty do not infect all who do business. Most transactions result with both sides smiling. If love of money is the root of all evil, then selfishness is evil's seed.

The Thai factory owners were eager to be rid of me along with anyone else who had been tarred by the brush of association with Edwards. It weighed heavily on me that we had let down our trusting and kind Thai associates. I was especially sorry to say goodbye to Charunee and inform her she must find another job.

Edwards had once confided to me, "James, I'm getting older and may not have many productive years remaining. I'm fighting for my legacy here." Some men busily gather and count their gold, seeking full pockets at the expense of others but instead come to discover they have built empty lives. How much richer they would be if they instead gathered an honest reputation and loyal friends of shared good character. Whenever I felt disheartened by my own position among the feuding parties in that business, I recalled Mei's comment to me back in Taiwan: "The prime minister's stomach can hold a ship," which is their way of saying that a leader must be capable of tolerating and managing a variety of conflicting voices. I was no prime minister.

In 1993, the Hans Christian company was sold to other luckless investors. Some of the hull and deck molds were eventually moved to a factory near Thailand's coastal resort town of Pattaya. The new factory was run by an expat New Zealander, but apparently production was limited to only a few boats.

The experience of the Hans Christian company was a story repeated in similar forms throughout Asia at that time and continues to this day. Many of the imported goods we purchase so indiscriminately are built on the cruel human gristmill of global economics. Tax havens and cheap labor are a perpetually moving target—Taiwan yesterday, Thailand and Philippines next, then on to China and Vietnam. Later, they will rediscover Africa and rush to exploit the labor there. And when there is no longer a cheap labor force to abuse, we can construct robots to build more robots. How ironic and inevitable it will be when the robots come to enslave their creators. Already we are willing prisoners to a technology that is so pervasive that we would likely starve to death in a month if the global economic-manufacturing system unraveled. Even today's sailors cannot venture beyond sight of their home port without an Asian-built satellite GPS to navigate for them. A lesson I took from this experience working in the global marketplace is that the more interconnected and co-dependent we become, the more self-sufficiency we lose and the more fragile our existence becomes. These issues reinforced on me how lucky I was to have found a life of modest needs aboard a small boat.

The Writer's Craft

Back aboard my boat in Hong Kong, my 20 months ashore in Taiwan and Thailand had left me eager to become a sea nomad again. Soon after I first sailed into Hong Kong I gave an interview about my travels to an editor of the local sailing magazine, called *Fragrant Harbour*. During its four-year history up to that time, it had grown from a four-page newsprint give-away to a glossy 70-page color publication with a wide circulation around the yachting centers of Asia. When I told David Robinson, the expat publisher and chief editor of *Fragrant Harbour*, that I planned to sail extensively through Southeast Asia, he suggested I write a monthly destination series on the interesting islands I found along the way. I contacted him on my return to Hong Kong and found the offer remained open. Even though the pay of $150 U.S. per feature-length article was not much, I readily agreed, since it gave me an opportunity to polish my writing skills and provided an incentive to explore the region thoroughly. Not that I particularly needed an incentive to travel to the distant shores of my dreams, but I appreciated how the job focused my attention on details of the islands and cultures I might have otherwise overlooked. Sharing my experiences sailing among some less visited islands with the wider cruising community was worthwhile in itself. Best of all, journalism gave me cover for my normal nosey questions, intrusive camera, and my innate need to imbed myself into the fabric of the islanders' lives wherever I went.

When I showed Robinson the 12-part series I had written about my trip across the Pacific for a Detroit-area newspaper, he gave it a quick glance and handed it back with the comment, "The pieces I want you to write need to be different. Fifteen-hundred words max, with photos, and drop the personal pronouns like 'I, me, or my.'"

Still not comprehending that he wanted my articles to read like a travel brochure, I asked, "Can I say 'we' instead?"

"No, the idea is to set your ego aside and remove yourself from the story."

It was quite a letdown to this presumptuous unlettered sailor to think my tales could be improved by reducing them to something like a terse impersonal account found in a newspaper or an in-flight magazine. Nevertheless, the valuable lesson I learned writing that series over the next few years was that a travel narrative need not be all about me. Whenever possible, the focus should be on the people, places, and events.

In a metaphor conflating the hard manual labor of the farm with the less virile, mental labors of writing, Thoreau declares: "A sentence should read as if its author, had he held a plow instead of a pen, could have drawn a furrow deep and straight to the end."

A good editor is "worth his weight in gold" because he ruthlessly deletes your carefully crafted clichés and harvests the essence of the story from the plowed-up roots littering the narrative field. If my editor and readers will forgive yet another metaphor, writing is a craft that takes time—lonely hours holding the pen and tapping out the revised drafts over and over on my portable typewriter until the manuscript becomes as vivid and tactile as the carved wooden storyboards of New Guinea. Both writer and woodcarver must pack their work with the essential elements needed to convey the events, without (cliché alert!) obstructing the forest by too many individual trees. It also helps to imagine my readers are new members of *Atom*'s crew. My obligation is to make them feel welcome and connected to my journey. All this was better brought into focus by the task of delivering a readable monthly travel story for the magazine.

Collecting my earlier journals and articles and expanding them into what became my first book was like a 25-year pregnancy. That travel narrative was not intended to be all about me, though a solo journey around the world is inevitably and unavoidably a discovery of self. Just as Michelangelo claimed he merely freed David from the marble, the writer of a memoir has all the material he needs within his memory and journals. He need only lay it all out and then whittle away the excess to reveal the heart of his story. This second book you hold was born of two years of reflective labors and, I hope, is not premature. In my mind, you are all fellow seekers, and it's my great privilege to have you aboard for this journey.

Atom Gets Spruced Up for Sea

I was now "sailor rich," having socked away enough money for an indefinite cruise through Southeast Asia. Unable to sit still on all my cash, I purchased a few items for the boat, including a new locally fabricated folding companionway dodger, new bunk cushions to replace the old flattened vinyl-covered foam, and a new mainsail to replace the old threadbare and patched hand-me-down sail that had brought me across the Pacific.

I also bought an English-built Lavac marine toilet. The toilet was added mainly to appease my more delicate guests who tended to turn up their noses and quickly return to shore when faced with using a bucket and then dumping it over the side. The Lavac was an ingeniously simple design that used a standard bilge pump mounted behind the toilet to create a vacuum when the gasket-sealed lid was closed. Pumping the handle simultaneously emptied the bowl while sucking in rinse water. It was foolproof compared with the other complicated, leaky, and clog-prone marine toilets on the market. The British designers got the unit just right, and it is still sold today. To be able to get the rinse water in and the wastewater out of the toilet I had to install two seacocks below the waterline. To do that I careened *Atom* on the shore of Hebe Haven by bringing her up to the beach at high tide and then installing the seacocks as she laid over on her side in the receding waters. Since she was high and dry for this job, I also scrubbed the hull bottom and added another coat of bottom paint. Once the port side was finished, the next day I turned the boat at high tide and painted the starboard side on the falling tide.

The day before departure, I made several trips ashore in the dinghy to provision with food and water for the trip of 600 miles across the South China Sea to the Philippines. Once I got to the islands I hoped to find crew to share my travels. But for this next offshore leg I was content to continue the solitary passage-making that had rewarded me in the past with such rich adventures. My muscles and mind unwound and relaxed. I felt the pride of being the master of my own destiny once more.

15 The Philippines – Galleons and Gold Mines

For a sailor, the islands across the next sea hold a limitless and bewitching allure.

Dervish Sailing; Fluid Confusions

As *Atom* and I drew within 60 miles of Luzon Island in the Philippines, the winds flowing down the mountains spilled onto the sea in an invisible mishmash of vortex currents. I expected some turbulence in the trades when closer to shore, but having the winds disrupted this far out was a surprise and a portent of a long and laborious struggle ahead. *Atom* turned and spun to the shifting winds. I worked like a whirling dervish, turning this way and that, throwing the tiller from one side of the cockpit to the other and back again, running ten steps forward to change jibs, turning aft to reef or unreef the mainsail, and rushing back to the cockpit winches to adjust the sheets. Far from bringing me to a state of dervish ecstasy, that often futile, maniacal routine frequently left me dismayed to see we were stalled again under backwinded sails. When fatigue and frustration set in, I again found solace knowing that for the first 99 percent of the history of sailing craft (before the engine was invented), sailors had had to deal with similar and even more difficult challenges than those I faced. There was nothing for me to do but persevere, as I tacked and inched my way along the mountain range of Bataan Peninsula for two days before reaching the entrance to Manila Bay.

From the start I anticipated that this voyage across the South China Sea from Hong Kong to Manila would be an arduous passage. Actually *experiencing* "arduous" turned anticipation to hard reality. On the first day the winds were light, and it took all the hours of daylight to sail the 15 miles needed for me to clear the uninhabited Chinese Lema Islands that stand like giant border guards between Hong Kong and the South China Sea. Numerous fishing boats and commercial shipping traffic passing me on all sides forced me to hand-steer through much of that first day and night. By dawn the islands and the heavy traffic lay far behind. The winter's northeast monsoon kicked in, providing steady winds that grew appreciably stronger by the hour. With the windvane steering engaged, I adjusted our course to the southeast, which brought wind and seas a few degrees forward of the port beam.

A day later, gale-force winds forced me to shorten down to three reefs in the mainsail with the storm jib sheeted in tightly. There was no opportunity for me to ease off the wind to a more comfortable downwind course until we had crossed the South China Sea. Until then, there was a risk of being driven so far to leeward that I would be unable to beat back into the monsoon to fetch the Philippines. To leeward lay the coast of Vietnam, whose officials at that time were not friendly to American yachts showing up uninvited on their coast. A gnawing anxiety settled in the pit of my stomach: I had strong winds trying to blow me away from my destination with a hostile country lying directly to leeward. If winds increased further or if anything critical broke on this passage, I could expect to be hailed by a Vietnamese gunboat and subjected to all the unpleasantness that would ensue.

Fast Sailing; Heavy Seas; Rogue Waves

The sheer thrill of sailing a fast beam reach distracted me from the body aches caused by the jarring pounding we took from the huge punishing seas. As my world heeled over at 30 degrees I watched from inside the security of the boat's cabin as the seas washed against the cabin windows. I knew the lurking danger of sailing beam-on to waves, lifting and dropping us 10–15 feet every few seconds. *Atom* relied on her shallow, lead-ballasted keel for a tenuous foothold in the sea to resist being thrown down the faces of the whitecapped waves like a piece of flotsam. Here, as on any open water passage, the average waves were nothing to worry about. Perhaps one in a hundred was significantly higher and steeper than the rest and would announce its arrival with a sharp slap against the hull that sent a fountain of spray showering over the deck.

What I feared most was a rogue wave. I scanned the approaching waves constantly, mentally bracing myself for The Big One. A rogue wave is that one in a few thousand that reaches double the normal height of its neighboring waves. A freak wave can end a voyage in a flash as it heaves the boat with explosive force into the wave trough ahead of it, nearly as hard as if she were falling on solid ground. In such an event, portlights and hatches can be stove in, hull to deck seams cracked open, and single weak points in mast rigging tested beyond their shock load range. I drew uneasy comfort knowing I had strengthened the boat's already solid hull, deck, and rig for just such punishment. Still, there was an unknowable limit to what she could take. In some situations it's preferable to slow the boat by heaving to, deploying a drogue or sea anchor, or by turning downwind under bare poles. But on this winter monsoon passage it wasn't feasible to prolong our exposure waiting for the winds to ease because it might be weeks before that happened. In this case, the best defense was to secure all hatches, reef down, and hold tight. Whatever would come next was beyond my control.

The physical laws that govern how various wave trains momentarily coincide were easily understandable, but knowing when that might occur is impossible. Every now and then over the next 600 miles, a minor rogue clobbered the boat, sending me flying to land painfully on whatever hard object lay in my path to leeward. Reefed down, *Atom* took the punishment without much complaint beyond shuddering from the assault, momentarily dipping the end of her boom into the sea, and filling the cockpit footwell with water. Mile after windswept mile, man and boat synchronized our focus of reaching a safe harbor.

The only serious navigational challenge on this leg was safely avoiding the low atoll and reefs of Pratas Island, located 150 miles southeast of Hong Kong. Navigation occupied a good chunk of my time as I attempted to take accurate readings of a cloud-obscured sun from the sextant while being punched and shoved around by the seas. I aimed closer to the atoll than I would have liked, in order not to be driven later so far to leeward as to be unable to fetch Luzon on one tack. But I knew I must stay on the leeward side of Pratas. Many ships steered by arrogant or hapless navigators have been shipwrecked while attempting to pass to windward of the reefs of Pratas. Wind and current in this region can wreck your boat on the reefs before you are even aware of their presence. Passing to leeward was my only safe option. A big part of navigating a small boat can be summed up thus: stay to windward of your destination, stay to leeward of your dangers.

Somewhere near Pratas, the waves grew confused among the crosscurrents, tossing themselves aboard from all sides as we continued bounding along tearing up the miles. I must have taken 10 sextant sights that day, attempting to average out the errors. My chart became cluttered with lines of position penciled in at various angles. The majority of the lines indicated I was passing about 20 miles to leeward of the atoll. Even so, I spent most of a day and night on deck peering into the spray-filled air for signs of waves breaking on reefs.

Danger in the Darkness of Manila Bay

Once we had fought our way inside the 25-mile-wide Manila Bay, I found more headwinds channeling between the mountain ranges that lie close to the north and south of the bay. At least the winds were fairly settled here, and sail changes were required less often. Another sleepless night passed as I sailed past the dark silhouette of Corregidor Island, which guards the entrance to Manila Bay like a giant tollbooth. In the darkness that night I watched the navigational lights of an approaching vessel. The green light on his starboard side with white light above indicated it was a motor vessel of some type. Using my handheld compass I noted the relative bearing between us changed enough over the next few minutes that it was clear he would pass safely in front of me if I held my course. Once he had passed, the course ahead looked clear. There was nothing to make me think this was anything other than another ordinary crossing situation. As I prepared to duck below to boil water for a cup of tea, I made one final visual sweep of the horizon. I was shocked to see a thick horizontal steel cable lift into the air a few feet above the water just two boat lengths ahead. I instantly leaned over to sight under the jib. The dark silhouette of an unlit barge surged towards me. In five seconds I would be entangled in the towline and then crushed under the barge's broad menacing bow. I leaped back to disengage the tiller from the self-steering and tacked the boat, clearing the barge by a scant few feet. Death lurks in darkness. Vigilance is all you have to stay alive out there, and vigilance demands endurance. The adrenaline rush shook me wide-awake and doubled my resolve to stay alert.

In open water a tugboat uses a towline that is several hundred feet long in order to reduce shock loads and provide a safe distance between themselves and the barge. According to international regulations, a tugboat pulling a barge is required to show a different navigational light scheme as well as carry a light on the barge itself. That captain had been lazy or ill equipped, which I've found was not unusual in Asian waters. I too was guilty of non-compliance by displaying only my white anchor light on the masthead. At least our small size and slow speed presented minimal threat to other shipping, and the single white light was normally the best choice for ensuring other vessels kept clear of us. In this case it was entirely up to me to avoid collision.

Unfragrant Harbor; Friendly People; Deep History

By sunrise I was within one mile of the yacht harbor. My head was reeling again. I was close to collapsing where I stood from lack of sleep as the dying wind ceased altogether. The high-rise buildings of Manila punctured the layer of smog hanging low over the waterfront ahead. Through binoculars I made out a hazy view of the yacht moorings, tantalizingly close, yet out of reach for now. I dropped my sails and then lowered an anchor into the flat calm waters. I stretched out on the cockpit seat, totally exhausted and instantly fell asleep. Two hours later I awoke to a hot sun piercing through my eyelids and burning my face. A light breeze brought the unmistakable stench of smoke, automotive exhaust, and sewage to my nostrils. I felt a perverse happiness since the mix of noxious smells also marked my approach to safe harbor. As I hoisted the anchor, a pair of American fighter jets screamed low along the waterfront and turned inland. I tacked my way up to the breakwater of the Manila Yacht Club basin and dropped my sails. Using my oar, I sculled through the closely packed boats and picked up an empty mooring to secure to our bow cleat.

While approaching the Philippines during the preceding days, I had listened intently to short-wave radio broadcasts on the BBC describing a bloody, ongoing coup attempt that had erupted against Philippine President Corazon "Cory" Aquino. When I imagined the scene of President Aquino being strafed and bombed by her own air force in her presidential palace in Manila, I couldn't help juxtaposing it in my mind with images of General MacArthur. In WWII, MacArthur and his army held out for months on their island fortress across the bay on Corregidor under relentless bombardment by encircling Imperial Japanese forces.

These were recent episodes in a long Philippine history that is marked by siege and counter-siege. Over a period of several thousand years, the islands had been populated by various waves of immigrants from Indonesia and mainland Asia. By the time of Ferdinand Magellan's arrival in 1521, Muslim chiefs had extended their power from Borneo as far north as Manila. At least 500 years earlier, the Chinese merchant ships of the Sung Dynasty had begun regular trading trips to these islands. The stage was set for an epic struggle of civilizations when permanent Spanish colonial occupation began in 1565. Within ten years the ruthless conquistadors gained control over most of the islands of what constitutes the present-day Philippines, from Mindanao Island in the south to Luzon in the north. The zealous Spaniards drove out

Muslim chiefs and converted the majority of the population to Catholicism, except for remote pagan tribes inhabiting the islands' mountainous interiors and a few firmly entrenched Islamic areas of Southern Mindanao. To this day, the Philippines (named for King Philip II of Spain) remain the only predominantly Christian country in Asia. After the Spanish-American War of 1898 until independence in 1946 the Philippines was a colony of the United States.

In 1574, the Spaniards successfully fended off a Chinese junk fleet carrying 3,000 pirates intent on sacking Manila. From the superb natural shelter of their base in Manila Bay they also held back other competing European forces and Muslim marauders for another 300 years. In contrast, the weary defenders of the shrinking Spanish Empire gave up with only a few token cannon shots of defense as U.S. Navy Commodore Dewey steamed into Manila Bay in 1898 to oust the Spaniards from the Philippines on the pretext of a spat with them over Cuba.

During WWII, it was America's turn to have her Asian empire downsized when the Japanese chased General MacArthur to Corregidor Island. Eventually he made a midnight escape on a PT boat to Mindanao where he was flown to Australia. "I shall return," he famously promised. And return he did, with a massive force of ships, troops, and planes to rain hell down on his previous tormentors. But MacArthur's triumphant return was brief. Soon he was off to Tokyo where he helped rule a defeated Japan. After the Americans peacefully handed over the islands to the Filipinos in 1946, years of political turmoil and the long dictatorship of Ferdinand Marcos ensued. Finally, fed up with the excesses of Marcos and his cronies, the mostly bloodless "People Power Revolution" brought Cory Aquino, the self-described housewife of an assassinated activist senator, to power in 1986.

As I sailed towards Manila, Aquino and the fragile Philippine democracy itself were under siege in the presidential palace. The possibility of her being ousted by a military coup was probably less humiliating to her than enduring the deeper embarrassment of relying on the fighter jets of the proud country's ex-colonial masters to tamp down the uprising. Hundreds of people had been wounded and nearly a hundred more killed before the traitorous faction of the military armed forces and Marcos loyalists had been defeated. By the time I arrived in Manila, the blood was being scrubbed from the streets as Aquino's forces negotiated the surrender of the remaining rebels who had barricaded themselves inside tourist hotels and high-rise buildings in Manila's Makati business district. With the army tenuously reunited, life in Manila quickly went back to what passes for normal.

My 650-mile passage from Hong Kong had taken eight days. Thanks to the unsteady winds of the final few days, the trip had been notably slower than our average pace of just over 100 miles per day in the trade wind regions. Since I had visited the Manila Yacht Club two years earlier when picking up a yacht to deliver to Hong Kong, I was able to reunite with past friends at the clubhouse and among the workers in the club's boat repair shop.

Manila was a city easy for visitors to dislike: the squalor of homeless people occupying cardboard boxes on the sidewalks; beggars, hustlers, and pickpockets trailing you on the street; arguing with taxi drivers over the fare because "the meter is broken"; top to bottom corruption; traffic noise and congestion; the heavy smog and the sweltering heat. The combination presented a less-than-welcoming impression. Yachts stopped here to clear in with customs and immigration, get provisions, make repairs, and then beat a hasty retreat. Yachties did not linger here. The main sewage outlet for the city emptied its foul brew straight into the yacht mooring basin, fouling the air with an eye-watering, sickening stench of sewage. Boat boys scrubbed the oily mess from the yachts' waterlines caused by frequent fuel spills. Even the decks required a frequent scrubbing to rid them of the atmospheric fallout of black soot. Although I was pretty hardened to third world harbors by then, even I felt the urge to leave almost from the first day, but first I had some repairs and provisioning to do.

Even with the unkind city environment, the Filipinos overall, even in Manila, were a surprisingly happy and friendly people. Despite reforms during the American colonial era and by the more liberal government since the Marcos years, there was a continuing Spanish colonial legacy of a few politically well-connected families owning a large percentage of land and big business. It was as if the country were entirely missing a middle class. The poor did not aspire to a non-existent middle class as much as they held a largely unattainable dream of joining the lower upper class.

As much as any other large city, Manila can be expensive or inexpensive, depending on the lifestyle you choose. For visiting sailors who exchanged dollars for pesos (at one dollar for 25 pesos) and avoided imported goods, it was easy to live cheaply. Use of the yacht club facilities by foreign guests cost only a few dollars a day. Altogether, I hung around in Manila for three weeks, doing maintenance jobs on the boat and provisioning for an extended sail through the more remote islands to the south.

Before I could sail south of Manila, I needed detailed charts of the islands. To cover even half of the archipelago would require well over one hundred charts. In most countries, that many charts would be a huge investment. Fortunately, the Philippine National Mapping office sold charts for the equivalent in pesos of about $1 U.S. each. On my way to the mapping office I walked down Roxas Boulevard along the Manila Bay waterfront. Within a mile, I passed the walls of the U.S. Embassy with its long line of Filipino visa applicants waiting outside the consular entrance.

As I ambled through the welcome open space of Rizal Park, I found myself in front of the remains of the four century-old walled city of Intramuros. These walls had been built after the Chinese pirate attack of 1574 that had nearly wiped out the poorly fortified city. At one time the 160 acres of land within the walled and moat-encircled city contained a fort, churches, schools, housing, markets, and everything else a colonial city required. When the American forces came to liberate Manila from the Japanese in 1945, the enraged Japanese Army took revenge on the civilian population, murdering tens of thousands of civilians, including women and children. The remains of the walled city of Intramuros that I walked past was a hollow shell of its former self after being almost entirely destroyed when American forces bombarded the Japanese defenders, pounding them into the blood-soaked rubble.

After crossing the bridge over the Pasig River into San Nicolas district, I was quite lost without a map, so I asked the driver of an idle horse-drawn carriage for directions. "Hop in, Joe. It's only 10 pesos," the man told me. "Joe" (from "G. I. Joe") or "*Kano*" (for "*Amerikano*") is what many Filipinos call Western foreigners. There's nothing offensive about the term, though some tourists always manage to find offense where none exists. Off we went in the ancient carriage pulled by an emaciated old horse, driven by an even older, leaner driver. The horse moved us along with traffic at a slow and broken trotting pace, hooves clomping on the centuries-old cobblestone streets. At my destination I pored over a navigator's mother lode of charts and topographic maps, selecting about 60 nautical charts and several detailed island maps covering the areas I expected to visit.

Looking over my bundle of charts and land maps of the Philippines, I let my imagination bring the intricate details of ink on paper to life. I imagined the harbors I would sail into and the mountains I would explore. The sheer number of islands contained on these sheets was staggering. One of my gripes with tourist brochures is their unabashed exaggeration. The Philippines tourism department claims there are exactly 7,107 islands in the archipelago, as if each and every one was counted and notable. Every travel brochure and article about the islands you read will parrot that number, despite the lack of an accurate source. But what constitutes an island? Does any barren islet or rock nearly awash at high tide qualify, or is it something more? Named islands are easier to count, and reportedly there are upwards of 2,000 of those in the Philippines, though I don't know if somewhere there exists a full catalog. Even if the tourist department's numbers were technically accurate, saying there are 7,107 islands is about as useful as a farmer expressing his crop size by the number of kernels of corn it held or describing the size of the land your house sits on as containing 21 million blades of grass. Although sources claim there are about 2,000 inhabited Philippine islands, looking at a detailed map you would be hard pressed to count 200. After sailing extensively around the island group, I would estimate the number of inhabited islands to be somewhere in the several hundreds, which is a grand enough number to consider and way more than any visiting sailor would attempt to visit.

On most of my trips across Manila and later travels into the countryside, I would jump into the back of the ubiquitous jeepney. The locally manufactured jeepney, whose origin is the American Jeep of WWII, is a stretched-out, diesel-engine-powered, jeep that serves as the primary means of public transportation throughout the islands. Jeepneys are unmistakable with their gaudy adornments of air horns, rows of extra lights, and emblems such as small aluminum horse statues. The exteriors are often brightly painted and carry religious names or are named after a prominent female in the owner's family. I stepped into one jeepney in Manila with the quirky name "Lover Boy" painted on its headboard. The cabs of some jeepneys are also garishly decorated by their owners in a hybrid pimpmobile/popemobile motif and play loud local music on their sound systems. Fares are only a few pesos for short runs, but some jeepneys will take you to the next town or even across the island at an affordable rate.

On a provisioning trip in Manila, I waved over a jeepney, entered the open back, and squeezed between the other passengers who were sitting on two benches running fore and aft. The jeepney didn't get beyond second gear before traffic stopped us. Even without the traffic, it was a slow trip across town because passengers wanted to get in or out at almost every street corner. Before long, being stuck in traffic, deprived of legroom and air conditioning, and forced to inhale jeepney exhaust motivated me to get out and walk or wave down a taxi. But it wasn't always that bad, and I came to prefer the jeepney to those predatory taxi drivers' wildly variable fares and broken meters.

When ready to disembark, if the music wasn't too loud, passengers often signaled the driver to stop by blowing a lip-smacking kiss in his direction. Otherwise, they simply tapped their pesos on the metal roof to get his attention. The driver's helper stood on the back step, clinging to handrails. He collects your fare and shouts *"Sige"* for the driver to continue once you are in or out. In the countryside, you may be packed in tightly with squawling babies, clucking chickens, and bags of produce filling the narrow isle. The driver cannot bear to refuse a fare, even when overloaded. There were times I rode hanging off the back bumper and handrails or on top clinging to the luggage rack. It's refreshingly cool to ride on top; I would watch the scenery go by, always on the ready to duck under drooping power lines or hanging tree branches.

Family; Tradition; Hospitality

Among the notable people I met at the Yacht Club bar was local yachtsman and club officer, Antonio Araneta. Tony was keenly interested in the details of my travels. When he discovered that I was working as a *"journalista"* of sorts and that we shared an interest in Philippine history, he invited me to his home for dinner. At his family home in the affluent Makati suburb of Manila, I met several generations of the Araneta family. Their house, better described as a mansion in colonial Spanish architecture, had a staff of 14 servants, including maids, security guards, and a personal driver. Seated at the head of the table was Tony's mother, the grand matriarch of the Araneta clan. She explained to me how their ancestors had come to these islands in the early 1700s from the Basque region of Spain. Later, after a bit of research, I learned that members of the Araneta family have long been leading figures in the Philippine political, military, and business communities.

Unlike the vast majority of Filipinos, the Araneta family bloodline was apparently as nearly pure Spanish as when their ancestors had stepped off a Spanish galleon over 250 years ago. Over the centuries, most Spanish settlers in the Philippines had intermarried with the local Asian and indigenous peoples and had shifted from speaking Spanish to the new national language of Filipino (also called Tagalog), which is based on one of the main indigenous languages on Luzon Island. Thanks to their American colonizers, English is a common second or third language for many Filipinos. But the Aranetas were the only family I met in the islands whose elder members continued to speak Spanish among themselves.

In Tony's library, the walls held portraits from the Araneta family tree, interspersed with law diplomas and photos of American and Philippine presidents who had visited the home. I noted that both Nixon and Marcos, two presidents with similar dramatic falls, had both been here for dinner. I hoped there wasn't a curse attached to visitors attending an Araneta family dinner.

After dinner I showed pictures on Tony's slide projector of my one and a half circumnavigations to date and gave a talk about my travels. Following that, Tony invited me into his library where he explained to me that he was attempting to organize an expedition to retrace the return route of Magellan's first voyage around the world. He asked if I would captain the yet to be built replica ship. He explained: "My plan is to sail from Manila, south through Indonesia, and then west across the Indian Ocean to round the South African Cape into the Atlantic, and then on to finish in Spain."

Part of me said: "Uh, ohhh . . . here we go again." Another part of me was intrigued by the possibilities of another adventure. We met several more times during the next week to discuss the details of such an expedition. But my earlier participation in the Marco Polo voyage fiasco put me on a fence. Tony then flew to Mexico, Cuba, and Madrid to continue his research. We stayed in communication over the next year, but unfortunately, as in most cases, the costs and organizational issues involved strangled his dream before it got beyond the planning stages.

However, I did learn a great deal from Tony and his library about the intriguing and complicated history of the Philippines.

The Philippines – Mix of Ancients and Accidents

From books I borrowed from Tony's library I discovered how the Manila galleon trade had been so essential to the centuries-long Spanish rule over these faraway islands. The Treaty of Tordesillas in 1494, in which the Pope divided the known and unknown world in two halves, designated the lands falling roughly from Brazil east to Africa and India as Portuguese territory. Lands west of Brazil to some vaguely understood meridian in the far western Pacific were to belong to Spain. Prior to the arrival of the Portuguese in the Spice Islands of Indonesia, the trade in spices, gems, silks, and other Eastern treasures had been restricted by the Egyptian sultans and Venetian middlemen who had regulated trade through the Red Sea. Once the Portuguese explorers discovered the sailing route around South Africa and found their way to India, they quickly dominated trade through the Indian Ocean. With the bulk of Asia-Europe trade goods passing around the Cape of Good Hope on Portuguese ships, the tremendous price of many of these Eastern goods was cut in half within a few years and then cut in half again.

After Magellan's pioneering circumnavigation, Spain seized on the alternate route to the Spice Islands and the China trade via the Pacific Ocean and the Philippines. Beginning in 1565, the Spanish discovered a trade route that allowed them to bring silver from their American colonies overland through Mexico to the Pacific port of Acapulco and then across the Pacific to their new Asian capital in Manila. Traders from China exchanged their goods in Manila for the pesos minted from silver from Incan mines, and the galleons returned to Mexico to complete the cycle. It was no easy route, though. Dutch and English pirates, typhoons, and navigational errors plagued the galleons. Fortunes of a lifetime were won or lost on the fate of every ship. These galleons were the largest craft ever built by Europeans up to that time. Some galleons were 160-feet long and carried large numbers of Spanish settlers along with their rich cargos.

The Spanish galleons had been crisscrossing the Pacific for over two hundred years before Captain James Cook discovered Hawaii in 1778. But how could it be that the Spanish navigators who had discovered the Philippines, the Marianas Islands, much of Micronesia, the Marquesas, the Solomon Islands, and New Guinea had somehow missed sighting the several high islands of Hawaii? The Manila galleons generally passed just south of Hawaii on the run in the trade winds westwards across the Pacific to Manila. Then on their return passage the prevailing winds forced them to sail north until near Japan before finding the zone of westerly winds that carried them north of Hawaii to make landfall on the California coast. In theory, they would not have sighted Hawaii on this route. But after hundreds of ships made the journey it seems all but impossible that not one of them took a slight detour or was forced off course by weather. My guess is that the galleons did discover Hawaii, but because they were running a trade route and not in the business of exploration, they left these islands mostly unmolested. In addition, since the Spanish guarded their galleon trade monopoly from other European powers, they had no reason to publish details of their route or their discovery of Hawaii.

Lapse of Judgment – An Awful Crunch; Touring the Islands

Once provisioned, I was ready to continue my own explorations of the islands. On New Year's Eve, I invited local friends to a pre-departure party aboard *Atom*. I served my guests a dinner of vegetarian spaghetti that some liked and some just picked at. Fish, pork, or chicken and rice, even seven days a week, was what most of them were used to and preferred. From just after sunset to well after midnight, the city was barraged with an unorganized display of firecrackers and aerial rockets. From every direction, a cacophony of sounds like the gunfire of execution squads and incoming mortar explosions rocked the city. It was as if the people were reenacting MacArthur's battle for Manila. A black powder blanket of smoke rose into the air and drifted out over the bay. Most cities around the world have a fireworks display in one location, but the 30-mile-wide stretch of barrios and towns linked together into greater Metro Manila competed with each other simultaneously. Meanwhile, anyone who could acquire firecrackers or rockets joyously contributed to the celebration. Every year, accidents from the fireworks fracas injure hundreds and sometimes kill people in Manila. Errant rockets have been known to burn down buildings. Occasionally, whole city blocks go up in a giant inferno as happened during Manila's 2015 New Year's bash.

Just after sunrise on New Year's morning 1990, while most of the city lay hung over and asleep, I dusted off the night's fallout of ash and shreds of fireworks paper from the deck. I hoisted the mainsail to the light land breeze and cast off from our mooring buoy. On all sides, the yacht basin was packed with local motorboats as well as a few visiting and local sailboats hanging on their moorings. With a fair wind behind me, I believed I could maneuver around the boats and past the breakwater into Manila Bay. Many times we had passed safely through similar crowded mooring areas in Hong Kong and other ports around the world. But on this day I made a tactical error. As soon as I had raised the mainsail and stepped to the bow to release our mooring line, the wind gusted and began driving us forward. I rushed back to correct the tiller, but the wind had forced her bow to turn in such a way that she would not react to the rudder in the short time available. We were less than one boat length from a nicely painted wooden motorboat when I realized we were going to collide no matter what I did. I rushed to the mast to release the mainsail halyard, but the pressure of the wind pinned the sail against the mast so that I only had time to lower it halfway before I had to give up and jump to the bow to ease the impact by using my outstretched arms to fend off the other boat. Despite my efforts, *Atom*'s pointed bronze stemhead fitting made a sickening crunching sound as it poked a six-inch hole into the stinkpot's pretty hull. It was remarkable to me how easily that hull plank gave way. This may rank as the stupidest thing I had ever done under sail. Now I knew why some stinkpotters hold blowboaters in such low regard. I should have taken the extra time and effort to scull out of the crowded basin or at least have hoisted only a small jib, which would have given me a chance to maneuver more easily than I could with the mainsail. Instead, I had been sloppy and complaisant. Now I had to delay my departure one day to contact the boat's owner and arrange to pay the boatyard for repairs.

Having cautiously sculled out of the yacht basin the following morning, I hoisted sail to run downwind out of Manila Bay. The fair wind held as I worked my way south along the mountainous coast of Luzon and tacked into a quiet and protected cove where I anchored for the night. At the first glow of dawn's twilight, I hoisted anchor and continued my passage south. Rounding the southwest peninsula of Luzon, I met with headwinds funneling down the channel between Luzon and Mindoro Island to the south. After tacking for several hours across Balayan Bay, I anchored in a partially protected indentation along the south shore of eight-mile-long Maricaban Island. Taking my kayak ashore, I found the beach was actually composed of pea-sized stones rather than sand. This corner of the island was uninhabited aside from a few cattle I saw grazing on the steep hillside. A scramble through the bush brought me to the top of the hill for a view of my next destination 12 miles ahead at Puerto Galera, on Mindoro Island. Below me, outrigger fishing boats, called *bancas*, propelled solely by paddle and multi-colored patches of sails, flitted butterfly-like across the white-flecked blue waters.

The next morning I again tacked into the headwinds, often sailing alongside those solo fishermen riding free in their double outrigger *bancas*. One man sailed up close enough that we exchanged greetings without the need to shout. He paced me for a mile so we could get a good look at each other's strange craft. His mini trimaran was comprised of a center hull of a hollowed-out log about 12 feet long with two flexible wooden outrigger booms attached to bamboo floats. The contraption appeared fragile and flimsy, with outriggers twisting up and down as he rode the choppy waters as lightly as a waterbug. He steered the boat easily by a combination of sail balance and an oar dipped into the water. With his other hand he frequently bailed water with a coconut shell as it spilled over the gunwales that rode just a few inches above the water. These minimalist sailing *bancas*, used primarily for fishing, were common throughout the Philippines wherever I sailed. Less abundant, but still common, were larger motorized versions that carried cargo and passengers from port to port.

That afternoon I tacked my way into one of the two narrow channel entrances leading to the mile-long indented harbor of Puerto Galera. An islet next to a twisted peninsula provided superb protection for the harbor. Beyond the small town at the head of the bay, the green mountains rose up over 8,000 feet in elevation within a few miles of the sea. This "Port of Galleons" certainly would have offered an excellent anchorage for the Manila galleons as they threaded their way through the archipelago to Manila. On that day the anchorage held six other visiting yachts from various countries. A few motorized *bancas* ferried handfuls of tourists from the town to the small-scale beach bungalow resorts located just outside the harbor.

In the Jungle; José's Gold

The day after I arrived in Puerto Galera, a fisherman paddled up to *Atom* in his sailing *banca*. The young sun-darkened man, named Emile Garcia, told me that when he wasn't fishing he worked part-time as a tourist guide and that he lived with his parents on the island across the harbor. Aside from Filipino, Emile spoke a fair amount of English. Like many Filipinos, he had picked up basic English in school. More recently, he was improving his English through his exposure to visiting yacht-folk and tourists who hired him for a one- or two-hour ride in his *banca*. When I suggested to Emile that I would be interested in a guided hike into the mountains behind town for a couple days he smiled wide and was eager to get started. "Is there any problem here with the NPA?" I asked, referring to the New People's Army, a communist-inspired insurgency that had been battling the government since the Vietnam War era. They were also rumored to operate as bandits who robbed and sometimes killed outsiders entering their territory. Emile replied that the rebels resided in remote parts of the island's interior and that we would avoid those places. In other parts of the island the rebels funded their cause by extortion, a.k.a. "revolutionary tax." The Philippine military had been hunting down the NPA and their spies all over the islands and had had some success in partially eradicating them. When President Aquino offered the NPA limited amnesty, many came down to surrender, but when some were then assassinated by the military, many others decided to hold out and continue the fight.

As I followed Emile up the forested footpath behind town, I was happy to return to an activity I loved as much as sailing—walking among the mountain footpaths, seeking the physical and mental challenge of summiting a high peak, and meeting the local people in places few tourists ever visit. I had learned on my walks across other islands in the past that it was a huge advantage on many levels to have a local guide, at least until I became familiar with the basics of the culture, language, and lay of the land. Since I only had a rough foundation in speaking Filipino, having Emile at my side the next few days would be another helpful boost to my language skills.

Several thousand feet above the town we paused at a clearing to look back over the folds of green hills to the harbor and beyond to the contrasting azure sea. Outside a one-room house built mainly of whole and split bamboo, called a nipa hut because of the nipa grass used for the roof, we met a slight, barefoot man dressed in mud-stained shorts and a shredded long-sleeved shirt. His wife was gathering green leafy vegetables from a garden as their young naked children played in the dirt. The man gave us his Hispanic name of José, which he used when speaking with outsiders. On his wrist he wore a broken-faced wristwatch as if it were a piece of jewelry. His curly hair and limited Filipino made it obvious he was from the Mangyan tribe, even though he was partially assimilated with the lowlanders with whom he frequently traded.

Up in the *bundoc* of Mindoro—*bundoc* being Filipino for "mountain" and coined into English as "boondocks"—live several tribes of indigenous Mangyan people. Each of the various Mangyan tribes has its own language, which is largely unintelligible to Filipino speakers. They survive mainly by farming root crops and fruit and by hunting small animals. These original inhabitants of coastal Mindoro migrated here by sailing canoes from various points in Southeast Asia thousands of years ago. From accounts of the traders aboard Chinese junks who visited these shores before the Spanish arrived, the Mangyan were peaceful fisherfolk, quite unlike the headhunters and warrior tribes they had encountered elsewhere. Faced with colonization by the Spanish and raids by slave-collecting Moro pirates, these gentle, outgunned people did not engage in futile battles. Instead, they gave up their fishing grounds on the coast and retreated to the rugged inland mountains where they could live a simple existence largely untouched by the menacing outside world. In recent generations these shy and reclusive people had continued their pacifist way of life, despite being exploited and discriminated against by lowlanders invading their lands.

Hanging from a string around José's neck was a glass vial no larger than a fingertip. When I asked what it contained, he held it up to my face and Emile translated: "It's gold flakes he dug from the river."

To supplement a meager income of selling vegetables from the family's garden to lowlanders, José scoured the *bundocs*, panning for gold in the mountain streams. After all, someone had named it Mindoro (Gold Mine) Island. The enticing name was a bit overstated in the same way that Greenland must have been a disappointment to gullible early settlers not expecting a mostly barren and frozen terrain. Mindoro never became the gold mine that tales had led the Spaniards to expect. But the Mangyans have managed to wrest just enough gold from the mountains to keep the legend alive.

Panning for gold with José

I suggested to José that if he would care to teach Emile and myself how to pan for gold from his river, we would pay him for the instruction by giving him any gold we found. José nodded his head in agreement. He grabbed a shovel, two wooden bowls, and a sack of supplies from his hut. We followed our barefooted guide up a slick, muddy footpath that tunneled through the forest canopy. Hours later, in the narrow cleft of a valley, we arrived at a clear stream less than a foot deep and small enough to cross in three steps. The bottom was a mix of sand, gravel, rocks, and clay. José pointed to a likely spot for gold, took his shovel and pried loose a large rock. We all grabbed it and heaved it up onto the riverbank. José reached into the depression left by the rock with his wooden dish and scooped up a pan full of gravelly sand. We watched him as he deftly shook and swirled the partly submerged pan, pausing from time to time to raise it out of the water to pick out the stones. After several minutes of this effort, the pan contained a cupful of multi-colored sand. We all looked intently as José spread the sand around the bottom of the bowl with his finger. With a sigh he tossed the goldless sand onto the bank in a ritual he must have repeated thousands of times over the course of his lifetime. We watched him run several more pans. Once we understood the technique, Emile and I worked the opposite bank. Pan after pan after pan came up empty as my back and knees grew weary and my fingers became numb in the cold water.

"Ginto!" (gold) Emile suddenly cried. José and I rushed over to see a single tiny fleck of gold on the tip of Emile's finger. Emile and I smiled enthusiastically as José unscrewed the cap of his necklace bottle and carefully transferred the fleck into it. I doubt that speck was worth one peso, but it kindled a heart-warming ember of gold fever in us that renewed our enthusiasm for the hunt. As darkness approached, we had added no more than a dozen of those tiny gold flakes to the bottle. Once the bottle was filled, which might take a month or more, José told us he would walk to town to exchange it at a general goods store for the few items his family needed that the land could not provide.

José led us to a campsite that he used when working this area of the mountain. In a fire pit, he roasted us some potato-like *gabi* roots (also known as taro) and cassava that we ate by peeling back the burned crust. I unrolled my one-man tent as José and Emile stretched out on a woven mat under the thatched lean-to. We spent a chilly night tending the fire in turns. In the morning as we warmed ourselves with the welcome heat of the rising sun, I shared my bag of oats and powdered milk with my friends, who choked it down while remarking what a poor substitute it was for rice. We worked another half day with just as unprofitable results as the day before. For José it was another average day of toil, no better or worse than most days on the mountain. When I think of José and his acceptance of much work for little gain, compared with those of us who are dissatisfied unless we amass a fortune in possessions (and debt), I'm reminded of the poem "To a Woman," by Filipino poet Conrado Pedroche:

> *You want the pearl beneath the sea,*
> *O you of many dreams?*
> *I have but cool, red clay, and sand*
> *Beneath my woodland streams.*

On the way down the mountain we stopped at José's gardens to pull ginger roots and cassava from the rich volcanic soil. Not having fertilizer, the locals rotate the crops. After a couple years a patch of land will no longer produce good crops. The farmers then abandon it and clear another patch. Eventually, an abandoned garden becomes reforested and fertile for clearing and planting once again. This practice has been going on in the highlands of Mindoro for many generations, and the Mangyan seem to realize that as long as a good percentage of the old-growth forest is left intact, the ecosystem will continue to flourish. Closer to the village of Baclaran we also harvested some jackfruit, called *lanka*, sprouting from the trunks of small trees. These elongated basketball-sized fruits weighed ten pounds or more each. Inside the rough green skin, the sections of rubbery fruit had a unique, slightly fermented flavor. Later, I found the flesh of the unripe jackfruit to be even tastier when boiled in a coconut milk broth.

An Excellent Tour; Emile Finds Lovlyn

Back at the boat, Emile was fascinated by everything aboard and kept telling me how he would love to crew on a yacht one day and travel through the islands. I had been thinking about making a counter-clockwise circumnavigation of the 90-mile-long island of Mindoro, so I invited Emile to join me. He could be my guide ashore, and I would teach him about sailing and living aboard a small yacht. A few days later, Emile beamed with anticipation as he gripped the tiller to steer us out of the harbor.

The next possible anchorage to the west of Puerto Galera was 60 miles away. Unable to make that in a daylight run, we had set off in the late afternoon for an overnight passage. Navigation was easy: the moonlight guided us along a straight and high coast, the waters ran deep to shore, and the winds held from astern. This passage between the two great islands of Luzon and Mindoro was known for its strong winds channeling through the straits. Through the night we reefed down sails progressively to the increasing winds. Having grown up bouncing in these same rough waters while fishing from small sailing *bancas*, Emile had no problem getting his sea legs and showed not a hint of seasickness. Sometime before dawn we rounded the western tip of the island at Cape Calavite. In the wind shadow of the mountains now, we sailed into a calm. Then, surprisingly, after sunrise the wind came at us from the south. As the great landmass of Mindoro baked under the sun, the heated air rose, drawing in a wind from the west. Now we could continue to sail south, but the onshore wind and waves along the open coast meant there was no suitable anchorage nearby.

Well-protected harbors with man-made breakwaters are uncommon among many of these volcanic islands. The 360-degree protection of Puerto Galera is a rarity. Most often an anchorage is chosen for the protection it provides from the prevailing winds. When the winds shift, you must seek out another anchorage. Because these islands are under the influence of prevailing seasonal winds, it is usually easy to find a satisfactory anchorage unless, as in this case, the island is so large and high that solar heating of the landmass creates its own wind system. We decided to carry on sailing through that day and the next night until we reached a more protected anchorage. At night we navigated by the lights of small settlements and the red lines of grass set ablaze by slash and burn farmers. There were also flaming fields of the dried-up remains after the sugarcane harvest.

We anchored the next morning off the town of San José. Our chart indicated the inner bay was too shallow even for our 4-foot keel, so we anchored in the outer bay, close to a beach where fishing *bancas* rested on the sand above the high tide mark. Facing the shore was a village of nipa huts on stilts. Children swam out to meet us, and I secured the rope ladder to the side so that some of them could board the first yacht they had ever seen. Wide eyes took in every detail as they peered through the hatches in amazement and chattered among themselves.

Because the boat rolled uncomfortably in the open anchorage, we stayed just the one night and continued on the following morning. After we sailed through a narrow two-mile-long channel between the south end of Mindoro and Ilin Island, we emerged into the full force of the northeast monsoon. Fully reefed, we beat into wind and wave for a couple of hours, making slow headway. I tacked north towards a peninsula of low land where we found enough shelter to anchor for the night. The force of wind caused *Atom* to heel and veer sharply as she tugged on her two anchors. By mid-afternoon the wind had settled down, so we rowed the dinghy ashore to visit the village of Tadlok. About 30 huts were built on the sand under the shade of coconut palms. Fishing *bancas* were pulled up next to the huts, and men sat around stitching up holes in their fishing nets as children played at fishing from the beached boats. A river passed alongside, and I noted that at high tide we might have been able to cross the river bar to moor in calmer waters, if needed. On the far bank of the river we could see sectioned saltpans where the crystals of evaporated seawater had been shoveled into snow-like mounds. I was struck by the total lack of rubbish or debris—the women had swept the sandy earth spotlessly clean from one end of the village to the other. A curious crowd of people gathered around us. Emile asked someone to introduce us to the "*barangay* captain." A middle-aged man stepped forth to shake our hands.

Emile advised me that it is customary when arriving at a new village to ask to see the *barangay* captain, who is an elected member of the community serving as a kind of mayor. *Barangay* originated from a Malay word meaning "sailboat." Naming a village a sailboat may have come from the idea that the sailing *bancas* that carried the early settlers to the islands contained families ruled by a chief who was also the master of the boat. It was only natural then to call the village mayor a captain. In pre-Hispanic times these *barangay* villages generally remained self-ruling. The lack of widespread coordinated resistance between the scattered *barangays* allowed the Spanish easily to conquer and rule these islands, except for south Mindanao, where the more organized Muslim settlements proved to be an ongoing challenge. Meeting the *barangay* captain to explain why you are there is a basic courtesy that repays the

visitor with several benefits. The captain is usually the best source for
local information and will almost certainly offer you his assistance for
any of your needs, such as where to buy provisions, recommend a
trustworthy guide, or identify someone who can help you fetch water.
He will also likely feel some responsibility for your safety and the
security of your yacht. Everyone in the village will soon know you are a
friend of the mayor, and this will help in your acceptance into the
community.

Suitably introduced to the *barangay*, I was barraged with questions
from the crowd. Emile told them about our trip to circle the island, and
in turn we asked them about the village. Not since my inland walks in
Tonga in the South Pacific had I encountered such a friendly inquisition.
I came to anticipate the standard set of questions that every traveler to
the smaller villages in the Philippines faces. It begins, normally enough,
with "What is your name?" which they repeat among themselves until
they get the pronunciation right. The next question in the familiar script
is always about where you come from. It doesn't matter that they never
heard of your hometown; it's somehow reassuring for them to know you
have a home somewhere and to know its name. The questions continue
in rapid fire: How old are you? What is your religion? Are you married?
If not, why not? Then follows a more detailed interrogation about your
family. If you counter by asking the same questions back at them, it only
encourages more questioning. Sometimes a senior woman will take on
the role of matchmaker and ask if you plan to get married in the
Philippines. My typical answer, "I don't know," sometimes brought the
comic follow-up quip, "Still negotiable?"

When I was asked why I was visiting a particular village, an answer
equating to travel for the sake of travel was seldom satisfying to the
interrogator. In their eyes, visiting such a dull and ordinary place as
theirs seemed not worth the effort to get there. The local people I
encountered in these islands were without question the most open,
hospitable people I had met in Asia. So many of them truly enjoyed an
opportunity to practice their English with tourists who wandered

through, even those of us who barely paused long enough to say hello and goodbye.

When I asked the Tadlok *barangay* captain for permission to walk around sightseeing in the hills behind the village, he selected a boy as our guide. Along the side of a cliff face we followed the boy into an expansive cave. Inside, the diffused sunlight illuminated a hanging garden of tree roots penetrating through the fissures in the rocks of the cave ceiling. Roots hung in the air a few feet above our heads, while others reached down to burrow into the rocky soil of the cave floor. Some roots had established themselves and grown thick and rigid as steel bridge suspension cables. Beyond the forest of roots at the back of the cave, we quenched our thirst from a pool of sweet, clear water.

The next morning we rose with the sun to sail around the windy southeastern corner of Mindoro. I learned I needed to start early before the trade winds began to increase in force as they typically did by late morning along a windward coast. Within an hour we were reefed down and heeled over, beating into the teeth of the trades. We made 15 miles to windward before tacking into the shelter of Bulalacao Bay, and sailed in as close to the shore as possible before dropping anchor in the shoaling water. We landed the dinghy and walked along the mile-long beach. Next to a village, numerous bamboo racks set above ground held small fish drying in the sun. Emile spoke to a fisherman who told us that schools of these sardine-sized fish, called *tolengan*, were so plentiful that all the local fishermen were currently employed in netting them from their boats. In another few weeks the run would be over, and these seasonal fishermen would return to their other jobs, such as gathering coconuts and tending their rice fields and vegetable gardens. A few of the men fished year round, staying out all night with pressure kerosene lanterns burning brightly to attract curious fish they would scoop one by one into hand nets.

A man paddled his *banca* across the river to meet us. It was the local ferry service, so we climbed in to cross over to the town of Bulalacao. Our fare was a half peso each (two cents U.S.). That typical small town of about a thousand people held the usual churches, vegetable market, and sari-sari stores. A sari-sari is a micro-sized convenience store found on nearly every street in every city and *barangay* in the Philippines. The stores are often run out of the front of the owner's house. Items for daily use ranging from cooking condiments to shampoo are repackaged into single portions to sell for a few pesos each. Even cigarettes are sold in single sticks. Regular customers are given credit and pay their bill on payday. Despite the higher long-term cost of buying in small quantities, the system works because many Filipinos live day by day and can't afford to buy in bulk.

Later that day we sailed a couple miles across the bay, passing between bamboo stakes marking several fish traps, to anchor in a well-protected cove. The water was deep close to shore, and I noted for future reference that this spot might make a good place to shelter from a passing typhoon. When we went ashore at the fishing village, the *barangay* captain treated us as special guests. He introduced us to each villager, who shook our hands warmly in the Filipino style, not by pumping your arm but by maintaining a prolonged clasp of hands in a handshake version of a hug. After we returned to the boat, some of the villagers paddled their canoes out to trade my spare bars of soap for their vegetables and fruit.

Because of a lack of protected anchorages further up the east coast on Mindoro, we tacked our way 30 miles east in moderate winds to gain the shelter of a string of smaller islands. From here there was a better wind angle to sail north. At Tablas Island we anchored next to some fishing boats in the two-mile-wide Looc Bay. Coming ashore, we met three jeepney drivers taking a break from work, sitting on a bench sharing a gallon bottle of fermented palm wine sap, called *tuba*. At their insistence we joined them to sample the acidic and slightly sour-tasting drink. In the islands, *tuba* is the drink of choice for those who can't afford bottled beer. Later we stopped at the town square where a beauty contest was taking place. After some speeches by the town council members and songs performed by a local choir, five lovely girls in long gowns were escorted onto stage. I coaxed Emile away to help me fill our water jugs at a tap behind the vegetable market before the final judging took place.

The next day we tacked against a north wind, sailing twenty miles further up the indented coast of the 35-mile-long island. On all sides of us were dozens of sailing *bancas* coming in from a night of fishing. We anchored off the village of Tanagon and went ashore to receive another friendly greeting from a crowd of people. We stayed ashore late into the evening and watched as men dragged their canoes down the beach for another night of fishing. Emile was especially happy to be sitting on the beach between three attentive girls, swapping stories and flirtations while the girls' brothers and fathers sat behind us drinking *tuba* and playing cards by lamplight. Being local tour guide had its social advantages.

In the morning we accepted an offer by the girls to guide us on a walk to visit another village a few miles away. The winding road passed over small hills and into valleys of rice paddies. On the way back, we met a lady tending the garden in front of her house. I complimented her on a Papaya tree that was so packed with fruit that the narrow trunk seemed ready to snap from the weight. She took my comment that it was "the most beautiful papaya tree I had ever seen" as a hint and asked us to wait a minute. She placed her wooden ladder against the trunk, climbed up five steps and twisted off several pieces of ripe fruit, which she presented to us as gifts.

The next morning Emile borrowed my kayak to go ashore to say goodbye to his new friend, Lovelyn, whose nickname she had told us was "Bic-Bic." He came back clutching a scrap of paper she had written for him that contained her mailing address. "For pen-pal only," he said when I looked too closely at the hearts and kisses symbols on the note.

We continued sailing north through the northern end of the region of the central Philippines known as the Visayan Islands. One of the welcome features of sailing these inland seas, surrounded by islands large and small, is that the swell of the open ocean was all but absent. When the wind laid down, so did the seas, leaving a calm surface to glide over instead of the tiresome heave and roll of an unceasing open ocean swell.

On our way back to Puerto Galera we stopped at Marinduque Island where I met the captain of an inter-island ferryboat. When I asked him about any navigable rivers in the region he told me there was a river 30 miles to the north near Lucena City in south Luzon that had depths of at least 12 feet for several miles upriver. Neither of us had a detailed chart, but he assured me the entry was straightforward. By now, Emile was keen to visit an actual city instead of all these boring fishing villages I had dragged him through. We departed early the next morning for a glorious sail with moderate winds on the beam, arriving off the river entrance at high tide. I hunted back and forth for a deep channel among the shoaling, sediment-filled water. What the ferry captain hadn't mentioned, or didn't know, was that there was now a shallow bar right across the river mouth. Giving up on finding the unmarked channel on our own, I dropped anchor a half-mile offshore in five feet of water and waited until a local fishing boat happened by. I waved him over, and we agreed on a price of 100 pesos for a tow over the river bar.

The tide was now as high as it would get. Even so, our towboat slowed to a crawl under full throttle, and the towline stretched to near the breaking point as he pulled *Atom*'s heavy keel through the mud. Once we were floating within the deeper water between the river's narrow banks, we cast off the towline and sailed upriver as children followed us along the shore, waving excitedly. *Bancas* carried passengers up and downstream at a fast pace while fishermen with handlines drifted downstream in the slow-moving current, sitting in inflated tire inner tubes. I nervously sailed under a couple of suspended power cables and then dropped anchor near a dock when I spotted a cable that was obviously too low for our 41-foot mast clearance.

As we went ashore the next morning, a local Coast Guardsman asked to inspect my passport and boat registration. Once he saw everything was correct, he told me ours was the first foreign sailboat he had ever seen in the river. Meanwhile, Emile ran off to the post office with a multi-page letter addressed to Bic-Bic.

Lucena City to me was just another city—like a small Manila—and held no particular attraction, so we left the following day. A fair wind hurried us downstream. We hit the sandbar again at high tide. With the press of full sail, we heeled slightly, and our keel cut a furrow through the mud bank like a horse-drawn plow through soft soil. We sailed overnight on the 50-mile passage back to Mindoro, taking turns hand-steering in two-hour shifts when the wind lightened too much for the windvane to hold an accurate course. Just after sunrise, the wind rose as usual to hurry us into Puerto Galera. We had been gone just three weeks but had visited several islands and had met many good people. I paid Emile for his help, and we promised we would see each other again. Within a few days I was ready to get underway once more. This time I would sail alone to more of those islands beckoning on the horizon.

16 Banton Island

Its people are the measure of an island's treasure.

Several mile-long tacks into the wind brought me through the Verde Island Passage between the islands of Mindoro and Luzon. A fortunate shift of wind then granted me a single-tack overnight passage across the remaining 60 miles from Puerto Galera to Banton. As on most passages through the central Philippines, navigation was easy because there often were at least two islands in sight at any time. Even without lighted navigation markers to guide me, on this passage I could discern the dark outlines of the islands under the light of a million stars. To fix my position I needed merely to take compass bearings on the islands and transfer those intersecting lines onto the chart. The sextant stayed in its box for the next few months.

Our cruise around Mindoro Island had given me a taste of what lay ahead on my travels through the Philippines. There was no guide book for cruising the islands I was now heading to. Everything ahead was unknown. But my charts indicated that the islands of Banton and Sibuyan, lying to the east of Mindoro, offered sheltered anchorages, at least during the current northeast monsoon season.

Small Islands, Warm Souls

Besides the necessity of finding a secure anchorage, smaller islands such as these intrigued me. To the wayward traveler, small islands open the better side of human nature. They provide an opportunity to know the land and the people on a more intimate level. In a large city, as a solo traveler I felt like a lost soul among strangers. There were times during my stay in Hong Kong, surrounded almost shoulder-to-shoulder by millions of people, when I felt disconnected from a faceless humanity. For many of us, our harried and distracted existence in the city leaves us too busy to allow time to let a stranger into our lives. But in a small island community you are soon among friends. Stepping onto an island is almost like joining the crew of a ship. At sea I reveled in the sanctuary of solitude. When I visited the world's out-islands, a deep need awakened in me to embrace society. There is no better way to do that than among the extended families of an isolated island.

A banca arrives to welcome me to Banton

I anchored within a protected bight on the west coast of Banton. My chart indicated a settlement here named Mainit, but there was no sign of a village on the shoreline of rocks, sand, and palm trees. In Filipino, *mainit* means "hot." The curious name itself was enough reason to bring me in for a visit. From the coast of this four-mile-wide island, I gazed upwards at a sea of coconut palms rising in a green wave up the half-mile-high slopes. By the time I had my main anchor down and then set a second anchor by dinghy, two men had paddled their *banca* out to greet me. Emilio Mingo and his son-in-law Winnie de los Santos stepped aboard and welcomed me to the island. The men told me that they were both farmers and fishermen and that they represented the only two families now living at Mainit. Though the unschooled Emilio only spoke Asi, one of the Visayan dialects limited to Banton and a few small neighboring islands, we became instant friends. Winnie spoke Filipino and a smattering of English, so his inquisitive father-in-law kept him busy as translator. "Where is your wife or crew?" Emilio asked in amazement after a quick scan of the empty boat. When I replied that I was sailing alone as I had done many times before, he smiled and put his hand on my shoulder in admiration, or sympathy, or a little of both, then invited me to come home with them for dinner.

Enchanted Springs, Black Fairies

Stepping ashore I immediately understood why the village had been named "Hot." Emilio and Winnie laughed as my bare feet danced across the burning mix of gravel and sand at the water's edge. The bottoms of their feet had built up thick calluses from years of walking barefoot, and they were nearly immune to the hot pebbles, although I did notice they too spent no more time than necessary on the super-heated stones. Winnie explained that the underground volcanic thermal heating there was most evident during low tide and that the pebbles were only pleasantly warm when covered by water at high tide. At low tide the locals sometimes dug a hole near the sea's edge to place fish or vegetables to cook in a natural earth oven. Thankfully, a dozen steps farther up the beach, the ground temperature returned to normal.

When I asked where I could get fresh water to fill my tank, they scooped out a shallow hole in the gravel near the high tide mark. The hole quickly filled with delicious, mineral-laden spring water that I later scooped out by the cupful to fill my water jugs. "It's an enchanted spring," Winnie told me. "It moves around underground and seeps up through the sand in different locations each season." He went on to explain that in the dry season the spring inexplicably runs more strongly, but in the rainy season it often becomes weak and sometimes even goes dry.

Camouflaged within the tree canopy and boulders above the beach was the nipa house of Emilio's family. His wife served us a dinner of rice, grilled fish, baked pumpkin, and *bibinka*—a delicious sticky cake made from grated cassava roots and coconut cream. Emilio's plot of land was so full of rocks that he used the larger ones for furniture in his dirt-floored house of woven split bamboo walls capped by a grass roof. We sat on these stones around the wooden dinner table while a group of children, temporarily banished from the house, stared and giggled at me through the glassless open window.

By the soft light of an oil lamp, we exchanged stories as we sipped fresh *tuba* that only a few hours earlier had been flowing sap collected from the top of a coconut tree next to their house. Along with the oddities of the hot beach and the spring that disappeared and reappeared, Emilio told me about the mischievous "black fairies" living in the mountains. According to Emilio, they take the shape of a chimp-sized monkey, which is three times the size of the real monkeys who inhabit the forests of Banton. A local farmer said he had shot and wounded a black fairy with his rifle. A few days later the man took ill and died, supposedly from the vague but lethal symptoms of black magic. The previous year, Emilio claimed, an old woman had been abducted by one of these fairies from her home and was never heard from again. The fairies are also blamed for casting a spell on a young married couple who climbed into a canoe one calm, moonlit night, paddled out to sea, and never returned. The mental image of that couple paddling off into the night haunted me. Were they seeking a new island in order to live away from disagreeable in-laws or under an intoxicating fatal spell?

When Emilio had married, the traditional courting ritual on Banton called for the man to declare his intentions by singing a love song called the *pamentana* outside the girl's window. Like characters in an opera, the girl would signal her acceptance of him by lingering in the window.

Later, the boy's parents brought gifts for the girl's family, and then the elders made plans for the marriage. The *pamentana* had gone away on Banton, although marriage still begins with a romantic courtship and then becomes a firm alliance between families.

My new friends gave me a ripe papaya and a bunch of bananas to bring back to my boat. The next morning, Winnie paddled out to join me for breakfast. I served up my favorite thick cornmeal pancakes. In place of syrup, I mashed the papaya and a banana into a jam, spread it over the pancake, and topped it with the fresh powder I grated from cinnamon tree bark and a hard, marble-sized nutmeg seed. As we ate in the cockpit, two teenaged boys in their *banca* joined us. Alongside them swam another young man. When I lowered the rope ladder and asked him to come on board, he bypassed the ladder, gripped the toe rail with his hands, and pulled himself up on deck. His legs were twisted and wasted, probably from polio. We don't often see polio victims in the Western world because since the late 1950s nearly all of our children have been vaccinated against this crippling disease. But even at a cost of pennies per dose, the vaccine has yet to reach all of the world's children.

The crippled teenager introduced himself as Boi. His friends later told me that Boi was too proud and independent to let them carry him and that crutches don't work on the sandy, stone-filled soil. His withered legs were a useless encumbrance to him on land, where he dragged himself along the uneven ground with excruciating effort. But in the water he had freedom of movement and an escape from a the brutal world of gravity that tested his endurance at every turn. His friends claimed he was one of the best divers and spear fishermen among them. I made a gift to Boi of my spare goggles and snorkel to replace his leaky, homemade, wood-framed diving glasses. In return, Boi offered to stay to watch over my boat while Winnie and I went on a foot tour of the island. I gave Boi a pancake and a glass of water, rigged an awning over the boom for some shade, and then departed with Winnie in his *banca*.

We stopped at Winnie's house where I gave his wife some antibiotic capsules from my medical kit for an infected cut on their daughter's leg that had turned into a tropical ulcer. She opened the capsule and poured some of the powder onto the girl's wound instead of having her swallow the entire capsule as I had expected. This was a common technique in poor communities. The people had learned that by applying small amounts of the powder directly to the wound, they could cure the infection with two capsules rather than needing to buy larger amounts for a week of oral treatment. It also made sense not to poison your entire body with drugs when a topical treatment could do the job as effectively. In the future, I employed their method on my own minor wounds, and it seemed to work better than the prepared antibiotic ointments.

The Long Stone Road

Behind their house, Winnie led me to a narrow road of hand-laid stones, the tops of which had been laboriously chiseled flat. The intricately constructed stone road circled the perimeter of the island, connecting the villages and making travel by foot much easier than walking the muddy footpaths that lead up into the interior mountains. Various heights of rock fill kept the grade of the road remarkably level as the land dipped and rose under it. Around each bend in the road were reminders of the rural lifestyle. People worked quietly in their tropical gardens or gathered piles of coconuts that had fallen throughout the forest during the previous night. Stone-sided fire pits for smoke-drying coconuts were everywhere, indicating that copra (dried coconut meat) was the island's chief export. In the sparse patches of soil between the weatherworn boulders, we passed crops of tobacco, banana, tomatoes, and taro. The name Banton, which means "stony," was an apt description of the entire island.

In a hidden interior valley on the western side of the island we entered the settlement of Tungonan. The village was set among mango, banana, breadfruit, and papaya trees, all competing for sunlight with towering coconut palms. Men had notched footholds into the bark of the trees with their machetes for easy climbing. I watched a man climb the tree as quickly as a monkey. He pulled himself between the fronds and onto the top where he retrieved a plastic jug that a day earlier he had tied to the cut-away stump of the tree's central flower stem. He hung the half-filled jug to a hook on his belt and descended to the ground. Winnie took a swig of the white liquid and pronounced it "very good." Gathering *tuba* required a skillful climber, and it was dangerous work. Many climbers had been killed or crippled when they grasped a palm frond that unexpectedly came loose and sent them plummeting to the ground.

At Tungonan we were stopped outside a high school by a teacher who brought us in to watch the students rehearse *Romeo and Juliet*. Next, we stopped at the *sari-sari* store where the woman who owned the store was weighing a baby in a basket hung under a scale normally used for weighing rice and flour. When I asked if babies were being sold by the kilo, the woman laughed and said, "No, we're measuring them to check for malnutrition." Mothers lifted the bigger children so that they could hang from the scale by their hands, while the storeowner, serving as a volunteer health worker, recorded their weight in her logbook. She then measured the children's height. "Filipinos like to be tall," she said. "Once a year at midnight on a full moon some parents stretch their children to make them grow. They call it *tubo* [grow]."

We left Tungonan to walk along the island's north shore where a narrow ribbon of concrete was gradually being laid over the old stone road. There was no assigned construction team for the project. Instead, each village had volunteers work on the section of road passing through their land. This ongoing project had kept many of the islanders employed for several years as they gathered and sorted small stones and sand from the seashore and leveled the road with pickaxes and shovels. A person was paid five pesos for each 50-kg bag of uniformly sorted stones he could fill and carry to the work site. At their slow pace, it seemed it would take another generation before the entire road was finished. The pace of work was slow and haphazard because there was no one in charge. There was no rush to complete the project, and why should there be? When the road was finished it would only attract the curse of motorized vehicles: something the small island community needed no more than they needed the invasion of a tourist industry that would turn them from self-sufficient stewards of the land to resentful stewards of demanding, credit-card-clutching tourists. On a beach along this north shore, some enterprising person had built a few nipa hut-style cottages to attract tourists to Banton. The scene reminded me of the uneasy choice between financial poverty and cultural destruction that faces so many island communities. A small island and its culture are fragile. A few cottages or a single guesthouse is bearable, but an influx of large numbers of tourists will unwittingly destroy the very thing they seek to discover. My hope is that communities such as Banton will choose to keep their lands out of the grasping hands of developers. I had to admit that I too was in some ways a tourist. But I carried my hotel and restaurant with me on my boat and sought to minimize my impact on the places I passed through instead of transforming them.

Defending Paradise: Pirates, Stones, and Church Bells

On the island's east coast is the main town of Banton. Here in 1663 the Spanish built a church and a fort out of limestone blocks to protect themselves and the local population from Moro pirates and slavers from the south who had repeatedly raided this peaceful isle. Like Puerto Galera on Mindoro Island, Banton was directly on the route of the Spanish galleons, sailing across the Pacific and through the San Bernardino Straits to Manila. The galleons could stop here for fresh provisions and anchor under the safety of the fort's cannon. Parts of the original fort and its cannon were still visible through the encroaching forest that had entwined the ruins with vines and tree roots. During the American colonial period the settlement was renamed Jones to honor a U.S. senator who pushed for voting rights for Filipinos. When the idea of Filipinos voting in American elections disappeared with independence in 1946, the town of Jones renamed itself Banton.

The people of Banton refer to their home as the "isle of peace and freedom." But there was a time when they defended it against invaders by hurling baskets of stones down from the cliffs. During the three years of Japanese occupation in WWII, to encourage obedience, many islanders had been summarily executed for minor offenses. Towards the end of the war their chance for revenge came when American planes sank a convoy of Japanese ships passing near the island. About 100 survivors reached Banton only to find the islanders waiting to greet their former masters with their baskets loaded with stones. The unarmed Japanese soldiers who had survived the initial barrage of stones retreated to the municipal hall. An angry mob surrounded them, pulling them out one by one and stoned them to death on the spot. Not one man was spared. I stepped into the same wooden building where the massacre had taken place and met the man who served as the island's postmaster, mayor, and sole policeman. Next to the mayor was an older man who proudly admitted to me that he had participated in the stoning, a scene unimaginable to me in a place of such serene and affable people. The kindnesses that nature had bestowed on the island were matched by the kindnesses its people had bestowed on me. But like the typhoons that occasionally sweep over the island, these amiable people are capable of rising up in fury when threatened.

The mayor informed me that the year before my visit to Banton, the island had again been invaded by pirates, for the first time since the Moros raids of centuries ago. The bandits in their *bancas* descended on the defenseless island from Luzon like a band of marauding Vikings. Brandishing rifles and machetes, the pirates entered the town, terrorizing the inhabitants and stealing whatever valuables they could lay their hands on. Since that incident, the islanders had organized their own coast guard with volunteers who rotated standing guard throughout the night. If a suspicious boat should arrive, the watchman would signal its arrival by ringing the church bells continuously. Another volunteer would run to nearby villages like Paul Revere warning of a British invasion. Hearing the alarm, the men of the island were then required to meet on shore to repel the invaders, while the women and children sought refuge hiding in the *bonduk*. Thankfully, bandits did not return and Banton's watch keepers have since returned to their beds.

Banton's connection to the outside world was via the weekly ferry from Lucena City and a monthly ferry from Manila. Few outsiders landed there because there was no hotel in town, though according to the mayor a guesthouse would soon be opened. The only other link with the outside world was the telegraph office where I watched a telegram being sent to Manila via short-wave radio by a woman tapping out the "dits" and "dahs" of Morse code on a wired brass key.

Mountain Gardens and Dynamite

On the way back from Banton town, we detoured to climb a steep, forested path to the top of Mt. Ampongo, the island's highest peak. We walked along the rolling ridgeline between Ampongo and the slightly lower Mt. Chaktak, which overlooked the anchorage at Mainit. On a narrow plain between these two peaks the fertile volcanic soil allowed some hardworking farmers to produce gardens of cassava and sweet potatoes. For two pesos I purchased two kilos of cassava roots direct from the lone farmer up here to use to make my own *bibinka* cakes in *Atom*'s galley. Beyond the cultivated fields, Winnie and I took turns cutting through the chest-high kunai grass so that we could make our way towards the edge of the cliff for a better view. Throughout much of the Philippines, this nearly impenetrable kunai grass had taken over the deforested lands, choking gardens and blocking any possible reforestation. We stepped as close to the edge as possible and looked nearly straight down at *Atom* as she lay securely in the anchorage. The blue waters stretching to the horizon were punctuated by islands like green stepping stones—Marinduque, the Tres Reyes (Three Kings), the

Dos Hermanos (Two Brothers), Mindoro, Maestro de Campo, Bantoncillio, Simara, and Tablas.

The day after touring Banton on foot, I exercised my arms by paddling my kayak around the island in a single long day. It was easy to slide through the calm waters on the island's leeward side, but it became a slow and tough slog to get through the choppy seas of the windward coast. There the turbulence of waves reflecting back from the bold rocky shoreline threatened to turn me upside down the moment I lost focus on maintaining my precarious balance. Once back in calmer waters, I was able to stop and rest my aching arms and back several times at isolated beaches set between the long stretches of boulders-strewn shores.

During these days Winnie was building himself a new outrigger sailing canoe. At night he was often out fishing beyond the anchorage with his father-in-law. I accompanied Winnie one day in his new sailing *banca* for the eight-mile round trip to Bantoncillo Island. With a fair wind behind us, our *banca* cut through the waters effortlessly. We hauled the boat up onto the perfect white-powder beach on the small, uninhabited islet, and I snorkeled among the shimmering coral reefs stocked with aquarium-sized tropical fishes. Winnie hunted the deeper waters for bigger fish with his sling spear. A couple more *bancas* approached, and Winnie waved me back to the beach just in time to avoid having my eardrums pierced by the thunderous explosions of dynamite sending up geysers in the waters in front of us. Fishing by dynamite was a serious problem in much of the Philippines because its overuse was killing the ecosystems of the reefs the fishermen depended on for long-term sustenance. But these men had hungry growing families waiting at home. Their thoughts were necessarily of food for the day at hand.

Halfway back to Banton, the fitful wind went calm, and I pointed out to Winnie what was obvious to him as well, that a contrary current was carrying us away from the island. Winnie handed me one of his paddles. Under a burning hot sun we rhythmically stabbed at the water with our short wooden paddles until reaching the beach at Banton two hours later.

Mother at the Loom, Children Flown Away

In search of more vegetables to bring on my upcoming trip to Sibuyan Island, one day I walked up a stony path leading to the village of Tan-Ag in the island's interior. A local woman who looked to be in her sixties was alone in the garden beside her house. For 50 pesos she cut enough green vegetables and cabbages from their stems to fill my bag. Through the open doorway of her little nipa hut I stared at an ancient wooden loom loaded with woven cloth. Seeing my interest, she and a younger neighbor woman gave me a demonstration. Using the foot treadle and quick, deft motions of her hands, she wove *buri* palm and *abaca* fibers into a roll of stiff cloth. Once a month she completed a roll of fabric that she carried to town for delivery to some Manila fabric merchant. In return she earned 500 pesos ($20 U.S.), which she said was enough to buy the few necessities she needed that couldn't be produced locally. Her husband, the loom's builder, had recently died and had been laid to rest in the island's cemetery. Her children had gone away years ago to live in Manila. Once each year one or another of them made a brief return visit to Tan-Ag. She reminded me of the other lonely old woman Mei and I had met in the abandoned Hong Kong fishing village. Both of these women had outlived their husbands and had watched their children go off to the city for a better education and jobs. It was a common theme in the countryside. Everywhere in the rural Philippines, I saw older people and children but not as many young adults. The adults I encountered either had never left their homes because of a legal or emotional need to keep the property that had been handed down by their parent's parents or had returned after failing to find a better life in the soul-crushing city. They came home to die and be buried in the soil of their ancestors. As I wondered if there was a way to bring some of the benefits of city life back to the country instead of enticing the young to abandon the old homesteads, I penned a verse:

> *Oh woman, where are your sons and daughters?*
> *Flown away to peck at the bitter fruits of the city.*
> *Will they fly home one day to bury you*
> *And mourn the loss of youth's bountiful orchards?*

A Mother's Son Returns

Reflecting on the woman at her loom tumbled me into the inner space of memories of my own mother and a sometimes troubled family life. I realized that I was not so different from her children. My mother died some years after my return from my 15-year-long second circumnavigation. She too had also spent many years without the comforts of family, just like the aging woman on Banton. Before I left on my first circumnavigation, my father had left her for a younger woman after years of leading a secret double life. My mother knew of some of his faults and shielded me from their marital troubles. Prior to the divorce and even after, this troubled man had shown a vengeful and abusive side of himself that I had not witnessed during my childhood. I bitterly resented his betrayal and bullying treatment of my mother. But some of my animosity was selfish: I equally resented the guilt his behavior placed on me when I left for my two-year voyage around the world. Before I departed, I cursed his existence and threatened never to speak to him again until he changed his behavior. Then I sailed out of his life. I vowed I would never be like him, which was an easy vow to keep. But there comes a time to let old wounds heal.

Twenty years later, when age had mellowed both our tempers, I finally forgave him, despite his continued prideful belief that no forgiveness was needed. An apology, however sweet to the ear, only robs forgiveness of its power. Just as the sea accepts all rivers, no matter how polluted or foul, who was I to build a dam against him?

I recalled that before he turned to meanness, his genius for invention and his strong work ethic allowed him to provide financially for his young family. He also taught me at an early age some of his considerable knowledge in engineering, metalworking and rebuilding classic cars in his workshop, hunting and wilderness camping, piloting a small aircraft, and the hundreds of other skills that a gifted father can teach his son. For a time, he provided the answers to all my questions. Skills passed from father to son gave me the assurance to go out into the world with full confidence in my abilities. Little did he know that I would use his knowledge of tools and his ingenious hands-on methods during my circumnavigations and later as I started my own business rebuilding sailboats and fitting them out for other sailors to roam the seas. I learned tools the way a child soaks up a foreign language, and the skills I acquired from my father at an early age are still with me today. I am my father's son, in the practical sense if not morally. Separating the truth of the flawed man from the myth of my childhood eventually brought an acceptance of things that cannot be changed.

While my mother outwardly encouraged my voyages, I know now how she silently wished for my return. I was too busy seeing the world to perceive her needs. But her heart was big. Her friends and volunteer work at the local hospital and various community agencies, as well as her part-time job as a director of county Senior Services, filled her life with joy and purpose. When I was a child, she had told me stories of how she had traveled in her youth with her girlfriend in an old beat-up Dodge car to Oregon and California in the early 1940s when it was not common for young women to go off on their own. They picked fruit in the orchards and then worked a year assembling aircraft components in a wartime factory. On days off, the small-town girls hunted autographs from Hollywood celebrities and danced at big band clubs with soldiers coming from or going to war. My father was one of those soldiers she danced with. Actually he was an engineer in the Merchant Marine who was running from his own tough upbringing under a stern father on a Minnesota farm. My mother brought that wandering mariner home to

Michigan to get married and live near her parents and three sisters. During her final years after all her relatives had died or fled from Michigan to faraway states, I could not convince her to come live with my family in warmer latitudes. She was understandably unwilling to leave the town that held her parents' graves, her church, her volunteer work for low-income seniors, and the few friends she had not outlived. She had grown old during the absence of her only child. Her steadfast pride in me was my secret embarrassment. Her love for me was so great that she wanted me to live the fullest life I could imagine, even if it meant years between visits home.

"My life has been wonderful," she told me as I gripped her hand on her deathbed. "You're here now, and I'm at peace to know we'll go through this together." I had finally returned like the Prodigal Son, to be at her side for her last days, to put both our souls to rest. I finally realized I was also there to seek forgiveness and complete my own cycle of redemption. My mother's pastor had seen events play out like this before and tried to assuage my anguish. I envy the peace of those who trust their God. But my grief was inconsolable. In a short time I understood that I cried not over the inevitable cycle of life and death but from the suddenly awakened guilt of a wayward son brought to death's confessional.

I had thought it sad when I saw that the children had left their mothers such as those I met on Banton and the Chinese woman in that abandoned village outside Hong Kong, without understanding at the time that I had done the very same thing. On one sorrowful night after my mother passed, I went to sleep in a funk of biting self-pity and dreamed of that woman of Banton at her loom. I watched from over her shoulder as she worked the machine alone. I wanted to speak to her, but she kept her back turned, pushing the foot treadle and concentrating on her work. Then she turned to me, and I saw her face was that of my mother with eyes that looked through me without recognition. There is always a toll to pay on freedom's road.

Women at the loom

Over the next three years, during my travels through Southeast Asia, I returned three more times to see my friends on Banton. On my final visit there, Emilio took me to a spot on his property on the hill above the anchorage. The palm trees framed *Atom* at anchor below us. "We will help you build a house here so you will have a place to live the next time you come back with your boat," Emilio generously offered. Banton was weaving itself into my soul. It was no longer just another island layover to me. That isle under the swaying palms embodied the essence of peace, grace, and discovery I had dreamed of as I wandered the world. I found it there in the richness of poverty and the benevolence of a tranquil people. Where nature is kind, people are kind. A hot, harsh desert may inflame the temper, but a small island community, pleasant climate, and abundant resources make for warm-hearted people.

As I raised anchor to leave this enchanted island, Winnie and his wife paddled out in their *banca* to hand me a basket of cassava cakes and bananas. "Come back soon—you have many friends here," they called, as our sails filled and carried us out to sea.

17 Lost Souls of Sibuyan

An adventure begins when you take the unknown path.

Braulio Rollon searched the misty heights of the mountain rain forest for rattan vines. As usual, he wandered alone within the clouds of Sibuyan Island's Mt. Guiting-Guiting, carrying little more than the essentials: a short *bolo* (machete), a flint to spark a cooking fire, and a small-caliber rifle that he used for hunting the increasingly elusive monkeys and wild boars. He foraged and lived off the land for days at a time, but because his island's forest was shrinking, he frequently found no more to eat than a few handfuls of wild edible plants. After he had collected all the vines he could lift onto his back, he would carry the bundle on an arduous two-day trek down the 6,000-foot-high mountain to sell them to a furniture maker in the coastal village of Taclobo. Only Braulio and a few other rugged men of the Mangyan Tagabukid tribe, who inhabited the interior of the island, continued to harvest the vines from these highest and least accessible areas of the mountain. Because the lower slopes of the mountain were rapidly being stripped bare by illegal logging and the lowlanders' encroaching mining operations, the search for rattan took Braulio higher and further into the jungle's hidden recesses each year.

As Braulio slashed through the bush on the steeply inclined slope, his *bolo* unexpectedly bounced off a metal object buried in the undergrowth. He bent down and uncovered a rusty iron cylinder about three feet long. When he tried to lift it he found it was too heavy. The strange metal object was a mystery but of no use to him, so he stepped over it and continued on his way along the mountain's flank. Soon his *bolo* hit another massive piece of metal. He reached down and uncovered a three-bladed object that he recognized as an aircraft propeller. Nearby, he found an engine, an aluminum airplane wing, and then the twisted fuselage. Strewn among the wreckage were machine guns, thousands of rounds of ammunition, and more of those rusty cylinders that he now realized were unexploded bombs. He was lucky his machete had not struck the bomb's triggering device. He looked around and found leather boots, jackets, goggles, and satchels of papers that had remarkably survived nearly a half century amid the perpetual wind and rain and riotous growth of the high jungle. He peeked inside the remains of the tangled fuselage. Braulio's excitement fell suddenly to deep sadness as he saw a complete skeleton leaning against the inside of the fuselage in a sitting position with arms cradling the bones of his comrade in arms. Both mortally wounded crewmen had died in each others' arms. Draped around their weathered bones were the stamped metal dog tags that identified them as American military. He knelt beside the skeletons, lit a candle he had made from tree resin, and said a prayer he had learned at the Catholic Mission to bless the lost men's souls. Braulio left the scene to report the find to the island's authorities.

Christ in the Mountain

After an overnight passage from Banton Island, I anchored off the small town of San Fernando on the south coast of Sibuyan Island. Surrounded on all sides by scattered islands, Sibuyan stands out boldly among its neighbors. Its craggy mountains tower nearly 7,000 feet above the 12-mile-wide, roughly circular island. Gazing up at the lushly forested slopes and jagged peaks disappearing under a stationary cap of clouds, I sensed that here lay an island of mysteries beckoning to be explored.

Sibuyan was the prominent, but still largely undiscovered, jewel in the necklace of seven islands that comprise Romblon Province. It was a bigger and wilder version of Banton Island. Strolling along San Fernando's placid main street of weathered wooden buildings, I passed a few dozen residences and followed my nose to a bakery where a slightly sweet *pan de sal* bread roll found its way into my hand for one peso. Next I stopped in front of a wooden shack that had "We Guard the Coast" painted in bold letters on its front wall. I thought the local Coast Guard officer might be interested in my arrival since visiting yachts are such a rarity here. I poked my head inside the open doorway to see the officer on duty stretched out flat on his back on a table. He snored blissfully, confident that the coast could look after itself during his siesta. Seeing that the sole coast guardsman here had neither weapons nor a patrol boat, I took it as a sign of an island at peace, far from the reach of the NPA (New People's Army) "infestation" or Moro pirates.

Moving on to the next building, I stepped into an office where I met Mr. Renion, the mayor of San Fernando. When I inquired about traveling into the island's roadless interior he suggested I first visit the Christ in the Mountain Mission to ask for a guide. Although I was prepared to walk the four miles to the mission, the mayor led me to the corner and directed me to step into the back seat of a pedal-powered tricycle. After watching the boy sweat and strain at the pedals under the hot sun for a few minutes, I asked him to stop and switch places with me. Making the circuit to towns and villages linked by this single road that encircled the island, a jeepney rolled by us with its passengers twisting their necks to gape at the unexpected sight of a pale *Kano* operating a pedicab.

Near the village of Taclobo, I stopped the pedicab next to a hand-painted signboard that read "Christ in the Mountain." As I walked up the neatly manicured grounds past flowering hedges to the church-shaped, oversized nipa house, a young Filipino man came out and introduced himself as Brother Frederico Molo. The mayor had told me that Brother Frederico's outspoken efforts to protect Sibuyan's magnificent remaining forests from illegal logging as well as his assisting the few remaining nomadic Mangyans to stand up for their land rights against the logging and mining companies had earned him a few enemies. I got the impression that the mayor agreed with Brother Frederico's work but not enough to stand against those powerful and dangerous forces himself. I came to learn that the Mangyans of Sibuyan were every bit as shy and non-confrontational as their counterparts on

Mindoro Island. Because their numbers and territory were so much smaller on Sibuyan, they were disappearing from their ancestral lands as fast as the old-growth forests.

Frederico brought me inside the mission house to meet a group of children sitting around a table scribbling lessons into their notebooks. "Welcome to our humble Catholic Mission for the orphan children," Frederico said. He then led me to see the smaller mission guesthouse set next to a gentle waterfall that emptied into a natural pool. He had constructed the house for occasional tourists to stay at when they visited the island, with the proceeds helping to fund the orphanage. "Shall you stay for viands?" Frederico asked. Although he spoke with a Filipino accent, I soon discovered that his English vocabulary was vast. It was as if he had memorized whole volumes of classic English literature, including a Victorian era dictionary, but had not heard the language spoken enough to know which words were too formal or archaic. His use of hypercorrect words not normally used in conversation gave his speech a charmingly formal and antiquated air. When I told Frederico I was looking for a guide to lead me to the top of Mt. Guiting-Guiting (Sawtooth Mountain), he replied, "I know a man who can guide us. In my own . . . uhm . . . perambulations in the forest, I have not yet endeavored to ascend that mountain. May I accompany you as interpreter?"

After setting a second and a third anchor to keep *Atom* securely moored in my absence, I returned to the mission the following day with my backpack filled with minimal provisions and camping equipment for a multi-day trek into the mountains. During the next few days I couldn't resist taking it upon myself to help Frederico unlearn some of his non-standard English. He, in turn, remained enthusiastic during the arduous journey ahead and was indispensable as an interpreter. Frederico instructed the older children at the orphanage to look after the younger ones for a few days during his absence. The two of us then set out for the village of Layag, which we reached after a few hours' slogging uphill along a trail partly overgrown with tangled bush.

The village turned out to be a single wooden house perched on a clearing on a saddle between the mountains. Noelyn and Lanie Ruga invited us into their combined home, schoolhouse, and medical aid station. These married lowlanders lived seasonally here in their government-sponsored schoolhouse where they taught the Mangyan children and provided basic healthcare for the people living in the mountains. The children who came here were from families of the semi-nomadic people scattered across several miles of mountains and valleys. The Mangyans mostly lived in rudimentary, temporary shelters, well camouflaged within the forest. By comparison the average lowlander's nipa huts built on cleared land were luxurious. The teachers explained that only one other family actually lived in the immediate area because each family preferred to keep to its own section of the forest where they could forage in a sustainable way without crowding their neighbors.

In Filipino, the word *layag* means "sail," which seemed an unlikely name for a mountain settlement. Standing on the front porch of the schoolhouse, I asked Lanie about the name. He pointed to the triangular, sail-shaped patch of azure sea visible below the horizon and a deep cleft between two mountains and said, "There is our *layag*."

Angeles, Man of the Jungle

When we told Noelyn and Lanie we were heading for Guiting-Guiting, they introduced us to a Mangyan man who lived nearby named Angeles Rollon. Angeles admitted that he had never actually been to the summit but claimed that he knew the way to get there. He pointed his *bolo* towards a mountain rising in the distance beyond the next valley, and then to another mountain behind it, and finally to a third distant peak that was Guiting-Guiting. With a silent nod of his head he agreed to act as our guide. His features reminded me of a tropical version of a Mongolian herdsman, with black hair hanging over his shoulders, narrow slits of eyes, and a long thin mustache that drooped over an unsmiling face. At his side hung his *bolo* in a wooden scabbard. The only other thing the barefoot man carried was an antique, small caliber rifle.

From Layag, Angeles led us on a steep descent along a muddy, eroded footpath to the Catingas River. We headed upstream, wading across the shallower sections and hopping between boulders in the more turbulent, narrow stretches. In one place, the river widened, and we saw that a couple of Mangyan families had planted gardens and built their huts on the low sandy riverbanks. During the typhoon rains that frequently affect the island, the people retreat up the mountain as the river floods and carries all before it—gardens, huts, and boulders—in a wild torrent down the canyon towards the sea. Later, the hardy mountain folk return to rebuild their grass and bamboo houses and plant new gardens.

As we made our way upstream, the canyon walls pressed in above us and slender waterfalls from smaller streams dropped like fluttering ribbons into the swift, clear waters of the main river. In places where the river had entirely cut away the riverbank, we inched our way along footholds in the cliff face with our bodies pressed against the dark, cracked volcanic rock wall. Somewhere near the headwaters of the Catingas River, we detoured up a rocky gulch. The sure-footed Angeles went ahead, scrambling over the boulders and unrolling a long rattan vine that he held for us so that we could pull ourselves up after him.

It was only after we were well up into the mountain hinterland that we left behind the background noise of chainsaws, wielded by men who were illegally cutting their way up the Catingas River Valley. Logging provided much-needed jobs for the island's growing coastal population, but the long-term effects of such rapid deforestation could mean the end of Mangyan culture. These forest dwellers were culturally ill-equipped to join the clamoring, impersonal masses in the competitive city. Many of the lowland settlers at the time considered the Mangyan barely human, and treated them like animals to be eradicated, pushed aside, or at best ignored. They could not see that these dignified and

gentle people required and deserved their wilderness homeland as much
as a bird needs the sky.

Children of the forest

Angeles could not bear to linger in the patches of red eroded earth
among the clear-cut logging zones that we passed through. He had been
offered work cutting and dragging timber back to the town lumber
merchant, but he refused to participate in the slaughter of the
wilderness, and ultimately, in his own destruction. It was sad to think
that within his lifetime much of the virgin forest might be reduced to
eroded sun-baked clay and patches of *kunai* grass as has happened on so
many of the once-forested islands of the Philippines. Modern island
nations too often ignore such examples as the warning lying among the
barren hills and silent Moai statues of Easter Island where
overpopulation caused the land to be stripped of its resources. When the
resources are gone, the culture withers as the people die off, move away,
or become slaves of a tourist economy—if anything of novelty remains
to attract the fussy tourists.

As we made our way down into the next valley, we surprised four young Mangyan children walking towards us along the forest trail. They froze in place, staring as we suddenly appeared in front of them. I aimed my camera, and they bolted into the bush as though I had pulled out a net to capture them.

Somewhere beyond the next mountain ridge we stopped to camp for the night. As a navigator, I couldn't help studying the contoured topographic map I carried and attempt to keep track of our position with my handheld compass. Much of it was guesswork in those interior valleys because we seldom had views through the forest canopy beyond the next fifty steps. As long as we had Angeles and his memory of every crag and fold in the land, there was no chance of becoming lost.

I unfolded my one-man tent, while Angeles and Frederico constructed for themselves a lean-to of branches and fronds to provide a rain shelter. A floor of bamboo kept them above the crawling insects and damp ground. Leeches were ever close. We had already pulled off several of those blood-suckers whose heads had fastened onto us as we passed through low-hanging vegetation. In the chill morning, we shared a pot of Frederico's finest "burnt rice coffee" from the remains of blackened rice stuck to the bottom of the pot of the previous night's rice and vegetable dinner. We shared my bread rolls, dunking them in Frederico's charred brew, which tasted better to me than drinking it straight from the cup.

Swift Jungle March

We got underway, following Angeles up, down, and up the mountains at a fast pace in hopes of reaching the final summit before nightfall. Angeles moved as silently as a shadow, was aware of everything, and spoke sparingly in soft tones. He seemed incapable of forming a smile, and shrank away from strangers, much like the *makahiya* (to be shy) plant, which magically curled its leaves shut as our legs brushed against it on the trail. As Frederico pointed to each new plant, Angeles told him its name and its use in a whisper, as if afraid the spirits of the forest would hear him reveal their secrets. One plant's leaves, he told us, were used as an antibiotic salve; another mint-flavored, crushed stem was good to clean your teeth; a certain chopped and crushed nut produced a paste to poison fish in the river, causing them to float to the surface where they could be caught by hand. My respect for his stamina and intelligence grew as we ascended the mountain. His lean physique was all sinew and muscle, his mind alert and perceptive. He roamed the forest like a cat with knowing eyes constantly scanning his environment. The jungle had taught him to move without announcement. His innate bush sense marked Angeles as purely aboriginal.

We hiked and climbed upward over rocks through tangled jungle on a fast pace with little rest. We finally stopped in a driving rain at the base of a crumbling vertical stone cliff that had us boxed in between two impassable ravines. The summit stood close now, just 200 feet of unassailable cliff face above us. Although the peak of Guiting-Guiting is a moderate 6,750 feet in elevation, when you begin your ascent at sea level and have to pass over several only slightly lesser peaks to reach it, your body then realizes you are climbing one enormous mountain. I hadn't known when we began our trek that the mountaintop was unreachable from this side of the island. I doubt Angeles had expected me to free climb that sheer rock wall. Instead, he probably led us to the dead-end because he attached no importance to standing exactly on top of the peak itself and didn't realize why a goal-driven foreigner needed to reach such a meaningless objective.

Later, I was told of a shorter and safer route beginning at the town of Magdiwang on the opposite side of the island. But even from there, the final ascent is filled with sections of treacherous rock climbing. The elusive summit of Guiting-Guiting had remained unclimbed until a group of mountaineers finally reached the peak just a few years before my own attempt.

The Lost Bomber

Several days after descending the mountain, I sailed away from Sibuyan. Two years later, I was drawn to sail back to the island after receiving a letter from Frederico that the wreckage of a long-lost WWII bomber had been discovered on the mountain. A report from the scene of the discovery would be a compelling addition to my series of magazine articles on the Philippines. Even without a journalistic excuse, I would have sailed back there to satisfy my own curiosity. To be paid even a small amount to indulge my wandering whims and to share the story was the ultimate joy of travel.

On my second visit to Sibuyan, I learned from the mayor that a couple of months previously, sleepy San Fernando had awakened with a flurry of activity when four officers visited them from the U.S. Army Central Identification Laboratory in Hawaii. Their mission had been to recover and identify the remains of the crew of an American B-25 bomber lost during WWII. The mayor had notified them of it immediately after Braulio Rollon had discovered the wreckage. He had found the wreck high up the flanks of Mt. Guiting-Guiting, not far from where his cousin Angeles had led us on my previous visit to the island.

The mayor showed me a signed receipt from the American team for items he had turned over to them, including "one boot, assorted bones, four pistols, one elbow joint, one radio transmitter," and other items that had been brought down from the site before the officials arrived. Although the army team members were thwarted from completing their search of the area by heavy monsoon rains, they did recover more bones and a couple of dog tags that identified the plane's crew. The plane and its skeleton crew had lain undisturbed for 47 years. But once news of the wreck had spread around the island, a few treasure hunters willing to tackle the treacherous mountain took other items from the site. Despite pleas from the mayor, anything portable and of use was taken for local recycling. For example, bullet tips containing hardened steel were reshaped to equip the island's fighting cocks with spurs, and aircraft aluminum had found its way into the construction of the local fishing boats.

When I expressed an interest in seeing the wreck site for myself, the mayor said that it was too difficult a journey for him to repeat but that if I went back to Taclobo Village, Brother Frederico would again find me a guide. At the mission, Frederico told me he had also been awaiting an opportunity to visit the bomber wreck. Without hesitation, he packed his bag, and we set off on foot together up the mountain in search of our guide.

We climbed back up to the village of Layag where we chanced to meet 30-year-old Braulio Rollon, who had discovered the plane wreck. He greeted us silently, looking us over carefully, judging if we were tough enough to keep up with him on the mountain trek or were just soft tourists who would be too weak to make the round trip. He warned us that it would require three days of difficult walking and climbing, often without trails to follow. At last he agreed to guide us to the wreck site.

On our first day we followed the same route up the Catingas River that we had taken two years previously. Carrying his hunting rifle in one hand, cooking pot in the other hand, and our heaviest pack on his back, the sure-footed Braulio led us away from the river up a steep path of loose rocks bound in place by vines and tree roots. Despite his cumbersome load, this 30-year-old expert woodsman moved swiftly and silently, stopping only to let us catch up. We passed men coming down the trail dragging bundles of hardwood planks from trees they had felled higher up. Frederico pointed out new areas of illegally cleared land that had been virgin forest during my previous visit. "I have been warned and threatened not to speak of this destruction of the habitat," he said solemnly. "But how can I ignore it? What will happen to us when this beautiful forest is gone and the erosion has turned our rivers to mud?"

At our campsite, Braulio lit a fire to cook a pot of rice soup and dried dog meat. I took a bowl full and picked out the bits of stringy dog flesh to give to my friends to eat. I was, after all, still vegetarian. Frederico smiled a sly grin, eyebrows bobbing twice, as he pulled a bottle of "Herbal Wine" from his pack. The label said: *Gives pep and life to the body. It is also good for anemics and nursing mothers. It will also help convalescents. Ingredients: 51 proof alcohol and Chinese herbs.* Frederico believed it also to be a suitable tonic for a mountaineering Catholic brother. The two men passed the bottle between them until it was empty. The wine put my friends into a quick and sound sleep. I followed them after listening for a few hours to the unidentified croaks, grunts, and songs of the jungle creatures and the wind rustling the forest canopy overhead.

Our guide on the mountain

The next morning we discovered that bush rats had torn through our bags during the night, ripping apart and ruining the rice and all the other foods we had brought. Braulio acted unconcerned, telling us not to worry because the forest would provide the food we needed. Like his cousin Angeles, he knew this forest intimately and intuitively. For his entire life he had foraged in the mountains and was able to survive extended periods in the bush with only his *bolo* and rifle, consuming only the food that capricious nature provided. Obviously, he was more used to the hardships of living in the forest with a nearly empty belly than we well-fed lowlanders were, but we pressed on regardless.

Several times Braulio stopped to check or set traps made of logs and vines ingeniously lashed together to trap wild monkeys when they reached for the fruit bait. When the traps failed and he lacked bullets for his gun, Braulio assured us his stealthy approach occasionally allowed him to catch a monkey barehanded. In a clearing on a mountain pass we found long bamboo poles with thorny branches lashed to their ends. At night, the Mangyan hunters used these giant fly swatters to knock bats out of the air as they swooped low over the hill's saddle. "Monkeys and bats roasted over a fire taste very good with rice," Frederico assured me. Two days later I became hungry enough to have happily devoured a roasted bat or monkey. Fortunately for the wildlife, Frederico and I were making far too much noise bashing through the undergrowth for our guide to shoot anything.

On our third day out, not far below the summit of Guiting-Guiting, Braulio casually warned us not to trip over an unexploded bomb that was partially hidden in the brush directly in front of us. A few steps ahead lay another unexploded bomb some salvagers had trussed up in bamboo and vines to haul down the mountain. Perhaps it proved too heavy for them, or they had thought twice about bouncing a 200-pound bomb down the rocky trail. A few cautious steps later we entered an eerie-looking scene of contorted aluminum wreckage, scattered machine guns and engine parts, all partially wrapped in the rain-soaked vegetation. Lifting up a piece of loose fuselage we found a leather bag that held a pistol, some old coins, and disintegrating leaflets that read, "MacArthur keeps his Pledge" and "MacArthur has Returned." During the war, thousands of these leaflets had been dropped over cities in the path of advancing U.S. forces in order to bolster the Filipino resistance against the Japanese invaders. I imagined a bombardier shouting, "You've got mail!" as he pushed the bags out the bomb bay doors.

Some in the American press at the time claimed MacArthur's arrogant statement, "I shall return," should have been "We shall return."

But back then, for many Filipinos, MacArthur was a loved and respected father figure. It was more important to them to know that he, rather than the American forces in general, had kept his pledge to return and liberate them from the Japanese menace. The Filipino people rallied to support him to a degree no other commander or Washington politician has ever experienced.

On the predawn morning of January 9, 1945, 22-year-old Lieutenant Wallace Chalifoux of the U.S. Fifth Air Force piloted his Mitchell B-25 bomber off an airstrip on Leyte Island. He and the other five young men in his crew were bound towards Luzon's Lingayan Gulf to support the U.S. troop landings there. The B-25 was a devastating weapon for strafing and bombing. She was powered by twin 1,850-hp engines on her 67-foot wingspan, was armed with twelve .50-cal. machine guns, and carried up to 6,000 lbs. of bombs.

In correspondence that I later had with Wally's relatives, I learned that the boy had recently graduated from high school in Chicago when the Japanese attacked Pearl Harbor. As soon as he could, he volunteered for flight training school and was then sent to the war in the Pacific. I can imagine the excitement the young men experienced as they lifted off for their bombing mission: the thrilling roar and vibration from the massive engines, the watchful gunner manning his machine-gun turret, and the final moment of terror when the cloud-shrouded Mt. Guiting-Guiting suddenly appeared through the mist in front of them. The official record of the crash states that another pilot in this 17-plane bomber group reported seeing two bright flashes appear near the peak of Mt. Guiting-Guiting. If so, I wondered why a search had not been made here after the war ended. It was incredible bad luck that the plane hit just a couple of hundred feet below the top of the highest peak in the region. If it had flown a slightly higher or slightly different course, the men would have slipped harmlessly past the peak to face the other hazards of war, perhaps even surviving these final months of war to return home to their families. Now that their remains had finally been brought home for the long-delayed burial, the airmen's fate was no longer a mystery.

That evening we prepared to bivouac in a windy driving rain. Our camp perched on a 45-degree slope under the minimal shelter of a twisted airplane wing. Frederico asked if I thought it was dangerous to be surrounded by all these unexploded bombs. "If they haven't blown up from the impact of hitting the mountain, I don't suppose they're likely to go off now," I said. "But I wouldn't build a fire too close to one." I knew the wind and rain made that impossible anyway.

Braulio seemed to be searching for something in particular when Brother Frederico asked what he was looking for. Hearing his reply, he turned to me shaking his head and said, "*Susmariyosup!* (Jesus, Mary, and Joseph!) He's looking for the leg bone he used as a pillow the last time he had slept here." Apparently sleeping that close with the dead was not one of the many superstitions held by our mountain man.

We spent a miserable night shivering together under a crumpled airplane wing on that pitched, rocky slope. With sleep all but impossible, we talked through most of the night. Now that we had gained his trust, the reticent Braulio began to share with us some of the legends and beliefs of the mountain people. He believed that the mountain spirits maliciously draw climbers to the summit where they become lost in the cold mists and eventually die of hunger. (I thought "So now he tells us.") He went on to relate how, in 1985, four climbers had died when the ravine they camped in turned into a thundering waterfall on a stormy night. (Another disturbing thought as the rain poured down on us.) The spirits were not all malevolent and sometimes fell in love with and protected those people who respected her rules. Even before the discovery of the bomber, the locals believed the mountain contained a kind of giant magnet that affects electronic instruments, causing aircraft to crash. Several years before my visit here, for example, a Philippines Air Force plane had been wrecked on the mountain. Another B-25 bomber, the *Lazy Daisy Mae*, was supposedly lost somewhere near the island and has yet to be found.

Witches, Boars, and Pythons

Apart from wild boars, Braulio claimed the only dangerous creatures on the island were the pythons that he believed were responsible for the occasional disappearance of children in the forest. He went on to explain that when the mountain people come down with a serious illness, it is frequently ascribed to *kilkig* (poisoning by someone practicing witchcraft). The only antidote is to drink an infusion of a certain type of boiled root of a plant that grows on the highest peaks. Throughout these islands, traditional healers were still sought out in preference to modern medicine, even by many of the devout Catholics in the cities. On Sibuyan, brass shell casings salvaged from the bomber's machine gun bullets had been fashioned into rings, which locals wore on their fingers to protect them against the "witches and black fairies" that inhabit the island.

The constant rain and cold wind and our growing hunger forced us to leave the wreck site the next morning. Frederico kept asking Braulio why he hadn't caught or shot anything for food yet. Obviously frustrated from listening to the same complaint over and over again, Braulio told him with uncharacteristic bluntness, "I can't hunt with you two chattering like a pair of excited monkeys and scaring the game away. Even when you stop talking you crash through the bush as noisily as two *carabaos* [water buffalo]."

In our haste to find food we gave up all pretense of being hunter-gatherers. We practically ran down the mountain. We stopped only to sip the rainwater, complete with drowned insects that had collected in the cup-shaped vessels of the carnivorous pitcher plants. If Braulio had shot a monkey at this point I'd have eaten it raw on the spot. If you want to go adventuring, extremes and discomfort are your common company. By now we'd experienced everything you might expect on a mountain trek—biting ants and blood-sucking leeches, the cold rain and wind, rocky terrain, jungle overgrowth—plus the added torment of hunger and thirst.

Señior Recto's Stew; Sleep Beneath the Monkey Skulls

In the evening twilight that comes early in the mountain-shaded river canyon, we stumbled up to a nipa hut beside the Catingas River. There we met Señior Salvador Recto who, seeing our wretched condition, kindly invited us into the hut to rest. Exhausted and starved from our trek, we were unable to carry on the usual small talk. Like pushy Hong Kong diners, we practically brushed him aside and sat in a semi-circle on the bamboo slat floor and focused on the pot next to the cooking fire. The middle-aged Señior Recto handed Frederico the pot. We each dove hands into the pot together and pulled out a handful of sticky rice, stuffing it into our mouths. Our host then passed around another blackened iron pot, and we each in turn slurped up an unidentifiable stew from a wooden ladle. A long row of monkey skulls stared down at us from a shelf on the wall. The stew tasted so wonderful after a nearly three-day fast that I never thought to ask what had gone into it. When I offered payment, Señior Recto just smiled and shook his head from side to side. Too exhausted to move and unable to continue anyway in the approaching darkness, we dropped into sleep where we sat. Señior Recto's wife and two children had run off as soon as we had arrived, and they stayed away the entire night at a relative's hut somewhere further down the river. This is the humanity of the jungle people; if strangers appear at your doorless house, feed them, let them rest, and make room for them by sending the children away.

The next afternoon, the children at Frederico's orphan mission prepared a meal for us as we soaked sore muscles in the pool under the waterfall. Frederico and I pondered the plight of the Mangyan we had met. Logging and mining companies posed an imminent threat to their way of life. Like the American airmen who had crashed here, the Mangyans seemed poised to perish within those mountains of lost souls. Perhaps more people like Frederico would awaken the local population to the need for conservation of these last remaining wild places before it's too late. An island is a fragile microcosm, and what was happening on Sibuyan represented what is happening to Earth, an island in space. We are a global society comprised of two cultures: those like the *Mangyans* who take only what they really need to survive and the rest of us "lowlander" types, who take all we can get, leaving nothing to sustain island Earth.

Though I soon sailed on to discover other alluring islands, I have ever since felt the pull of Sibuyan's magnet. In quiet moments my memories of Sibuyan's generous people in their sanctuary of wildness still call to me. I hope my friends there and their children had the chance to go on with their lives undisturbed.

18 On a Distant Sea

These ancient, well-traveled sea routes remain pathways always new.

After my first visit to Sibuyan Island I sailed alone back through the jumbled mix of islands of the Sibuyan Sea to Puerto Galera on Mindoro Island. Since I had been in the Philippines for three months it was time to revisit the office of immigration for a visa extension. I also needed to find a bank that could arrange a money transfer because the traveler's checks and cash that I had stuffed into *Atom*'s hidden locker while in Hong Kong were now running low. These tasks couldn't be accomplished in Puerto Galera, but it was a secure place to leave the boat while I caught a ferry to Luzon Island and then a bus to Manila. My friend Emile Garcia asked to join me on my visit to Manila so that he could buy a battery-operated radio and some other items for his family.

Mistaken in Manila

We arrived in Manila late in the evening after a full day on the bus and ferry. From the Manila bus terminal we caught a motorized tricycle that took us to several nearby hotels that were either full or cost way more than I was willing to spend. The tricycle driver then took us to the Ermita district, known for cheap hotels as well as a raucous row of girlie bars that catered to male tourists. We moved along the bar strip among the human wreckage of pimps and beggars. White-haired grandfathers pumped up by the Purple Pill walked arm in arm with teenaged hookers. We fell in line behind a group of four buddies in wheelchairs, a bit drunk and wobbly on their wheels after rolling out of a noisy strip bar. The doorman/bouncer opened the door for us to follow the disabled tourists into the next bar, but I stopped to ask him to recommend a cheap hotel. His smile turned sour, and he cursed as he looked at Emile. Then he silently pointed down the road. Apparently he thought I was a sex tourist here to have fun with local boys like Emile. Watching the endless parade of foreign men hunting young women was apparently acceptable to him, but abusing the boys too, well, that was too much to take. Finding a hotel here was beginning to look like a bad idea. We walked another two blocks beyond the row of bars and stepped through a gate in an eight-foot high cement block wall. We entered a dilapidated single-story building where a lone red light illuminated the doorway. Inside the lobby, the clerk looked up from his television and told me a room would cost 100 pesos per hour. "We just want a room for the night . . . to sleep only. Have you got a nightly rate?"

He scribbled some numbers on a piece of paper as if he had never been asked a question so complicated, and replied, "Eight hours will be 800 pesos."

We negotiated seven hours for 400 pesos. A boy unlocked our room. I saw it had one twin-sized bed, a floor lamp, a fan that rattled, a filthy toilet, and nothing else, not even a chair. Going back to the clerk, I told him I had asked for a room with two single beds. "I'm not a damned sex tourist, all right."

"Sure, it's okay," he reassured me with a slight wink as if he was helping me cover up my charade. No doubt he had seen strange actors before. To make me happy, he had his boy bring in a second stained mattress and dumped it on the peeling vinyl floor.

"Since there's no air conditioning, I guess we won't bother asking for a sheet," I told Emile with a shrug. As I lay fully clothed on top of the bed in an effort to make as little contact with the soiled mattress as possible, I set my wristwatch alarm, closed my eyes and said to Emile, "We're on the clock now. I'll see you in six hours."

Having taken care of my banking, visa extension, and Emile's shopping, we returned to Puerto Galera. Emile said he thought that the trip to the city was great fun and that we should do it again soon. It was the last time I wanted to visit any city, though that feeling faded almost as quickly as a sailor swears off returning to sea after a storm passage.

Fellow explorer from s/v Mariposa

During our absence a newly arrived junk-rigged wooden sailboat named *Mariposa* had moored next to *Atom*. I rowed over in my dinghy to visit the crew of four young, German-speaking Swiss men and one of their Filipina girlfriends. I learned that three of these Swiss adventurers had recently rebuilt the one-time Vietnamese fishing boat with the help of traditional boat builders on Negros Island in the southern Philippines. Since then the guys had been roaming the islands looking for a place where they could set up a tourist diving business, which they eventually did on a nearby island. The crew slept in hammocks slung above and below deck. Aside from her powerful diesel engine—which was often needed to move the heavy hull and its minimal sail area—she was a simple, honest sailing boat, unencumbered by much of the equipment and comforts found on the average cruising yacht.

The three co-owners and their other friends divided their time between working in Switzerland and vacationing on *Mariposa* as she traveled through the islands. One of the temporary crew, Theo Bodmer, told me he had quit his job as a computer programmer in Switzerland and had been living aboard *Mariposa* for the past couple of months. He was now looking to gain further sailing experience on a more conventional sailing boat, with plans to go cruising on his own boat one day. Two years before this first sailing vacation, the footloose 25-year old and a buddy had made a motorcycle trip through Europe and India, living as backpackers on a shoestring budget. When I told Theo that I planned to sail to the central and southern Islands of the Philippines and that he could come along as crew, he accepted without hesitation. Theo had already been to a few of those islands I was aiming for, and his knowledge of the region would prove helpful.

Theo moved into *Atom*'s forward cabin, and we prepared to get underway. "You know, my Swiss friends on Mariposa were shocked to hear you have a toilet on board but no engine. They think that's crazy," Theo said. I replied that I was equally surprised that they had the reverse mentality. To them, motor-sailing on their passages between islands was essential, but use of even a toilet bucket was too civilized. I couldn't help noticing—and I tried very hard not to notice—that some of them preferred to defecate into the harbor by hanging their bare backsides over the bulwarks in full view of the boats anchored on all sides of them. This particular dead-end corner of the harbor had little natural flushing action, so the lingering evidence floating around our boats was impossible to ignore. But that didn't stop my Swiss friends from diving off their deck and swimming around in their own toilet bowl. I really had nothing to complain about because I also liked the idea of the simplicity of using a bucket, but at least the pump on my toilet macerated the waste before it went discreetly overboard and then quickly biodegraded.

On an April morning, Theo and I sailed east through the Verde Island Passage and then turned south. From the start we enjoyed a rare northwest wind on the stern, galloping along 70 miles to our first anchorage at Maestre de Campo Island (the peculiar Spanish name means "the capitán general's chief of staff"). For most of those miles we enjoyed an extra boost from the spinnaker that I rarely used alone because it required constant trimming and hand-steering.

At Maestre de Campo we anchored between two sheltering peninsulas next to the town of Conception. Ashore we met Father Dennis Mckillip, an expat American Catholic priest who had resided here at his parish for the past 30 years. He introduced us to Hidalgo Famarin, who guided us on a one-hour walk through the mostly deforested hills, overgrown with waist-high kunai grass, to the highest point on the island at Mt. Baguntor. The island reminded me of a smaller and slightly less rugged version of its peaceful cousin, Banton Island, that we could plainly see lying 18 miles away on the eastern horizon.

Balut – Eggs-istential Male Enhancement Secret?

We sailed next to Banton where we had a brief reunion with my friends Winnie and Emilio. At Emilio's house I was introduced to a much-loved Filipino snack food. Knowing I was vegetarian, Emilio had some fun with me by offering me a boiled duck egg known as *balut*. Those of sensitive eye and stomach may want to avoid that common street food, which is a boiled, fertilized duck egg containing an all-too-recognizable partially formed duck embryo. The multi-textured mix of meat, fluid, and yolk is made by allowing the embryo to grow for about 17 days and then boiling it before it has formed bones and feathers. Emilio cracked open the shell, loudly slurped the liquid, and then bit the head off of the gelatinous baby bird. Given the lightly feathered skin and the hard beak that Emilio picked out of his mouth to show me before plopping it back in with a crunch between his teeth, this particular *balut* had been left to develop a few days too long. I stifled a rising gut retch when he thrust the remainder of the half-eaten duck fetus under my nose. Emilio howled laughter and then smacked his lips satisfyingly. He then thrust up his forearm with a fist to express his faith in *balut*'s reputation for boosting male sexual prowess. That was one more day in which my vegetarian diet made perfect sense and gave me a good excuse to avoid those types of exotic local delicacies.

Before departing Banton, we filled our water jugs again from the delicious spring waters bubbling up through the magical beach of Mainit. In Banton, I introduced Theo to my tropical island breakfast of cornmeal pancakes smothered in mashed papaya, mango, and banana from Winnie and Emilio's fruit trees. The mango we particularly appreciated because ripe mangoes were a rare find in the Philippine provinces. Most Filipinos preferred to harvest the mango unripe and eat its sour, tart, and crispy slices sprinkled in salt.

Beached in Boracay

The mid-sized mountains of Banton blocked the light trade winds on the morning we departed. To get underway, I demonstrated to Theo the twist and pull technique of my sculling oar. We sculled in turns for an hour until the winds filled in a mile outside the anchorage. Sailing south in the calm waters behind the string of islands in the Tablas Strait, we arrived the following morning at Boracay Island. Today's well-known resort island of Boracay was then a partially developed enclave of mostly young backpacking tourists who came to enjoy the island's two-mile-long, sugary white beach, water sports, and lively beachside discos. Theo had been here before and let me know that it would be unforgivable to sail past the island without stopping. I also wanted to stop and check in on an artist friend from Hong Kong named Ray Chang, who had invited me to visit his vacation home located in Diniwid Cove on the island's northwest coast. We sailed past two other yachts in the open anchorage on the southwest corner of the island and carried on inside the reef that runs parallel to the shore. Small, motorized outrigger ferryboats, as well as sailing *bancas* carrying tourists, plied the lagoon as we cautiously sailed over the shallow waters just a couple boat lengths off the beach. When our keel touched the sandy bottom I knew I was a bit too close to shore and turned the boat to a slightly more offshore course. With Theo on the bow directing me to steer around the isolated coral heads, we continued gliding over the sand for nearly two miles with only inches of water under the keel.

We turned into a cove where *Atom*, tiny as she is, still had no room to swing on a single anchor, so we anchored her from the stern, and took a line from the bow to secure on a rock ashore. Then we climbed up the bamboo terraces and ladders to a split-level hut perched on the edge of the cliff overlooking *Atom* in the cove below. Every piece of the structure and its sparse furniture and decorative art looked as if it had been produced from local materials, giving to the place the effect of the fantasy treehouse seen in the movie *Swiss Family Robinson*. Lounging about were several of Ray's Bohemian artist friends who told us Ray was currently back in Hong Kong. I wasn't comfortable leaving the boat in this precarious spot between the rocky shores, so we sailed back south along the beach until Theo directed me to anchor off one of his favorite beach bars. We dropped the bow anchor and then buried a stern anchor on the beach so that we could pull her stern up to the shore and have the bow pointed out in case we needed to make a speedy departure if onshore winds picked up. We were so close to the beach that we waded the few steps to shore. At low tide *Atom*'s keel rested on the soft sand, lightly thumping on the bottom to the wakes of passing *bancas*. That night we danced at the disco with tourist gals and transplanted Manila hookers, while within a beer bottle throw of *Atom*. The party carried on back to the boat where Theo kept our guests happy with refills of cheap Tanduay Dark Rum mixed with fruit juice.

The beach at Boracay

The next morning, while Theo slept in, I began a daylong kayak journey to circle the five-mile-long island. As I paddled along the windward coast, I saw the initial signs of the rapid development taking place in step with the more congested western side of the island. This ancestral domain of the *Ati* negrito tribe had been gobbled up by land developers and foreign settlers who found they could legally buy cheap property in paradise by marrying a local girl. Walking along a footpath on one of the few remaining patches of forest on the island, I met up with a German man and his Filipina wife who invited me up to their house on the top of a small cliff. Inside their modern cement home he showed me artifacts he had collected from New Guinea, and we exchanged tales of our mutual travels there. The man worked from this home as a painter of pictures, many fine examples of which hung on their walls. He had come to Boracay before the island was discovered by tourists, and he lamented bitterly the changes that developers and tourists had brought to his island sanctuary, without realizing that like the Post-Impressionist painter Paul Gauguin in Polynesia, he himself was an unwitting publicity agent in opening the floodgates to the forces he detested. These expats were the modern-day equivalent of the Vikings who had raided and settled the coast of parts of Medieval Europe, except that these islands were overrun with cash instead of swords.

Tourists are brought in by the sometimes well-meaning local politicians to stimulate the economy. The realization that the more stimulated the economy, the deader the society, arrives too late for the indigenous people. Island cultures can usually sustain themselves while hosting a few foreign residents, but sleazy over-development and throngs of cash-rich tourists inevitably spell the end of any meaningful island culture. The nomadic *Ati* people had arrived in Boracay and the larger neighboring island of Panay perhaps as many as 20,000 years ago, crossing over what was then a partial land bridge from Borneo. They had withstood encounters with Moros, Chinese traders, and Spanish and American colonists, but tourists had finally defeated them. The tourists will never know the good people they pushed out. I tramped from one corner of Boracay to the other, crisscrossing the entire island during the week we stayed there, and I did not see one *Ati*.

Rovers, Raconteurs, and Old Birds of Paradise

After a week, even my more sociable crewmate was ready to move on from the endless beach party on Boracay. We continued sailing south with stops along the west coasts of the islands of Panay and Negros. I had expected the winds of the northeast monsoon to last at least into the first part of May before the southwest monsoon set in, but we found ourselves sailing in mostly light and variable winds that made for a sedate three-knot passage. With such erratic winds, we kept pressing on to reach the better protection of Port Bonbonon, also known as Tambobo Bay, located at the southern tip of Negros Island. This port was a turning point for many yachts. Here sailors faced the choice of heading back north or continuing south to the troubled waters of Mindanao, the second largest island in the Philippines. In this country of over 90% Christian population, a faction of the Muslims who predominated in parts of Mindanao was demanding an autonomous Muslim state. They had been waging a low-grade, on-and-off campaign of terrorism, kidnappings, and piracy that continues to this day. It was not an outright civil war but more of a tolerable conflict, something akin to the Irish "troubles." Even though the Muslim troubles were at that time mainly limited to southwestern Mindanao, most sailors considered the entire island of Mindanao off-limits.

To enter Port Bonbonon safely, we skirted around a coral ledge extending from the western shore more than halfway across the narrow inlet. Inside the reef, the deep, winding bay resembles a placid river, well-protected from all winds in a region far enough south that direct hits from typhoons were rare. Near the beach on the western shore of the bay sat about a dozen houses of mixed cement, lumber, and nipa-style construction. The eastern shore comprised an undeveloped mix of small cliffs and mangrove forest. Village activity centered on fishing. Men hung their nets up between the palm trees to dry and repaired their *bancas* on the beach while women carried the catch home to be cooked over wood fires.

The first electricity had reached Tambobo only one year before our arrival. Although tourists follow electric power lines that lead towards a beach as surely as hunting dogs sniff out a rabbit trail, for the moment the little undiscovered yacht haven remained untrammeled because there was no resort to house the tourists. A sign of things to come happened when a local resident with a house on the beach celebrated the arrival of electricity by installing a karaoke machine. He daily crooned Sinatra's "My Way" in high decibels that reverberated across the harbor. Apparently, it was the only song he knew, and he wanted to perfect his delivery. The crowing roosters at dawn included at least one early hour reveler that needed his circadian clock reset forward a few hours. The combined clamor of cocks, afternoon karaoke, and evenings of hooting and hollering from rum-filled fishermen whose boats sheltered in port during foul weather caused us to relocate to a quieter anchorage around the next headland at the head of the bay. Further up the bay the water shoaled into a muddy mangrove estuary and wildlife preserve. In this land-locked section of the bay, the only noises were the splash of jumping fish and the knocking of fishermen's paddles against the sides of their *bancas* as they herded the fish into their nets.

We shared the anchorage with eight other foreign yachts hailing from Germany, Switzerland, France, Australia, England, and the United States. Some of these sailors had come and stayed. One American couple in their fifties sailed into port while we were there. Within a few days the wife had seen enough of the cruising life and flew home with uncertain plans to return. A week later the husband had acquired a local girlfriend and was making plans for a divorce.

On another boat was Bruce from South Dakota, recently retired from the U.S. Navy, living on a small pension on his 26-foot fiberglass sloop *Iwalani*, with his young Filipina girlfriend, Maryann. He had bought the boat in Guam where he had been stationed in the Navy and had sailed alone downwind for a thousand miles to the Philippines for a well-deserved retirement in these blessed islands in the sun. Somehow the two of them managed to get along on a boat filled to capacity with all the gear needed to sail and maintain it along with some optional items like a house-sized microwave oven powered by a portable gasoline generator sitting on the afterdeck. Once we heard the hum of the generator at sunset we knew it was time to join Bruce and Maryann for popcorn and sundowners in the cockpit. "If it wasn't for my ex-wife, I'd be sitting here on an Ericson 30," Bruce lamented. One story Bruce loved to recount took place at the island of Homonhon, where he had made his first landfall in the Philippines. He went ashore to witness a cockfight and found himself almost too close to a drunken brawl that ended in a blood-letting knife fight that enthralled the betting spectators even more than egging on the spur-wielding roosters. The next morning a pair of unmarked *bancas* sped past his anchored boat. A man in the bow of the chase boat sprayed the anchorage with bullets from a fully automatic rifle. Those in the boat being hunted replied with sporadic shots until they both slipped out of view around the corner of the island. Bruce found out the next day that one man had been killed. It turned out that one of the boats was the Philippine Coast Guard shooting it out with members of the local police after the police had refused to let the Coast Guard continue smuggling and reselling unregistered, stolen motorcycles.

We sailors met on different boats each night for sundowners and yachtie gossip. On one yacht I met Claude, who was from Belgium, as I recall. He was a likable guy, obviously infatuated with Bridget, his much fawned over Filipina wife. Despite his amiable personality, trouble followed Claude like an afternoon shadow. Bridget's family hated Claude, probably because of his attempt to buy land from the wrong people and start a business here. For months he had been in a hopeless cycle of threat and counter-threat and had finally hired a lawyer who further complicated the mess. Offending people and then calling in the lawyers was a common mistake made by foreigners who came to these islands to settle. They wanted things done their way and done now. Poor Filipinos distrusted corrupt legal authorities; they relied on their neighbor's sense of honor, which let them down all too often. For the wealthy, well, they always had influence and connections to sort out their problems. The Filipinos are exceptionally tolerant, but even these friendly people often ended up hating the pushy foreigners encroaching on them.

Another sailboat anchored next to the beach was owned by Jeff, a Cockney taxi driver from London's working class East End who, until the previous year, had been living free and wild as a bachelor sailor. He then sailed into Bonbonon and married a local girl. When she got pregnant he paid local carpenters to build them a new nipa house in the village. Between building the house and assisting his needy extended family, Jeff soon found his savings had vanished. Lately, he divided his time between swinging from the hammock on their porch while playing guitar, doing maintenance jobs on his boat, and driving a taxi back home to finance his lifestyle in the islands.

On the point of land next to where we anchored lived Eric, a Swiss friend of Theo's. Eric and his local wife Bing had built a sprawling nipa-style house on the hill overlooking the anchorage. He kept his classic wooden sailboat *Boy Willie* on a mooring near his dinghy dock. The couple hosted parties for us visiting sailors and provided a dinghy dock and a place on the beach below their house where sailors could do projects such as dinghy repairs. Eric was a dealer in rare seashells and gems that he collected during his travels around Southeast Asia. He could daily be seen in his sarong, jumping around with a watering can, tending his banana trees and young flowers on the steep slope below his house. A hand-operated pump provided his water, which he shared with us sailors to refill our water jugs. His house was equipped with an electric guitar and synthesized keyboard. Other sailors brought their guitars, banjos, and harmonicas for jam sessions at his house or barbecue parties on his beach.

Not far down the shore from the houses and yachts of resident expats, I met an elderly couple living in a 10-foot-wide hut on the beach just two steps from the high-water mark. I stopped to visit them and share simple conversations in Filipino. Their *banca* was pulled up on the beach, and I recalled having seen them paddling across the harbor together to fetch firewood from the opposite shore or drifting in the lagoon fishing with handlines. For a toilet they simply stepped knee-deep in the water and squatted. They were here because they had always lived this way. Their children lived in more comfortable houses in a nearby inland town. At first I thought how odd it was that their children would leave them in their seemingly frail condition to fend for themselves in utter poverty and as close to homeless as could be imagined. They had no visible possessions in the hut, no furniture, not even a pillow or blanket to cushion their bony old bodies from the hard bamboo floor. Then they told me they could go to stay with their children at any time, but they loved to live here together on the water with easy access to their *banca*. They grilled fish on the beach, and friends and family brought them rice and vegetables. They were happy, and it made me happy to see them there together after all those years.

I had been told the reason that the old couple could live as squatters on a beach in front of a more valuable house was that the Philippine government recognized the rights of free people in an island nation to have unrestricted access to the water. You could own waterfront property here, but you couldn't own the beach within a certain number of feet of the high tide line. More and more, around the world, whether in the United States or less developed countries, local people are displaced from their access to boats and the water. Land gets paved over, fences go up, and taxes increase. The people get pushed out either by a resort development or by private estates. Living on a sailboat may give you a nearly free pass to anywhere, but many places bar your access to the shore just as they restrict their land-bound neighbors from accessing the water.

Over the next couple of years I sailed in and out of Port Bonbonon several times and took many leg-stretching hikes through the countryside, which consisted of patches of forest and cornfields. In the dry season the land lay dusty and brown. When the rains came, the fields instantly turned green with new fast-growing corn stalks. Walking along a path through the young corn, I paused to listen to guitar music coming from a farmhouse. A smiling farmer stood in the doorway of his hut and waved for me to join him. Romel led me inside where we sat on a mat next to his six-year-old son who strummed a Spanish guitar so big he could barely get his arms around it. Romel looked on approvingly as the boy sang the simple plaintive love song his father had taught him:

> *Kong ikaw ay lumayo* (If you go away)
> *Kung ang isip moy hindi* (And if you think not of us)
> *Sa pagtolo nang luha* (Tears will fall)
> *Ako ngayon ang may dusa* (And I will regret)
> *Hindi namin mahal muli* (We will never love again)

We communicated in a mix of Filipino and Visayan since nobody in the family had been taught a word of English at school. In the corner of the one-room hut the boy's mother turned a grinding stone by hand while his sister fed the last precious kernels of dried corn from the previous year's harvest onto a hole in the top of the stone. Slowly, particles of coarse corn meal spilled out the bottom onto a mat. Under an open lean-to attached to the house, a pot of water mixed with meal boiled over a wood fire. The mother then mixed the thickened meal with coconut cream and served the tasty snack to me wrapped in a banana leaf. She claimed they had already eaten as all eyes watched me eating alone. There was still a month to wait before the new crop would be ready to pick. I felt guilty when I noticed not a speck of food visible aside from the near empty corn sack. I hoped I was not eating this year's seed corn. It was obviously a hungry time at their little farm. Telling them I'd be back soon, I ran across the fields and dinghied back to the boat, raided my food lockers for gifts, grabbed my guitar, and hightailed it back to the farmhouse. In exchange for the food gift, Romel spent the day teaching me to play several Filipino folk songs on my guitar.

The agricultural village of Bonbonon is located a half mile up an inclined dirt road from the port. The old settlement consisted of a few houses, a *sari-sari* store, and a church. There was also an outdoor basketball court that served as a disco on Friday nights when children and teenagers from the village and surrounding countryside farms danced to the screeching old record player with its single speaker, which hung from a tree branch.

Pure Filipino – Jeepney Packing and Talking Eyebrows

Since Tambobo and Bonbonon villages offered little more than beer, bread, and soap at their *sari-sari* stores, getting provisions or anything else required catching an infrequent jeepney for a half-hour trip from Bonbonon to the small town of Siaton and then transferring for a two-hour jeepney ride to Dumaguete City. Our typical jeepney trek was a lesson in the Third World law that states personal space does not exist. The two benches were crammed to beyond capacity with passengers. Under our feet were sacks of produce bound for the town markets. Extra baggage was lashed to the roof, and more passengers clung precariously off the back of the vehicle. Our pace was tortoise-like as we stopped at nearly every crossroad or farmer's hut along the route and rolled by woven mats or plastic sheets filled with unhusked rice drying in the sun on the edge of the road.

In the bustling college town of Dumaguete, I entered a stationary shop. When I asked the sales girl if they carried notebooks, she replied with a quick flash of raised eyebrows. In Filipino, briefly raised eyebrows means "yes." A prolonged eyebrow raise may mean "please repeat." When I asked where the notebooks were located, the clerk wordlessly pointed with twisted puckered lips as if giving an imaginary friend a kiss on the cheek. The black centers of her eyes followed the direction of her pursed lips, accompanied by a slight turn of her neck in the direction of the object. I saw this same reaction over and over again with Filipinos, especially from women. Maybe it was low latitude languor or an unwillingness to resort to the overt action of finger pointing. I doubt that anyone knows exactly why this is done; they just do it. But the pantomime always delighted me.

Back in Bonbonon, with the boat fully provisioned, Theo and I pored over my charts of the Philippines, looking for islands off the well-worn cruising path. Ever since I was a child in school, I've had a weakness for maps. A well-drawn map pulls me from its two dimensional image to a dream world where I conjure up images of inaccessible jungles, mountains, and sea shores—strange lands with strange inhabitants. My cartophilia naturally carried over to the world of nautical charts. It was intoxicating to be aboard my boat surrounded by hundreds of islands, as I sorted through piles of detailed charts. I read a chart as a priest reads Holy Scriptures, searching for revelations in place names. Around us were the islands of Limasawa (five wives), Lapu-Lapu (a town named after the Filipino chief who slew Magellan in Cebu), Camiguin (the pearl-shaped "island of ebony trees"), and Cayagon de Oro (River of Gold). To this day, I can lose myself for long periods in a chart of some island I once visited or one I'll likely never get to visit. The next island to the south of us—the great, twisted landmass of Mindanao—was hard to ignore, despite its dangerous reputation. Upon the uncertain winds of May, Theo and I set sail for Mindanao.

19 Moving with the Monsoon

We ride the wind along the awesome lonely pathways of the sea.

Sailboats in the Philippines still follow the course of the ancient Chinese junk fleets that sailed these waters a thousand years ago—run south before the northeast winter monsoon, lay up on a comfortable island during the transition months, then run back north with the southwest summer monsoon. Above all, because the frequent typhoons can occur in almost any month, we keep a sharp eye on the weather and our nearest safe harbor.

Throughout the Philippines, the cooling northeast trade winds blow from October to April. Locally called the *amihan*, the northeast monsoon is the time of most consistent winds for sailors. The southwest monsoon (*habagat*) that prevails from May through September is less steady, with hotter temperatures and more rain. The transitional months of May/June and September/October are the least welcomed by sailors due to the light and variable winds. Visiting yacht skippers often swear that this period is completely windless and that making an inter-island passage on an engineless boat is impossible. Proving them wrong was a simple matter of patience and perseverance over haste.

When I reached Cebu Island, located square in the center of the Philippines, a cruising sailor told me he had motored three days to get there without encountering a breadth of wind. I had just traveled the same route at the same time, and I'd enjoyed sailing in flat water with the light winds that he believed were nonexistent. Motoring at six knots, that skipper created a six-knot headwind, making him oblivious to any new subtle wind that springs up. He may have been a victim of urban time anxiety syndrome, which drives people to get from point A to B on a firm time schedule. Such sailors also depend heavily on technology, which makes them shallow and out of touch with the skills needed for sailing in the state of grace that I seek when I venture on the sea. The shallow sailor is unaware that sailing can be enjoyed moment to moment, independent of regimented time and burdensome gadgets. They may look for excuses or belittle those of us on a different path. That is not to say every sailor needs to rip out the diesel engine to know how to sail, but it does intensify the experience and leads to greater awareness and competence.

Crossing the Caribbean Sea and Pacific and cruising extensively for several years in Southeast Asia without the aid of an engine had taught me the skills needed for the art of natural sailing in the ancient way, with mindful attention to detail, flexibility, and an uncommon degree of forethought and patience. Beyond the mental requirements, the physical elements useful for engine-free cruising are a boat of moderate displacement like the Triton, which sails well in light air, a full sail inventory, including light air sails, and a sculling oar. Oh, and be physically and mentally prepared for hard work, some sleepless days and nights, and more than a little risk of shipwreck. That is what voyaging under sail has always been, along with a guarantee of adventure. Alas, the greater the adventure, the greater the danger.

For example, typhoons can occur in any month in the central and northern Philippines, but their main season is May through November. During November of my first year cruising the Philippines, I picked up a radio broadcast warning of a powerful typhoon approaching the Visayas. I hurriedly departed from an island offering marginal shelter and sailed for Puerto Galera. Once tucked into the sheltered corner of the harbor, I set all four of my anchors to the four points of the compass. Close on my heels, the typhoon cut a wide swath of destruction through the central Philippines. It ended up passing about a hundred miles south of Puerto Galera. Fortunately for us, we saw sustained winds of only 40 knots. Yet even in those moderate conditions, there were ferries, fishing boats, and yachts dragging their anchors all over the harbor. Though *Atom* was unscathed by that storm, another boat could have easily dragged anchor and collided with us. For this reason I believe the best place to be in a typhoon is tucked inside a small river, moored between the mangroves, and safely out of reach of other craft.

Gale force winds are rare in these islands, aside from typhoons and occasional times of reinforced monsoon trades, or when caught within a short-lived thunderstorm. My crew Theo had brought with him a primitive portable SSB radio receiver that he fussed with for hours at a time, attempting to tune in to weak signals broadcasting voice weather forecasts for the area from the USCG station on Guam. When radio wave propagation was good and the temperamental radio was tuned just right, we occasionally received half a useable forecast. We also listened in on the daily SSB radio program called Rowdy's Net, which took place every morning. Cruising sailors with transmitting radios aboard got together there to relay weather forecasts, hear security warnings, and make contact with friends on yachts who had moved on to other locations.

A Filipino Welcome in Dapitan

After a month of socializing in Tambobo and exploring the southern regions of Negros Island by kayak, foot, and jeepney, Theo and I sailed across the straits to Mindanao. We made the crossing of 30 miles in seven hours, tacking and shortening sail to accommodate the shifting wind. *Atom* flitted in between the vertical cliffs that form the approach to Port Taguilon with sails fluttering like giant, slow-motion butterfly wings in the invisible eddies of winds swirling down off the mountains. By attentive sail trimming we eventually stemmed the slight current of an ebbing tide. Inside the mile-wide bay, two sailing *bancas* kept pace with us as they returned home with the night's catch of fish piled in the bottoms of their canoes. Along a rocky shoreline, punctuated by narrow strips of beach, children gathered outside their huts to stare and wave excitedly at the sight of a strange sailing boat entering the bay. Since they had no concept of our heavy lead keel hidden underwater, *Atom* seemed to them an impossibility as she mysteriously balanced herself upright without the support of the outriggers found on all local craft.

We tucked the boat behind an islet in the bay, so well protected by land on all sides that we could ignore the vagaries of the weather. After landing our dinghy at a dock on the mainland, we walked along a road over the hill to the ocean side of the peninsula and found ourselves within the grounds of the newly-built Dakak Beach tourist resort. Not a single tourist was visible along the perfect white beach, in the glistening freshwater swimming pool, or in the grass-roofed dining area. The numerous thatched bungalows sat empty. Perhaps it wasn't tourist season, or the resort hadn't been discovered yet. The emptiness of the place, the way the gardens and streams blended in with the natural forest, the low buildings that seemed more bamboo and palm than concrete—all gave it the rare quality of an abode where the works of man actually improved on the nature surrounding it.

In fact, the entire port was far too quiet for Theo, and a couple days later we sailed out of the otherwise perfect bay to anchor five miles away in a more open, two-mile-wide bay next to Dapitan City. Along the way we took care not to run into the low floating rafts where seaweed was cultivated. Once sufficiently grown, the seaweed was harvested for processing into an agar gelling agent used in the local jello-like desserts.

Dapitan is said to have gotten its name during the pre-Hispanic era from a Visayan word meaning "to invite" when a local chief invited a tribe from another island to settle here. The local people were no less welcoming when we landed there. According to Alberto Te, the Chinese Filipino whom we met behind the counter of his waterfront bakery on Sunset Boulevard, ours was the first yacht to visit the town in more than a year. Alberto welcomed us strangers like dear friends, taking us on a walking tour of the town and then returning to the bakery to fill a bag for us of cakes and breads for which he would accept no money. At his insistence, we came back to their attached house that evening to join his family for dinner. Much of Filipino cuisine is as forgettable, even regrettable, to foreign visitors as, say, English food is to the French. But like any place, they have their successes. Alberto and his wife served us piles of tasty thin noodles, called *pancit*, chicken *adobo* with potatoes in a vinegar and soy sauce, and a salad of fresh-off-the-raft, lightly steamed seaweed, called *guso*, dressed with lime juice and more vinegar.

The mid-sized town of Dapitan was relatively prosperous by Philippine standards. The lightly trafficked, smoothly paved streets led past well-kept homes, assorted shops, parks and gardens, all lit by electric lamps at night. In Sibuyan Island, I recalled the men mostly hid in their houses at night to drink beer. More than one man told me he feared poisoning or sickness by "moustache transfer" if he shared his drinking glass with a passerby. In Dapitan they cheerfully drank together in little groups, bringing their chairs into the street to converse and exchange gossip with their neighbors.

José Rizal – Filipino Patrick Henry

We took a half-hour bus trip down the coast to the vegetable market at the larger and busier town of Dipolog, but we found there little of Dapitan's small town charm. Dapitan City is best known as the former residence of Filipino patriot and scholar José Rizal. The Spanish colonial government labeled Rizal a *filibustero* (subversive) for his anti-colonial writings and had him exiled from Manila to distant Dapitan for several years in the late 19th century. While in Dapitan, the young revolutionary organized and supported with his own funds the building of a school, hospital, city water supply, and horticultural projects, all of which appear to have left a lasting mark on the city. In 1896, the 36-year-old martyr was executed in Manila for refusing to abandon his support for reforms in the Philippine colonial system. Although he was Gandhian in his belief of non-violent reform, his execution served to ignite the festering Filipino Revolution until an expanding colonialist America ultimately sidetracked it. The Americans supported the ascension of Rizal to Filipino national hero since he had espoused a non-violent, semi-autonomous Philippines, rather than full independence. Rizal's other shining quality to them was that he was already safely dead.

A tricycle pedicab took me to Rizal Park, site of Rizal's restored home on the shaded banks of the river alongside a museum and library devoted to his life and writings. Like many revolutionaries in history, he was a well-educated member of an upper-class family, possessed a great intellect, and had a keen sense for detecting injustice. He also had a penchant for troublemaking among the ruling class. In his writings he repeatedly railed against what he called the "double-faced Goliath" of corrupt Catholic clergy and repressive government. Rizal was a true polymath, a learned and well-traveled liberal reformist, expert in the wide-ranging fields of medicine, engineering, arts, languages, and poetry. The long list of his vocations also included novelist, farmer, surgeon, sculptor, historian, and insurrectionist. Rizal might have been considered the Philippines equivalent of America's Patrick Henry, George Washington, Thomas Jefferson, and Benjamin Franklin—if the British had managed to hang them all during the American Revolution.

Filipino public rhetoric was at times somewhat loosely affiliated with reality. From what I heard at the time in the local news, from the lips of the politically active, and from virtually all college students, everything bad that had ever happened to the Philippines, from the problematic state of its electrical grid to its chronic poverty, was the fault of the United States because of something it has done or failed to do. Of course, some politicians and educated people, and even more of the less educated, knew this was absurd. But the need to place blame on outside forces was too great to resist. The other myth expounded to me most often by many Filipinos was that their country was "rich in natural resources." This was believed despite the obvious facts that over-fishing, deforestation, and truly limited resources divided among a large population that was growing at a frightening rate were enormous obstacles for Filipinos as they attempted to move forward. I often heard Filipinos say they were most proud of their "national pride." It had never occurred to me before that one could be proud of simply being proud. While not a problem in small doses, an over-abundance of national pride, whether in the Philippines or elsewhere in the world, gives people an unearned sense of achievement, provides an excuse to avoid self-criticism, and stocks a ready market for perceived insults.

The Filipino people largely retain a Confucianist belief in conformity and respect of others. Their code of *Hiya* (shame) gives them a guiding sense of propriety. Their shared sense of community helps them get through hard times. Whether it be fault or virtue, the Filipino is at heart fatalistic. If there is such a thing as a national expression, in the United States it could be "do it my way." In Thailand it must be *mai pen rai* (it doesn't matter). The Filipino version would be *bahala na* (leave it to God).

Theo and the Saldon family of Dapitan

While we were in Dapitan, our new friend Alberto introduced Theo and me to Dr. Manuel Saldon, who came out with his teenaged children in their *banca* to visit aboard *Atom*. Dr. Saldon invited us on the spot to stay at his family's vacation home located above the beach around the next headland. After securing their *banca* on a towline we hoisted anchor and set sail. None of the family had been on a monohull sailboat before, so when we heeled sharply to the wind, they all shrieked, scrambled to the high side, and prepared to abandon ship. I put in an extra reef and reassured them we always sailed that way, which calmed them down. By the time we arrived at their secluded cove, they were all enjoying the ride.

At the doctor's insistence we stayed overnight in his house on the low cliff overlooking the bay. After breakfast with the family we hiked uphill about a thousand feet to the peak of Love Mountain for a sweeping view of the peninsula and off-lying islets. Theo and I returned to the boat that afternoon with bags of fruit and vegetables from Manuel's garden. The hospitality we experienced there was characteristic of uncounted places we visited in the Philippines. Small communities make for easy friendships and sharing. The Filipinos' balance of self-reliance and willingness to help one another is in many ways suggestive of Thomas Jefferson's ideal agrarian society. These sun-soaked islands were a glorious place for the sailor to come in from the wilderness of the sea and join the human communities inhabiting its Elysian shores.

Another Tugboat Encounter; Islands of the Central Seas

After departing from Dapitan, we sailed east into the Mindanao Sea. Although land was still in sight on the horizon, I pulled the sextant from its box for the first time in three months to teach Theo the art of celestial navigation. I hadn't needed it in these island-studded seas, but he wanted to master the technique in order to fulfill his dream to cross oceans one day on his own boat. We handed the sextant back and forth, shooting the sun over and over. At dusk we shot a round of stars from pinpoints of light that had traveled light-years to reach our eyes. In the morning twilight we shot another star and two planets as well. Theo sorted out the basic math quickly. After a few more lessons he became fairly proficient in getting accurate readings on the sextant and transferring those intersecting lines to our charts. Celestial navigation is like a magician's inscrutable trick that becomes a simple matter of method once someone takes you through the process step by step. At least it was simple in the calm waters we encountered. Later, he would have to master the less easy juggling act of taking sights while sailing on his ear in tumbling seas.

Meanwhile, during that first night the wind sputtered and stalled. The air became so nearly calm that it required all my attention to discern any prevailing tilt from the flame of an exposed candle I had set on deck. During his watch, Theo grew frustrated of studying sails, candle, and compass through his thick eyeglasses. Each time I got us on course and moving at a barely perceptible quarter knot, I handed the tiller over to him. Before long we were drifting in a circle. I would turn the boat back on course with several sharp pulls of the tiller and then trim the sails for each barely detectable puff of wind. We chased the elusive zephyrs that were never quite strong enough to fill the slatting sails. But those used to light-air sailing know that a well-designed boat can be moved by the force of as little as one knot of wind speed. Even when the sails appeared empty as they panted lightly from the boat's gentle roll, by sensing the touch of the faint current of air on my face, by noticing the slight preference for the sail to flop more to one side than the other, and by paying careful attention to the helm, we achieved up to a half-knot of speed through the water. The job can seem as impossible as coaxing a butterfly to land on one hand while attempting to clutch a handful of smoke in the other. When the wind speed increased enough for Theo to detect it, I suggested that he "Think of the sails like vertical airplane wings. Don't let their angle of attack stall their lift." That didn't seem to help. Soon after I went back to my bunk I noticed we had spun off course as I saw the stars shifting overhead through my open hatch while I heard Theo tramping around the deck, muttering curse words in German. Under the circumstances, I couldn't blame him.

During my midnight watch, I sighted the lights of a boat on the otherwise empty starlit horizon. After watching for a minute, I was wary but not overly alarmed. After all, what are the chances of two boats miles apart actually hitting each other on a calm night of good visibility in the middle of a wide-open sea? As he drew closer, I recognized the navigation lights he carried indicated he was a tugboat pulling a barge. The visible red and green running lights indicated he was coming straight at us. Now we were in trouble. While there was plenty of sea room for him to alter course, I knew from my close encounter with a Manila Bay tug that the tow cable and barge presented a serious threat even if the tug itself took evasive action. At that point we were absolutely becalmed and as immobile as if sitting in a sea of molasses. The tugboat, apparently confident in his right of way, stubbornly held to his track long after it was obvious to us that we were on a collision course. We assumed he was seeing our masthead light and my flashlight illuminating our sails. He probably assumed it was up to us to start our engine to get out of his way. We were all making dangerous assumptions.

Theo pumped up our pressure kerosene lamp and held up its brilliant light in front of our listless white mainsail. I set the sculling oar over the transom and pulled hard to one side with the oar until the boat was set on a course perpendicular to the tug. I then began sculling with as much concentration and physical effort as I could muster. The gentle ocean swell lifted the oar blade from the water. Then when the stern dropped under the passing swell, the blade hit the water, causing the oar socket to lift off its pivot pin. Between the waves, I managed to build up a fraction of a knot of boat speed before coming to a standstill the next time the oar came loose. The two miles between us became one, then a hundred yards and closing.

As the tug bore down on us I called out to Theo, "Set down the lantern and prepare to launch the dinghy." With hands welded to the oar, I looked up to see the tugboat finally alter course. He would barely avoid ramming us, but his unstoppable barge, I knew, would not change its course so quickly. The tug passed us closely enough that his bow wave slapped hard under our overhanging transom and lifted us to surge forward a few yards. Theo had our grab bag of survival gear on deck.

The dinghy and oars were unlashed and ready to launch. The straining tow cable hung taught in the air like a grim reaper's scythe about to remove our heads. I continued my furious effort on the oar and gained a few more precious yards. Finally, the barge brushed past our transom about 30 feet away. I dropped the oar and sat down in the cockpit, unable to feel my numb hands for several minutes. It was another case of engineless David versus a powerful Goliath, except mere evasion was the victory we sought.

Tropical Torpor; Dodging Thieves; Looking Penniless

We carried on with little to no wind for the remainder of the night. The following morning our patience was further tested as the calm reached the point where even I gave up my attempts at sniffing out a whiff of wind. In the full tropical summer, the sun rose high overhead and seemed to hang nearly immobile at noon for several blistering hours. "We'll be sailing again before you know it," I said at least once each hour to keep Theo's spirits up as the sun threw down its midday fire. On deck the hard-edged shadow from the mainsail grew shorter until it became as thin as the sail itself. Our choice was between roasting on deck and steaming below from the combined deck and hull radiating the sun's heat inward. I was reminded of summer days in Detroit while working in the factory welding pit, brazing together cracked cast iron punch press frames as they simmered red hot over a half ton of flaming charcoal. Theo and I doused ourselves in buckets of warm seawater. We yearned for the relief of sunset, just as I had ached for the release of the four o'clock factory whistle.

By late afternoon my predictions came true when we were rewarded with enough wind to fill the sails. Predictions of this sort are too easy, since wind is never absent for long in our turbulent atmosphere. Twenty-six hours later we had traveled 90 straight miles along the irregular coast of Mindanao to anchor off the city of Cagayan de Oro. Much of the coastline along the bay had water too deep for easy mooring, so we anchored close to a squatter settlement next to the shipping terminal. The low-lying shore supported a maze of wood and tin shacks built on decaying stilts driven haphazardly into the mud. Seeing no better place to land our dinghy, we tied it to the bottom of a ladder beneath a house and called up to the occupants in the shack above us. A woman leaned out of her window and waved us to climb up to the rickety bamboo porch. The dinghy was safe there, she told us, and gave us directions to town. We walked carefully along bendy narrow planks serving as elevated alleyways for the settlement, until we reached a road on solid ground.

I always used security bars in my companionway hatch when anchored off a large town or squatter settlement. The welded stainless steel bars that slid into the companionway track did give a comical appearance as if we were looking out of a prison cell, but they functioned well to allow ventilation while keeping out intruders. The only thing ever stolen from my boat up until that time, which included 12 years of cruising in 32 countries, happened that night in Cagayan de Oro when a pair of shoes I had left on the afterdeck were likely snatched by a midnight swimmer. Going ashore the next morning in my flip-flops, I couldn't help staring at the feet of every man and boy I passed in case I might recognize my only pair of shoes. At the least, I could deliver to the thief my spare pair of shoelaces. Considering that my $40 leather boat shoes represented an average month's salary for many people there, I took to wearing cheaper shoes.

The affluent Western traveler to poor regions may not know that he carries the scent of money on him the way a rat carries fleas. As seen by the desperately poor families inhabiting the shanty towns on the fringes of large cities, the typical yachtie on a large and opulent yacht is a direct representation of the social rottenness of our world. The yachtsmen come blazing through the anchorages on high-powered inflatable dinghies that cost more than double that of the locals' homes, clutching a platinum credit card while demanding this or that service. Because they bring more than they need to these poor countries, some locals figure they deserve to have it taken from them. It's a wonder to me that the locals don't steal every possession from every yachtsman they encounter and then hang them by their own halyards. Yet, by some miracle of human nature, and a fear of police retaliation, that never happens.

By contrast, I rowed ashore in my pitiful 6-foot patched plastic dinghy, carrying only empty water jugs. I'd come to hear about the lives of my hosts, to be guided and informed, seeking nothing beyond the ordinary and displaying no prideful advantage over them. From the welcoming and helpful reception I got almost everywhere I went, you might think I had washed ashore half-naked, clinging to a piece of shipwreck flotsam.

Within a few days, Theo had had his fill of that particular big city—a place of promise and disappointment, much like any other city. I couldn't help but notice again how a city in decay incites in the visitor a hardness of the soul, while a return to sea inspires dreams. We sailed back along the coast of Mindanao and then north towards the island of Cebu. Along the way we anchored off Dumaguete City on Negros Island, 25 miles north of our old haunt in Port Bonbonon. The anchorage was wide open to the northeast. But now that the monsoon had shifted to the southwest, the north/south trending coast provided a reasonably safe shelter, even though the afternoon winds tended to parallel the coast, filling the anchorage with an uncomfortable roll-inducing chop.

Hiking Mt. Talinas; Ramming Speed; So Long, Theo

When I visited the library at Silliman University in Dumaguete, a professor asked me to give a talk and slide presentation to his students about my journeys around the world. In return, a student from the university's mountaineering club invited me to join them on a weekend climb to the peak of nearby Mt. Talinis. Theo agreed to stay behind and watch the boat in the bouncy anchorage, while three of us caught a jeepney to Valencia, a quiet town virtually buried under a cloak of flowering gardens. From there we hired two motorized tricycles that hopped and jerked along trails of rocks and holes, better walked over. Going downhill, we rode. Going uphill, we got out and pushed the underpowered tricycles. Eventually, we found local resident and mountain guide, Rene Vendiola, who was assisting his friend in loading ears of corn into a cart harnessed to a water buffalo. Rene agreed to guide us on foot that very day to the mountaintop. First, we detoured through the forested countryside to visit Casaroro Falls. The sunlight came through the trees here and there in piercing columns as we descended hundreds of feet down a steep trail until we reached a river. By scrambling over rocks on the riverbank, we suddenly stood below a torrent of water where it cut a deep columnar hollow into the rocks as it dropped into the river. We took a quick refreshing swim in the cool waters.

It was a more grueling uphill march back out of the river basin, which continued as we gained elevation on the mountain. Tropical alpine lakes appeared through shrouds of drifting clouds below us. We made camp before sunset in the solitude of Talinis's peak and were rewarded with views between the clouds of the forested hills and a cerulean sea flecked with distant islands.

Our visit to Dumaguete was also memorable when a couple days after our descent from the mountain, a 60-foot-long double-decked ferryboat lost steerage as it came into the harbor one morning. Instead of swinging around the ferry pier as it usually did, to my horror it came straight at us with no apparent reduction in speed. Fortunately, I was on deck at the time. I leapt to the bow to release the anchor rode just as the ugly steel bow rammed into my bow pulpit, instantly bending the 1-inch stainless steel railing back. I hadn't had time to release both anchors, so the ferry kept shoving us backwards, stretching our rode to near the breaking point as it dragged our second anchor through the seabed. Finally, we were both aground in shallow water. Fortunately, the tide was rising, and the water was calm. In a couple hours the ferry's crew had repaired their motor and returned to the dock. The captain told me he had lost steerage and reverse thrust when the motor died. "Don't worry," he said, "the ferry's owner will pay you for any damage." But the owner proved elusive, and I was unable to track him down. Theo and I disassembled and bent the pulpit back into its approximate shape as best we could and sailed out of Dumaguete a few days later.

We rode the southwest monsoon winds north to Cebu, the Philippines' second largest city. Theo departed from there on a flight to Manila and then home to Switzerland. He had been one of the most helpful and uncomplaining crewmates I'd ever shared a boat with. He was every bit as intelligent as you'd expect from a multi-lingual, well-traveled computer programmer. Theo also had the lungs of a dolphin. He free dove to fifty feet, holding his breath for an extraordinarily long time, which was useful more than once to retrieve a fouled anchor or items accidentally dropped overboard. During those three months Theo had become a competent sailor and good friend. "Next year, when I've saved enough money, I'll come back to buy myself a boat like *Atom*," he told me. I believed him and looked forward to helping him find a boat and fit it out for his own first voyage.

Cebu City was Manila Lite: crowded and blistering hot ashore when it wasn't raining; a magnet for beggars, thieves, and displaced people from the rural provinces; and the water in the harbor a filthy soup that often carried a hull-staining film of oil on its surface. It was also where yachts came to get provisions and sailors sought entertainment in the bars. The life expectancy for a visiting yacht's inflatable dinghy and outboard motor where measured in hours. One night I was awakened by gunfire when an American yachtsman anchored next to me shredded his awning with a shotgun blast while trying to scare off a *banca* full of thieves intent on making off with his dinghy, even though it was lashed on deck and chained to the mast. That type of brazen thievery was almost unknown outside of Cebu and Manila.

The best place to land a dinghy there was at the dock next to the house of an American retired couple named Don and Bev. They had sailed to Cebu several years earlier, built their American-sized brick house in the middle of the run-down port area of Oano, while keeping their boat moored in the harbor. It was a mystery to me why the couple had chosen to build their retirement home on the waterfront of a decaying commercial port. Don was very pleasant and helpful to visiting sailors, providing us a safe place to land our dinghies and a tap to fill our water jugs. He was also a daily voice on the SSB net, providing weather reports and other local information. Bev was an unhappy woman who spent most of her time tending her plants, watering her lawn, and chasing Pinoy trespassers off their property at the end of her broom. She enforced her loudly spoken policy of "no prostitutes on our property!" by confronting sailors who used their dinghy dock to ferry their local girlfriends to their boats. When three girls who worked assembling electronic components in a local factory came to visit my boat, I had the embarrassing job of trying to explain to an irate Bev in front of the girls that they were not prostitutes Although we male sailors treaded lightly around Bev, we were happy to have the use of the couple's dock and water tap.

In Cebu I renewed my visa once again and gathered the provisions that were hard to find in the provinces. One week after I'd arrived, I sailed out alone, daysailing to several more ports along Cebu's 122-mile length. Ten miles outside Cebu City I stopped at Liloan anchorage, which offered good protection in the southwest monsoon and a safer environment than in the heart of the nearby city. Between Liloan and Port Carmen a few more miles up the coast, I met several resident expat sailors, including an Australian whom I assisted with launching his homebuilt catamaran by rolling it down the beach on logs at high tide. In the next harbor, Mike Allen owned a shop where he built and repaired sailboats. Labor was cheap, but importing specialized yacht gear at the time was a difficult and expensive process. In his younger years, Mike had sailed his 20-foot pocket cruiser, a Pacific Seacraft Flicka, through these islands before swallowing the hook in Cebu.

From Cebu, I continued my solitary wanderings by sailing east and then south, stopping nearly every night at a new anchorage as I explored the islands between Cebu and Leyte, and then sailed back to Mindanao. It made sense to return to Mindanao to avoid the summer typhoons, which track further north. My progress from harbor to harbor, from one fishing village to the next, was steady yet unhurried.

When underway, I often sailed past fishermen, who would frequently become nervous, frantically waving me off so as to avoid sailing into their drifting nets. To calm them down, sometimes I complied by altering course and making a long detour around the nets. Other times I just sailed straight over their nets while smiling innocently and waving back. Being on an engineless boat, I had no propeller to entangle fishing nets. Years ago, I had also installed a short keel extension to cover the inch-wide gap between the rudder and keel, making it impossible for us to snag anything floating or submerged such as fishing nets. With our long, smooth keel we simply glided over the nets, leaving them perfectly intact as they popped up in our wake.

While visiting fishing villages, I saw there was nothing like a maximum legal size fish catch or minimum size for individual fish caught in the Philippines. Anything catchable was fair game. Whole communities made their living off fish smaller than your little finger. The fry were dried, salted, mashed, soaked in vinegar, and bottled for flavoring dinners that for many of the impoverished people might otherwise consist of little more than plain rice.

Sailing south along a peninsula on the northeast tip of Mindanao, I turned to enter the mouth of the Agusan River. By taking frequent depth soundings, I managed to avoid grounding on the charted rocky shoals at the river mouth and other banks of shoal waters further upstream. Using the one-knot incoming tide and fluky winds, I tacked and drifted upriver, passing a *barangay* named after Magellan, who was the first European explorer to leave a record of having visited there. The Agusan is the third largest river in the Philippines, running over two hundred miles through an immense valley in the heart of Mindanao. For hundreds of years, this area known as the Kingdom of Butuan had been an important source of gold mining and was the trading and cultural center of the region. Its Buddhist leaders had maintained contact with traders from Persia, Southeast Asian kingdoms, as well as China and Japan.

I followed the meandering earth-colored river past swampy, mangrove-lined shores for six miles upstream where a low bridge prevented further progress. There I moored the boat with bow and stern anchors along the edge of the river just clear of a commercial dock near Butuan City. Along the shore, vacant sawmills and half-sunk barges marked the decline of a logging industry that for decades had ravished the once plentiful forests of the interior plains.

Hey, Joe, Where Are You Going?

Walking from the port into Butuan City, the children of the *barangays* cried, "*Kano*" when I passed. As in many other places in the Philippines, the older children and young adults practiced their English by shouting, "Hey, Joe! Where are you going?"

Hearing that greeting for about the hundredth time, I began to get annoyed. An unusually large number of strangers I passed in the Philippines all wanted to know where I was going. A reply of "Nowhere" seemed to satisfy them as well as laying out my actual itinerary. It took me a while to understand that *saan ka pupunta* (where are you going?) was often used among Filipinos when greeting each other just as Americans use the phrase "How's it going?" Even so, I learned it was better not to say, "What's happening?" or "What's going on?" when greeting Filipinos. Those phrases were used when asking about some specific problem such as when there's a fight going on. When hearing that greeting, Filipinos are likely to respond with an embarrassed grin, locally known as an "uncooked smile."

Although I had been warned that parts of Mindanao were infested with anti-government rebels, pro-government militias, and Islamic extremists, I saw none of them where I sailed. Regardless, Butuan City held little attraction to me once I had seen it. I had come here merely to satisfy a vague curiosity after seeing the river look so inviting and prominent on my chart.

Marooned in Mindanao – the Kindness of Strangers

With the help of a two-knot current I sailed back down the Agusan and was swept into the Mindanao Sea. I sailed west along the coast, investigating every anchorage that my chart indicated could provide good shelter. Each place was memorable in its own way, but nowhere did I find the same combination of friendly people, beautiful atmosphere, and secure anchorages as I had in the Dapitan area further west.

I stopped again at Cagayan de Oro simply to rest overnight. The following morning I got underway early with a light land breeze that carried me less than ten miles. The wind vanished, leaving me adrift on a calm sea about a mile offshore. I pulled a bunk cushion from the cabin and lay down on it in the cockpit to close my eyes for a short nap. I left the sails up and the self-steering engaged in order to get moving again as soon as the wind came up. Perhaps I was too comfortable because I slept too soundly. The next thing I knew, the boat shuddered and her keel made the unmistakable grinding noise of fiberglass on rock. She had struck the inshore reef and skidded sideways, parallel to and only a long jump away from a gravel and sand beach. I stood up in utter shock. A new wind had gradually sprung up from a different direction during my sleep, had filled the sails, and had driven us ashore. Our insignificant-looking U.S. flag fluttered from the backstay as if shortly to be a marker of *Atom*'s final resting place. I could have banged my head against the hatch in frustration at my stupidity, but I was too busy. Breaking free of my trance-like state, I rushed to save the boat. First, I dropped the sails and then dug through the cockpit lockers for an anchor. Pulling out a bag of tangled rode and a light anchor, I looked up startled to see dozens of people gathered on the beach ten steps away. Other people were still running towards us from the village of huts under the palm trees. Could they help me somehow? Would they see me as a stranded traveler in need or as potential salvage once the building waves had split open the hull? Was this a Muslim or Christian village and would it even matter?

As the building waves bounced us on the rocks of the dead reef, several men pulled themselves aboard. I ignored them until I had locked the hatches to the cabin. I then launched the dinghy and ran around like a madman attempting to keep more men from climbing aboard.

"*Kung nasaan ako?*" (Where am I?) I asked the eldest man on deck.

"San Salvador" (the Saint Savior), he replied. That was also the name of Columbus's first landfall in the Americas. I hoped that being washed ashore into the hands of a savior saint was a portent of better fortune ahead.

Nobody appeared to speak English. I tried to calm my nerves and organize my own rescue by giving the men tasks in Filipino. Either these were some of the roughest looking brigands I had yet seen in the islands, or my fear of them had made that transformation for me. I asked one man to stand on deck and feed out line to me as I rowed offshore to drop an anchor in deeper water. Unfortunately, when they pulled on the anchor line we found the water near shore was so deep that the anchor was hanging nearly straight down at the end of its 125-foot nylon rode. There was only one option remaining. I needed to harness the muscle power of the gathering crowd to actually lift the boat off the rocks while I used the sails to gain deeper water. I put two reefs in the mainsail, exchanged the larger jib for the storm jib and sheeted them both tight. We needed just enough sail to drive to windward without having too much wind pressure forcing us further aground. I ordered everyone off the boat except for one man on the foredeck who held a strain on the anchor rode.

At least thirty volunteers waded into the chest high water and placed their shoulders under *Atom*'s hull. Having no idea that the combined displacement of boat and ballast was a whopping 8,000 pounds, they assumed it would be an easy lift. In unison I directed them to push each time the breaking waves lifted the keel off the rocks. For a while nothing happened. Then they got serious, shouting directions to each other and bringing more people into the water to place their hands against the hull. We bumped again and moved a few inches forward. Again and again we bumped and moved inch by inch. Suddenly we were afloat. I told the man on the bow to pull in the anchor while I held the tiller over to bring us closer into the wind. *Atom* heeled slightly and responded. After we made a few more yards to windward I pulled a handful of pesos from my pocket and handed them to my anchor man and asked him to share it with his friends who had helped me. He waved the wrinkled peso notes in the air for his friends to see and then dove into the water to swim to shore one-handed while the other hand held his precious pesos above water.

Atom sailing along Mindanao

Once I had gained a few more boat lengths from shore, I checked the bilge and found it dry. We had steerage and watertight integrity, so no serious damage had been done. With the relief of a condemned prisoner getting a last-minute pardon, I felt I had slipped the noose from around my neck. I waved and shouted triumphantly back at the throng of people on the beach. A rising chorus of cheers went up from the crowd. The "better angels" residing in the unknown village of San Salvador had saved me after all. Every mile we sailed from then on was because of their kindness toward a potentially marooned sailor. No doubt these good people would pass the story of that day on to their children, just as I'm passing it on to you. A hundred arms or more continued to wave farewell as we slipped away offshore.

Oversleeping when close to shore had nearly shipwrecked me. That was an unavoidable hazard of sailing alone. Sailing engineless was another risk I took with full knowledge of the potential consequences. I had a need to experience the challenge of sailing the way it had been done before engines and other mechanical aids eliminated much of the risk. My goal was to test my boat and myself. Of course, it would have been safer, easier, and more practical to have an engine. Not one sailor in a thousand can, or will care to, make any significant engineless passage. I feel no need to convince them to do otherwise. In fact, recounting here some of my misadventures may serve just the opposite purpose. So be it.

Captain Joshua Slocum undertook the first solo circumnavigation (without an engine) when he was in his fifties. Slocum was an exceptional seaman with a lifetime of voyaging experience under his belt. For the rest of us mere mortals the highly physical and mental sport of sailing alone and without an engine is best tackled in the vigor of youth. There's no getting around the fact that an extended cruise in a purely sail-driven craft is a dangerous pursuit, particularly because young sailors may lack the experience and hard-earned skills to make sound decisions. But of the four sailing friends I've known who were lost at sea, none of them were solo sailors, and all of them had bigger boats with engines. Having crew and an engine and a big boat didn't bring them home to safe harbor. Safety cannot be bought so easily, if it can be bought at all. To make a voyage in any craft is to risk your life. But to live out on the deck of the world you must turn off that fear-driven, negative inner voice that holds you back or you risk losing much of the very things that make life worth living.

On a sail-only vessel, the sailor learns to pay attention to nature's signals. He sees or senses the minute currents and wind eddies with the same intensity of observation as a bushman tracking game on the African savannah. Just as the land environment shapes the cultures of the people who inhabit its mountains, desserts, islands, jungles, and seashores, a sailor's life is shaped by the implacable, indifferent, demanding, yet inspiring sea. That he died as he lived—in love with the sea, yet defiant and unsubmitting until the end—is a sailor's rightful epitaph.

A sailor lives on the heaving breast of an inspiring and alluring sea. Personifying the sea does not mean her harsh and elemental realm is any more concerned with human need than is the most forbidding desert. It's true the sea is open to all. She has no preference or respect for your money, social position, morals, or education. No pleading or bargaining can win your passage; it must be earned with good planning and determination.

An engineless passage is like running a marathon: you may run it once or twice or a dozen times, but who would expect you to run it every day of your life, forever? On one end of the spectrum lies the sailing purist I had been during this portion of my second circumnavigation. At the opposite end are people who use their sailboats as sail-assisted motorboats; they motor almost everywhere and occasionally hoist some sail when conditions are optimal. Most sailors reside happily somewhere in the middle. There came a time when I no longer felt the need to run those epic saltwater marathons and tacked toward the center by adding a small outboard motor to *Atom*'s equipment inventory. Even so, my uneasy alliance with an outboard motor remains preferable to me than the sooty curse of cohabitating with and maintaining an inboard diesel engine. Our differences are irreconcilable.

My boat could be considered merely a well-crafted tool, a home that traveled. But in my eyes she was so much more. She became my protector and seemed to possess a soul of undeniable grace. Sailing is a spiritual and transforming endeavor to one who is receptive. It is the antidote to a closed mind and a hardened heart. The reality of voyaging under sail is even richer than the fantasy. Your mind opens as wide as the horizon. Time disconnects from the metronome of the Protestant work ethic. On a sailboat you can once again be that child you recall being during your first exploration of a captivating forest or the winsome seashore.

A sea passage to foreign lands can teach us to be inspired by what we don't know instead of being afraid and judgmental. The years rush by like a succession of waves heading to who knows where. Like a seascape, our lives are ever-changing. A capricious society demands that we change our direction in the same way the wind guides the waves; if we resist, we find ourselves broken and drowned under the breaking seas. We praise what we are or what we think we are—in my case the self-sufficient purist, the libertine libertarian, the dedicated anti-authoritarian. My happiness abides in living in peace among my peers, relying on myself as far as possible, and being self-responsible. At sea alone and out in the world's society I learned to trust conscience as my sole legislator. Some people may consider my brand of individualism to be selfish. Yet the fight for the survival of the individual spirit is also a fight for all individuals, for all cultures, for human nature, and for nature herself. What is life if it is not lived your own way? To marry self-indulgence with acts of service to others is the ultimate reward. I pass my story on to others not for them to follow in my steps but in hopes of inspiring them to furrow new paths.

In one of my guiding passages by Henry David Thoreau, I found a sentiment similar to what I discovered on my own travels:

> *I learned this, at least, by my experiment: that if one*
> *advances confidently in the direction of his dreams, and*
> *endeavors to live the life which he has imagined, he will*

meet with a success unexpected in common hours. He will
put some things behind, will pass an invisible boundary;
new, universal, and more liberal laws will begin to
establish themselves around and within him; or the old
laws be expanded, and interpreted in his favor in a more
liberal sense, and he will live with the license of a higher
order of beings. In proportion as he simplifies his life, the
laws of the universe will appear less complex, and solitude
will not be solitude, nor poverty poverty, nor weakness
weakness. If you have built castles in the air, your work
need not be lost; that is where they should be. Now put
the foundations under them.

To challenge yourself, to place those foundations under your castles in the air, is to begin an adventure that is more precious than merely gathering possessions while clinging to the myth of security. The cemeteries are filled with tombstones that might as well read: "He died from complications of not living." I hope your own life contains an epic voyage, and that you affirm the voice within telling you that you mustn't wait until you are dying to discover you should start living.

As we watch the heavenly bodies that push and pull the tides, the ticking clock, the birth and death of all nature's gifts around us, we may pause to ask, "Where did the time go? Where will we go now?"

Just as earliest man gazed across a wide river and needed to know what lay on the other side, I too saw my future across the sea. Those early people may have been driven primarily by the hunger of the body. But I believe they too were also compelled by the soul's universal hunger to explore.

Once we had freed *Atom* from the reef on Mindanao, I again set my course for the next distant sea.

Epilogue

Those who sail beyond familiar shores find a life of adventure, seeking, and learning.

After a full year of cruising the Philippines, I sailed *Atom* from Mindanao back through the islands to Manila and then again across the South China Sea to Hong Kong. I had now fulfilled my dream for the voyage, which had begun four years earlier in Florida. The journey had brought what I'd expected and more.

At this point I was ready to move on from the extreme minimalist, almost austere, and mostly solitary voyaging of those years. *Atom* and I entered a new phase; something different lay ahead for us. I went back to working on boats for Simpson Marine and writing for *Fragrant Harbour* magazine in Hong Kong for one year. In my spare time I used the lessons I had learned at sea and in the boat building industry to refit *Atom* to make her more comfortable and seaworthy.

My sailing friend, Theo, had meanwhile earned enough money as a computer programmer in Switzerland to buy his own boat. I was happily surprised when he flew out to Hong Kong, and I was able to assist him in selecting a well-used 28-foot sailboat of a similar design to *Atom*. For a couple months we worked side by side on our boats to prepare for another voyage. We traveled far during the next several years, sometimes sailing in company from island to island and across the oceans.

My first journey around the world had taken two years. During that time I packed a lot of living into a short period of time. That first circumnavigation now seemed like a sprint compared with the marathon of the present world voyage that was as yet only half finished. My voyages had certainly not been all fair winds and red rose-bottomed clouds drifting above the sunset, but there were more than enough rewards to lure me back to sea again and again. After another 11 years of further adventures, I found my way home to complete a second circumnavigation. Mei eventually joined me in Trinidad, where we were married, and then sailed together on the last leg of the journey home. In the years since, Mei and our worldly ship *Atom* have both been by my side.

Since our return to the U.S. our world has remained all about boats and sailing as we began our own small business to refit our customers' boats, provide consulting service for new sailors, and undertake yacht delivery trips. To assist in the launching of other sailors' dreams is a fulfilling thrill, reminiscent of embarking on my own voyages.

If readers need to know why I would undertake a long voyage on a small sailboat, they need look no further than the explanation from Henry David Thoreau in *Walden*, published in 1854. Although his adventure is set in a cabin in the woods, his experience could equally reflect the spiritual journey of solo voyaging:

> *I went to the woods because I wished to live deliberately, to front only the essential facts of life, and see if I could not learn what it had to teach, and not, when I came to die, discover that I had not lived. I did not wish to live what was not life, living is so dear; nor did I wish to practise resignation, unless it was quite necessary. I wanted to live deep and suck out all the marrow of life, to live so sturdily and Spartan-like as to put to rout all that was not life, to cut a broad swath and shave close, to drive life into a corner, and reduce it to its lowest terms, and, if it proved to be mean, why then to get the whole and genuine meanness of it, and publish its meanness to the world; or if it were sublime, to know it by experience, and be able to give a true account of it in my next excursion.*

The first step in publishing the "meanness" or transcendence of my own adventure was the recent retrieval of a tattered old logbook from *Atom*'s locker. Thumbing through the pages was a passage through a sea of remembrance. In it was a list of the names of every port I had visited, the weather conditions along the way, the miles sailed, the meridians and time zones crossed. In the back of the book was the guest log, containing hundreds of signatures with "Best Wishes" and "Fair Winds" from so many friends from all walks of life. Although I sailed mostly alone, my voyage was far from solitary.

Crossing oceans alone by sail and oar might be seen as an acute form of self-denial and selfishness but never as the bigger crime of denial of self. My simple desire was to sail and discover the world and, in doing so, to discover myself. I've now recounted the first half of the story from that logbook and look forward to telling the second half in a future book. Meanwhile, *Atom* has a new log with blank pages waiting to be filled.

Acknowledgments

Like solo sailing, writing is a lonely occupation. But that burden was eased immeasurably by a collaboration among friends with a mutual interest in sailing and in stories of sailors on the sea. I'm grateful to the considerable editing and publishing help that I received from the following people.

John Lane, attorney and veteran from the early days of modern hang gliding, who also happens to have a wide range of literary pursuits, gave me many welcome suggestions to improve the prose and flow of the story.

Matthew Fike, author, professor of English, and sailing enthusiast, further helped to clean up the general chaos of the manuscript. The flaws that remain are entirely my own.

Steve Dunmeyer, who sails his own Pearson Triton (the same model boat as Atom), assisted in converting the files and publishing them to ebook and paperback format.

Special thanks are also due to all those persons I met along the way who assisted in many ways to make my travels easier.

Made in the USA
Middletown, DE
20 November 2016